SPEECHES AND PAPERS

RELATING TO

THE REBELLION

AND THE

OVERTHROW OF SLAVERY.

BY

GEORGE S. BOUTWELL.

BOSTON:
LITTLE, BROWN, AND COMPANY.
1867.

CAMBRIDGE.
STEREOTYPED AND PRINTED BY JOHN WILSON AND SON.

This Volume

IS

RESPECTFULLY DEDICATED TO MY FELLOW-CITIZENS OF THE ANCIENT TOWN OF GROTON,

TO WHOSE

GENEROUS AND UNWAVERING CONFIDENCE AND SUPPORT, FOR MORE THAN A QUARTER OF A CENTURY, I AM CHIEFLY INDEBTED FOR MY OPPORTUNITIES FOR PUBLIC SERVICE.

CONTENTS.

SPEECHES.

JEFFERSON.

SPEECH DELIVERED AT BOSTON, APRIL 13, 1859, AT A FESTIVAL ON THE ANNIVERSARY OF JEFFERSON'S BIRTHDAY.

IT is a distinguished honor to be permitted to preside on a festive occasion, when the virtues and political principles of Thomas Jefferson are remembered.

For this honor, I am indebted to the undeserved partiality of the committee who have invited and organized this gathering, that here, within the limits of the Commonwealth which first resisted British aggression, we may acknowledge our obligations to the men and the principles of a sister republic in the great struggle for liberty in America.

Public justice, in a large sense, is often slow, but always sure; and, on the hundred and sixteenth anniversary day of the birth of Jefferson, we encourage our faith in humanity by the reflection, that his principles, and the purity of his private and official life, have been relieved from the rancor and obloquy of personal strifes; and that he now stands the chosen leader of a majority of the people of the nation, who either accept his principles, or claim that he would, if living, accept theirs.

The world permits some men to be immortal, and Jefferson is one of the chosen few. Some are immortal on account of their goodness or wisdom; some on account of their love of freedom, or services in its support; and some because the record of the world's life would be incomplete without their names and doings. In addition to these high qualities, Jefferson is immortal because he attached himself ardently and faithfully to principles in which all men of all ages must be interested.

There can be no history of America, without a history of its great Revolution; there can be no history of that Revolution without the Declaration of Independence; and there can be no history of the Declaration of Independence without the name, the services, and the character, of Jefferson.

Moreover, the history of the American Revolution, with its actual and possible results, is no longer local, or even continental: it is for the world.

We are also building up a language, which, if not destined to be a universal dialect, shall yet borrow something of the learning and something of the speech of every people, and which is finally to be spoken and understood in all civilized nations.

The principles of the American Revolution have, then, a common interest for all mankind; and the English language, as a medium of universal communication, shall make those principles, and the contest itself, everywhere known. Hence the name of Jefferson is to be more widely diffused, and the principles which he declared are to be generally accepted, because they awaken sentiments as universal as the love of life. Jefferson is not, then, a star merely in our own firmament, but a central sun, whose light and heat, in the revolutions of the world's political system, are for every zone and every people. Other men participated more largely in the contests of the Revolution; but none understood better the principles on which it was waged, or sought more zealously to secure its advantages through the theory of human equality as the basis of the equality and sovereignty of the States.

In the catalogue of great names, Washington is first. Exhibiting a patriotism loyal and unselfish, a wisdom circumspect and practical, he was always a leader, because the instincts of men discovered in him a greatness far superior to that of others; and they consequently yielded a willing obedience to his authority. After Washington are many whom we can neither compare nor contrast. Each had a record that cannot die; each had a life that—

> "Closed without a cloud.
> They set as sets the morning star, which goes
> Not down behind the darkened west, nor hides
> Obscured among the tempests of the sky,
> But melts away into the light of heaven."

In Jefferson was combined a high order of political philosophy, with profound, sagacious, far-seeing statesmanship. The cardinal idea of the nationality which he encouraged and cherished is the equality of all men by nature and before the law, as the basis on which the States, as independent sovereignties, are associated together for mutual protection, but without the right anywhere to oppress the smallest Commonwealth or the humblest citizen.

The minimum of power under this sacred right, is the power of each State to decide for itself, by its own great tribunal of the jury, whether any man found within its limits, be he a citizen or not, shall be transported to another State, there to suffer the penalty of crime, or to endure the oppression of slavery.

Mr. Jefferson believed in the right of revolution as a sacred right; and now, as when the Declaration of Independence was adopted, all experience has shown that mankind are more disposed to suffer while evils are sufferable, than to right themselves by abolishing the forms to which they are accustomed.

Thus far in our history, the revolutionary spirit has not been evoked often, except in resistance to despotic, irresponsible power; and thus far the results have proved ultimately favorable to liberty. While this great right of the people can never be abridged, it is the glory of our institutions that they provide for every probable emergency under the government.

Mr. Jefferson was an example, but not a solitary nor even a distinguished one among the patriots of the Revolution, of purity in official life. Possessing and enjoying a considerable fortune, he gave himself for forty years to the duties and labors of the public service, and retired without the smell of the smoke of corruption on his garments.

Jefferson saw and reverenced the principle of human equality, and he maintained a consistent hostility to every form of human bondage. He was, by birth, training, and association, allied to the slaveholding class: yet, in youth, he strove to abolish slavery in his native State; and, in old age, he breathed a prayer and a lamentation for his country, whose sky was overcast by the lowering clouds of civil and servile war, made possible by the influence of a system which he had denounced in the draft of the Declaration of Independence as it came from his pen. In the original paper, the King of Great Britain was accused, indicted, and condemned in language which should be read and remembered by all.

"He has waged cruel war against human nature itself; violating its most sacred rights of life and liberty in the persons of a distant people, who never offended him; captivating and carrying them into slavery in another hemisphere, or to incur a miserable death in their transportation thither. This piratical warfare, the opprobrium of infidel powers, is the warfare of the Christian King of Great Britain. Determined to keep open a market where *men* should be bought and sold, he has prostituted his negative for suppressing every legislative attempt to prohibit or to restrain this execrable commerce. And, that this assemblage of horrors might want no fact of distinguished die, he is now exciting those very people to rise in arms among us, and to purchase that liberty of which he has deprived them, by murdering the people on whom he also obtruded them; thus paying off former crimes committed against the *liberties* of one people, with crimes which he urges them to commit against the *lives* of another."

These words ought, as a ray of Divine light, to illumine the minds of the people, that they may see the enormity of the crime of opening the African slave-trade, of extending on this continent the area of slavery, or of increasing the number of markets where men are bought and sold.

Jefferson accepted the Union, and labored for its perpetuity; but he considered the rights of the States as equally important, and he regarded the rights of man as more sacred than either.

Justice is at once the foundation and the object of the Union, — to the States justice, whose ministrations are the only security for their equality and sovereignty in the Confederation; to the people justice, which must recognize the equality of men, that is, the absence of any natural decree by which subordination is required of any, or authority is conferred upon any.

Slavery is the enemy of justice; and therefore it is the enemy of the Union, and the only enemy the Union has cause to fear. Freedom is an element and an ally of justice; and therefore it is a supporter of the Union. While, then, the Union stands upon the sovereignty of the States as one element of political justice, and while, consequently, we have neither the disposition nor the power to interfere with any State institution, we must yet so assert the supremacy of right in the Territories of the nation, and upon the high seas, as to secure the country against the further extension of a system which is not only a wrong to those who writhe under its power, but it is to us a tyrant, that robs us, by every accession it makes, of some portion of our just share in the government, and, through the treasury, the army, and the navy, takes security that its own authority shall not be disturbed.

Mr. Jefferson had faith in principles and in men. Let us accept the teachings and the experience of his eventful life.

Mr. Jefferson participated in two revolutions. *We have seen a third; and a fourth, more important than either, approaches.* When James Otis pronounced his famous speech against the writs of assistance, power departed for ever from the despotic judges and royal governors of Massachusetts. When Patrick Henry anathematized George the Third, through the examples furnished by Cæsar and Charles the First, Thomas Jefferson, then a youth of twenty-two, listening at the door of the lobby of the House of Burgesses, heard the thunders of that coming Revolution which was to shake and finally to rend in pieces the British empire. Thirty-five years afterwards, Jefferson himself was called to inaugurate a new policy in place of that of the Revolutionary period; and he thus saved us from the possibility of ever being tempted to imitate the monarchical institutions of Europe.

In less than thirty years more, the child of one war and the hero of another accepted a policy by which the government was entirely separated from those moneyed institutions that in other countries have proved the efficient allies of despotism.

These contests were not settled upon personal grounds, nor did they relate chiefly to the patriotism or the ability of the men engaged on either side; but the country having in some measure outworn and outgrown its former policy, having accepted new ideas, and having, under the pressure of circumstances, framed new issues, it necessarily demanded new and legitimate exponents of its judgment and will.

The great issue with slavery is upon us. We cannot escape it. The policy of men may have precipitated the contest; but, from the first, it was inevitable.

The result is not doubtful. The labor, the business, the wealth, the learning, the civilization, of the whole country, South as well as North, will ultimately be found on the side of freedom.

The power of the North is not in injustice. We are bound to be just; we can afford to be generous. Concede to our brethren of the South every constitutional right without murmuring and without complaint. Under the Constitution and in the Union, every difficulty will disappear, every obstacle will be overcome. But, rendering justice to others, let us secure justice for ourselves; and we of the North, not they of the South, shall be held responsible, if the slave-trade upon the high seas is openly pursued or covertly permitted, if new territory is consigned to slavery, or if the gigantic powers of this government are longer perverted to the support of an institution dangerous to the welfare of the people and hostile to the perpetuity of the Union.

MR. DOUGLAS: POPULAR SOVEREIGNTY.

PUBLISHED IN THE SPRINGFIELD REPUBLICAN, 1859.

MR. DOUGLAS deserves consideration. He is a bold man, a persevering man, a successful man. All this may be true, and yet Mr. Douglas be neither wise nor honest. Mr. Douglas is doing what has been done by two men only in this country, Mr. Jefferson and General Jackson, — making a platform for his party. He is doing, moreover, what has not been accomplished by any man, — making a platform which is hostile to the opinions of three-fourths of his party, and doing this defiantly, perseveringly, unscrupulously. But Mr. Douglas is not content with this. He denounces the President, who is the recognized head of the Democratic party; he caricatures and ridicules the President's domestic policy; and, finally, he announces, in anticipation, what the Democratic platform, to be built in 1860, shall not contain. Will he succeed in all this? Is it in the power of Mr. Douglas to inflict a fatal blow upon the integrity of the Democratic party of this country? These questions wait for a full development of the temper and tone of the Southern wing of the party. It is barely possible, — an assumption, we confess, that shocks every moral sentiment, — yet it is barely possible that Mr. Douglas is acting in unison with leading Southern politicians, who say, "Go just as far as may be necessary to secure the requisite number of votes in the North, and leave us to manage the rest." Or it is again possible that the South may have so lost courage as to accept and support Mr. Douglas, as only not as dangerous as the candidate of the Republican party. In either case, Mr. Douglas may succeed; but, in either case, the lesson to Mr. Douglas and his coadjutors is the same. Having acquired power by the votes of his enemies, through the influence of threats which appealed to their fears, he will not hesitate to maintain himself, and to secure a re-election by the same means. If, in 1860, the South shall accept opposition to the slave-trade and a zealous support of the doctrine of popular sovereignty in the Territories, because votes cannot be obtained by any smaller concession, will their leader, with his ambition quickened, but not satiated, hesitate, in 1864, to take any position which the temper of the North may demand? If Mr. Douglas, out of power, can subsidize, delude, and coerce the South, how greatly will his opportunities be increased when he has a hundred millions annually at his disposal! The South may yield the government of the country to the Republican party, and carry on, while out of power, an independent and honorable opposition; but the election of Mr. Douglas by such means will introduce the slave States to a *future* answering to the *past* of Ireland, — *that Ireland* that was deluded, corrupted, deceived, and betrayed by its leading men.

But Mr. Douglas's *principles* are not dangerous to

the South. Socially, pecuniarily, and politically, he is the ally of slavery. He thinks the institution ought to be extended wherever it can thrive, and that it can thrive wherever the legislation of Nature has not been unfriendly. His political principles are with the South; his religious tendencies are towards the Catholic Church; but his policy is for the advancement of his own interests. Hence he does not succumb to all the dogmas of the South. Slavery, to be sure, is right; but, inasmuch as it has not been established in the Territories by the Constitution, it can have no existence there until introduced by positive law. The South, under the authority of the Dred-Scott decision, maintains the doctrine, that slavery exists in all the Territories of the Union; and this opinion has been endorsed by Mr. Buchanan. One portion further maintains the opinion that Congress cannot pass laws unfriendly to slavery in the Territories, but that it is a duty to legislate in its favor; while another party looks to the Supreme Court for all necessary protection. Mr. Douglas dissents from these opinions, and asserts "that the Constitution of the United States neither establishes nor prohibits slavery in the States or Territories beyond the power of the people legally to control it; but leaves the people thereof perfectly free to form and regulate their domestic institutions in their own way, subject only to the Constitution of the United States." This is Mr. Douglas's platform; and it is to be observed that he concurs with the extreme men of the South in maintaining the doctrine that Congress cannot interfere with slavery in the Territories. It is probable that he here concedes to the slaveholders all that can be of practical use to them, for it is quite unlikely that Congress will ever establish slavery; but he denies to the North what is of signal importance, — the right to prohibit slavery in the Territories of the Union.

It is a remarkable fact in the history of the metaphysical doctrine of popular sovereignty, as taught by Mr. Douglas, that its chief success is due to a single sophistical statement, on which his whole system depends. The chief article of his creed, which we have already quoted, declares that the Constitution of the United States neither establishes nor prohibits slavery in the "States or Territories," &c. If we omit *Territories*, his creed is true: if we include *Territories*, his creed is false. The Constitution treats with *States* in regard to slavery; but it does not deal with *Territories* at all in this respect. The Constitution is not only entirely silent in regard to the *rights* of people in the *Territories*, but it does not even assume the *existence* of people in the Territories. What, then, can be more absurd than to assert any thing as the law of the land in regard to slavery in the Territories, from the fact that the Constitution neither establishes nor prohibits it? As the States are, by the terms of the Constitution, subject to their own will in regard to slavery, and as the Territories are not mentioned, it follows that they are excluded from the operation of the rule which is applied to the States, and the law of their political existence must be found elsewhere. Mr. Douglas may assume, that, by analogy, the right of the people of a State in regard to slavery is the measure of the right of the people of a Territory.

Our answer is, if this law of analogy applies to slavery, it applies to every thing else; and we have, consequently, no longer a Territory, but that complete organization which we call a State. Whenever any distinction, however unimportant, is made between the condition of a State and a Territory, Mr. Douglas's doctrine of popular sovereignty in the Territories is fatally undermined. All distinctions, therefore, are carefully avoided; and he constantly speaks of States and Territories as equivalent organizations. Give a wider application to Mr. Douglas's slavery logic, and the absurdity of the reasoning is seen. *The Constitution of the United States neither establishes nor prohibits any institution whatever in the Territories, beyond the power of the people legally to control it, but leaves the people thereof perfectly free to form and regulate their institutions in their own way, subject only to the Constitution of the United States;* and therefore, we say logically, the people of a Territory have all the rights of the people of a State; and, therefore, there are no Territories belonging to the American Union; but all are, by the silent, negative operation of the Constitution of the United States, converted into independent, sovereign members of the North-American confederacy. We commend this system to the advocates of popular sovereignty. It offers many advantages. It will not be possible for the people or the Congress of the old States to resist the admission of new States, inasmuch as their consent will not be asked. It avoids all unpleasant issues. It provides for new slave States; it disposes of Utah; it settles, in anticipation, all questions that may grow out of the annexation of the Catholic Mexican States; and it permits the immigrants from the celestial empire to re-establish their institutions, and take their places as members of this imperial republic.

Does any one suggest that we have carried the doctrine of popular sovereignty so far that it is either dangerous or ridiculous? It is certainly ridiculous enough in theory, and it would be infinitely dangerous in practice; but Mr. Douglas went as far at Columbus the other day, when he asserted that there was no difference between States and Territories. But, we may humbly ask, if there is no difference, why appoint Committees of Congress on Territories? Why consume the time of senators and representatives in framing governments for people who have full and complete rights of their own as citizens of perfect States? Why has Mr. Douglas himself stood patiently and laboriously at the head of the Committee on Territories, until he was dethroned by his political friends? Is there any such Committee on States? Would it be proposed by anybody? Would it be tolerated by anybody? If Territories are States, why haggle, as did Mr. Douglas in the case of Kansas, about their admission into the Union? Why, indeed, is there any question at all? If, as Mr. Douglas asserts under the pressure of the necessity of his own theory, Territories are "subject only to the Constitution of the United States," and Territories are equivalent to States, why are they not, from the first, sovereign members of the confederacy, and entitled to representation and consideration as such? If popular sovereignty is so sacred a right in this country, is it too much to suggest that some portion ought to reside in the citizens of the States? that they may very properly have an opinion, under the Constitution of the United States, concerning the admission of new States into the Union? Yet all this is theoretically denied by Mr. Douglas's dogmas. It seemed hard enough that the thirty million of people in the old States should have no opinion concerning the institutions of Territories that had been acquired by their valor, wealth, and enterprise; but now, under the new political dispensation, these thirty million can have no opinion concerning the admission of States which may have established Catholicism, Mohammedanism, polygamy, or even slavery.

Further, Mr. Douglas's doctrine of popular sovereignty is not freedom, but tyranny, — tyranny for the old States, in that they are compelled to accept new States as equal copartners in the confederacy, without the right to a separate, independent judgment of their own; tyranny to the Territories, or to the State-territories, as Mr. Douglas will undoubtedly call them by and by, in that they are compelled to accept the sovereignty of the Constitution of the United States, to which they have never assented. It is the essence of freedom in a political organization, that the people shall either have formed, or assented to, the constitution or fundamental law. In violation of this great principle, Mr. Douglas, from the beginning, puts the Territories under the Constitution of the United States, and, by the operation of the same Constitution, forces these State-territories into the American Union. The Constitution of the United States is but an institution, and therefore, according to Mr. Douglas's doctrine of popular sovereignty, ought to have received, in some way, the assent of all who live under it; yet he asserts over a new Territory the supremacy of an institution to which the people have never assented, and, by virtue of that supremacy, transforms the Territory into a State, and then forces the State into the Union.

The preamble to the Constitution of the United States is a sufficient exposure and refutation of all Mr. Douglas's absurd vagaries and theories: —

> "We, the people of the United States, in order to form a more perfect Union, establish justice, insure domestic tranquillity, provide for the common defence, promote the general welfare, and secure the blessings of liberty to ourselves and our posterity, do ordain and establish this Constitution for the United States of America."

It is quite plain that the Constitution was formed by the people of the United States, and that its jurisdiction was limited to the United States.

Another delusion under which Mr. Douglas labors, is, that the people of a Territory derive their authority to establish and regulate their domestic institutions from the Constitution of the United States; while, in fact, the right exists because they are *men*, and it would be just as perfect had the Constitution of the United States never been formed. In truth, the Constitution of the United States, as a constitution, can never apply to the people of a Territory until they have formed a constitution for their own government as a State, been admitted into the Union, and accepted the terms of admission. The underlying truth of republicanism — a truth which Mr. Douglas unceasingly disregards in his hot zeal for popular sovereignty — is, that every man, at some period in his life, has a right to a voice in the establishment of the government under which he is to live.

With our opinion of Mr. Douglas's character for boldness and perseverance continually enhancing, as we have disentangled his inconsistent propositions from each other and from the delusive arguments by which they are supported, we turn to examine his quality as an historical authority upon matters of government. Mr. Douglas misapprehends or misrepresents the political character and condition of the American colonies; and therefore all inferences drawn from, or arguments based upon, his statements are erroneous and fallacious. The American colonies never had an incipient or inchoate existence; but they were perfect political organizations from the very first. By the operation of the feudal law, the lands discovered in America by the subjects of England were for the benefit of the sovereign; and we have only to refer to the early charters, to see that all grants made were made by the king. The lands in America were never the property of the people of England, nor subject to the jurisdiction of their Parliament. By the charters, granted without the authority of Parliament, the people of the respective colonies were recognized as perfect political bodies. It is the theory of the British constitution that all power originally resided in the king; and our ancestors maintained that by the charters, under the feudal law, and in conformity with the long-established usage of Great Britain, the people of the colonies were independent of the Parliament and people of England. The colonies were separate governments, having the same head, to be sure; but the people of England had no rights of legislation over the people of America. The king was the acknowledged head of the colonial governments, and the rights enjoyed by the people of England were the measure of colonial rights. Neither the Parliament nor the people of England had jurisdiction in America. Your jurisdiction, said the colonies to Parliament, is confined to the English realm. America is not within the realm. As the king granted to you the right of legislation for the realm of England, so has he granted to us the right of legislation for and within our respective colonies in America. As the king has granted to you lands within the realm by the feudal tenure, so has he granted to us lands without the realm by the same tenure. As the conditions on which you exercise authority are expressed in Magna Charta, the great charter of British liberties, so the conditions on which we exercise jurisdiction over our lands are expressed in our respective charters, which are the charters of American liberties. As the king has agreed that he would not levy an aid nor assess a tax upon his subjects within the realm without your consent, so he has agreed that he would not impose a tax upon his subjects in America without the consent of their representatives in general assembly met. As the king had and has the right to cede a conquered territory without the consent of the Lords and Commons, so he had the right to convey to us this region, which was acquired without any expense of the blood and treasure of his British subjects. In fine, that America is a part of the dominions of the king of England and his successors, and owes allegiance to him and them; but is no more subject to the people and Parliament of England than the people and Parliament of England are to the king's colonies in America.

In harmony with this logical and constitutional exposition of American rights is the undisputed fact, that the Declaration of Independence was not made against the Parliament or the people of England, but against the king himself. It is a chief allegation, that the king had "combined with others to subject us to a jurisdiction foreign to our constitution, and unacknowledged by our laws; giving his assent to their acts of pretended legislation." Here is the whole argument in a brief statement. The king had combined with Parliament in an effort to substitute the power of Parliament for the legislative rights of the colonies; and for this violation of the constitution he was deposed. Every colony, from the moment when its charter was granted, was as really sovereign, in regard to its own affairs, as were the people and Parliament of England in regard to the realm itself.

Upon this view, no argument can be drawn from history in support of Mr. Douglas's theory of government in the Territories of the Union. On the other hand, the reasoning from analogy, based upon the truth of history, would be this: the colonists admitted that the sovereignty, including jurisdiction and property, was in the king; and they claimed the free enjoyment of those rights which the king had granted to them: hence it follows, as jurisdiction and property in the Territories are in the United States, as a sovereign sole, that the people of the Territories may take and enjoy such rights, and such only, as may be conferred upon them by the government of the United States. This doctrine would require qualification in practice; but it is the only legitimate deduction from our colonial life and history. The *war* of the Revolution was against the people and Parliament of Great Britain; but the *Revolution* itself was against the king, who was deposed because he conspired with Parliament to deprive our ancestors of those rights which were conferred and guaranteed by the respective colonial charters. The theory of the British government is unlike our own in these particulars; and Mr. Douglas's inferences are, consequently, without force.

Mr. Douglas appears to be equally unsound in his legal and political ideas concerning what is called *jurisdiction*. An acquisition of territory implies, first, unqualified jurisdiction over the territory acquired; and, secondly, a right of property in all lands not held by a legal title derived from the previous government. The essence of cession of territory is the transfer of jurisdiction; and jurisdiction is the right of exercising authority, which includes the power of governing or legislating. If, then, there can be no cession of territory without a transfer of jurisdiction, and if jurisdiction includes the power of governing, it follows necessarily, that the right to legislate for the Territories of the United States is in the Congress of the United States primarily, to be exercised by that body or transferred to another, — a territorial legislature, for example. Inasmuch as jurisdiction is an unavoidable element in territorial possession, no occasion existed for a constitutional recognition of the right of Congress to legislate for the Territories; and nothing can be more absurd than Mr. Douglas's inference that the absence of such recognition is evidence of want of power. The power is inherent in the fact of possession, through purchase, conquest, or discovery; and, without such possession, there can be no occasion or opportunity for the exercise of the power. The two co-exist; and, when the United States are in possession of territory, they can abandon the right of jurisdiction, or be deprived of it, in one of the following ways only: —

1st, By *non user*, in which case the occupants of the territory, whether few or many, would have an undoubted right to assume the duties of government.

2d, By a transfer of power to a local legislature, in which case the powers of the local legislature would be limited by the terms of the act transferring the power.

3d, By conquest, in which case jurisdiction would pass to the conqueror.

4th, By revolution, in which case the rebels, made patriots by success, would exercise jurisdiction over the territory seized.

The logical absurdity of Mr. Douglas's position is seen in the fact, that, while he cannot deny to the

United States jurisdiction over acquired territory, and while he does not show the way by which jurisdiction passes from the general government, he yet assumes the right of the people of a Territory to legislate for themselves; and the practical absurdity of his position is apparent in the fact that no attempt has yet been made to introduce popular sovereignty into any Territory, and in the fact that Mr. Douglas himself, and as if in refutation and derision of his own argument, declares that "the right pertains to the people collectively, as a law-abiding and peaceful community, and not to the isolated individuals who may wander upon the public domain in violation of law;" and, finally, that "the principle, under our political system, is that every distinct political community, loyal to the Constitution and the Union, is entitled to all the rights, privileges, and immunities of self-government in respect to their local concerns and internal polity, subject only to the Constitution of the United States," but that the right "can only be exercised when there are inhabitants sufficient to constitute a government, and capable of performing its various functions and duties, — a fact to be ascertained and determined by Congress." The logical deductions from these contradictory absurdities are, —

1st, None shall enjoy the right of self-government, or be people sovereigns in the Territories, who are not "loyal to the Constitution and the Union."

2d, "Isolated individuals who may wander upon the public domain in violation of law" are not popular sovereigns; but the "right pertains to the people collectively, as a law-abiding and peaceful community."

3d, None shall enjoy the right of sovereignty in the Territories unless their numbers, condition, power, and purposes shall have been first "ascertained and determined by Congress."

Therefore popular sovereignty is not a right inherent in the people of the Territories, but a privilege which may be granted or withheld by Congress.

Do we, then, deceive ourselves, when we say that Mr. Douglas offers no new theory of territorial government, and that he stands just where the Republican party stands? We now judge him by his conclusions, and not by his arguments. He admits the supremacy of Congress over the Territories, he admits that his vaunted doctrine of popular sovereignty is not inherent in the people, for he denies it entirely to certain classes and conditions; and, finally, he claims that Congress is the judge of the time when the concession of the power of self-government may be made to the popular sovereigns in a Territory.

There is no occasion to follow Mr. Douglas further; but, if we had his ear for a moment, we should state the following propositions as essential to and consistent with the proper government of the territories:—

1st, The right to acquire territory is inherent in every government; and, in our own case, it is not derived from the Constitution of the United States.

2d, As the essence of a cession of territory is the transfer of jurisdiction, the United States necessarily acquire jurisdiction over all territory obtained by discovery, conquest, or purchase.

3d, As jurisdiction is the right of governing or legislating, the right of the United States to govern the Territories is legitimate.

4th, The right of self-government is inherent in every man, and may be exercised lawfully whenever he can perform the duties that are inseparably connected with the right. The same law applies to communities; and, if Congress does not yield this right to the people of a Territory when they are able to perform the duties of a perfect government, they may assert their rights, and vindicate them at all hazards.

5th, The Constitution of the United States may be extended over a territory by the treaty of annexation, or by a law of Congress, in which case it has only the authority of law; but the Constitution, by the force of its own provisions, is limited to the people and the States of the American Union.

6th, When the people of a Territory are equal to the establishment and maintenance of a State government, they have an undoubted right to set up such a governnent; and it would be an invasion of true popular sovereignty, which is a right more sacred than the right of territorial jurisdiction, if Congress were to hinder or interrupt the action of the people.

7th, A State, so formed, may apply for admission into the Union; and Congress is entirely free to accept or reject the application.

There is no difficulty, theoretically or practically, in reconciling the jurisdiction of Congress with the right of the people to form their own institutions, because the latter right is a practical right only when the ability to discharge the duties of a perfect government exists. And when this ability, in the progress of events and the increase of numbers, is secured, the jurisdiction of Congress, the lesser right — a right that, in the nature of things, is temporary — must yield to the greater right, the right of a people to govern themselves, — a right that is not only permanent, but sacred as the life of man.

The Territories are the children of the Union, and the government of the Union should be conciliatory and paternal. There can then be no higher duty than the protection of the infant Territories against those institutions that are at war with progress, with civilization, with Christianity.

SLAVERY THE ENEMY OF THE FREE LABORER, OF PRODUCTION, OF BUSINESS, AND OF THE UNION.

SPEECH DELIVERED AT CAMBRIDGE, NOV. 1, 1860.

I PROPOSE to speak to you to-night, upon those topics that are before us in this campaign. The time for deliberation passes rapidly away, and the moment for final action approaches. I know not but that it would have been wiser for you, gentlemen, to have devoted the minutes of this evening to the details and labors of the canvass; but I assume that in Massachusetts, and especially in this district, where the Republican forces are led by one of the most valiant and trustworthy men of the country, there will be no lack of honorable effort to secure the triumph of the Republican party.

It is my privilege to address you upon political topics, at a moment when the supporters of freedom, fortunately, are relieved of all anxiety concerning the result of the pending canvass. The mind of the nation halts not between two opinions or among many. The events at Charleston in April, and at Baltimore in June last, rendered it certain that no one but the nominee of the Republican party could be elected President by the votes of the people; and the events in Indiana and Pennsylvania on the 9th of October rendered it certain that the nominee of the Republican party would be elected without the intervention of the House of Representatives or the Senate of the United States. Unhappily for the peace of the country and the integrity of the Union, there are bodies of men in this and the neighboring cities, in this and the neighboring States, who, having lost hope in the success of the parties to which they are attached, now seek, by combinations and menaces, to embarrass and thwart the administration of a Republican President; and thus, indirectly, they give aid and comfort to those enemies of the government who, in other sections, conspire for its overthrow.

I question not the motives of these men. Purity of purpose is an *apology;* but in political affairs, where wisdom and ordinary sagacity are wanting, it can never be a defence of those measures which bring ruin or grievous ills to a state. The party of which I speak would first make its power felt in this Commonwealth by the election of two gentlemen in the 4th and 5th Congressional Districts, who, though marked by the respectable characteristics of citizenship, are, politically considered, but the relics of a great party, which, in the fulness of its strength, and when led by master minds, exhibited a marvellous incapacity for the business of government. The masses of the party once dominant here and powerful everywhere, true to their ancient love of liberty, find in the Republican organization sufficient security for the perpetuity of

Freedom and the Union. This new party is already called to the responsibility of administering the government of the country; and for you the question is, Shall Boston and the surrounding cities and towns, illustrated and ennobled as they are with the evidences of learning, industry, and wealth, be represented by men whose experience and political associations will enable them to act efficiently for the protection of labor, the extension of commerce, and the development of all the material interests of the metropolis?

Legislative power, in a great country, is due to the personal ability and integrity of the representatives of the people, and to those political associations which characterize a free state. Shall the labor, the business, the prosperity, of Boston, and of the cities that are held in her gentle embrace, be made dependent upon a Congressional minority, led by Southern men of extreme and hostile opinions; or will you confide your fortunes to the noble and generous West, whose sons cherish the life and history of this old Commonwealth, from whence so many of them have gone forth? If there are men among you who believe in slavery, and who, consequently, desire to see all the great powers of this government wielded for its extension and protection, to them I make no appeal. They cannot consistently vote for the Republican candidates, however much the interests of trade and business might be advanced thereby. If there are, on the other hand, those who hesitate to sustain the Republican party, though no barrier of principle is interposed, I call upon them to consider whether Boston can afford, by a defiant Congressional and Presidential vote, to separate her interests from those of the great producing and consuming States of the country? The census of 1860 will show a population in Ohio, Michigan, and the States westward this side of the Rocky Mountains, equal to the white population of the fifteen slave States.

I ask no man to vote for the advancement of his pecuniary interests, as he would thereby deserve my contempt rather; but I unhesitatingly declare that the time has come when slavery is the apparent as well as real enemy of the free laborer, of production, of business, of the constitutional administration of the law, and of the Union of the States.

Failing or succeeding — failing, I think, but succeeding or failing — in these districts, the enemies of the Republican party hope to transfer the election of President from the people to the House of Representatives. Disappointment waits upon this hope; but to-night I treat our political enemies according to their claims, and without reference to their prospects. The supporters of Mr. Bell are the leaders in this movement. The friends of Mr. Douglas, with broken ranks, with uncertain step, and marshalled by unskilled men, take the place in the dismal procession to which they are assigned by their ancient enemies; while the officers of the old Democratic legions, now happily destitute of soldiery, either foot or mounted, patiently wait for the result of a contest in which they have no risks, make no sacrifices, but whose advantages, if any, are sure to inure to them.

Mr. Breckinridge maintains the doctrine of the

equality of the States; Mr. Douglas flaunts the doctrine of popular sovereignty; Mr. Bell claims special credit for supporting the Constitution and the Union; and yet the partisans of these leaders unite in a policy which denies the sovereignty of the people, which offensively asserts the equality of States while it denies the equality of men, and puts the existence of the Union at the mercy of desperate and hostile factions.

The election of a President by the House of Representatives is in the highest degree anti-republican; and constitutional authority was given therefor only to protect the country against the evils of a dissolution of the government in consequence of a failure by the people to elect a chief magistrate.

There have been two elections of a President by the House of Representatives, and there is nothing in our experience to invite a third trial. Each State is entitled to one vote; and the votes of a majority of the States in the Union are necessary for a choice. The doctrine of popular sovereignty is disagreeably illustrated, when little Delaware, with hardly half the population or wealth of the county of Middlesex, exerts the same influence as New York, when Arkansas and Florida are set off against Pennsylvania and Ohio. But can there be an election? The Republicans control fifteen States, with the possibility of a sixteenth, and no hope beyond. Mr. Breckinridge can command eleven States; and the remainder either have divided delegations, or will support Mr. Bell. Mr. Douglas cannot be a candidate before the House of Representatives.

It is an error to suppose that the Republican party, which is in possession of more political power in the House of Representatives and in the country than any other party, will yield its position or compromise its future. If it were possible to secure its defeat in 1860, it is yet sure of ultimate success. We cannot doubt that the Republican States would maintain their position at all hazards and against all odds. Would the supporters of Mr. Breckinridge unite in the election of Mr. Bell? Certainly not; for, when the people have once failed to elect a President, the government is irreversibly given over to the Southern wing of the Democratic party until 1865.

There could, then, be no election of President by the House of Representatives; but who can foresee the consequences of a struggle among men already inflamed by ambition, disappointment, and personal and sectional hatreds? The disunionists of the South would seize the opportunity to advance their schemes; and for that opportunity they would be indebted to the so-called Unionists of the North. A vote against the Republican party strengthens the hands of the disunionists. Failing in an election by the people, and failing in the House of Representatives, the eyes of the nation are turned to the Senate. There the candidates for the Vice-Presidency are limited to two; and none can doubt that Mr. Hamlin and Mr. Lane are the persons who will receive the highest numbers of electoral votes. At that moment, the government of this country will be in the custody of thirty-four men, twenty-nine or thirty of whom are from the slave States of this Union. They will elect Mr. Lane, of Oregon, and thus secure the complete triumph of the pro-slavery Democracy.

Happily, the men who advise you to aid in the defeat of Mr. Lincoln are powerless for the accomplishment of that object. Were it not so, they would bring upon the people such calamities as we have not yet been called upon to endure. Disunion in the South is the fruit of timidity in the North. Mr. Lincoln is a conservative man; the Republican party is pledged to the Constitution and the Union by its most solemn declarations; and, whenever the North shall declare itself for freedom and the Constitution by decisive and unwavering majorities, the cry of disunion will be silenced for ever.

The Republican party will protect the rights of States, — the rights of Virginia as carefully as the rights of Massachusetts; but it is only by allowing it to administer the government that the South can be satisfied of its ability and disposition to protect the rights of all.

Believing in the success of the Republican party, we yet plead for large majorities, knowing that the power of the secessionists will diminish as the numerical, moral, and political strength of the free States is combined in favor of Mr. Lincoln.

We are aware of the nature of the contest that is before us. The slaveholders will not loose their grasp upon the treasury, the army, the navy, all the chief offices of government at home and abroad, without active, possibly not without violent, resistance. The lovers of power and the enemies of the Union will combine.

We cannot shut our eyes to the fact, that, in the South, there are many men hostile to this Union, not so much for what it has done as for what they fear it will do. They have seen with alarm the growth of the free North, and they have anticipated the most violent attacks upon their rights. The sooner they are undeceived, the better for all, South and North.

The success of the Republican party will bring peace; but the success of the factions will continue the strife.

Some twenty or more years ago, Mr. Calhoun was driven out from the administration of General Jackson. In connection with that expulsion commenced the war against the Union. Mr. Calhoun, soon after, published an Essay on Government, in which he denounced this Union, and declared that it was a failure. General Jackson, for the moment, was able to crush out the disunionists. He wrote a letter in 1833, just after the secession movement was over, to a gentleman of Georgia, in which he said: "The disunionists are destroyed. They ought to have been hung on a gallows as high as Haman. We know," says he, "that the tariff question," which was then the question before the country, "was a mere pretext: the next pretext will be the slavery or the negro question."

These doctrines of Mr. Calhoun have been disseminated over the South; they have infected, to a great degree, the public mind: and to-day we find leading men in that section of the country, both of the Breckinridge and the Douglas parties, pledged, in case of the election of Mr. Lincoln, to disunion,—Mr. Yancey; Colonel Orr, of South Carolina; Mr. Foote, of Mississippi; and others. Mr. Foote claims to be a friend of Mr. Douglas; but, in a speech made by him at Saratoga, he declared, that, if Mr. Lincoln was elected, he was pledged to go home and join hands with the extreme South in opposition to the Union. Mr. Wise, of Virginia, is an avowed disunionist. How many of these men in the South are sincere, and how many are merely "men in buckram," I cannot say. I rather think, from a short article I saw in a letter from Norfolk, that Mr. Wise may be classed among the latter. At any rate, I do not think a great deal is to be feared from such men. In a speech made in Virginia lately, he said: "He wanted men to organize and be on the alert; he wanted minute-men,—men who would stand by the South: men who would fight for the South, who would die for the South: men who would be ready at a minute, in a moment, to protect the South: men who would meet the Wide-Awakes of the North, when the time should come, first with cannons loaded with grapeshot, and rifles and muskets and guns, if we can get them;—if not, then with swords and short-swords and bowie-knives; and, if we cannot get them, we will fight them with pickaxes and scythes and shovels and pikes, and, if we cannot get them, then I shall lead the van, and go in for fighting them with the weapons that God Almighty gave us." You see how his valor oozes out. It reminds us of De Quincey's essay in which "murder is considered as one of the fine arts." A member of a club in which murder was practised and discussed as one of the fine arts thus advises a young man who offers himself as a servant: "For, if once a man indulges himself in murder, very soon he comes to think little of robbing; and from robbing he comes next to drinking and sabbath breaking, and from that to incivility and procrastination. Once begin upon this downward path, you never know where you are to stop. Many a man has dated his ruin from some murder or other that perhaps he thought little of at the time."

We need in the North large majorities, in order that we may control at once this spirit of disunion, whether it is real or assumed; and I take it for granted that the men of the North will not allow this Union to be broken up in order that slavery may govern the country. If the question is ever presented, which I trust will never be presented, — Shall this Union be dissolved, and slavery be allowed to stand? — I believe that the great mass of the people of the North will say, that the institution of slavery, having been the destroying power in this government, shall not be allowed to exist longer than the government. We hold, in the North, the right of the States, — the right of Virginia to hold slaves, if she will; not because it is right to hold slaves, but because it is the right of Virginia to decide for herself whether she will hold slaves or not. But when they ask us to extend the institution of slavery to new Territories, whether under the guise of protection by Congress, or by the Supreme Court, or by the doctrine of "popular sovereignty" as in New Mexico, it is our right and our duty to resist such extension by every power conferred upon us by the Constitution: and we have a right to call in aid the authority of Congress; we have a right to call in aid the power of the people in the Territories themselves.

You recollect, very likely, that Mr. Yancey, of Alabama, came to Massachusetts during the last month, and in Faneuil Hall attempted to put upon Massachusetts the responsibility of the existence of the slave-trade from 1789 to 1808. In order that I may not misrepresent Mr. Yancey, — because I propose to review some of the positions which he took, — I choose to read to you what he said in regard to that provision of the Constitution by which the slave-trade was permitted from the year 1789 to the year 1808. He says: —

"Now we say, that, when that compact was formed, in all the States, save one, slaves were held as property; slaves were held by our fathers, who fought the battles of the Revolution; slaves were held by the very men who formed the compact that exists to-day between Massachusetts and Alabama. Now, then, these fathers who formed that compact put into that instrument certain provisions with reference to that property. What were those provisions? Why, one of those provisions — the most striking of all those provisions, as applicable to the great issue now, that no more slave States ought to be formed, that slavery ought not to be extended into the Territories — one of those compacts with reference to that issue is this, that the slave-trade which was carried on by our fathers, and especially, men of Massachusetts, by your fathers, that that trade should not be prohibited before the year 1808. Our fathers did not leave it to the legislative policy of the country to determine whether it ought to be prohibited or not. And not only that, but our fathers put into the Constitution this other guarantee, with reference to the slave-trade; viz., that the Constitution should not be altered, so far as that article was concerned. You might amend the Constitution with reference to the representation; you might amend it with reference to the commerce between the States, and with reference to the treaty-making power, and all other matters: but it was guaranteed in the Constitution itself that the article which secured a continuance of the slave-trade until the year 1808 should not be amended. Why did our ancestry do this? At whose instance did they do this? At the instance of Massachusetts: Massachusetts was in favor of the slave-trade section."

It is to that declaration of Mr. Yancey that I wish to call your attention, for the purpose of showing that there is no foundation in truth for his statement that Massachusetts was the author of the provision in the Constitution by which the slave-trade was legalized for twenty years.

In the Convention of 1787, there was a "Committee of Detail," as it was called. That Committee made a report of a draft for the Constitution; and in that draft it was provided (in Article VII.) that "no tax or duty shall be laid by the Legislature on articles imported from any State, nor on the migration or importation of such persons as the several States shall think proper to admit, nor shall such migration or importation be prohibited." This provision, as it was originally presented to the Convention, left the slave-trade open for an unlimited period of time. The delegates from the North refused to agree to any Constitution which contained that provision. Eleven of the old States had prohibited the African slave-trade; it was kept open only by Georgia and South Carolina. But it is to be observed, when we consider what it was expedient for the men of that day to do, that the Articles of Confederation contained no provision by which it was in the power of the Continental Congress to prohibit the slave-trade. It was left to each State to act upon its own judgment in that matter. South Carolina and Georgia had, thus far, kept the slave-trade open; and there was no power anywhere, except in those States, by which it could be controlled. Mr. Charles Pinckney, of South Carolina, said, "South Carolina can never receive the plan [of the Constitution], if it prohibits the slave-trade." So we see, and it is to be borne in mind, that, in the very beginning, South Carolina determined not to come into the Union, unless she could have her own way in regard to the matter of slavery. And it is also to be borne in mind, that, at that early period, certain States of the South entered systematically upon a crusade against the great interest of the North, which was the navigation interest. The original draft of the Constitution contained a provision, that no law for the encouragement of navigation should be passed, except by a two-thirds vote of each house of Congress; thus taking the subject of navigation out of the ordinary range of legislation, which was none other than a systematic and well-directed attack upon the great interest of the North.

General Pinckney, of South Carolina, declared it to be his firm opinion, that, if he "and all his colleagues were to sign the Constitution, and use their personal influence, it would be of no avail towards obtaining the assent of their constituents. South Carolina and Georgia cannot do without slaves: as to Virginia, she will gain by stopping the importation," — alluding to the well-known fact, that Virginia was then, as now, engaged in the slave-trade; that is, in raising slaves and sending them further South for sale. The argument of South Carolina and Georgia was, that, if the slave-trade was abolished immediately, the supply of slaves would become a monopoly in the hands of the Northern slave States.

General Pinckney again, after discussion, "held himself bound," as he said, "to declare candidly, that he did not think South Carolina would stop her importation of slaves in any short time." He moved to commit the clause, that slaves might be taxed with other imports; yielding a little to the judgment of the North, yet not willing to relinquish the right of the South to engage in the slave-trade.

Mr. Rutledge, of South Carolina, seconded General Pinckney's motion, and said: "If the Convention thinks that North Carolina, South Carolina, and Georgia will ever agree to the plan, unless their right to import slaves be untouched, the expectation is vain. The people of those States will never be such fools as to give up so important an interest."

Upon the motion of South Carolina, the provision relating to the slave-trade was recommitted; and, on the 24th of August, Governor Livingston, of New York, made a report "that the importation of slaves should not be prohibited prior to the year

1800," thus giving them twelve years, "and that a duty might be laid upon them to an amount not exceeding the tax on other imports." That was the proposition of the Committee, when their second report was made.

August 25, the day following, General Pinckney moved to strike out 1800, and insert 1808. It was a compromise, undoubtedly, by which South Carolina and Georgia were allowed to continue the slave-trade for twenty years. But it was a calumny upon Massachusetts, which ought not to have been made in Faneuil Hall, and which ought not to have been cheered by any one of Massachusetts, to assert that the old Commonwealth was responsible for the slave-trade. To be sure, Mr. Gorham, of Massachusetts, seconded the motion of General Pinckney, of South Carolina; but it was under the pressure of the declaration of South Carolina and Georgia, that they would not come into the Union unless they had a period of twenty years in which to supply themselves with slaves: and, as we had neither the power to compel them to come into the Union nor the power to compel them to prohibit the slave-trade, it was simply accepting, for the North and for the whole country, the best terms which the States of South Carolina and Georgia would offer. Therefore there was no other course, except to reject the Union entirely, or else establish a Union with South Carolina and Georgia outside, but still with the right to introduce just as many slaves as they pleased. And the declaration that I make now, that South Carolina and Georgia were responsible for this provision in the Constitution, is fully sustained by the declaration made by Gouveneur Morris, of Pennsylvania, in the Convention, when this amendment was adopted, providing that the slave-trade should be continued until 1808. "I am for making the clause read, at once," said he, "that importation of slaves into South Carolina and North Carolina and Georgia shall not be prohibited;" and he said, further, "he wished it to be known that this part of the Constitution was a compliance with those States." And that declaration of Gouveneur Morris, made in the Convention, in the presence of men from all sections of the country, — South Carolina, Georgia, and North Carolina included, — was not denied by any man there; and therefore the evidence is conclusive that the provision in the Constitution, by which those States that chose were permitted to continue the slave-trade for twenty years, was introduced in compliance with the express demand of South Carolina and Georgia, coupled with the declaration that those States would not come into the Union if the slave-trade were prohibited immediately. Luther Martin, of Maryland, in his letter (Elliot's Debates, vol. i. p. 418) says, "We were told by the *two first* of those States [Georgia and South Carolina], that their States would never agree to a system which put it in the power of the general government to prevent the importation of *slaves*, and that they, as delegates from those States, must withhold their assent from such a system." And yet Mr. Yancey comes to Massachusetts, with this historical record known to him, and in Faneuil Hall charges upon the ancestry of the people of the Commonwealth the great crime that they, by their will, continued the slave-trade for twenty years!

And coupled with that is the declaration that they caused to be put into the Constitution another provision, — that the provision allowing the slave-trade for twenty years should be irrepealable. I put Mr. Madison against Mr. Yancey, and ask you to find the truth. Mr. Madison, on the 10th of September, moved to take up the clause relating to amendments of the Constitution. Mr. Rutledge, of *South Carolina*, — not any man from Massachusetts, — said, "he never could agree to give a power by which the articles relating to slaves might be altered by the States not interested in that property and prejudiced against it." "In order to obviate this objection," says Madison, "these words were added to the proposition: 'Provided that no amendments which may be made prior to the year 1808 shall in any manner affect the fourth and fifth sections of the seventh article.'" (In the Constitution, the fourth section became the first clause of the ninth section of the first article.) So, again, it was due to the suggestion of South Carolina — to the *demand* of South Carolina, indeed — that the clause allowing the slave-trade to be continued for twenty years was made irrepealable. This is the second important falsehood Mr. Yancey uttered in reference to the men of Massachusetts.

Next, Mr. Yancey said, that, by keeping the slave-trade open for twenty years, Massachusetts imported one hundred thousand slaves, by which she made a profit of ten millions of dollars, which, by the thrift and economy of the State, now amounted to *one hundred million*, or one-eighth of the accumulated capital of two hundred years of labor and economy by our people. I thought it worth while to inquire as to the truth of this statement; and I found, upon an examination of the census, that it was as false as the other statements concerning slavery. By the census of 1790, there were 697,897 slaves in the country. In 1810, there were 1,191,364 slaves. You will observe that this period covers the entire period of the continuance of the slave-trade after the adoption of the Constitution. The increase in those twenty years was 493,467. We find, by examining the census of 1810 and 1820, — a period when there was no slave-trade legitimately carried on in the country, — that the annual increase was a trifle over two and six-tenths of one per cent. Applying this ratio of increase to the slave population of 1790, we find, that, in 1810, it would have amounted to 1,167, 364, or only 24,010 less than the actual number of slaves in the country. It is undoubtedly true, that, during those twenty years, many slaves escaped, and others were emancipated; so that the number of slaves imported was larger than the number shown by the census. But it is susceptible of exact proof, — as nearly as any thing can be, — that the number imported did not exceed sixty thousand: and it is also susceptible of proof, that South Carolina and Georgia imported at least one-third of those slaves; that Baltimore, New York, and Rhode Island were also engaged in the slave-trade; and yet Mr. Yancey comes into Massachusetts and into Faneuil Hall, and not only exaggerates the number of slaves imported fully fifty per cent, but charges upon Massachusetts the responsibility of the slave-trade for twenty years!

In the next place, he says that we made ten million of dollars on the hundred thousand slaves imported, or one hundred dollars profit on each slave. When you consider that the slave-trade was free, that it was legalized, that nothing stood between the merchant and the trade except his own conscience, is it to be believed that the average profit on the slaves imported from Africa was a hundred dollars, when the price did not probably exceed two hundred dollars in the extreme States of the South?

I come next to the action of Virginia in reference to the freedom of the territory north-west of the river Ohio, as set forth by Mr. Yancey; and notwithstanding these calumnies upon Massachusetts, as uttered by Mr. Yancey in Faneuil Hall, I think it was a compliment to Massachusetts that he came here. His whole speech is the speech of a dispirited man. It reminds us of the scenes in ancient Rome, when the defeated warriors of other countries were carried through the streets in the triumphal processions of the victors. It is a compliment to Massachusetts, that he came here, to Faneuil Hall, to plead with us that we should not attempt to control the country by the influence of our opinions; recognizing the fact that Massachusetts leads the public sentiment of the country against the extension of slavery to-day, as she led it against the despotism of Great Britain nearly a century ago.

He asks us, substantially, to be generous to the

South in this matter of slavery, because, as he says, Virginia has been generous to us. The declaration is, that Virginia, of her own motion, gave to the country the territory out of which have been formed the great States north-west of the river Ohio. He asserts, without any qualification, that, by the compact between Virginia and the other States of the Union, the Ordinance of '87, in its sixth article, by which slavery or involuntary servitude, except as a punishment for crime, was for ever prohibited in the territory north-west of the Ohio River, became a necessity. He claims for Virginia the credit of the exclusion of slavery from that territory, and says that the exclusion was provided for in the original compact. I thought I had read the history of the country in that particular; but I took pains, after Mr. Yancey made his speech, to examine the act of the Legislature authorizing the cession, and the deed of the territory made by Mr. Jefferson and his two associates, as far as Virginia had interest in it; and there is not to be found one word in either in reference to the exclusion of slavery. The territory, as far as Virginia had any rights, was conveyed to the nation without any declaration whatever as to the exclusion of slavery.

The credit he claims for the cession on the part of Virginia is very much diminished when you know what the facts are. In the first place, there was no jurisdiction actually existing in any State which was acknowledged by the other States. Several of the States claimed that this territory, which was then unsettled, lying west of the Alleghany

Mountains, had been obtained from Great Britain by the common blood and treasure of the whole people, and therefore it could not belong to any State. You remember, that, by the treaty of 1783, our territory was bounded by the great lakes, the Mississippi, the river St. Mary's, the Gulf of Mexico, and the Atlantic. There were thirteen colonies lying on the easterly slope of the Alleghanies; and, of course, the country west of that range was unoccupied. There were also, in addition to this claim of the United States to the territory west of the Alleghanies, conflicting claims by the States, growing out of the colonial charters, which were granted at a time when the extent of this continent was but imperfectly understood by the British Government; and the result of that ignorance was, that the charters granted to several of the colonies were conflicting.

For instance, the charter of Massachusetts included all the territory between two lines, one drawn from the head-waters of the Merrimack, and the other from the head-waters of Charles River, to the Pacific Ocean. The Colony of Connecticut had, by its charter, a right to all the territory lying between two lines drawn from different points on Narraganset Bay to the Pacific Ocean. The charter of the New-York Colony corresponded in character; and the charter of Virginia, which was the oldest of all, — dated in 1609, — covered the territory lying between two lines, one drawn from a point two hundred miles south of Point Comfort, now Old Point Comfort, and another line drawn from a point two hundred miles north of Old Point Comfort to the Pacific Ocean; and, of course, it included a large part of what is formed into the present Union.

These claims were conflicting. Those States that had no rights in the Western territory by their charters, maintained that all charter rights were annihilated by the Revolution, and that the territory belonged to the republic as a whole. Massachusetts made claims; Connecticut made claims; New York made claims; Virginia made claims. On the 16th of September, 1780, the Continental Congress passed a resolution calling upon the several States to relinquish their claims to the general government. What did Virginia do? Did she relinquish her claim? No. New York moved first. On the 4th of March, 1781, she ceded her rights in the Western territory to the United States. The cession by New York was followed by the cession of the rights of Connecticut; but it was not until the first day of March, 1784, that Virginia ceded her rights in the territory north-west of the river Ohio to the United States.

What next? In the month of April, 1784, Mr. Jefferson, from the committee to devise a government for the territory north-west of the river Ohio, reported a plan; and in that plan was a resolution that slavery should not exist in the territory north-west of the river Ohio after the year 1800. What then happened? Each State had one vote in the Continental Congress; but the vote was made up of several parts. The vote of Virginia was made up of three parts; Virginia having three delegates in the Continental Congress. Mr. Jefferson voted for the slavery prohibition, the other two delegates against it. The vote of Virginia was against the slavery restriction, and not for it; and therefore Virginia, not only by the deed of cession and by the act of her Legislature, was silent in regard to the institution of slavery in the great North-west, but in 1784, when she had the opportunity, under the lead of Mr. Jefferson, of prohibiting slavery in that territory, she voted against the prohibition.

With what propriety, with what justice, then, I ask, could Mr. Yancey come to Massachusetts, and claim that it is to Virginia that we are indebted for the freedom, the power, and the strength of the great States north-west of the river Ohio. It was not until, by general consent of all the colonies, a form of government was established for the territory, that Virginia, in harmony with the other States of the Union, assented to that famous ordinance by which slavery or involuntary servitude, otherwise than as a punishment for crime, was for ever prohibited in the territory north-west of the river Ohio.

Mr. Yancey next, or in the course of his speech, proceeded to speak of the prosperity of the South, and said that the exports of that section were about two hundred million of dollars annually, and the exports of the North only about one hundred million; and from these facts he asked us to infer that the South was much more prosperous than the North. In the same speech, you will remember that he spoke of the expenses incurred in the South for the maintenance of the slaves. He estimated that there were four million of slaves; that half of them received two pairs of shoes a year; and that the expense of furnishing shoes was about ten millions.

Then there was the expense for clothing, — some thirty millions more, or forty millions in all. He also stated that the Southerners were in the habit of travelling in the North, visiting our watering-places and our mountains, and expending large sums of money — a hundred or a hundred and fifty million of dollars — for the maintenance of the white population of the South. So you see, upon his own statements, when you consider them together, that, though the South might raise cotton of the value of two hundred million of dollars, still the larger part is expended in the maintenance of the slave population and free population of the South. Such is the fact. One of you, who might be able to buy a hundred bales of drillings upon a credit of twelve or eighteen months, and export those drillings to India, and obtain the returns in season to meet your notes at maturity, could just as well claim to be the exporter of the cotton drillings, as the South claim to be the exporter of two hundred millions of cotton.

The commission merchant, or the corporation that manufactured the goods, was really the exporter of the hundred bales of drilling, you being but the agent doing the work. So it is true to-day that the slaveholders of the South, who produce two hundred millions of cotton, are but the agents of the capitalists at the North. The "Charleston Mercury" has disclosed the truth in an article recently published, in which it commends the scheme of dissolution, and advises the South to put that scheme in operation immediately, because, it says, the South is now indebted in large sums to the people of the North; the next year's crop has already been advanced upon; and, when we dissolve the Union, we shall not only break up this government, but we shall have a court of insolvency, without assignees or dividend. That, gentlemen, is the truth in regard to this whole question of Southern prosperity. It is Northern capital which furnishes the means by which the production of cotton is carried on in the South.

The exports of a country are not a measure of its prosperity; nor are the producers of the particular articles exported usually the most prosperous. The opposite is more frequently true. The exports and imports must be considered together. We feed and clothe the South, and, through our commerce, furnish the country with the products of other countries. It is the whole country, South and North together, that exports cotton and gold and grain. The prosperity of a country or a State is ascertained when you know the average production of the industry of the people, the degree of social and domestic comfort, and the gross accumulations of labor and trade; and, in all these respects, the slave States are the least prosperous of American States.

You will see at once that there can be no real prosperity in the slave States, and for this reason: the slaveholders are not themselves laborers; they produce nothing. In the next place, men who do not labor, who live upon the proceeds of the labor of other men, are expensive in their habits. Therefore you have, in the South, a large non-producing class, and a class that consumes largely. They contribute nothing to the public prosperity. In the next place, there is not in any slave State, nor can there ever be, an efficient system of public education; therefore the white men of the South, with the exception of the slaveholders, are, as a general thing, in a state of ignorance; and, not being intelligent and educated, their labor is comparatively unproductive. Unless it be the slaves themselves, I know of no class of men in this country more to be pitied than the white laborers of the South,— unable to compete with the blacks, ignorant themselves, and despised by the slaveholders.

There can be no respect for labor or for the laborer in the presence of slavery; and therefore it is that we appeal to the laboring population of the North to stand by those doctrines, by which the Territories of this nation are to be secured to freedom, and made hereafter the homes of an intelligent and industrious laboring population, where labor shall be respected and honored. It is one of the peculiarities in the history of men, that the sons of Ireland, for example, who have fled from despotism in the old world, should come here, and, by their votes, do what is in their power to establish a despotism in this country. Whatever we may say of Russia or of Austria or of Italy, whether under the rule of the Bourbons or the Pope, there is no despotism so oppressive as the despotism of the slaveholders in the extreme slave States of this Union. In those States, there is to-day no liberty of speech, no liberty of the press; and I think that we may appeal to all citizens, whether native-born or adopted, to so exercise the elective franchise that this despotism, so oppressive in the slave States, shall not be extended to territory that would otherwise be free.

The next element in the polity of the South is to be found in the fact, that the producing class, the slaves themselves, are under two influences, both antagonistic to individual and public prosperity. The slave, — what is his interest? It is to produce as little as possible, and to consume as much as possible. And how does he differ from the free laborer, who enjoys the fruit of his own industry? The free laborer produces as much as possible, and consumes as little as possible; therefore there is, as the result of his energies, a surplus, more or less, which goes to the credit of individual, and ultimately of public, wealth. There is, in the free States of this country, no considerable number of non-producers; hence the North has this advantage over the South, that there are few non-producers and a large number of producers. Every man is interested in adding as much as possible to his own wealth, and therefore interested in adding as much as possible to the wealth of the community. Hence it is that the free States to-day are rich and powerful, and the slave States are poor and weak.

It is not for us of Massachusetts to disparage Virginia, or any other of the slave States; but, when we are called upon to consider whether we will extend slavery into new territory, it is a matter that concerns us to inquire what has been the effect of slavery in the States where it exists. Especially are we justified in examining into the pecuniary and financial condition of the South, when a man comes here from Alabama, and in Faneuil Hall boasts of the superior wealth of the South, as contrasted with the condition of the North. Under the influence of these two ideas, the extension or non-extension of slavery to new territory, and the fact that Mr. Yancey had boasted of the wealth of the South, I thought it well enough to look at Virginia, and ascertain what her condition is. There were no statistics in regard to Alabama, or I should have taken pains to make inquiries into the condition of his own State; but, concerning Virginia, there are statistics.

Look at Virginia as a whole. Consider the extent of her territory,—many times the size of Massachusetts. She has an inviting climate; she has, by nature, a fertile soil; she has valuable mines of iron and coal, and even stores of the precious metals; she has navigable rivers, that penetrate to the interior of the State; she has an extensive sea-coast; and she has water-power sufficient to turn all the machinery of New England. Under such circumstances, if there were the proper degree of enterprise and public spirit, you would find great wealth. But what is the condition of Virginia to-day? She has a public debt of thirty million of dollars, which is increasing at the rate of a million dollars a year. Her six-per-cent stocks, that have thirty years to run, sell for ninety cents; while the six-per-cent stocks of the State of New York sell for $1.12, and the five-per-cent stocks of the State of Massachusetts are worth more than par.

I ask you, to what is this difference to be attributed? It is to the fact that financial men in this country and in Europe have not confidence in the ability of Virginia to pay her debts. And there is an historical fact which is worth considering in this connection. No despotism has ever yet paid its debts, because the expense of maintaining a despotic government is always large, and its resources relatively are small. Very likely, Virginia may pay her debt; but it will only be when she has relieved herself of the weight of the institution of slavery. If she shall see fit, by her own motion, to provide for the emancipation of her slaves; if she shall encourage free labor, and develop her internal resources thereby, — then she will be able to pay her debt. But, if Virginia allows the institution of slavery to remain for fifty years, she is bankrupt, and her scrip is not worth thirty cents on a dollar for any man who invests for his children.

How has Virginia disposed of the money she has borrowed? She has put, of the public money, eighteen million of dollars into railways; her citizens have invested between nine and ten million more. Bear in mind, Virginia, a Southern State, whose wealth is the subject of Mr. Yancey's boast in Faneuil Hall, invests, of the wealth of her citizens, as I have said, nine or ten million in her railways. The citizens of Massachusetts have invested more than fifty million of dollars in railways within her own limits, and fifty to a hundred millions more in railways lying in other States. We could buy all the railways in Virginia without producing any perceptible effect upon the money market.

What next? The railways of Virginia pay an annual dividend, over and above the current expenses, of two per cent: the railways of Massachusetts, good and poor together, pay a dividend of between six and seven per cent. Where, then, is the wealth, where the prosperity? Is it in Massachusetts, or in Virginia?

Next, we know what the trade of Virginia is. In her impoverished condition, she taxes all the goods sold in her limits; and we find, that, in one year, the goods sold amount to only forty-one million of dollars in the great State of Virginia! When Mr. Yancey visited Boston, I could have shown him, in ten minutes, a dozen merchants who sell more goods, each year, than are sold in the whole State of Virginia; and yet he comes here and boasts of the prosperity of the South!

I say not these things for the purpose of disparaging Virginia, but to ask the men of Middlesex and of Massachusetts whether upon the slopes of the Rocky Mountains, east towards the Mississippi and west towards the Pacific Ocean, you are willing to establish yet other Virginias with the institution of slavery. If you are not, there is but one way to prevent it, and that is to vote the Republican ticket, because all the other parties, either covertly or openly, are in favor of the institution of slavery. There are but two parties, there can be but two parties, in a country like this, when an issue of the importance of the extension of slavery is presented to the people.

Mr. Breckinridge and his adherents are open, bold, and defiant supporters of the institution of slavery; and the parties that stand between the Breckinridge party and the Republican party will be crushed and annihilated in the great struggle that is going on. It is not enough for the exigencies of the occasion, that men say, as Mr. Douglas says, that they "don't care whether slavery is voted up or voted down."

The free men of this country *do* care whether "slavery is voted up or voted down." They mean, wherever they have the power to bring the elective franchise to bear upon the question of slavery in the Territories, to vote it down. We have the right in the Territories to vote it down; and we will exercise that right. We have the right to prohibit the foreign slave-trade, which to-day is permitted, if not recognized; we have a right to vote the foreign slave-trade down, by putting into the government of the country men who will see that the laws are executed against the slave-trade, as well as for the recovery of a fugitive slave who happens to escape to the North.

And I say further, gentlemen, that the success of the Republican party is as important to the South as to the North; indeed, I think it is more important to the South that the Republican party should succeed than it is to us; and it will be written of the Republican party, and of the men who have led it in these days, as by Mr. Bancroft it has been written of James Otis, that "he builded better than he knew."

We are working for the interest of the whole country, and in this respect, chiefly, that it is only by and through the Republican party that the way is to be opened for the escape of the South from the calamities that are already foreshadowed. Do you hear the rumbling, the muttering, sometimes in Virginia, sometimes in Texas, sometimes in Tennessee, as when, in 1856, after the defeat of Colonel Fremont, the slaves of Mr. Bell rose in insurrection?

It is only by the success of the Republican party that the weight of despotism that rests upon the border slave States can, to some extent, be removed. When the government of this country shall be in the hands of patriotic men; when officers shall be appointed in the border slave States who are not devoted entirely to slavery, as they may be in Virginia and Kentucky, — there will be freedom of speech and freedom of the press; and the people will begin to consider and to discuss the question, just as we discuss it here to night, whether slavery is, upon the whole, advantageous or otherwise. When they are permitted to discuss this question, they will reach precisely the same conclusions that you reach, — that it is an evil, morally, socially, and financially.

And, when the people of any State — for instance, the State of Delaware, where there are not two thousand slaves to-day — shall discuss the question, and decide that it is not wise to continue the institution of slavery, there is nothing in the question beyond the capacities of the most ordinary statesmanship. Ways and means will be devised by those States, of themselves, without the intervention of the general government, or the States of the North, for the peaceful emancipation of the slaves in the border slave States. When that shall have been accomplished, instead of their coming North to compete with the free white laborers here, the black men of the North will go South. You recollect that Mr. Yancey told us how the slaves enjoy basking in the sun, with the temperature at one hundred and ten degrees. Do you think they come North for that purpose? No: they come here because they cannot be allowed to remain in that climate which is best adapted to their constitution.

Therefore the emancipation of the slaves does not portend evil to the laboring people of the North, but rather benefit. When the slave population of the South has the hope, that, some time or other, ways and means will be provided for emancipation, they will be quiet, whether that emancipation be five, ten, twenty, or thirty years hence. But I am one of those who believe that there is not power enough in this government, however ardently it might be desired by those who administer it, to keep the slaves in subjection, however religiously we may observe the provision of the Constitution which requires the suppression of insurrections,—I say, I am of those who believe that there is not power enough in this government—aye, I believe more, that there never was a government powerful enough—to control the five and six and seven and eight and ten million of slaves that are to be in this country in the next fifty years, if some means be not devised for their emancipation.

They are already under the control of the same influences that control their masters; they are becoming, in a degree, more and more intelligent every year; they comprehend the doctrine of human rights; and it will not be in the power of this government, or of any other, to keep these men in submission twenty, thirty, forty, and fifty years. Therefore whoever furnishes an opportunity for the free people of the slave States to consider this matter for themselves is a benefactor of our country; for, if the South shall be deluged with blood in consequence of a servile war, the calamity will be one affecting the whole nation. Hence it is hardly less our interest than it is theirs to pursue the discussion of this question, but yet with an earnest desire to advance the fortunes of the whole country.

Whenever the Republican party comes into power, the moderate and conservative and upright minds of the South will see that we contemplate no injury to them. The most that can happen is, that, by a proper and constitutional administration of this government, there shall be freedom of speech, freedom of the press, freedom of the mails, in the slave States; and, as the result of this freedom, the people themselves will proceed to discuss the question of slavery, and finally to devise means for its abolition.

My friends, I do not propose to keep you longer. I wish, in conclusion, to ask you to consider how great the question is that you are called upon to determine. It is none other than the question of the freedom of these vast Territories, from the summits of the Rocky Mountains towards the Mississippi River on the one side, and the Pacific Ocean on the other, — Territories sufficient to form ten or twenty new, influential, and populous States. Would it not be, not only a calamity, but a disgrace, to the people of this country, if at this moment, when Russia has emancipated her millions of serfs and provided for their education; when Hungary is already contemplating her own redemption from Austria; when Italy is freeing herself from the Bourbons and from the Pope; when, in the language of one of our poets, —

> "Voices from her mountains speak,
> Appenines to Alps reply,
> Vale to vale and peak to peak
> Toss the old, remembered cry,
> 'Italy shall be free!'" —

the millions of people on this continent should desecrate to slavery a territory equal to the thirteen original States of the Union?

SECESSION.

AN ADDRESS DELIVERED AT CHARLESTOWN, MASS., ON THE EVE OF THE EIGHTH OF JANUARY, 1861.

IT is a melancholy circumstance in our experience, that an assembly of American citizens should be convened under the shadow of Bunker Hill, and within sight of Faneuil Hall, to consider whether, and by what means, the Union of the American States can be preserved. But it is only by exigencies and trials that the greatness possible to an individual or a nation is developed; and, under Providence, I yet believe that the wisdom and virtue and power of the American people are sufficient to exact of posterity, for the men of this generation who are at once true to Liberty and Union, the admiration and homage which we accord to those of our ancestors who inaugurated a system of popular liberty, and organized the Union of the States on this continent. Yielding what is due to difference of civilization and circumstances, our experience corresponds to that of the renowned nations of ancient and modern times.

Institutions may protect the rights of a people; but they have never essentially changed the character of men. Personal ambition, envy, disappointment, and hatred, organizing themselves in base and dangerous conspiracies, have waited upon every prosperous commonwealth. Vain hope it was, in the founders of these States and of this confederacy, that they and theirs should escape the evil to which free governments have been ever exposed!

But, oh, what excellency of wisdom it was, that in free schools; a free press; a religion untrammelled by law; a clergy identified with the interests, the hopes, and the fortunes of the people; the right of every citizen to bear arms; and the recognized though limited sovereignty of each State,—they secured liberty to all the generations of men on this continent, and set an example which the nations of the earth shall gladly imitate! Nor is it improbable, that the trial through which we are passing will demonstrate, more than any previous experience, our capacity to reconcile liberty and law.

No citizen ought now to be surprised or alarmed. And I may appeal to those of you who honored me with your presence on a former occasion, that nothing has yet transpired, of which you were not, in general terms at least, fully forewarned. Looking to events subsequent to the 6th of November, I then said: "The slaveholders will not loose their grasp upon the treasury, the army, the navy, all the chief offices of government at home and abroad, without active, possibly not without violent, resistance. *The lovers of power and the enemies of the Union will combine.*" The conspiracy against the Union, of which, alas! there is now but too ample evidence, was then announced, and some of the conspirators pointed out. We knew then that unbridled license and unblushing corruption existed in the government: but we did not know that three traitors to the Union were members of the President's Cabinet; that the President himself—unwittingly, as we may now hope—was the instrument of their designs; that munitions of war in great abundance were distributed in Southern forts and arsenals; that these forts and arsenals were purposely kept in a defenceless state, that their contents might easily and surely fall into the hands of the secessionists; that our small navy was unnecessarily employed in distant seas; that the strongholds of the nation were wilfully exposed to the attacks of the enemies of the Union; and, finally, that a chief officer of the government, the head of the War Department, had, without the knowledge of the President, entered into an agreement, by which South Carolina, the leader of the rebellion, was put in a position to seize the forts in the harbor of Charleston, without danger to those engaged in the treason.

One simple act of instinctive patriotic devotion to the country has precipitated events, disclosed the plot, startled the traitors, awakened the President to his duty, aroused and concentrated the energies of the people. So long as the incorruptible integrity of the captors of André shall be remembered; so long as men shall be moved to sympathy by the winter horrors of Valley Forge; so long as the common trials and common dangers endured by the men of the South and the North shall be recognized,—so long will the people of this country cherish the wise act and sturdy patriotism of Major Anderson. Nor is it to be deemed among the least of the fortuitous circumstances of that movement, that its author is a son of the South and a citizen of Kentucky. And I doubt not the time shall come, when the States of the South, with one accord, shall acknowledge their indebtedness to the commander of Fort Sumter. Nor should any man of this generation forget how great the relief he experienced when the intelligence reached him that the exposed band at Fort Moultrie, numbering scarcely one-fourth as many as the defenders of Thermopylæ, had taken refuge in Fort Sumter. Men realized then how powerless secession is and ever must be in individual States, while the general government holds fortifications in the harbors, that can neither be taken nor wisely attacked nor safely menaced. And though, in the long annals of our national life, it shall here and there be written that occasionally and temporarily passion usurped the throne of reason, and madness was installed in the seat of justice, it will also appear that the power and integrity of the nation were everywhere displayed, and the banner of the republic, without one star dimmed or one stripe erased, everywhere proclaimed the truth that only in the Union is there peace.

The world's history will furnish few chapters more interesting and instructive than a true record of the events of the last sixty days in America, — how a mighty nation found itself suddenly the victim of a widespread and dangerous conspiracy, and disseverance of territory and civil war imminent; how the government was corrupted, its chief officers engaged in treason, and, under one pretext and another, fleeing from the capital; how its treasury was drained, and its credit destroyed; how confidence was impaired, industry paralyzed, business prostrated; then how reason resumed its sway, justice asserted its supremacy, men rallied to the support of the republic; then how the misled escaped from the meshes of traitors, the wavering became loyal, and the people, regardless of party ties and the calls of weak or treasonable leaders, announced the doctrine that not one inch of territory shall be severed from the American Union; and, finally, how, in all and through all and above all, were seen the forms and heard the voices of two heroes of two wars, — one born in the South and the other in the North, — who rebuked treason, defended the Union, and gave assurance to the country that the army of the republic would prove true to the interests of the republic.

We may anticipate, but we cannot fix, the judgment of posterity concerning these events; and, indeed, what more interests us is the discovery of a safe way of escape from the dangers that remain.

The first necessity of this inquiry relates to the causes, the means, and the steps by which we have become involved in the present difficulties.

At the foundation of our public and national troubles lies the institution of African slavery. All theories concerning the causes of the present disturbances rest upon this foundation.

To be sure, there was, independently of slavery, a distinctive difference between the settlers of Virginia and the country south, and the settlers of Pennsylvania, New York, and New England. But this difference could never have disturbed the harmony of our national relations.

The disturbing influence of slavery is due to the fact that it is recognized in the Constitution of the country. But slaves are not recognized as property, nor is the rightfulness of slaveholding recognized; though slavery, as an institution, is recognized as an element of political power in the government of the country. And, by this recognition, the extension of slavery to Territories that might ultimately seek admission as States into the American Union became a question of interest and of right, under the Constitution, to every citizen of the republic.

Various expedients for the limitation of this right, or the transfer of its exercise, have been devised; and all have signally failed. Whether the citizen is to be deprived of a portion of political power by the extension of slavery to a new Territory, the ultimate admission of that Territory as a slave State into the Union, a partial representation of its slaves in the House of Representatives and in the Electoral Colleges, are questions of individual personal right in the government of the country, which cannot be transferred properly to the settlers of the Territory, or to the Supreme Court, but can be disposed of only by the action of the people who are already in the Union as citizens of the several States. This democratic republican doctrine would never have been denied, had not the cotton culture assumed majestic proportions, and had not the increase of free States alarmed the ambitious leaders of the South. From the first fact is derived the significant and menacing expression, *Cotton is King;* and, from the latter, the conciousness of power which leads the States of the North to imitate the example of the Antonines; and, regulating their conduct by justice, they are as little disposed to endure as to offer an injury. As between the *States* of this Union, free and slave, there is no conflict whatever. The duty of each and all under the Constitution is plain. If the States had been left to themselves, that duty would have been, generally, freely and faithfully performed.

But as between the claim of the slave States to extend the institution of slavery to the Territories, and the counter claim and purpose of the free States to consecrate all these Territories to freedom, there is an irrepressible conflict. The troubles between the States are due to the re-actionary influence of the revolutionary policy connected with, and the events that have transpired in, the Territories.

The policy of excluding slavery from the Territories is older than the Constitution. It dates from 1784, when proposed in the Continental Congress by Mr. Jefferson; and there has never been a moment of time since when the free States were not in favor of its exclusion. No change in this particular can be expected, and probably none is expected, by the South.

That the South has been greatly disappointed in the increase of wealth, population, and number of the free States, there is no doubt. In 1819, a writer in Niles's Register assumed, as the basis of his predictions concerning the future of the two sections, that not more than one free State would be formed out of the Illinois country, as he called the North-west, previous to 1850. In 1860, that same country, with the addition of the single State of Ohio, contained a population equal to the free inhabitants of the fifteen slave States; while Florida, which the writer proposed to set off against the Illinois country, is in the Union, but with a single representative only in the lower house of Congress.

Each census since 1810 has disclosed the important fact, that the increase of population is chiefly in the free States; and each decennial apportionment of representation in Congress has transferred political power from the slave to the free States. Hence four decennial periods have been periods of intense excitement; and at each the friends of the Union have been alarmed for its safety. The years 1820, 1830, 1850, and 1860 are marked as crises in the affairs of the country; and we necessarily connect the revolutionary spirit manifested at each epoch with the sensible realization of the loss of political power. The vigor with which General Jackson, in 1832, wielded the authority of the government against nullification, had paralyzed South Carolina, and destroyed her men; so that, in 1840, there was neither capacity nor spirit for rebellion. Moreover, the promise of the annexation of Texas, though never reconciling the more comprehensive sagacity of the statesmen of South Carolina, yet served for the moment to divert the attention of the Southern mind from the threatening preponderance of the North. The Mexican war is more intimately connected with our present troubles than is generally believed. Many ambitious men took an active part in the field. They saw at once the wealth and the weakness of that enervated and effete republic. Especially was it apparent to those interested in slavery, that Mexico and Central America offered golden opportunities for the extension of territory and the increase of power.

It may be well to bear in mind the fact, that the major part of the general officers of the Mexican war, who were called from civil life to the army, have since been found acting together in the political affairs of the country; and, as early as 1850, a secret organization was contemplated by which the policy of the Democratic party was to be controlled.

It was in 1850, also, that the first of a series of congressional measures was adopted that threatened the integrity of the Union. I refer to the Fugitive-slave Law, with its denial of right of trial by jury. Had this been secured in the State where the alleged fugitive was found, or in that from which he escaped, there would have been a substantial and general acquiescence in the enforcement of the law. But the secessionists, neglecting the example of General Washington, who only desired the return of a fugitive if it could be secured without offence to the feelings of the people among whom the slave might be sojourning, demanded the passage of a law unnecessarily repugnant to the inhabitants of the free States. Thus was the work of alienation commenced, and thus did mutual hostility supplant a common loyalty to the Union. Nor was it an ordinary insult to the integrity of the people of the free States, that the law was framed upon the theory that a jury of the country would not find the fact according to the evidence. It is my firm and conscientious belief that the verdicts of juries would have been governed by the testimony and the law, and that the exceptions would have been so few as not to have excited attention anywhere. Nor is it improbable that a provision for trial by jury, under the supervision and direction of judges of the United-States courts in the States from which the escape was alleged to have been made, with proper securities for the return of persons who might be found entitled to their freedom, would have relieved the North of all serious apprehensions concerning personal liberty. But neither course was adopted; and hence the Fugitive-slave Law of 1850 has been the occasion of unmitigated evil to the country, and was the first of a series of measures designed to effect a separation of these States.

Next, the conspirators against the Union, misleading Mr. Douglas, and probably abusing the confidence that he reposed in them, secured the repeal of the Missouri Compromise. Like all measures ostensibly for peace that have marked our public proceedings for ten years, this act imbittered and intensified party and sectional strifes at Washington, and involved the nation itself in civil war on the plains of Kansas.

Those unhappy results were all foreseen. When Congress refused to declare the condition of a Territory that was inviting both to free and slave labor, what else than civil war could have been expected? Indeed, war could not have been averted. Congress virtually invited the twenty-five million of American people in these States, entertaining opposite and hostile opinions upon slavery, to assemble by their representatives, and decide whether Kansas should be free or slave. The decision of the question, so submitted and so made, was necessarily offensive to the defeated party; and hence we had, not only civil war in Kansas, but alienation of sentiment throughout the whole country, with a tendency specific and powerful to disunion and civil and servile war, in whose lurid flames men are to-day, like spectres, walking.

Next, in 1856, the Democratic party was required to accept, as a part of its platform, a resolution, on which the right of a State to secede from the Union can be logically based.

I read from the Cincinnati Platform of 1856: —

"*Resolved*, That we recognize the right of the people of all the Territories, including Kansas and Nebraska, acting through the legally and fairly expressed will of a majority of the actual residents, and whenever the number of the inhabitants justifies it, to form a constitution, with or without domestic slavery, and be admitted into the Union upon terms of perfect equality with the other States."

By this resolution, one question only — the question of population — is reserved to the old States: this being settled affirmatively, then the right of a Territory to admission into the Union is declared to be absolute and final. Thus, upon the absolute right of a Territory to admission into the confederacy without the free consent of the existing members is naturally, fairly, and logically based the right of a State to secede from the Union, without regard to the wishes or opinions or power of the Union itself. And thus, in 1856, did the Democratic party accept the doctrine of secession as a constitutional doctrine.

Following the inauguration of Mr. Buchanan in March, 1857, and foreshowed by his inaugural address, came the opinion of the Supreme Court in the case of Dred Scott. I forbear to comment upon the opinion itself; but it widened the chasm, already fearful, between the two sections of the Union.

So logical are events in this country, and so inflexible are the laws which govern the increase of population and the distribution of political power among the States, that the application of the doctrine of secession and the overthrow of the Union could not have been postponed beyond 1860, unless, indeed, they were indefinitely deferred.

The census of 1860 numbers the swarming myriads of the North, and measures and fixes the representative power of the two sections for ten years. This is, in itself, a revolution such as takes place in no other country on the globe. The South were forewarned by the censuses of 1840 and 1850; and they foresaw that in a national Democratic Convention, acting under the two-thirds rule, they would be able barely to dictate the nominee of the party in 1864. This fact also measures the loss of power in the country and in Congress.

Since 1850, for the first time in the history of the country, the free States have commenced the work of colonization over the border. This work will go on. Not offensively, nor by plan, but in obedience to laws of migration and population which no mere human power can resist or permanently control. This colonization threatens the abolition of slavery in Missouri, in portions of Texas and Virginia, and in Delaware.

From and through Kansas we may expect a line of migration southward, over New Mexico and Arizona, into Sonora and Chihuáhua. Across the Isthmus there will be one or more lines of free States under English or American rule, and in either case hostile to slavery. The construction of a railway to the Pacific Ocean promises to unite the country east and west more firmly; and hence the importance of action by the South before the consummation of these schemes for enlarging and strengthening the Union.

The first act of 1860 in the drama of secession was the destruction of the Democratic party; for I feel bound to admit, that, while the integrity of the Democratic party was preserved, it was difficult, if not impossible, to destroy the Union. Not that the Democratic party was more loyal to the Constitution or the Union than other parties; but, being ever swift to obey the calls of slavery, it was not easy for slavery to make an issue with it.

Hence, in the Convention at Charleston, an issue was forced upon the party for the express purpose of driving it from power. Eight States withdrew from the Convention before a candidate was nominated or a platform adopted. It was a blow struck at the Union over the falling body of the Democracy. The manifest purpose was to sever the Democratic party, give the election to the Republicans, whether by numerical strength they were entitled to it or not, divide the Union, seize the capital, prevent the inauguration of the new President, hold the archives of the government, usurp the command of the army and the navy, and, upon the basis of legitimacy and right even, to re-form and reconstruct a military slaveholding empire in the South, which should command the Gulf of Mexico, the mouth of the Mississippi, stretch to the Pacific between Upper and Lower California, and finally absorb Cuba, Mexico, and Central America. Thus, under the corrupting and dechristianizing influences of slavery, is it the purpose of these leaders to convert the fairest portions of the American continent to the rule of a military despotism.

Governor Pickens, of South Carolina, in his inaugural address, says the new government will be more military in its character than the old one. This is a considerate and significant statement of the policy of the South. Thus far, they have failed in nothing; and it is now too plain to require proof, that the Democracy united would have commanded the electoral vote of the country in 1860. In the natural order of events, the Republican triumph should have been deferred to 1864. But the Republican party has triumphed, not so much by its own inherent strength, as by the systematic and pre-arranged divisions of its opponents. It seeks by constitutional means, and in constitutional ways, to administer the government of this country. The secession leaders are now able to rally the people of their respective States upon an issue favorable to their treasonable schemes. South Carolina, with a defiant and warlike spirit, abandons the Union. The seven other States that went out of the Charleston Convention will soon follow South Carolina. If the question of secession is submitted to the people of North Carolina,

Maryland, and Virginia before the 4th of March next, they also may join the rebellion against the Union. The leaders resolve upon separate secession, because they well know that no union among themselves can ever be effected unless they first cut the cords that bind them to the existing government.

In this juncture of affairs, we anxiously ask, what more remains to be done? I infer, from what I see and hear, that most of my countrymen believe that the election of Abraham Lincoln to the Presidency is to be declared in the customary way, and that he is to be inaugurated at Washington on the 4th of March next. The intentions of men are hidden from our view; but the necessities of the seceders we can appreciate, and the logic of events we can comprehend. It is a necessity of the South to prevent the inauguration of Lincoln. If he is inaugurated at Washington on the 4th of March, the cause of the secessionists is lost for ever. In all their proceedings, they have been wise and logical, thus far; and I assume that resistance to the inauguration of Lincoln is a part of their well-laid scheme. No man can now tell whether this scheme will be abandoned, whether it will be tried and fail, or whether it will be tried with success. I believe it will be tried.

True, the administration has put itself on the side of order; the city is alarmed for its existence, knowing full well, that, if it is given up to the military or the mob, and the representatives of eighteen free States are, for a single hour only, fugitives from the capital of the country, its reoccupation will be upon terms less agreeable to the inhabitants of the District and the neighboring States. The possession of Washington does, in a considerable degree, control the future of this country. Believing, as I do, in the stern purposes of these men; knowing, also, that Maryland and Virginia can command, on the instant, the presence of large bodies of volunteers,—I deem it only an act of common prudence, for the free States, without menaces, without threats, with solemn and official declarations even that no offensive movement will be undertaken, to organize, and put upon a war footing, a force of one hundred thousand men, who may be moved at any moment when desired by the authorities of the country.

What, then, will be our position? The way ought to be open for the inauguration of Mr. Lincoln; but there are those who demand a compromise as a step necessary and preliminary to that event. I do not now speak of the demand made upon States, in their sovereign capacity, to repeal certain laws, concerning personal liberty, alleged to be unconstitutional.

The duty of States in that particular is plain. If they have laws upon their statute-books that are unconstitutional and offensive, they should be repealed, as an act of duty; if they have laws that are offensive and unnecessary, they should be repealed, as an act of comity: but if constitutional laws exist, that are necessary for the protection of the rights and liberties of citizens, though they be offensive to other men and States, they must stand, though the heavens fall. Action upon such laws, whether ending in revision or repeal, is in no proper sense a compromise.

The compromises of which I speak are the various propositions before Congress, or its committees, which proceed upon the idea that the election by the people of a President of the republic, in constitutional ways and by constitutional means only, shall not be consummated by his peaceful inauguration, unless the character of the government is previously fundamentally changed, or pledges given that such changes shall be permitted. I see no great evidence that these demands are to be acceded to; but I see that the demands themselves attack the fundamental principles of republican liberty. If disappointed men, be they few or many, be they conspirators and traitors or misguided zealots merely, can interpose their will, and arrest or divert or contravene the public judgment, constitutionally expressed, then our government is no longer one of laws, but a government of men.

I am not of those who hold that the Constitution of the country is perfect, and ought never to be changed; but I do hold, that, while it exists, it should be observed. Let, then, Mr. Lincoln be peacefully inaugurated; let him declare his own views; let him administer the government, that men may judge his administration by experience: then, if there be persons or States whose rights need additional securities, I doubt not that he and his friends will readily grant them. But the secessionists know that their only hope is in the precipitancy of their measures and the extravagance of their demands. The leaders understand that the masses are deceived, and that even a brief delay will rekindle their loyalty to the Union, and that, in two or four years, the confederacy would be stronger than ever before. If, then, present compromise be impracticable; if seceding States deny a delay, as they probably will; if they plunge the country into the horrors of civil war by the actual shedding of blood, — is it not wise to submit to a peaceful dissolution of the confederacy? This depends, gentlemen, upon your readiness to affirm one of two propositions, — either that secession is a right secured to each State by the Constitution; or, denying this, but admitting the right of revolution, that the seceding States are too powerful to justify resistance on our part.

If secession is a constitutional right, it is a right appertaining to each State; and, if it is the right of each State, it is the right of a mere majority of the citizens of the smallest State in the Union to decide whether the Union shall longer exist. And hence it follows practically that we have no government. A question, then, in which we are all vastly more concerned than we are in any thing that it is possible for the seceding States to do, is the settlement for all time of the question of the right of the American Union to exist; not the right to exist in subordination to the will of a State, but an original, supreme right, derived from the people of the whole country, from the people of all the States.

If secession is not a constitutional right, then all organized, formidable, open, belligerent movements for the disruption of this Union are rebellions; and all persons engaged in them, and their aiders and abettors, are rebels and traitors. It is the essence of all governments, that they have power to suppress insurrections; and, by the Constitution of the United States, special authority for this purpose is given. Coercion, then,—not of a State, which is too intangible for that purpose, but of the people of every State and Territory who may be in resistance to the authority and laws of the Union,—is a right in the federal government, derived alike from the Constitution and from the necessities of national life. Nor does it follow that the State governments are subordinate to the general government; but each has a sphere of its own, and each is supreme in that sphere. The opposite doctrine is the source of our difficulties. In 1831, on the 4th of July, Mr. Calhoun gave this toast at Pendleton, S.C.: "The State and general governments: each imperfect when viewed as separate and distinct governments, but, taken as a whole, forming one system, *each checking and controlling the other*, unsurpassed by any work of man in wisdom and sublimity." And in 1860, South Carolina, failing to accomplish all that she desired in the control of the general government, enters upon the suicidal work of secession. I do not say that active and warlike coercive measures are necessary and wise immediately; but it should be understood that the government of the Union has both the ability and the purpose, in its own time and in its own way, to suppress insurrections and rebellions. The recent shock to public credit and individual enterprise was not owing to the attempted secession of one or many States, but to the fact that the illogical views taken by the President in his message destroyed the government itself by denying its right to exist. We may as well admit the right of secession in a State, as to deny to the general government the right of coercion. Practically, in either case, the government is at an end.

Will the people maintain the Union by the exercise of force? Ultimately, they will, if it prove necessary; and for that purpose the free States will become a unit. We have no alternative in this matter. The reasons which impel us to resort to force are too powerful to permit a choice on our part.

I. *Geographical considerations.* — From the British possessions trending southward are three great slopes, two single and one double, distinctly separated from each other, yet neither is so divided or broken by natural lines or barriers as to permit its division for political purposes, — the Atlantic slope, the Mississippi valley, and the borders of the Pacific Ocean. The writers of the "Federalist" well thought it practicable to form one confederacy between the Atlantic Ocean and the Alleghanies, and another between the Alleghanies and the Mississippi River. The rapid advance of civilization, and the construction of railways and telegraphs, have dissipated this idea. The Rocky Mountains are still a barrier sufficient to mark the limits of independent States. The railway will solve the problem of the union of the Pacific with the

Atlantic. But we search in vain, on any parallel of latitude from the Lakes to the Gulf of Mexico, for a line or barrier that can mark the boundaries of independent States. Nature has put the seal of unity upon each of these three great continental divisions; and Nature's order will not be disturbed permanently by the power of man.

II. *The trade of the Gulf of Mexico.*—After the Mediterranean Sea, the Gulf of Mexico is the most important water for commercial purposes on the surface of the globe. It is filled with fertile and productive islands; it touches the entire cotton-growing region of North America, that seems to hold this inland sea in its majestic embrace; it is the region of valuable woods, of precious minerals; it is the thoroughfare to the Pacific by the shortest overland routes on the continent; and, above all, it receives the contributions of the Father of Waters, in whose valley, within a hundred years, there shall dwell in peace and plenty a hundred million of human beings. Other men may expect peace while the inhabitants of the Upper Mississippi follow the windings of the waters, that trickle from their own hills, through a foreign country, to the sea. I do not. And may we not here suggestively remember, that migration has always forced itself southward, and that the Roman armies, enlisted in ancient Pannonia, marched a thousand miles beyond the Tropic of Cancer towards the equator?

III. By dissolution, we abandon the trade of the Pacific and of the islands and continents of the East.

IV. The business and wealth of all our cities have for their foundation the unity of the country.

When this foundation is removed, the wealth of New York, Philadelphia, Boston, Chicago, St. Louis, New Orleans, and Baltimore will be essentially and permanently diminished. We should be oppressed with attempts to establish conflicting custom-house regulations, and with an extensive and defenceless frontier.

These considerations apply with equal force to the South, and will deter them in a degree from pursuing the course marked out by the leaders. There are also additional reasons that apply exclusively to the South.

I. *An expensive government and direct taxation.* — The suggestion of Governor Pickens must be followed, and the South will be burdened with a heavy military organization. A change of government will not create manufactures or commerce. No one supposes that a line from the Atlantic to the Pacific can ever be defended against contraband traders; and hence the custom-house duties of the two sections would in the main correspond. The North could never consent to a lower system of duties in the South, and the result would leave commerce in the hands of those who enjoy it to-day. We shall have two governments, — the Northern cheap, with large revenues, and the Southern expensive, with small revenues. In the Northern, direct taxes and debts for general purposes would be unknown; in the Southern, debts and direct taxes would paralyze industry, diminish the price of property, repel immigration, — and finally the free States would assume the control of the continent outside of the slave States.

In every government, there is a limit to the power of taxation. The citizen can contribute a portion, great or small, of his annual income; but, whenever the accumulations of former years are taken, the citizens and government are soon involved in a common ruin. The South has no credit; nor can it ever have, for the basis of credit is wanting. Its net annual income is small. Commerce it cannot create; the power of taxation will be insufficient for a state of peace even; and the power to borrow money in the North or in Europe is denied to her by well-remembered circumstances in the history of individual States, as well as by the recognized influence of her social and industrial policy.

II. Cotton ceases to be king when the American Union ceases to exist. This event would be injurious to us all. It is well that cotton is king of commerce, but we can never allow it to subjugate liberty. A division of the Union will diminish the cotton crop to the amount of twenty or thirty per cent annually, during the continuance of the strife between the sections. Cotton may be raised, with differing success, over a belt of seventy degrees of latitude. Nowhere is there so large a tract of lands fitted to produce cotton of superior staple as in the United States; but the cotton regions of Central America, South America, Africa, and Asia are quite sufficient to supply the present demand of the world.

The political disturbances that have already taken place have given an impulse to the English mind which will ultimately prove pernicious to the great interest of America. Lands are not needed for the growth of cotton, but the presence of qualified laborers upon those lands. Now that the interests of England and Continental Europe are put in jeopardy by the movements of the South, we may look for more vigorous efforts to procure supplies of cotton from other sources. These efforts will be crowned with success, partial or complete; but it behooves the South to put an end to a controversy which will give no additional security to slavery, and which may result in the overthrow of the institution itself, and the surrender of the cotton-growing power to other sections of the globe. A diminution in the supply of American cotton works an increase of the article elsewhere, or else a change in the manufacturing industry of America and Europe. In either case, the South first, and the whole country secondarily, must suffer. The reign of King Cotton must be peaceful: by war, he will be dethroned.

III. The movements of the secessionists encourage and forbode servile war. I fear that men who have defied the flag of the republic may yet have bitter experience touching the institution of slavery. By the Constitution, we are bound to suppress servile insurrections; and the North would doubtless, whenever the exigency should arise, act in conformity to the requirement. But who can or will be responsible for the four million slaves, when the flag of the Union is no longer recognized in the slave States, and hostility to the North takes possession of men, who, more than any besides, are interested in promoting loyalty to the government? Nor will it be easy for the North to prevent hostile incursions into the South. If men sought the overthrow of slavery in blood, the destruction of this Union would be at once the beginning and the accomplishment of their design.

IV. The Southern States cannot form a lasting Union among themselves. Being the weaker section, the politics and diplomacy of the North would be directed to promote divisions and estrangements. The northern slave States would gradually lose their interest in slavery; and finally the Northern confederacy would aid in the emancipation of their slaves by purchase, and receive them into the Union of free States. Slavery cannot advance northward: freedom, with the Union or without it, will advance southward, and, by its gentle allurements, bring back State after State into the Northern confederacy.

If, then, peaceful secession were possible, there is nothing beyond inviting to either section, and destruction surely awaits the South. But peace for any number of years is not possible; secession is war, and those who weigh the circumstances will so treat it in the beginning.

Will fugitives from slavery be surrendered? Will the territorial questions be answered? Will strife cease on the borders of States or Territories? Will there not be bitter and bloody struggles for the possession of New Mexico and old Mexico? — for the control of Central America and the routes to the Pacific?

And, for the North, there is the additional consideration that we cannot consent to the establishment of a slaveholding, military oligarchy upon our southern side. We must first, then, give to the existing administration whatever support may be needed for the execution of the laws and the preservation of the Union.

We must look for the peaceful inauguration of Mr. Lincoln, and be prepared to secure his inauguration at the capital of the country, and at the appointed time, by the presence of such force as may be demanded by those officials who are bound to keep the peace. Then there must be time given for the organization of the conservative men of the South, who are at present borne down by an audacity and tyranny unknown since the revolutionary era of France. This interval will at once exhaust the revolutionists of the seceding States, and diminish the number and force of the prejudices in the Southern mind, that have no basis, except in misrepresentations made for political purposes.

Nor should I deem it unwise for the North, if it may do so without serious division and loss of strength, to announce its readiness to aid those States that desire to adopt a plan of emancipation, by the assumption, on the part of the general government, of a portion of the pecuniary burden. In so far as the evil is general, its removal should be sought through common and mutual sacrifices.

But if, unhappily, neither a spirit of justice in us, nor the presence of obstacles in the way of the secessionists which cannot be overcome, nor the exhaustion and sacrifices on their part of a condition of war without any of its customary honors or glories, shall recall them to their loyalty to the Constitution and the Union, there will then be no alternative but to preserve the one and compact the other by the exhibition of such force as may be needed.

When all things else have failed, *force* is the last resort of States, whatever may have been the theory of their organization. And we shall, I doubt not, if these but possible extremities of public and national life are finally to be presented and accepted, preserve the freedom of the citizens and the sovereignty of the States.

It is, indeed, possible, yet not probable, that the leaders of the South, maddened by ambition and disappointment, and deceived by a few men who misrepresent the opinions and purposes of the North, may seize the pillars of the temple of the nation, and bring it down in ruins upon us all. But, for one, I fear not any such catastrophe; and I accept the future of the country with the utmost confidence that Liberty and Union are to be hereafter, as now, one and inseparable.

The words which I addressed to Kossuth, when, in the name of the people of Massachusetts, I sought to cheer him with the hope that Hungary would be restored to nationality and freedom, I now address to myself and to you: "Liberty can never die. The generations of men appear and pass away; but the aspirations of their nature are immortal." Slavery may die. The republic shall live!

CONCESSION AND COMPROMISE.

SPEECH MADE IN PEACE CONGRESS, FEB. 18, 1861, AS REPORTED BY L. E. CHITTENDEN.

I HAVE not been at all clear in my own mind as to when, and to what extent, Massachusetts should raise her voice in this Convention. She heard the voice of Virginia, expressed through her resolutions, in this crisis of our country's history. Massachusetts hesitated, not because she was unwilling to respond to the call of Virginia, but because she thought her honor touched by the manner of that call and the circumstances attending it. She had taken part in the election of the 6th of November. She knew the result. It accorded well with her wishes. She knew that the government whose political head for the next four years was then chosen, was based upon a Constitution which she supposed still had an existence. She saw that State after State had left that government, — *seceded* is the word used, — had gone out from this great confederacy, and that they were defying the Constitution and the Union.

Charge after charge has been vaguely made against the North. It is attempted here to put the North on trial. I have listened with grave attention to the gentleman from Virginia to-day; but I have heard no specification of these charges. Massachusetts hesitated, I say: she has her own opinions of the government and the Union. I know Massachusetts; I have been into every one of her more than three hundred towns; I have seen and conversed with her men and her women: and I know there is not a man within her borders who would not to-day gladly lay down his life for the preservation of the Union.

Massachusetts has made war upon slavery wherever she had the right to do it; but, much as she *abhors* the institution, she would sacrifice every thing rather than assail it where she has not the right to assail it.

Can it be denied, gentlemen, that we have elected a President in a legal and constitutional way? It cannot be denied; and yet you tell us, in tones that cannot be misunderstood, that, as a precedent condition of his inauguration, we must give you these guarantees.

Massachusetts hesitated, not because her blood was not stirred, but because she insisted that the government and the inauguration should go on in the manner that would have been observed had Mr. Lincoln been defeated. She felt that she was touched in a tender point when invited here under such circumstances.

It is true, and I confess it frankly, that there are a few men at the North who have not yielded that support to the grand idea upon which this confederated Union stands that they should have yielded; who have been disposed to infringe upon, to attack certain rights which the entire North, with these exceptions, accords to you. But are you of the South free from the like imputations? The John Brown invasion was never justified at the North. If, in the excitement of the time, there were those to be found who did not denounce it as gentlemen think they should, it was because they knew it was a matter wholly outside the Constitution, — that it was a crime to which Virginia would give adequate punishment.

Gentlemen, I believe — yes, I know — that the people of the North are as true to the government and the Union of the States now as our fathers were when they stood shoulder to shoulder upon the field, fighting for the principles upon which that Union rests. If I thought the time had come when it would be fit or proper to consider amendments to the Constitution at all, I believe that we should have no trouble with you, except upon this question of slavery in the Territories. You cannot demand of us at the North any thing that we will not grant, unless it involves a sacrifice of our principles. These we shall not sacrifice: these you must not ask us to abandon. I believe, further, — and I speak in all frankness, for I wish to delude no one, — if the Constitution and the Union cannot be preserved and effectually maintained without these new guarantees for slavery, that the Union is not worth preserving.

The people of the North have always submitted to the decisions of the properly constituted powers. This obedience has been unpleasant enough when they thought these powers were exercised for sectional purposes; but it has always been implicitly yielded. I am ready, even now, to go home and say, that, by the decision of the Supreme Court, slavery exists in all the Territories of the United States. We submit to the decision, and accept its consequences. But, in view of all the circumstances attending that decision, was it quite fair, was it quite generous, for the gentleman from Maryland to say that under it, by the adoption of these propositions, the South was giving up every thing, the North giving up nothing? Does he suppose the South is yielding the point in relation to any territory which by any probability would become slave territory? Something more than the decision of the Supreme Court is necessary to establish slavery anywhere. The decision may give the *right* to establish it: other influences must control the question of its actual establishment.

I am opposed, further, to any restrictions on the acquisition of territory. They are unnecessary. The time may come when they would be troublesome. We may want the Canadas. The time may come when the Canadas may wish to unite with us. Shall we tie up our hands so that we cannot receive them, or make it for ever your interest to oppose their annexation? Such a restriction would be, by the common consent of the people, disregarded.

There are seven States out of the Union already. They have organized what they claim is an independent government. They are not to be coerced back, you say. Are the prospects very favorable that they will return of their own accord? But *they* will annex territory. They are already looking to Mexico. If left to themselves, they would annex her and all her neighbors, and we should lose our highway to the Pacific coast. They would acquire it, and to us it would be lost for ever.

The North will consider well before she consents to this, before she even permits it. Ever since 1820, we have pursued, in this respect, a uniform policy. The North will hesitate long, before, by accepting the condition you propose, she deprives the nation of the valuable privilege, the unquestionable right, of acquiring new territory in an honorable way.

I have tried to look upon these propositions of the majority of the committee as true measures of pacification. I have listened patiently to all that has been said in their favor. But I am still unconvinced, or, rather, I am convinced that they will do nothing for the Union. They will prove totally inadequate; may perhaps be positively mischievous. The North, the free States, will not adopt them, — will not consent to these new endorsements of an institution which they do not like, which they believe to be injurious to the best interests of the republic; and if they did adopt them, as they could only do by a sacrifice of principles which you should not expect, the South would not be satisfied: the slave States would not fail to find pretexts for a course of action upon which I think they have already determined. I see in these propositions any thing but true measures of pacification.

But the North will never consent to the separation of the States. If the South persists in the course on which she has entered, we shall march our armies to the Gulf of Mexico, or you will march yours to the great lakes. There can be no peaceful separation. There is one way by which war may be avoided, and the Union preserved. It is a plain and a constitutional way. If the slave States will abandon the design which we must infer from the remarks of the gentleman from Virginia they have already formed, will faithfully abide by their constitutional obligations, and remain in the Union until their rights are in *fact* invaded, all will be well. But, if they take the responsibility of involving the country in a civil war, of breaking up the government which our fathers founded and our people love, but one course remains to those who are true to that government. They must and will defend it at every sacrifice, — if necessary, to the sacrifice of their lives.

THE CONSPIRACY: ITS PURPOSES AND ITS POWER.

ADDRESS BEFORE THE PHI BETA KAPPA SOCIETY OF HARVARD UNIVERSITY, JULY 18, 1861.

IN troublous times like the present, men are anxious about what is doing, and take but little interest in what is said. Your invitation of honor and command contained a stipulation that I should speak upon those subjects that concern the welfare of the country, engross the attention of the American people, and disturb the maritime and commercial states of Europe. In this, as well as in all things else around us, is evidence of the common anxiety and of the existence of gloomy apprehensions concerning the future.

The anniversaries of this ancient and learned society have been thus far, as I understand, literary festivals; and the change indicated by the directions which I am to observe is no slight evidence of the eventful character of the times through which we are passing. Yet how impotent are all words, and surely such words as mine, when every highway resounds with the tread of armed men, and twenty million hearts beat warmly in response to the call of the country!

The effort of a strong man combating in the presence of a deadly danger, or struggling in the embrace of death itself, awakens at once our sympathies, our fears, and our hopes; but, for the last ninety days, our eyes have been fixed continually upon the sublime spectacle of a mighty nation, born of the purest patriotism that the world has ever seen and nourished by the genial influences of liberty, struggling to escape from the grasp of traitors and tyrants. As no other rebellion of which history speaks was so causeless in its origin, so none was ever so base in its character, or dangerous in its design. It is a formidable rebellion. Foreign nations have not over-estimated it: the American people have not, I fear, comprehended it. Nor let us be surprised or maddened, that Europe, on the moment, seemed ready to accept the dissolution of the Union as an accomplished fact. From the 4th of March, 1837, to the 6th of November, 1860, there was no successful, indeed there was no formidable, resistance to the domination of the now seceded States in the government of this country.

Wonder not, then, that the present generation of European statesmen and diplomates impulsively accepted the will and the purpose of the Southern mind as the law and the destiny of this continent. Educated and systematic statesmanship is usually paralyzed by a rebellion; and, in our own experience, it is observed that the early struggles in behalf of Secession drove from places of trust and influence the major part of the statesmen of the North in whom the confidence of the country would otherwise naturally have reposed. Wonder not, then, that Europe lost faith in our institutions and government, when familiar and trusted statesmen disappeared from the public councils. But neither they nor we knew the people of America. A quarter of a million of men have already answered the call of the President, and a quarter of a million more will take the field whenever the first authoritative summons reaches them. The instincts of the people are trustworthy. This rebellion is against them: its object is the overthrow of their government. "Not one common soldier or common sailor," says the President, "is known to have deserted his flag."

On the 24th of April last, two officers of the regular service, of inferior rank, but of that modesty of manner and nobleness of character which exact universal respect, reported to General Wool, in New York, that they were in command of eight hundred soldiers of the army of Texas, which General Twiggs had then recently abandoned, having first failed in his design to carry it to the camp of the traitors. These eight hundred men were soon followed by fifteen hundred of their comrades. Thus did this army, deserted by its commander, deprived of the means of transportation or subsistence or defence, stand firm in its fidelity to the government and the Union, and await and create an opportunity to return to the loyal States. No event in the history of this memorable rebellion is more worthy of being transmitted to posterity; and I trust that the names of these men will yet be known, and their faithfulness rewarded.

In disgraceful contrast is the conduct of the major part of the officers of the army and navy from the South. A small number of honorable men have been true to the country. Theirs are names that cannot die. But in what associations of infamy will history place the names of Ingraham and Twiggs and Maury and Lee, and all who, like them, have enjoyed the favors and the honors of the republic, who were its children by a double tie, and yet who have for years plotted treason while in command of armies, in command of squadrons, or, even worse than all, while enjoying the confidence of General Scott himself!

This, then, is not a rebellion of the people against tyrants; but, for the first time in the annals of mankind, we behold a rebellion of tyrants against the people, — a rebellion of tyrants against the people, a rebellion of tyrants against humanity, a rebellion of tyrants against justice, a rebellion of tyrants against law, a rebellion of tyrants against liberty, a rebellion of tyrants against the sovereignty of the American States, a rebellion of tyrants against the integrity of the American Union, a rebellion of tyrants against the hopes of the whole human race in the capacity of the people to govern themselves. Tyrants whose aims are so hostile to mankind could not be otherwise than false to every sentiment of truth, justice, and honor, as well as traitors to the country whose fostering care they had received. Being tyrants and traitors, they were prepared for the meanest acts and the vilest crimes. The law of their conscience, then, was not violated, when, under the pressure of their necessities, they stole the public money, seized the public arsenals, bombarded a starving garrison, and laid sacrilegious hands upon a hospital filled with the sick, and dedicated to humanity and to God.

Nor is it otherwise than according to a law of their nature that they have thus far failed to exhibit one chivalrous trait of character, or to perform one heroic deed. The war has been, on their part, that of a banditti. Do you, on your part, propose to conduct it as though they were brethren who had yielded suddenly to temptation, or gentlemen who are occasionally a little awry in their manners, or Christians temporarily forgetful of the requirements of the Decalogue? The apologists of these men refer us to the parable of the prodigal son. But, when he went out, he took only the portion which fell to him, and that by the judgment of his father; and, though he wasted his substance in riotous living, he made no war upon the homestead, but returned in contrition and humility. Other rebellions have had justifying causes or palliating circumstances. This has neither. High above all others, and alone, it stands distinguished for its criminality. The annals of nations furnish no counterpart to the baseness of States, and the treachery of individual men, which have characterized all these proceedings. Look at Louisiana. She was purchased with a price: her leading industry was fostered by a tax upon the commerce and the labor of the whole country. She has not now, nor has she had during her entire life as a Territory and a State of the American Union, an inhabitant who can with truth say that the government has done him any wrong, even the least, or failed to yield him ample and speedy protection in all his rights. Yet Louisiana went out of the

Union like a thief in the night, regardless of the ties of loyalty and of gratitude which should have bound her to a common country. And now she assumes to stand at the gateway of nations, and essays to control the outlet of that valley where are soon to dwell a hundred million of people. If the freemen of the North, and especially of the North-west, consent to this upon any terms or for any period of time, then history will say that slavery came to them no sooner than they deserved it.

But how are we to speak of the impotent treachery of Florida? — purchased as she was as a key to the Gulf of Mexico, rendered possibly habitable for civilized man by the expenditure of fifty million of dollars and the sacrifice of noble lives in an inglorious war, admitted as a State when she had not one-fourth of the productive power of the ancient county of Middlesex; and now, assuming upon her position, for which she is indebted to the generosity of the nation, she strikes a feeble but malignant blow at the Constitution and the Union.

Another outpost of the nation is Texas. We held her by the triple bond of voluntary annexation, conquest, and purchase. With a subsidy of ten million, we quieted a groundless claim that she made upon New Mexico; we allowed her property in all her immense public domain; directly or indirectly, we furnished means by which she inaugurated a system of public schools, a system of internal improvements, and by which her people were relieved of the burdens of taxation. We kept upon her frontier one-fourth of the army of the republic, and sought to facilitate her commercial relations with the States of the Pacific, as well as with those of the Atlantic. With much hesitation, and with singular uncertainty concerning her future, Texas, too, has abandoned the Union.

Of the old States, Georgia and North Carolina left the Union with hesitation and reluctance; South Carolina, early and defiantly; while Virginia treacherously remained until she hoped by her departure to paralyze the government, seize the capital, and secure the triumph of treason. Of all the States, old and new, South Carolina had an historical claim to be disloyal. She was subjugated out of the union with Great Britain by the armies of the North. She was induced to adopt the Constitution by a trade which was demoralizing to her people; and her career had been characterized by hatred and contempt of the other States of the confederacy. It must, however, be admitted that her recent movements have been marked by an appearance of respectability to which the other seceded States can lay no claim.

Of Virginia higher hopes were entertained. She had given great men to the service of the country, and to its history great names. The Declaration of Independence, which asserted that "all men are created equal," was hers by a peculiar right. She had a large part in the achievement of the national freedom; the Constitution was, in an eminent degree, her work; and no State had shared with her the homage of the whole country. Statesmen and leadership seemed to be hers by a divine right. In February last, twenty-one States assembled by her request to consider whether, and by what means, the

Union could be preserved. The nation believed in the sincerity of Virginia; but that summons was made in the interest of treason. Of her five delegates, three were then traitors, and a fourth made haste to be numbered among the enemies of his country. Her duplicity and hypocrisy may well be chronicled in the fact, that John Tyler, President of the Peace Congress, in his valedictory address thrice invoked the blessing of heaven upon the Union and upon the work of that Congress, though he had himself voted against the most essential resolutions. He then went to Richmond, and in forty-eight hours, even before the Congress of the United States or any State could be consulted, denounced the entire proceedings.

Mr. Rives was a professed Union man in February, and an open traitor in May. The treachery of Virginia was accompanied by a singular stupidity; and to-day her territory is invested by sea and land, a hundred thousand men are marching over her borders, and she madly accepts her melancholy doom. Bankrupt in treasury, dishonored in name, public and private resources exhausted, her pride broken if not humbled, she awaits the regenerating influences of a truer civilization. Her doom is certain and melancholy, whatever may be the fortune of the war. Missouri and Maryland have involved themselves in local and civil strife; and Kentucky seems destined to bring upon herself the same dire calamity.

These leading facts in our recent experience indicate the course of events during the last eight months. They indicate, moreover, the nature and extent of the conspiracy formed for the overthrow of the government. This conspiracy, at the time when its machinations were first revealed, was supported by the executive departments in fourteen or fifteen States, and by the legislatures of an equal number. It had corrupted most of the officers of the army and navy, who by birth were allied to those States; and freedom of speech and of the press was there already crushed. The conspiring States, having first destroyed freedom at home, proceeded to overthrow the institutions of freedom throughout the country.

I need not here and now detail the events of those dreary months of December, January, and February, when the country was paralyzed by corruption and imbecility, nor speak of the anxieties and forebodings which April brought when the fall of Sumter was followed by a wild crusade towards Washington.

The administration was divided, and members of the President's Cabinet abandoned the capital and their places, to identify themselves prominently with the rebellion. The capital of the country was in imminent danger; and a regiment of our own troops was attacked in the city of Baltimore, and its members massacred. Washington itself was besieged, and for days the country was ignorant of the fate of its capital. Then communication was opened by a circuitous route, over which men connected with the army, or otherwise in the service of the government, were permitted to pass. The call of the President for seventy-five thousand soldiers dissipated all idea of peace except through war.

So much of the country as remained loyal responded with alacrity. But the States of Delaware, Maryland, Missouri, and Kentucky, though nominally in the Union, refused to comply with the requisition. Thus had the conspiracy acquired the control of fifteen States, including six of those that carried on the war for independence.

The loyal States have met the issue thus forced upon them. They will, we trust, maintain the cause of the Union to the end. Yet how great are the sacrifices! Commerce impeded, manufactures paralyzed, and the claims due from citizens of the seceded to citizens of the loyal States at once and completely repudiated and abandoned. The first shock to credit and business, and the positive losses by repudiation and bankruptcy, have diminished the resources of the country to the amount of five hundred million of dollars.

To this must be added and superadded the cost and losses of the war itself. Of the half-million of men we are to put into the field, possibly one-tenth will never return to their homes. Our annual expenditures in the prosecution of the war will be not less than two hundred and fifty million of dollars. This expenditure, however, is not a positive and complete loss. It furnishes employment to farmers, artisans, and manufacturers; but the impoverishment of the nation will exceed a hundred and fifty million a year, besides the loss of life and of the otherwise productive services of the army in the field. This is a crude but not an exaggerated estimate of the burdens we are assuming in defence of the Union and for the restoration of the Constitution.

It would be a fallacy in reasoning, and a folly in statesmanship, if we failed to make the most searching inquiries concerning the causes of the private and public calamities in which we are involved. If we are too timid to search for the causes, or, searching, are not able to discover them, then indeed is our way dark, and the nation without hope. There is, however, no difference of opinion as to the remote, the ultimate, cause of all these difficulties. It is SLAVERY. States North and States South, States loyal and States discontented, agree in this. How, or in what way, these evils have been produced by slavery, men are not agreed. They may have been produced by heated and hostile enthusiasts, who have attacked slavery when and where they had no right to attack it; they may have been produced by its supporters, who made claims in its interest that were repugnant to the principles of the nation; they may have been produced because too much was yielded to slavery, or because too much was withheld; or they may have been produced because the rapid growth of a great nation under a free Constitution is incompatible with a system of servitude.

And as no man whose opinions are sought at all has a right to withhold them in an exigency like this, however unimportant they may be as aiding the solution of great difficulties, so I express mine with freedom, and as fully as the occasion and the time will permit. I put, then, but little responsibility to the account of individual men or upon political parties. Something, no doubt, men and parties have done or failed to do, that, doing or failing, has contributed to the disorder of the times. We are experiencing the shock to which the country was from the first exposed. Nor was the danger hidden. It was seen by Washington, Jefferson, Hamilton, Madison; it was feared by the leading statesmen of the intermediate generation. That they warned the country against the danger is not evidence that the danger itself might have been avoided. They spoke of the magnitude of the peril, and gave utterance to their fears as well as to their faith and hopes.

Slavery existing in one-half of the States of the Union was necessarily, within those States, a subject of individual, domestic, and public concern. Hence its support became a matter of political importance. Slavery was the great interest of those States; and hence there arose a policy looking to its security and advancement. For these purposes the State governments could do but little, and the national government could do much. Hence there came to be in the slave States a fixed and general opinion that the national government should be administered for the protection and extension of the system of slavery. Hence the exigencies of the slave States were never met by the admission or the assertion of the right of each State to settle the question of slavery for itself; nor by the concession that a Territory had the right to do the same thing; nor by the execution of the Fugitive-slave Law as faithfully as other national laws are executed; nor by the declaration of political parties and of Congress that there was no power under the Constitution, and no purpose among the people of the free States, to interfere with slavery where it exists.

But none can deny that freedom is aggressive; and there can be no doubt that it has been the purpose of the people of the free States, with singular unanimity and without regard to party, to administer the government in the interest of freedom, but yet according to the Constitution. It is a fact well worthy of observation, that no theory of the Constitution, or of the rights and duties of individuals or States under it, adopted by any political party in the North, has ever been accepted by those who now lead the rebellion. From Mr. Calhoun to John Tyler, they have uniformly repudiated the Constitution, as insufficient for slavery and the slave States.

The amendments demanded by Mr. Calhoun in his speeches and essays, and by John Tyler in his resolutions offered in the Peace Congress, proposed such alterations in the Constitution as would have rendered the government inoperative, unless it acted under the control of the slave States. Does any one say that he thought or believed that we have a Constitution which is neither for freedom nor for slavery? Is there a human mind that is not for freedom or slavery? a human heart that is not for freedom or slavery? a pulsation that is not of life or of death? So there is no Constitution that is not for freedom or slavery, no people that is not for freedom or slavery, no nation that is not for freedom or slavery. And hence our Constitution, being for freedom, (with gratitude to our fathers and to God be it ever spoken and for ever remembered!) — our Constitution, being for freedom, is repudiated by those who seek to establish a government which shall be for slavery and against freedom.

In February last, I met for the first time Mr. Seddons, of Virginia. Said he, with great frankness and without delay, "There is no reason why we should attempt to deceive each other. This contest is for the government of the country, — whether it shall be governed by the South in the interest of slavery, or by the North in the interest of what you call freedom." "And further," said he, "we are not disturbed by what you have done, but we are alarmed at what we apprehend. You are drawing a line around us, either by positive law or by immigration. You say we shall not go with our slaves over that line. No matter where the line is, near or remote; the time will come when we must pass over it. We are now eight million, and our slaves are four. Somebody must leave. You say the slaves shall not: then the masters must, and our country is given up to the negro race."

This is the view of a philosophical, transcendental secessionist. I do not stop now to refute it. It is substantially an assertion that the country must be governed in the interest of slavery, and that freedom should be restrained within certain limits by positive law. On this foundation the conspiracy and the rebellion are to establish a government of which human slavery is to be the corner-stone; whose lines shall extend, like the parallels of latitude, across the American continent, from sea to sea; and over which neither freemen nor freedom, nor the institutions of freedom, can ever pass.

We thus the better comprehend the magnitude

of the contest in which we are involved, as we perceive more fully the value of the stake to be lost or won by those who have inaugurated the war.

We have seen Europe a good deal disturbed by the transfer of the comparatively unimportant provinces of Nice and Savoy from Sardinia to France. Any question of territory upon that continent now excites the gravest apprehensions. These apprehensions are due to the ambitions and rivalries among states corresponding to each other in territory and power. The extent of our territory on this continent has saved us from similar anxieties; but the division of the country, as contemplated by the rebels, involves a sacrifice so great that peace ought not to be welcomed, if accompanied with any limitation of our boundaries, even though the war last through the century. I share your surprise, that, by suggestion or statement, I should admit the possibility of a division of the territory of the republic under any circumstances whatever. Yet we all know that this war means separation, or it means nothing.

And I foresee that when you have prosecuted it for a time, I know not how long, with such varied success as you may, there will appear men who will advocate a division of the country for the sake of peace. Our hope is that the machinations of all such will fail, and that the war will be brought to a speedy and triumphant end. But it is not the part of common prudence, to say nothing of wisdom, to omit recognizing the fact that eleven States are in open and systematic rebellion; that two others are avowedly hostile; that two others have not taken a position upon the question; and that nearly all the men in that vast section, accustomed to participate in public affairs, are involved in the conspiracy beyond all hope of escape, except by the accomplishment of their design.

It is safe, also, to assume, further, that the governing class of the South, including the slaveholders, though constituting, it may be, only a minority of the people, are animated by the bitterest hostility to the Union, and to the citizens of the free States. Secession is —

> "A gulf profound as that Serbonian bog,
> Betwixt Damiata and Mount Casius old,
> Where armies whole have sunk."

The Southern masses will soon learn that they have been deceived in regard to the courage and capacity of the people of the North. I trust that we shall not, in like particulars, underrate them. In 1774, Mr. Burke, in his speech on conciliation with America, gave a sketch of Southern character; and, though his opinion of the invincibility of Southern men was not confirmed by what happened afterwards, his views are not destitute of interest at this time.

He was at the moment chiefly desirous of refuting the argument drawn in favor of the English interest in the South from the fact that the Church of England formed a large body in that region. "There is, however," said he, "a circumstance attending these colonies, which, in my opinion, fully counterbalances this difference, and makes the spirit of liberty still more high and haughty than in those to the northward. It is that, in Virginia and the

Carolinas, they have a vast multitude of slaves. When this is the case in any part of the world, those who are free are by far the most proud and jealous of their freedom. Freedom is to them, not only an enjoyment, but a kind of rank and privilege. Not seeing, then, that freedom, as in countries where it is a common blessing and as broad and general as the air, may be united with much abject toil, with great misery, with all the exterior of servitude, liberty looks among them like something that is more noble and liberal. I do not mean, sir, to commend the superior morality of this sentiment, which has at least as much pride as virtue in it; but I cannot alter the nature of man. The fact is so; and these people of the Southern colonies are much more strongly, and with a higher and more stubborn spirit, attached to liberty than those to the northward. Such were all the ancient commonwealths; such were our Gothic ancestors; such in our day were the Poles; and such will be all masters of slaves who are not slaves themselves. In such a people, the haughtiness of domination combines with the spirit of freedom, fortifies it, and renders it invincible."

This description of slaveholders as a class is not strictly accurate; but we are dealing with men who boast some of the qualities named, if they do not actually possess them. As American slavery is the worst slavery of modern times, I cannot doubt that its effects upon the masters have been proportionately pernicious. With these qualifications, I am willing that Mr. Burke's description shall stand. We are dealing with men who are proud, haughty, and vindictive; who believe that liberty is a privilege, not a right: and, consequently, they are hostile to the American Constitution and Union, because it is the theory of our government, that liberty is a right, and not a privilege.

These remarks apply to slaveholders as a class, and not to the entire population of the South. We are also dealing with men and communities that are animated and controlled by personal and local ambitions which are natural, and from which none of us are entirely free. Some have personal ambition to gratify; some have wrongs to avenge; while Baltimore and New Orleans are indulging the delusion, that, under a new government, they would advance to the position now occupied by New York; and Memphis destroys herself in the vain attempt to equal Cincinnati. I am not ignorant of the existence of a public opinion that regards the view I am taking as altogether too serious, as well in reference to the causes of the rebellion as to the character and purposes of the men engaged in it.

It seems to be very generally believed that there is no danger of a severe contest, and that the exhibition of power by the national government will be followed by a retreat of the rebel armies and a return of the seceded States to their allegiance. Nothing could be more welcome to us than the acceptance of the Constitution by the rebellious States. But I have no hope that this will be accomplished immediately. I assume, on the other hand, that the war will be conducted with what vigor the rebels may command upon the land and upon the sea, and that in all military movements we shall be ultimately successful. The prosecution of the war will demand and develop a policy on our part. What is this policy likely to be? or, rather, what is it wise and proper for the national government to do?

For the present, undoubtedly, the prosecution of the war is the chief concern; and I am not without the hope that success on our part will be followed by a revolution of public opinion in the seceded States, so signal and so universal that nothing further will remain to be done, except to exclude from public employment and to banish from the country all who have taken a leading part in this great rebellion. But if your victories are not followed by a revolution in public opinion, if your authority is not re-established in the seceded States by the consent thereto of a majority of the people, if they still regard themselves as aliens and beyond your legitimate jurisdiction, what, then, is to be done?

Some will say, consummate secession by permitting and agreeing to a partition of the territory of the republic. But this suggestion affords no relief. Separation is the end of the Union and the overthrow of the Constitution, and, of course, the abandonment of those objects of sacred historical interest for whose preservation the war is now prosecuted. Reject, then, this suggestion you must; and one great good still remains which ought never to be abandoned, — the integrity of our territory. If the Union must end, if the Constitution must fall, let us still abide in the shelter of the grand historical idea that the great central portion of the North-

American continent is always and ever to be the abode, the country, of one people.

The settlers at Jamestown and Plymouth did not merely found towns or counties or colonies, or States even: they also founded a great nation, and upon the idea of its unity. Their colonial charters extended from sea to sea. Their origin, their language, their laws, their civilization, their ideas, and now their history, constitute us one nation. In the geological structure of this continent, Nature seems to have prepared it for the occupation of a single people. I cannot doubt, then, that continental unity is the great, the supreme, law of our public life.

A division such as is sought and demanded by those who carry on this war would do violence to our traditions, to our history, to those ideas that our people, South and North, have entertained for more than two centuries, and to the laws of Nature herself. An agreement such as is desired by the discontented would only intensify our alienations, embitter the strife, and protract the war upon subordinate and insignificant issues. Separation does not settle one difficulty at present existing in the country; while it furnishes occasion, and necessity even, for other controversies and wars, as long as the line of division remains.

Nor can we doubt, that when, by division, you abandon the Union, acknowledge the Constitution to be a failure, the contest would be carried on regardless of State sovereignty, and finally end in the subjugation of all to one idea and one system in government. Whatever may stand or fall, whatever may survive or perish, the region between the Atlantic and the Rocky Mountains, between the great lakes and the Gulf of Mexico, is destined to be and continue under one form of government.

And now again I ask, if your victories are not followed by a revolution in public opinion, if your authority is not re-established in the seceded States by the assent thereto of a majority of the people, if they still regard themselves as aliens and beyond your legitimate jurisdiction, what then is to be done? In the opinion of many, it may be wise to re-organize the State governments, as we are now doing in Virginia, by the election of men who are friends to the Union and the Constitution. The movement in Virginia answers a salutary purpose for the moment; and, if the war is followed by a change in public sentiment, the organization will become a legitimate government, deriving its powers from the consent of the governed.

But if you assume that Virginia is hostile to the Union, and if she shall remain so after battles and victories won by the army of the republic, what then is to be the fate of the new government? If you abandon it, the men who ruled at Richmond will come to Wheeling, take possession of the government by the authority of the people, restore it to Richmond, and there be ready to aid again in embarrassing or overthrowing the national administration.

If, otherwise, you maintain this government by force, then the sovereignty of the State is annulled, and the rule is no longer that of a majority. While, then, the organization of loyal governments by the loyal people of the rebellious States is a measure eminently wise, as affording an opportunity for wresting local authority from the hands of the rebels, we cannot look to it as a permanent means of maintaining the Union in name, if, unhappily, our military successes should not be followed by a re-action in public sentiment.

It would of necessity happen, in connection with the organization of loyal State governments, that the national troops would hold, for naval and commercial purposes, the principal cities and forts, as Baltimore, Richmond, Norfolk, Charleston, Mobile, New Orleans, Memphis, and Galveston; but the holding of these places, however valuable in a military and commercial aspect, is not the restoration of the Union, which exists by consent and not by force. There can be no doubt that the possession of the central points named would have a salutary influence through all the South, and, in so far as fraternal feelings were promoted, would tend to the restoration of the Union; yet we ought not to forget that the measure is one of war, and not the legitimate action of our republican system in time of peace.

Again I ask, for the purpose of leaving with you such thoughts as the times force upon an unwilling mind, if your victories are not followed by a revolution in public opinion, if your authority is not re-established in the seceded States by the assent thereto of a majority of the people, if they still regard themselves as aliens and beyond your legitimate jurisdiction, what then is to be done? This is, indeed, to my mind, the most embarrassing question of all, far exceeding in difficulty, and outweighing in importance, those military problems on which public attention is now exclusively fixed. These I have not attempted to consider; for, with the great majority of my countrymen, and with faith and confidence unshaken, I trust the conduct of the war to the foremost military chieftain of the age. The political difficulties remain; and eventually the country will be compelled to consider them.

One political difficulty is the insecurity of the national capital. Successes in Virginia, the siege of Richmond and its capture, do not overcome this difficulty. Will you remove the capital? You ought not; you will not. It is a part of the nation. Washington is the capital of the republic; it is incorporated into our history; it is interwoven with our traditions. If you remove the capital from the Potomac, and especially if you do this from a feeling of incertitude concerning its safety, then your action is more prejudicial to the Union than was the secession of all the States that rest upon the Gulf of Mexico. Will you make the capital secure where it is? How? Shall it be by the presence of a standing army? Is the country willing to strengthen the hands of the executive, and thus peril the liberties of the nation and the hopes of mankind? If we are to be and continue a nation, we must have a capital. That capital must be secure; it must be secure in peace and freedom, and not merely safe under the protecting power of the bayonet.

The war must demonstrate to the rebels, to the country, and to the world, not only that the objects for which it was undertaken cannot now be accomplished, but that all these grand schemes of treason and disunion must be abandoned. Success on our part in battle does not demonstrate this. We leave the States the same, the institutions the same, the people the same, chastened to some extent, but rendered vindictive also by defeat, as well as taught by experience to pursue a career in the future similar to that which they have pursued in the past. Is it hoped that the spirit and purpose of this rebellion can be controlled by the punishment of the leaders? Justice demands that heavy penalties be visited upon these men. I trust that the demands of justice will be met; but was ever a country pacified, or a numerous people intimidated, by such means? If you leave to treason the same sphere of action; the same motives for action; hopes strengthened, rather than weakened, by the belief, universal under the circumstances, that former errors might be avoided, — then you reserve for the country and the next generation a repetition of our own experience.

The overthrow of nullification seemed, for the moment, disastrous enough to the leaders: yet Mr. Calhoun, the apostle of the heresy, came afterwards into the Senate, was promoted, by the consent of that body and of the country, to the chief seat in the Cabinet of President Tyler, promulgated his pernicious opinions in State papers, corrupted the mind of the South concerning the true theory of our government, and, more than any other man, contributed to the disasters which have befallen the republic. Did any man doubt about Mr. Calhoun's opinions,—that they were hostile to the Union? And, after this experience, is it reasonable to expect that all the leaders even of the rebellion are to be excluded from public employments? But, if this were possible, there will not be wanting those who, nurtured under similar influences and entertaining similar opinions, will organize a new rebellion, which, in another generation, will menace the existence of the country.

I come now to a proposition which has, as I believe, the general support of history and experience. Whenever a rebellion is based upon a dissimilarity of institutions, the rebellion is finally to be controlled only by a modification of the institutions themselves. To the substance of this proposition I think the country must ultimately come. If, in the prosecution of the war, there is developed a strong Union sentiment, I should much prefer to rest upon that than upon any policy of our own. But, in the exigency that I anticipate, we shall be obliged to address ourselves to the question of slavery, so far, at least, as to render the national capital secure, and to demonstrate to the slaveholders, by a loss of power on their part, that slavery cannot control the government; that its positive and relative force, which can be applied to the work of dissolution, is less than ever; and that a renewal of the contest is likely to be followed by a further loss of power and consideration in the country.

By the Constitution, authority is given to Congress "to suppress insurrections." It does not follow that military force is the only means by which insurrections are to be suppressed; indeed, we might well infer that other means are to be resorted to when practicable. If Congress finds Maryland and Virginia in a state of insurrection, and especially if the insurrection is carried on by the governments, as in Virginia now, such means must be used as, in the judgment of Congress, are adequate to secure a permanent peace. Nor can Virginia say, that, by the Constitution, the question of slavery is reserved to the States themselves. It is true of the Constitution; but the difficulty is that the people of Virginia have repudiated that instrument, made open and treasonable war, and hence it is our province to decide whether or not we will deal with them as though they were true citizens of a loyal State.

Having rejected the Constitution, they render inevitable the arbitrament of war. If, by the fortunes of war, the national troops occupy and possess Virginia, and this occupation is not followed by evidence of returning loyalty on the part of her people, Congress must consider whether any means exist for the suppression of treason, for the suppression of the insurrection. Or are we to admit that the power of the government to suppress the insurrection is exhausted when the territory of the rebels is occupied by a military force?

The idea of the rebels, high and low, seems to be that the national government is solemnly bound to secure to them all the rights and privileges guaranteed by the Constitution, while they make war upon the Constitution, the Union, and the right of the nation to exist. And I know not but that there are some among us who believe that this war, with its vast expenditures and gigantic appliances, is to be carried on for months, or even years, for the twofold but inconsistent purpose of protecting the government against rebel slaveholders, and of protecting the rebel slaveholders against rebel slaves.

If your victories are not followed by a revolution in public opinion, if your authority is not re-established in the seceded States by the assent thereto of a majority of the people, if they still regard themselves as aliens and beyond your legitimate jurisdiction, then, inasmuch as the enjoyment of the right of the nation to exist is the supreme necessity of all, as the safety of the capital is essential to the enjoyment of that right, as the presence of slavery in Maryland and Virginia is inconsistent with the safety of the capital, no alternative remains but to provide for the extinction of slavery in those States at such times and upon such conditions, always including compensation to the masters who are not under the ban of the law of treason, as may be compatible with the welfare of the States themselves and the preservation of the Union.

By so doing, we wrong no man in his right of property, we give safety to the capital of the nation, we demonstrate to the South that slavery no longer has power to rule or to ruin the country, and we thereby take most ample security for the future peace of the republic.

I am aware that the prosecution of the war will develop a policy. Necessity is a stern master; and our exigencies are likely to be such that we shall yield private opinion to the public good. Let us all remember, as a bond of union between us, that the struggle in which we are engaged is for the existence of the government, and does not relate to questions of administration.

Our strength is in the justice of our cause, and in the fact that the interests of all sections are concerned in the preservation of the Union. Whether reason will be consulted by the Southern leaders we cannot foresee. Our course is plain. There must be a vigorous prosecution of the war, the restoration of all public property, the possession of the Mississippi River and of the principal commercial points on the seaboard. Moreover, the loyal citizens of the several States are entitled to, and must receive, the protection of the national government. The war on the part of the rebels is for the doctrine that the nation has no right to exist, if a single State, at any time or for any purpose, withholds its assent.

The war on their part is against all government, — that which they have attempted to set up, as well as against that which they inherited from Washington and Jefferson.

We maintain the right of the nation to exist, not in the favor of any State, small or great, Florida or New York, but by the will of the people of the whole country, acting in the light of our traditions and history, and in obedience to our necessities. The nation, the Union indeed, existed long before the Constitution was formed. The Constitution itself was framed to form a *more perfect Union.* This is a war for national existence.

It is now nearly two centuries since the weak

colonies that then clustered around Plymouth Rock, menaced in their right to exist, carried on a war against King Philip, who, for his courage and comprehensive policy, well deserved the name of the great ruler of Macedon. In that contest, every tenth house in Massachusetts was burned, and every thirtieth person was slain or carried into captivity.

Philip captured all our remote garrisons, and destroyed our towns on a line within twenty miles of the sea-coast. Our ancestors never once thought of peace or negotiations while an enemy remained within their borders.

So let their example bind us to the duty of maintaining the right of this nation to exist; to the duty of maintaining the Constitution as the supreme law of the land. But let us with joy and thanksgiving welcome the return of men and States to their allegiance, justly due to a government that, for three-fourths of a century, has protected all and injured none.

EMANCIPATION: ITS JUSTICE, EXPEDIENCY, AND NECESSITY, AS THE MEANS OF SECURING A SPEEDY AND PERMANENT PEACE.

AN ADDRESS DELIVERED IN TREMONT TEMPLE, BOSTON, UNDER THE AUSPICES OF THE EMANCIPATION LEAGUE, DEC. 16, 1861.

I DO not speak in a representative capacity, and the responsibility for what I say is not to be divided or assumed by any one. No person is better aware than I am that he who undertakes to give public advice in times of public peril assumes a grave responsibility. Nor is the responsibility materially lessened by the fact that he who assumes it has but slight claims to public consideration. In every free government, and especially in our own, the mature and considerate judgment of the people ultimately controls the administration of public affairs. As the river which drains and fertilizes half a continent bears upon its bosom the navies and commerce of an empire, and refuses to be subdued or controlled by any power save that of the ocean itself, is but the combination of minute rills, which, in the mountains where they had birth, escaped observation; so the current of public opinion, on which a nation is borne to its destiny, is but the union of individual thoughts, that, in their expression, seemed powerless for evil or for good. And as the river is dependent for its existence, as well as for its purity, upon the mountain rills, so the current of public opinion is dependent for its majesty and vigor upon the minute contributions that are made to it from distant and unobserved sources. Hence no thought is lost, no contribution is unimportant; nor can any one escape responsibility, however he may shrink from duty. Nor ought it to be admitted, whatever the circumstances of peace or war, that measures affecting the welfare of the nation are not to be discussed by and before the people. But such discussions may have evil effects, unless conducted with moderation, and under the influence of a sturdy patriotism.

So, too, in times of public trial, the details of the public service must be left to the discretion of those intrusted with the conduct of affairs. There must, moreover, be liberality — indeed, a broad and unquestioning generosity — in the judgment we form of those on whom the responsibility rests.

But, on the other hand, whenever a people, through ignorance or timidity, are incapable of examining and considering matters of public concern in a proper spirit and with wise reference to legitimate ends, then are their liberties in greater peril than they can ever be from the hostilities of foreign or the machinations of domestic enemies.

I have come to-night to speak with great freedom, but not in the language or spirit of complaint or doubt. We have seen how, by the energy of the administration, the loyalty of the States, and the patriotism of the people, an army of two-thirds of a million of men has been raised, equipped, and put into the field; how a navy carrying more than twenty-five hundred guns has been created; how resources to the amount of more than two hundred million of dollars have been gathered from the voluntary offerings of all classes. Hence we have confidence in the future. Moreover, the country confides in the President. To style him honest is but an inadequate expression of the nice sense of justice — the highest human attribute — which distinguishes him among men. He also possesses what Locke calls a large, sound, roundabout sense, that enables him to form opinions with care, and to act with discretion. These qualities are supported by a courage undismayed in hours of severest trial. He was among those at Washington, who, after the disaster of Bull Run, were unmoved either by fears for their personal safety, or apprehensions of danger to the fortunes of the republic. He is surrounded by able and patriotic men; and there is a united opinion in favor of giving to the administration a loyal and generous support. Nor is it any indication of a want of confidence, that the people of Boston, who in times of trial were accustomed, in their assemblies, to consider public questions, have now convened to contribute, if they may, to the restoration of peace, the re-establishment of the Union, and the return of our former political and commercial happiness and prosperity. But I may say to you, my friends, in the beginning, that I have no suggestion to make, the way to which is not clearly laid open in the recent message of the President. His recommendation to the Congress that territory should be acquired to which the black population of the United States may be removed, contains the opinion that the slaves are to be emancipated, either as an incident or a consequent of the war. It is, moreover, the teaching of experience, that great civil contests, based upon questions of domestic policy, must be settled by statesmanship; and when, as with us now, a nation's existence is in peril, questions of policy affecting that existence must be settled by a bold, vigorous, comprehensive, foreseeing statesmanship. For —

> "Not to the ensanguined field of death alone
> Is Valor limited: she sits serene
> In the deliberate council; sagely scans
> The source of action; weighs, prevents, provides,
> And scorns to count her glories from the feats
> Of brutal force alone."

In speaking of the justice, expediency, and necessity of emancipation as the only speedy means of crushing the rebellion and restoring the Union, I impose on myself three limitations, and desire you to connect them with all that I may say: —

1st. That a military necessity exists for doing what is proposed; and that I shall undertake to prove.

2d. That this necessity does not require us to take any action in reference to the loyal States.

3d. That I always and everywhere contemplate compensation to loyal men.

And I first inquire, what constitutes a military necessity? I assume that a military necessity does not depend upon the exigencies of the army in the field; but the great military necessity is to save the government, and whatever is necessary for the salvation of the government is clearly within the right and the duty of those who administer it and control the military department thereof. I think our Constitution has plainly indicated what a military necessity is, in that provision which declares that the writ of *habeas corpus* shall not be suspended, unless, in cases of rebellion or invasion, the public safety may require it. And what do we see to-day? That all of us are here deprived, by the exigencies of the times, of the right which, from the days of *Magna Charta*, with here and there an exception, has been the security of all Englishmen, and of all men who inherited the rights and the privileges of Englishmen. And why? Because it is believed by those intrusted with the administration of public affairs, that the public safety requires it. We have given up the great security which we had, that, whenever our liberty was taken from us, we had a right to an inquiry as to the reason therefor; and that right has departed, at the bidding of the government, and in obedience to the public exigencies.

If we demonstrate that the public safety requires the emancipation of the slaves, here or there or anywhere, then we have demonstrated that a military necessity exists. My friends, you are assembled with anxious countenances to consider how the country shall be saved; and you instinctively trace our peril backward to the institution of slavery, and are convinced without argument, that, had slavery not existed on this continent, there would not be a State—no, nor a county nor a parish nor a man—in all this republic to say that this Union ought not longer to exist. Therefore we charge home, with instinct and logic, the responsibility of the whole matter to the institution of slavery. And if, by the emancipation of the slaves, we can hasten by one day the return of the power of the Union and our lost prosperity, does not a military necessity exist?

I hear a suggestion from many quarters, which means, if I understand it, substantially this: that South Carolina and her ten associates in this rebellion are still entitled to the protection of the Constitution of the United States; and therefore we are bound to treat those States as we treat the States that are still loyal to the Union. If we yet labor under that delusion, then God save us! for not to the hands of man is intrusted the salvation of this republic, if we still indulge in the delusion that South Carolina and New York, that Florida and Pennsylvania, that Mississippi and Illinois, that Texas and Minnesota, are to be treated by the government of the country as enjoying equal rights and equal protection under the Constitution.

We have not thrust them out of the Union: they have gone out deliberately, freely, without compulsion; and, in all that relates to the subjugation of the territory and of the people of the rebel States, we must treat them as enemies, as belligerents. Are we to ask whether we are in war with these eleven States, when our frontier, from Kansas to the Chesapeake, is menaced by their forces, and when we, boasting that we have six hundred and sixty thousand men in the field, have been outnumbered at every point? If you indulge the delusion that we are not at war, and that these people are not to be treated as enemies, then the destruction of the country is near. We *must* treat them as enemies. When they came into the Union, they gave to the Union jurisdiction over their territory. That jurisdiction they now deny: let the armies of the republic go forward; let the statesmanship of the country secure the right that was guaranteed to us, and which we have not abandoned, however the rebels may desire to put off the responsibility from themselves.

Whatever is necessary to be done for the reestablishment of the government of the Union over the rebellious States we have a constitutional right to do; for the Constitution, if it secures any thing, secures the integrity of the territory over which and to which the Constitution applies. The rebels have no right to complain. We secure constitutional rights, as far as we can, to all the loyal States: disloyal States are enemies, and we must so treat them.

Suppose there are a few loyal men in South Carolina, North Carolina, Georgia, and Texas: are they to stand in the way of the salvation of this country? I trust not. When the war is over, when this territory is restored to the Union, the government of the country re-established, then, if these people have suffered by any thing that we have done, make them the compensation that is then in our power. But we cannot stop now, when the Union is in peril, when the lurid flames of war light up the horizon on every quarter, to inquire whether, in South Carolina or in Georgia or in Tennessee, there may be men who, if they could, would be loyal to the Union.

We have, my friends, labored under two or three delusions. First, we did not believe, twelve months ago, when the nucleus of the "Confederacy" (as it is now called) separated from the old Union, that a great conspiracy existed. We could not believe that men intrusted with important duties — Senators and Representatives in Congress, officers of the army and the navy who had been supported in luxury from the treasury of the nation, Judges of the Supreme Court, men high in authority throughout the fifteen slave States of the Union — had conspired criminally, traitorously, with perjury upon their lips and in their hearts, against a government which, as far as we knew, had never pressed too harshly upon a single citizen of the republic. We could not believe it. It was not strange that we did not believe it. But now, after a brief and sad experience, we find that for thirty years this conspiracy had existed; that it covered the whole slave territory of the Union; that it had given rise to the annexation of Texas, to the compromise measures of 1850, to the repudiation of the Missouri Compromise in 1854, to the division of the Democratic party at Charleston in 1860; that it had entered systematically upon the scheme of destroying the best government which the world had ever seen. It was not strange that we did not believe it; but now, now we know that it existed, and we know, too, full well, that it had its origin in the institution of slavery. And ought not the judgment of this country to be visited upon that institution as a part of the retribution for this foulest of human crimes?

It was a delusion, also, that we did not believe in the unanimity of the South upon this matter. We thought that the movement was instigated and carried on by a few hot-brained persons, whom we proposed to separate from the great majority of the people, and dispose of without special ceremony. But we have found, as the war has gone on, that it either included originally in the conspiracy all the chief men of the South, or that they have been drawn, unwillingly or willingly, into it; so that now there is no excuse for the man who believes that there is any lack of unanimity in the eleven seceded States. We are not more unanimous in this hall or in this State, or in the free States of the Union, in favor of maintaining the Union, than they are in favor of breaking down this government, and disgracing free institutions in the presence of the world and before posterity.

Let us no longer abide in the delusion that there is a want of unanimity in the South.

Another delusion in which we have indulged, to this very hour, is, that they had not resources sufficient to carry on this war, and that very soon they would be exhausted. I shall have occasion to discuss this subject further, as I go on. But we have found, as a matter of experience, during the last twelve months, that they have exhibited no evidence of a want of resources. Have they not put men enough into the field? Have they not, as far as we know, equipped them sufficiently for the service? Have they not had enough to eat, to drink, and to wear?

Then, as far as the year's experience goes, we

have been laboring under a delusion as to the power of the South.

It may be well enough to explore briefly the causes of the rebellion, as developed in the institution of slavery itself. And the proposition I make is that the institution of slavery is of such a character that hostility to this government was inevitable, sure to come at some time or other.

A change of opinion has been going on in the slave States, which perhaps I may well illustrate by a short chapter from my own experience. In 1857, in the month of November, I was at Lexington, Kentucky; and, on the sabbath, I attended service at what I understood to be the oldest Methodist Episcopal church. I listened to an able discourse. It was devoted to the maintenance of three propositions, which, as far as I could judge, were accepted by that congregation. They were, first, that the Saviour never said any thing in favor of human equality; secondly, that he never said any thing in favor of universal education; and thirdly, said the preacher, what we need is authority in the Church.

Do you not see, if those propositions be taken as indicating the public sentiment of the South, that slavery has worked two radical changes in the people, both of which are antagonistic to free institutions, and upon which free institutions cannot long be maintained? One is the denial of the equality of man; the other is the denial of the right of individual opinion in matters of religion.

And next I maintain, that the Constitution of

the Union, having been established for the purpose, as declared in the preamble, of securing liberty to the men who framed it and to their posterity, was inadequate to meet the wants of the slaveholders.

We have in the Constitution a provision giving to the government authority to put down insurrection. But do you not think that the time was foreseen when, on the plantations of the cotton districts, the slave population might rise and sweep away the white inhabitants in a single night? How powerless then would be the provision of the Constitution, even if the government were wielded by slaveholders! Hence it is, that, since the revolt commenced, they have steadily marched towards the establishment of a military, slaveholding oligarchy; for it is the necessity of the institution of slavery that it shall be maintained by a stronger government than that for which our Constitution provided. And, in the next place,—I do not propose to discuss it, but in the next place,—it was a necessity of slavery that it should acquire new territory, because it exhausts the land on which it fastens. These, then, as I believe, were the causes of the rebellion. There were pretexts, such as agitation in the North; but they were mere pretexts.

There were also inducements to the rebellion, one of which was a belief that the North would not act unitedly and energetically for the overthrow of the conspirators. I may state here what I think will be sustained by some gentlemen whom I see around me; and, inasmuch as the injunction of secrecy upon the Peace Congress was removed on the last day of the session, I assert, but not for the purpose of arraigning any man before this assembly or before this country, that in that Congress a Representative from a free State — a State that has with great alacrity furnished its quota of men to the army — announced to slaveholders and to non-slaveholders, that, in case the government undertook to put down the South "by force," the North would furnish a regiment to fight with the South as often as it furnished one to fight against it. In justice to the people of the country, we ought to say, in this connection, that the South has been entirely disappointed. The people, with great unanimity, have rallied to the support of the government; and not one regiment, possibly not one man, has been found to join the forces of the South. But such inducements undoubtedly operated to lead the people of the South forward in the rebellion they had undertaken.

Another inducement to the rebellion was the bankruptcy of the South. From two to three hundred million of dollars have been repudiated by the rebellion. It is well enough to remember that as long ago as 1792, I think, Mr. Jefferson wrote a letter to General Washington, urging him to accept a second term for the Presidency: and one of the five or six reasons which he gave for the request was the danger of secession; and a reason why he feared secession was, that the South was largely indebted to the North. This indebtedness of the South to the North, wiped out for the last fifty years at the rate of two or three million a year, and finally consummated by the repudiation of two or three hundred million, has always been an obstacle to a firm union between the two sections. Another inducement, by which the South has been combined as one man, was the cry, raised for the first time in that section of the country not more than five or six years ago, "Negroes for the negroless!" Thus every poor white man in the South, who ignorantly believed it to be the height of human ambition to own a negro, was inspired with a hope, that, at some future day, he might become a slaveholder, if the rebellion could be carried on successfully, the South separated from the North, and the African slave-trade opened. This is one of the means by which the rebels have been able to combine the Southern strength. Another reason — I will not stop to discuss it — was wounded pride, mixed with poverty; always a source of discontent.

In passing, I may say that I believe the Southern States, the Gulf States, have deceived, to a great extent, the border slave States, — Maryland, Kentucky, and Virginia; for, when the time should have come that they could secure the separation of the slave States from the free States, or the Southern States from the Northern States, they would incline to leave these border States with the North, as a bulwark against the spread of anti-slavery opinions southward, knowing, that, under the Constitution, we should return fugitives to these border States, and the border States, by State legislation, would return fugitives from the seceded States.

Will the rebellion exhaust itself? Consider the

extent of the territory that it includes. Consider the resources of that country in soil and climate. Consider the fact, that, in consequence of the existence of slavery, they can put in the field and equip, allowing the institution of slavery to remain, one-tenth or even one-eighth of their entire white population. And though, with the blockade, we close up the ports, so that they are deprived of certain luxuries and necessities of life, they yet can command those great staples on which their armies will depend for subsistence. They possess one power which we have not yet attained, and which, I trust, is not in store for us: they repudiate their debts as fast as they are contracted, "leaving the things that are behind, and pressing forward to those that are before." It was the estimate of Napoleon, that no nation could keep more than one in forty of its population in the field. The State of Indiana has put one in twenty of its entire population into the army; other States, one in twenty-five, one in thirty, one in thirty-five, one in forty. If it be assumed that the free States can put into the field, and keep in the field, one in thirty of the entire population, our army will not consist of more than about seven hundred and thirty thousand or seven hundred and forty thousand men; and, if you allow the institution of slavery to remain, the three and a half millions of men and women in the revolted States to continue upon the plantations, guarded by white women, aged men, and children, all armed,— if you allow the three and a half millions to remain upon the plantations and produce subsistence for the army, they can keep one-tenth or one-eighth of their entire white population in the field. If you strike from the resources of the South the supplies which are furnished by the three and a half million of black people, do you not see that a portion of the men who are in the army of the South must go home to produce supplies? Therefore the effect of allowing the institution of slavery to remain is to give them an equal opportunity with us in every contest. But, if we deprive them of the support they derive from their slaves, then a portion of their army must return to the plantations, and they would be reduced to one hundred and fifty thousand or two hundred thousand men, and the war would be at an end.

We may very well inquire whether this rebellion, if it go on, is to exhaust us. I do not propose to pursue the financial inquiry; but it is sufficient to say that the Secretary of the Treasury estimates that the public debt, on the 30th of June, 1863,—a year from next June,—will amount to nine hundred million dollars. If it shall happen in consequence of the check that is given to the exportation of cotton, and in consequence of a good supply of breadstuffs next year in Europe, that there shall be no demand for any of the products of this country, and there should be a demand for specie in consequence of excessive importations made inevitable because of an increase in your circulating medium, who does not see that bankruptcy is before us? And it is well to consider whether, if we have no regard for the black man,—it is well for the merchants of Boston and New York, the men who have four million tons of shipping on the ocean, a million in the East Indies, to consider whether we are willing to involve ourselves in a common bankruptcy, rather than to strike, while we have the power, at the foundation on which this rebellion rests.

It is a necessity that this war shall be closed speedily. We have tried the blockade. It has been to a good degree effectual. But do you not see that it is powerless with reference to producing that which we expected from it,—the suppression of the rebellion? Though our ships line the whole coast, from Galveston to the Chesapeake; though we keep out foreign supplies of every sort; though we cut off the export trade in cotton,—still these slaves produce that on which the rebel armies, armies in the field, depend. You may say we can, by one decisive battle, settle this matter. We have had one hundred thousand, one hundred and fifty thousand, for aught I know two hundred thousand, men on the banks of the Potomac for the last sixty or ninety days. Possibly by battle we might settle this matter; but we run a great risk. We thought, when in July our army went forth with banners and trumpets, they were marching to victory. Our soldiers fought well, victory seemed within their grasp, and yet defeat — temporary defeat — to our arms resulted. And who knows, that, with new leaders and new men, we are to gain a decisive advantage? When there are other means to settle this matter, will we risk the existence of this republic — risk freedom, and its name and fame in all the nations, and throughout all time — on the capacity of generals on the Potomac? I say no, if it can be avoided. Wars and battles are not the worst of evils, but they are to be avoided when and where we can avoid them. The life of the nation is involved in this contest, to say nothing of the men. All of us have sent our friends, brothers, kindred, — those who are dearer to us than our own lives; and shall we peril them on the Potomac, in Kentucky, in Missouri, in South Carolina, at the mouth of the Mississippi, — where my own friends and neighbors and townsmen are to-night, — shall we risk their lives rather than strike at the institution of slavery, when we know that the rebellion rests upon slavery, and will go down when slavery ceases to support it? Have you yet other men whom you wish to sacrifice upon this altar? Ellsworth, Lyon, Baker, and others of equal virtue and equal patriotism, with names unknown, have gone down upon bloody fields, sacrificed at the shrine of slavery; and will you offer up more, and yet more, of the best blood of the country — the young men, the hope of the nation, the strength of the future — in order that slavery may longer last?

I say, then, it is a necessity that this war be closed speedily. By blockade it cannot be: by battle it may be; but we risk the result upon the uncertainty whether the great general of this continent is with them or with us. I come, then, to emancipation. Not first, — although I shall not hesitate to say, before I close, that, as a matter of justice to the slave, there should be emancipation, — but not first do I ask my countrymen to proclaim emancipation to the slaves in justice to them, but as a matter of necessity to ourselves; for, unless it be by accident, we are not to come out of this contest as one nation, except by emancipation. And first, emancipation in South Carolina. Not confiscation of the property of rebels: that is inadequate longer to meet the emergency. It might have done in March or April or May, or possibly in July; but, in December, or January of the coming year, confiscation of the property of the rebels is inadequate to meet the exigency in which the country is placed. You must, if you do any thing, proclaim at the head of the armies of the republic, on the soil of South Carolina, FREEDOM, — freedom to all the slaves in South Carolina, — and then enforce the proclamation as far and fast as you have an opportunity; and you will have opportunity more speedily then than you will if you attempt to invade South Carolina without emancipating her slaves. Unsettle the foundations of society in South Carolina: do you hear the rumbling? Not we, not we, are responsible for what happens in South Carolina between the slaves and their masters. Our business is to save the Union; to re-establish the authority of the Union over the rebels in South Carolina; and, if between the masters and their slaves collisions arise, the responsibility is upon those masters who, forgetting their allegiance to the government, lent themselves to this foul conspiracy, and thus have been involved in ruin. As a warning, let South Carolina be the first of the States of the republic in which emancipation to the enslaved is proclaimed, and as a penalty for her perfidy in this business, which began at the moment that her delegates penned their names to the Constitution when it was formed. Treachery was in their hearts then, and they have adhered to their disloyalty through evil report and through good report; but I trust the day is now near when, by the reconstruction of South-Carolina society, we shall there have a State which, in process of time, will be loyal to the Constitution and the Union.

Next, Florida. Impotent in her treachery; purchased with the money of the people; with less than one hundred and fifty thousand inhabitants; with property, I suppose, not of equal value to that which might be found in a single ward in this city,—she has undertaken to lend herself to this conspiracy. Emancipate the slaves that are there, and invite the refugees from slavery in the South, for the moment, to assemble there, if they desire, but without compulsion, and take possession of the soil. If that is not sufficient, let the penalty upon South Carolina be increased by dividing her soil among those whom she has heretofore held in bondage.

And next in this work of emancipation I name Texas; for, if we read the history of the last twenty-four months aright, these people have gone out of the Union because they see they cannot extend slavery in the Union. It was not because a few abolitionists in the North hated slavery; it was not because some of us went to Chicago in May, 1860, and nominated Abraham Lincoln for President, and then elected him: but it was because men of all parties and all persuasions and all ideas, in the North, had come to the conclusion that slavery should not be extended. It was the doctrine of churches, the doctrine of homes and hearth-stones, that slavery should not be extended; and hence the slave States went out of the Union. Which way do they expect to extend slavery? Southward, through and over Texas, into Mexico and into Central America, thus cutting us off from the Pacific, separating us from our possessions west of the Rocky Mountains, and rendering another division of the Union, by the line of the Rocky Mountains, inevitable. Now, then, let us teach them, by emancipation in Texas, that, in the Union or out of the Union, slavery is not to be extended. Emancipate the slaves in Texas; invite men from the army, from the North, from Ireland, from Germany; invite the friends of freedom, of every name and of every nation, and bid them welcome in Texas, where we have one hundred and seventy-five million acres of unoccupied land, or shall have, when we confiscate it to the government of the United States. Thus we form a barrier of freemen, a wall over which or through which or beneath which it will be impossible for slavery to pass.

I do not pursue the subject of emancipation further. These three States will be sufficient for warning and penalty, for refuge and for security against the extension of slavery; but I certainly would have it understood distinctly, that, by the next anniversary of the birth of the Father of his Country, we shall emancipate the slaves in all the disloyal and rebellious States, if they do not previously return to their allegiance.

"What will you do," says one, "if you emancipate the slaves?" My friend, what will you do if you don't? What are we doing now, when we have not emancipated the slaves? I want to tell you what Mr. Jefferson thought, more than sixty years ago, and I ask you if that which he feared is not in process of completion to-day? He says, in a letter to St. George Tucker, dated Aug. 28, 1797: —

"Perhaps the first chapter of this history which has begun in St. Domingo, and the next succeeding ones, which will recount how all the whites were driven from all the other islands, may prepare our minds for a peaceable accommodation between justice, policy, and necessity, and furnish an answer to the difficult question, Whither shall the colored emigrants go? And, the sooner we put some plan under way, the greater hope there is that it may be permitted to proceed peaceably to its ultimate object. But if something is not done, and soon done, we shall be the murderers of our own children."

Terribly prophetic words! Terrible in the possibility of their fulfilment!

What will you do with the negroes, if you emancipate them? As between what we may or can do with them and the salvation of this country, we ought not to hesitate a moment. They are but four million; and, though in their weakness they plead, here are five and twenty million of men who ask a country; all the coming generations of this continent rise now and demand sacrifices of us all, that we may secure and preserve a country for them. Mankind everywhere gaze with anxious eyes upon this contest, lest the last hope of liberty should go out in this our land; and if — I do not hesitate to say — if the salvation of the country demanded the sacrifice of four million on this continent, black or white, slave or free, North or South, it would be a sacrifice well made for so great a cause. But, my friends, it demands no such sacrifice. These four million of people are able to take care of themselves. Have you considered what it requires to take care of one's self? I do not mean, when I say that these four million are able to take care of themselves, that they can build cities, that they can set afloat a vast commerce; I do not say that they can immediately become proficients in the arts and sciences,—I do not know that they ever can: but do you not see, on the face of things, that the slaves of the South have to-day possession of those industries, are accustomed to the exercise of those physical and mental faculties, on which society primarily depends? They are able to take care of themselves.

I should like, my friends, to spend a moment in stating some facts in regard to the British West Indies, because I believe that the public mind has been, to a great extent, deceived by the representations that have been made, through the agency of slavery, in reference to the results of emancipation in those islands. If you will pardon me a moment, I will read certain statistics, which, in their results, show what has been accomplished by the black population of the West Indies, emancipated by the British Government seven and twenty years ago. I venture to anticipate what I am to say, by expressing my belief, that, with the exception of Greece, where, thirty years since, there was hardly a house with a roof on it, there are no people on the face of the earth who have made more progress than the emancipated slaves in some of the British West Indies. What have they done? Take, for example, Barbadoes. They have opened schools, and, with a population of 140,000, have some 7,000 children in the schools; and they have over 3,000 landholders. In Antigua, with a population of 35,000, they have more than 10,000 children in the day and Sunday schools; and 5,000 landholders among those who were slaves seven and twenty years ago. In Tobago, there are 2,500 land-owners, with a population of 15,000. In St. Lucia, with 25,000 inhabitants, there are more than 2,000 land-owners. And even in Jamaica, which is the exception to the West-India Islands in the matter of prosperity since emancipation, in a population of some 400,000, they have 50,000 freeholders.

So, then, if you test that people who came from slavery and barbarism seven and twenty years ago by the two tests of primary civilization, cultivation of the soil and education of the children, they have made great progress. But it is well worth while to remember that Barbadoes is one of the most populous portions of the globe. Of the 106,000 acres of land, 100,000 are under cultivation; and the price of the cultivated land is from four to five hundred dollars an acre.

If we show that in one single instance emancipated slaves have been able to take care of themselves and make progress, though there may be twenty instances of failure, still the one instance of success demonstrates their capacity; and their failures are to be attributed to misfortune and the influence of circumstances.

In the next place (although I do not intend to go into the financial aspect of the question), I will read the results of the cultivation of sugar, which is the great article of export in those islands; and I know very well that the commercial community is interested in whatever relates to exports and imports. The dependencies of Guiana, Trinidad, Barbadoes, and Antigua, previous to emancipation, produced 187,000,000 pounds of sugar; and, in 1856–7, they produced annually 265,000,000,—showing a gain of nearly 78,000,000 a year: and their imports went up from $8,840,000 to $14,600,000 a year. And the present Governor-General of Jamaica, Mr. Hincks, whom some of you may remember as the former Attorney-General of Canada, and who was here in 1851 at the railway celebration, as it was called, states, from his own knowledge and observation, that, on an estate in Barbadoes, ninety blacks perform the work formerly done by two hundred and thirty slaves; and that the produce of each laborer during slavery was 1,043 pounds of sugar, and the produce of each laborer since emancipation is 3,660 pounds, annually. He also states that the cost per hogshead, under slavery, was £10 sterling; while, in 1858, it was produced at a cost of £4 sterling. So we see, that, whether we test the black population of the British West Indies by the fact that they have established schools, by the fact that they have become landholders, or by the fact that they export of their main staple more than they did formerly, they still have demonstrated their capacity to take care of themselves.

But I say further, my friends, that it is not a matter for argument, but within the range of the commonest observation, that the time is approaching when the emancipation of the slaves in this country must take place. It is inevitable; and we have now, I think, only a choice of ways. Emancipation may take place by the efforts of the slaves themselves; it may take place by act of the government of the United States; it may take place by the action of the slaveholders themselves, who led in this rebellion. But, for us, it is first a matter of justice. I said I would not omit that consideration, and I will not, as a matter of justice to the slaves themselves, who certainly have been subjected to a sufficient apprenticeship under slavery, through two centuries, to prepare them for freeedom,—which these gentlemen have told you is the legitimate and natural result of apprenticeship in slavery,—if they are ever to be prepared. Justice to the slaves demands emancipation. I will not make for myself, though others may for themselves, the nice distinction which you remember was made by Mr. Croswell, when he wrote a letter endorsing and explaining the speech of Colonel Cochrane. He says, "The difference between the abolitionists and the Union-defenders is this: the abolitionists are in favor of emancipation because it would be a benefit to the slaves; we are in favor of emancipation because it would be an injury to or diminish the power of the rebel masters." I do not care about this nice distinction. It reminds me of what Macaulay says of the Puritans. "The Puritans," says Macaulay, "hated bear-baiting, not because it gave pain to the bear, but because it gave pleasure to the spectators." Whatever your opinion may be, if you are in favor of emancipation, I do not greatly care whether you favor it as a matter of justice to the slaves or as a punishment to the masters. And we must agree, my friends, to the Declaration of Independence. The fundamental difference on which the North and South have divided for thirty years is on that part of the Declaration of Independence which says, "All men are created equal." The South has denied it: we have undertaken to maintain it. We ought to consider (if you will allow me a moment by way of explanation) that the Declaration of Independence was prepared as a political document. It did not relate to those differences among men which we see, which we recognize, which are natural, which are divine, which are not to be complained of. But Jefferson meant, when he penned that provision, that no person was by birth under any political subserviency to any other person. That is what he meant. Not that men are of equal height or weight, equal moral influence or intellectual capacities; but that all are equal in this, — that no one is born under any subserviency, politically, to his fellow-man. Let us maintain the doctrine now. These slaves are men: Jefferson did not hesitate to call them "brethren." In a letter to M. de Munier, explaining the reason why neither Mr. Wythe nor himself had proposed to insert a clause for emancipation into the slave code of Virginia, he says: —

"There were not wanting in that assembly men of virtue enough to propose, and talents to vindicate, this clause. But they saw that the moment of doing it with success was not yet arrived; and that an unsuccessful effort, as too often happens, would only rivet still closer the chains of bondage, and retard the moment of delivery to this oppressed description of man. But we must await with patience the workings of an overruling Providence, and hope that that is preparing the deliverance of these our suffering *brethren*. When the measure of their tears shall be full, when their groans shall have involved heaven itself in darkness, doubtless a God of justice will awaken to their distress, and by diffusing light and liberality among their oppressors, or, at length, by his exterminating thunder, manifest his attention to the things of this world, and that they are not left to the guidance of a blind fatality."

These slaves are men. The declaration concerning the equality of all men applies to them as to us; and, now that in the progress of events the South has relieved us of responsibility in regard to eleven disloyal States, let us stand forth as a nation in our original strength and purity, maintaining the ideas to which our fathers gave utterance, but which, under the circumstances, they were not able always and everywhere to enforce. Let us in the presence of these slaveholders and rebels, and in the presence of Europe, proclaim the equality of all men.

As to the expediency, still further: Have you ever considered that the South has taken possession, by circumstances and by skill, of the best territory, in soil and climate, upon this continent? This territory has been given up to slavery; and the men of Massachusetts, of the North, have not the power to go there in the presence of slavery, and develop the natural resources of that extensive country. We have taken possession of the fertile lands this side the Rocky Mountains; and it is a necessity of our existence that freedom should go South. Therefore it is a necessity that slavery should disappear. Have you, merchants, considered — have you, manufacturers, considered — that the seven hundred thousand negroes of the South, engaged in the cultivation of cotton, have a monopoly of the best cotton lands on the surface of the globe, and that their interest is to produce just as little as possible? What is your interest? Your interest is to have these lands developed so that they shall produce as much as possible. From 1845 to 1857, the supply of cotton in all the markets of the world diminished nine hundred thousand bales; and the price went up from the producing price of five or six cents to ten, twelve, fourteen, and sixteen cents a pound; the manufacturers working all the time upon short products of the raw material, and paying famine prices. We are told by statisticians that the whole population of the globe is ten or eleven hundred million. The total product of manufactured cotton goods has never exceeded seventy cents for each inhabitant of the globe. Produce cotton by free labor on the productive land of the South, develop it in Egypt, in India, in South America, — wherever, on the broad zone of seventy degrees, cotton can be raised at five or six cents a pound, and pay to the producer a good profit, — and your manufacturers in New England, in the free States, in England, in France, will double and treble the amount of goods now produced.

Is it not a matter of some consequence to manufacturers, to the people, to the laborers everywhere, that we should take these fertile and productive cotton lands out of the control of these seven hundred thousand slaves; make them free men; stimulate them by wages; invade those cotton lands, which can be worked by white labor, as one-eighth of the cotton lands of the country are now worked by white labor, and thus increase the product of cotton twenty-five, fifty, seventy-five, and, in a few years, one hundred per cent.; and stimulate the industry, and increase the comforts and conveniences, of all mankind?

If you look at this matter merely in a commercial point of view, will you allow slavery to retain the best cotton lands, and allow these lands to remain in possession of slaves?

I heard a suggestion just now, from the other part of the hall, to the effect — if I understand it correctly — that, if we emancipate the slaves, a great many of them will come this way. Have you ever thought, my friend, if you do not emancipate the negroes, that, in consequence of the disturbed condition of affairs, they will escape and invade the free States, and you will have the negroes here, whether you will or not? But, if you emancipate the slaves in the South, — assuming what Mr. Yancey said in Faneuil Hall last year, — the negroes of the North will go South; for he said they enjoyed nothing so much as basking in the sun, with the temperature at one hundred and ten degrees. If the slaves be emancipated, what with their own natural ability and such aids and appliances as the government and twenty million of people in the North can furnish, they will get employment, pay, and subsistence.

Another consideration that ought to be taken into account by the commercial men of the North is, that if we emancipate the slaves, and dedicate this country to freedom, the process of bankruptcy and repudiation, as a general thing, will come to an end, instead of your being called every year, in ordinary times, to contribute one, two, or three million to the support of the South. The time has come, after sixty, seventy, or eighty years of experience, when it is a right which we may demand, that the people who occupy the best portion of the North-American continent shall earn their own living, and pay their own debts.

The other consideration, as a matter of necessity, to which I invite your attention, is this: Having been involved as we are by slavery, and a conspiracy and rebellion based on slavery, we have a right to take security for the future, that there shall be no other conspiracy, that there shall be no other rebellion, that there shall be no other war reserved for future generations, growing out of this institution. Slavery, in its essential characteristics, is a despotism; and you will search long, and be disappointed often, when you seek for a slaveholder who is in heart desirous of supporting free, democratic, republican institutions. If you would take security for the future peace of the republic, it must be by dedicating this territory to freedom. Nothing else will give the country security for the future, or freedom to the States that are now engaged in the rebellion.

Emancipation is inevitable, first, possibly, by the act of the slaves themselves. I ask whether you—I do not ask whether the people of Charleston, with their city in flames, with the power of the slave population in some way or other felt in this their great calamity,—I do not ask whether they prefer the emancipation that took place in Jamaica, or that which took place in St. Domingo; but I ask you if, now, after the sacrifices you have made in the service of slavery, the expenses in which you are involved, the just and righteous hatred you have for the leaders in rebellion,—I ask you if, after all this experience, you ought not to choose an emancipation such as took place in Jamaica, rather than reserve this question of slavery until emancipation takes place as it did in St. Domingo. You cannot hesitate, whether you look to your own interest, to your own comfort, or whether you regard the interest, the comfort, the welfare, and the safety of the slaveholders themselves. And bear one thing in mind,—that, in Jamaica, thirty insurrections occurred in the century preceding emancipation, the last of which involved the destruction of eight million dollars of property, and was only put down at an expense of six hundred thousand dollars. Since emancipation, there has not been an insurrection of the blacks in that island; and it is a contradiction of all human experience to assume, that, when these people are emancipated, they will turn round and cut the throats of their former masters. If the United States shall lead in the emancipation, even at the head of the army, the emancipated population can be so controlled that they will not commit those excesses which have characterized conflicts between the oppressor and the oppressed in other countries and other ages.

But I made a suggestion, which I propose now to consider. It is, that if we do not emancipate the slaves, or if they do not speedily take the matter into their own hands, the probability is that they are to be emancipated by the rebels themselves. You think, possibly, that it is absurd to suggest that when they have involved the country in war, when they have staked every thing on the institution of slavery, they should, under any circumstances, be tempted or induced to destroy it. But have you considered that there are ten thousand men in the South, in civil positions and in the army, who, if this rebellion be put down and the government of the Union re-established over the revolted States, have only the choice between hanging and exile? Do you believe, when you remember the sacrifices they have already made; when you consider, that, on the coast of Carolina, they apply the torch to their own property, — that, in the extreme exigency to which they may be reduced if we are successful in the prosecution of the war, they will not emancipate their slaves, and claim the recognition of France and England, and the alliance of foreign governments, which alliance, we see, will be but too readily accorded?

My friends, I have not been startled by the intelligence from England to-day, because I have seen that we were drifting steadily and certainly to a foreign war; and nothing, I believe, can avert that calamity within a few months, except emancipation of the negroes in the South, so that we can say to the people of England, to the people of France, If you make war against us, you make war in the interest of slavery. I believe, although I was educated in that school which had but little faith in English politics or in the political principles of Englishmen, that, if we write emancipation on our banner, there is yet remaining in the heart of the English nation virtue enough to say to their ruling classes, whatever their desire may be, and to the manufacturers, whatever their exigencies may be, You shall not interfere to re-establish slavery where it has been struck down. I believe, also, that the French nation, which, in 1778, was in alliance with us; which regarded the extremity of Greece; which fought for an idea in Italy, and restored the unity of that ancient seat of power and of majesty in the affairs of the world, — I believe that the millions of France would say to the Emperor, if he were otherwise disposed, This is a war in which we can take no part. By emancipation, we shall be left to ourselves; but, if we do not speedily strike a blow somewhere — in South Carolina or Florida or Texas — as indicative of our purpose, I see not any way to avert a foreign war, adding untold calamities to the difficulties and horrors in which we are at this moment involved.

Do you think that England is without inducements? History teaches something. She has her traditions of the Revolution, and of the war of 1812; her governing classes are in sympathy with the governing classes of the South; her manufacturers desire the raw material; her merchants now urge the government on, and guide it, too, in a policy which looks either to the restoration of the Union or to separation, and, whatever may be the result, with equal sagacity. They see very plainly that here is a breach between the North and South that cannot be repaired in one generation; and they know, that, when the war closes, they will have the sympathy of the South, if they show sympathy to the South now. They expect a monopoly of the trade of the South; and if the slaveholders bear sway when peace comes, whether it come by union or disunion, that monopoly will be secured. It is only by a reconstruction, to some extent, of Southern society, that the people of the North can participate hereafter in the trade of the South.

Then there is a feeling, not only in England, but throughout Europe, that we are advancing too rapidly. Conscious as we have been, boasting as we have been, it is possible that, after all, we have not estimated the prosperity and greatness of the republic as it has been estimated abroad. Extending from the great lakes to the Gulf of Mexico and the Rio Grande, from the Atlantic to the Pacific; covering the continent; threatening Mexico and Central America with the process of annexation,—they cannot look otherwise than with anxiety and apprehension upon a nation which promises in the course of the present century to contain a population of one hundred million of freemen.

Therefore I say, in reference to the future, that we are in the greatest peril, unless we place the nation, and that speedily, in a position where we can defend ourselves as the supporters of freedom, and appeal to the yeomanry of England, the peasantry of France, and ask them to keep the peace, while we restore to its fair proportions a government such as the world has never before seen. Our country will move on in a career of prosperity which shall know no limits in this generation, if we escape from the perils in which we are involved by slavery.

Our interest and our duty require us to avert the calamity of foreign war by any sacrifice, save that of justice and honor.

With one word more, my friends, I leave this subject. In the exigency in which we are placed, we must support the government. We may maintain our opinions, believing that in due time those opinions will possess influence; but the government, that must — for it is the only means by which the rebellion is to be put down — from day to day, with the highest wisdom and on principles of established justice, execute all the requirements and provisions of the Constitution.

This contest is between slavery on the one side, and the government on the other. Both cannot stand. Either slavery will go down and the government remain, or the government will be destroyed and slavery triumph over us all. For slavery it is that we have made our sacrifices; for slavery it is that we are involved in these troubles; for slavery it is that we incur these expenditures; for slavery it is that manufactures are paralyzed; for slavery it is that commerce is interrupted; for slavery it is that our foreign relations are disturbed; for slavery it is that foreign war threatens our borders; for slavery it is that free institutions are perilled throughout the world, and among all the coming generations of men. Are there still further sacrifices demanded for the institution of slavery? Remember the dead that have fallen in defence of the country; remember the living who are perilled on the battle-field and in the camp; remember your friends who have gone out to fight the battles of the republic; and say whether you can lie upon your pillows, and feel that you have done your duty to them, to your country, and to your God, unless you exert such influences as you can command to bring to a speedy termination the cause of all our trials.

OUR DANGER AND ITS CAUSE.

PUBLISHED IN THE "CONTINENTAL MONTHLY" FOR FEBRUARY, 1862.

IT is certain, that, when this page comes under the eye of the reader, the relations of the United States, both foreign and domestic, will have been changed materially. At the present moment, however, the condition of the country is unpromising enough, yet not so gloomy as to preclude the hope of a fortunate issue. The sacrifices and sufferings of the people are greater in civil than in foreign wars; and the ultimate advantages and benefits are proportionately large. We speak now of those civil wars which have occurred between people inhabiting the same district of country, — as the civil wars of England. Other contests, as the revolutions of Hungary, Poland, and Ireland even, were not, strictly speaking, civil wars. The parties were of different origin, and had never assimilated in language, customs, or ideas. The struggle was for the re-establishment of a government which had once existed, and not for the reformation or change of a government that, at the moment of the conflict, was performing its ordinary functions.

The civil war in America does not belong to either of the classes named. To be sure, in Missouri, Kentucky, and Western Virginia, the contest has been between the inhabitants of the several localities, aided by forces from the rebel States on the one hand, and forces from the loyal States on the other. But those States, as such, were never committed to the rebellion; and the struggle within their limits has demonstrated the inability of the so-called Confederate States to command the adhesion of Missouri, Kentucky, and Western Virginia by force; but it does not, in the accomplished results, demonstrate the ability of the United States to crush the rebellion. The border States were debatable ground; but the question has been settled in favor of the government, as far, at least, as Western Virginia and Missouri are concerned.

In the eleven seceded States, there is no apparent difference of opinion among those in authority, or among those accustomed to lead in public affairs. The sentiment of attachment to the old Union has been disappearing rapidly since the secession of South Carolina, until there are now no open avowals of adherence to the government, unless such are made by the mountaineers of Eastern Tennessee and Western North Carolina. These men are for the present destitute of power. Should our armies penetrate those regions, the inhabitants may essentially aid in the re-establishment of the government. For the time, however, we must regard the eleven States as a unit in the rebellion. Thus we are called to note the anomalous fact that the rebels seek a division between a people who speak the same language, occupy a territory which has no marked lines or features of separation, and who have, from the first day of their national existence, been represented by the same national government. Hence it is plain, whatever may be the immediate result of the contest, that there can be no permanent peace until the territory claimed as the territory of the United States is again subject to one government. This may be the work of a few months, it may be the work of a few years, or it may be the business of a century. Without the re-establishment of the government over the whole territory of the Union, there can be no peace; and, without the re-establishment of that government, there can be no prosperity.

The armies of the rebel States will march to the great lakes, or the armies of the loyal States will march to the Gulf of Mexico. We are, therefore, involved in a war which does not admit of adjustment by negotiation. In a foreign war, peace might be secured by mutual concessions, and preserved by mutual forbearance. In ordinary civil strife, the peace of a state or of an empire might be restored by concessions to the disaffected, by a limitation of the privileges of the few, or an extension of the rights of the many. But none of these expedients meet the exigency in which we find ourselves. The rebels demand the overthrow of the government, the division of the territory of the Union, the destruction of the nation. The question is, *Shall this nation longer exist?* And why is the question forced upon us? Is there a difference of language? Not greater than is found in single States. Indeed, Louisiana is the only one of the eleven where any appreciable difference exists; and the number of French in that State is less than the number of Germans in Pennsylvania. Nor has nature indicated lines of separation, like the St. Lawrence and the lakes on the north, and the Rocky Mountains on the west. The lines marked by nature — the Rocky Mountains, the Mississippi River, and the Alleghanies — cut the line proposed by the Confederates transversely, and force the suggestion that each section will be put in possession of three halves of different wholes, instead of a single unit essential to permanent national existence.

Do the products of the industry of the two sections so conflict with each other in domestic or foreign markets as to encourage the idea, that, by separation, the South could gain in this particular? Not in the least. The North has been a large customer for the leading staple of the South; and the South is constantly in need of those articles which the North is fitted to produce. The South complains of the growth of the North, and vainly imagines, that, by separation, its own prosperity would be promoted. The answer to all this is, that there has never been a moment for fifty years when the seceded States had not employment, for all the labor that they could command, in vocations more profitable than any leading industry of the North; and, moreover, every industry of the North has been open to the free competition of the South. Not argument, only statement, is needed to show, that by origin, association, language, business, and labor interests, as well as by geographical laws, unity, and not diversity, is the necessity of our public life. Yet, in defiance of these considerations, the South has undertaken the task of destroying the government. Nor do the rebels assert that the plan of government is essentially defective. The Montgomery Constitution is modelled upon that of the United States; though the leaders no longer disguise their purpose to abolish its democratic features, and incorporate aristocratic and monarchical provisions. They hope, also, to throw off the restraints of law, bid defiance to the general public sentiment of the world, and re-open the trade in slaves from Africa. It remains to be seen whether the desire of England for cotton and conquest, and her sympathy with the rebels, will induce her to pander to this inhuman traffic.

It has happened occasionally that a government has so wielded its powers as to contribute, unconsciously, to its own destruction. But our experience furnishes the first instance of a government having been seized by a set of conspirators, and its vast powers used for its own overthrow.

It is now accredited generally that several members of Mr. Buchanan's Cabinet were conspirators, and that they used the power confided to them for the purpose of destroying the government itself. Hence it appears, whatever the test applied, that the present rebellion is distinguished from all others in the fact that it does not depend upon any of the causes on which national dissensions usually have been based.

The public discontents in Ireland, in their causes, bore a slight analogy to our own. There were existing in that country various systems and customs that were prejudicial to the prosperity of the island. Among these may be mentioned the encumbered estates and absenteeism; and it is worthy of remark that whatever has been done by the British government for the promotion of the prosperity of Ireland, and the pacification of its people, has been by a reformation of the institutions of the country.

Rebels in arms may be overthrown and dispersed by superior force; but the danger of rebellion will continue so long as the disposition to rebel animates the people. This disposition cannot be reached by military power merely: the exciting cause must be removed, or, at least, so limited and modified as to impair its influence as a disturbing force in the policy of the country. As we have failed to trace this rebellion to any of the causes that have led to civil disturbances in other countries, it only remains to suggest that cause which, in its relations and conditions, is peculiar to the United States. All are agreed that *slavery* is the cause of the rebellion. Yet slavery exists in other countries,— as Brazil, for example,—and thus far without exhibiting its malign influence in conspiracy and rebellion. This is no doubt true; but it should be borne in mind, that, in the United States, slavery has power in the government as the basis of representation, and that the slave States are associated in the government with free States. If the institution of slavery had not been a basis of political power, or had all the States maintained slavery, it is probable that the rebellion would never have been organized, or, if organized, it could never have attained its present gigantic proportions.

We have now reached a point where we can see

the error of our public national life. The doctrine announced by President Lincoln, while he was only Mr. Lincoln of Springfield, that the nation must be all free or all slave, was not new with him. The men who framed the Constitution acted under the same idea, though they may not have expressed the truth so distinctly. There is, however, abundant circumstantial evidence that they so believed, and that their only hope for the country was based on the then reasonable expectation that slavery would disappear, and that the nation would be all free. It was reserved for modern political alchemists to discover the idea, on which the leading politicians have been acting for thirty or forty years, that one-half of a nation might believe in the fundamental principle on which the government is based, and the other half deny it, and yet the government go on harmoniously wielding its powers acceptably and safely to all. This is the error. Our failure is not in the plan of government; the error is not that our fathers supposed that a government could be based and permanently sustained upon slavery and freedom advancing *pari passu.* They indulged in no such delusion. The error is modern. When slavery demanded concessions, and freedom yielded; when slavery suggested compromises, and freedom accepted them; when slavery, unrebuked, claimed equal rights under the Constitution, and freedom acknowledged the justice of the claim, — then came the test whether the government itself should be administered in the service of slavery or in behalf of freedom. Two considerations influenced the slaveholders. First, even should they be permitted to wield the government, they foresaw that its provisions were inadequate to meet the exigencies of slavery. No despotism can be sustained by the voluntary efforts of its subjects. Slavery is a despotism, and, as such, can be supported only by power independent of that of the slaves themselves, and always sufficient for their control. The slaves were yearly increasing in numbers, and gaining in knowledge. These changes indicated the near approach of the time when the slaves of the South would re-enact the scenes of St. Domingo. The plantations of the cotton region are remote from each other; and the proportion of slaves on a single plantation is often as many as fifty for every free person. The sale of negroes from the northern slave States has introduced an element upon the plantations at once intelligent and hostile, and, of course, dangerous. The time must come when the white population of plantations, districts, or States even, would disappear in a single night. In such a moment of terror and massacre, how, and to what extent, would the United-States Government, acting under the Constitution, afford protection, aid, or even secure a barren vengeance? These were grave questions, and admitted only of an unsatisfactory answer at best. The government has power to put down insurrections; but for what good would a body of troops be marched to a scene of desolation and blood a fortnight or a month after the servile outbreak had done its work? These considerations controlled the intelligent minds of the South, and they were driven irresistibly to the conclusion that the government of the United States was insufficient for the institution of slavery, even though the friends of slavery were intrusted with the administration. What hope beyond? They dared to believe, that, by separation and the establishment of a military slaveholding oligarchy, to which the public opinion and public policy of the seceded States now tend, they would be able to guard the institution against all tumults from within and all attacks from without.

If, however, success were to crown their present undertakings, is it probable that the government contemplated would be strong enough for the task proposed? If Russia could not hold her serfs in bondage, can the South set up a government which can guard and defend and secure slavery? Or will a French or English protectorate render that stable which the government of the United States was incompetent to uphold? These questions remain; but the one first suggested is settled, — that the government of the United States, howsoever and by whomsoever administered, constitutionally, is inadequate to meet the exigencies of slavery.

Secondly, the leaders of the rebellion foresaw, a long time since, that they had no security that the government would be administered in the interest of slavery. The admission of California, followed by the admission of three other free States, forced the slaveholders into a hopeless minority in the Senate of the United States. The census of 1860 promised to reduce the delegation of the slave States in the House of Representatives. Previous to 1870, other free States were likely to be admitted into the Union; and thus, by successive and unavoidable events, the government was sure to pass into the hands of the non-slave States. It would not be just to the South to omit to say that apprehensions there existed that the North would disregard the Constitution. These apprehensions were fostered for unholy purposes; and so sealed is the South to the progress of truth, through the domination of the slaveholders over the press and public men, and by the consequent ignorance of the mass of the people, that these misapprehensions have never been removed in any degree by the declarations of Congress or of political parties in the North.

The mind of the South was thus brought logically to two conclusions: first, that the government of the United States was inadequate to meet the exigencies of slavery, even though it should be administered uniformly by the friends of slavery; secondly, that the administration of the government would be controlled by the ideas of the free States.

These conclusions would have been sufficiently unwelcome to the Southern leaders, if they had had no purpose or policy beyond the maintenance of slavery where it exists; but they had already determined to extend the institution southward over Mexico and Central America, and they knew full well the necessity of destroying the Union and the government before such an enterprise could be undertaken with any hope of success. Hence they denied the right of the majority to rule, unless they ruled in obedience to the will of the minority. Thus the slaveholders came naturally and unavoidably to the denial of the fundamental principle of the government; and, having denied the principle, there remained no reason why they should not undertake the overthrow of the government itself. And thus the conspiracy and the rebellion sprung naturally and unavoidably from the institution of slavery.

Further, slavery is the support of the conspiracy and the rebellion, both in Europe and America. However disastrous slavery may be to the mass of the whites, it affords to the governing class the opportunity and means for constant attention to public affairs.

In all our history, the North has felt the force of this advantage. As a general thing, a Northern member occupies a seat in Congress for one or two terms, and then his place is taken by an untried man. And, even during his term of service, his attention is given in part to his private affairs, or to plans and schemes designed to secure a re-election. The Southern member takes his seat with a conscious independence, due to the fact that his slaves are making crops upon his plantation, and that his re-election does not depend upon the hot breath of the multitude. He enjoys a long and independent experience in the public service; and he thus acquires a power to serve his party, his country, or his section, which is disproportionate even to his experience. A good deal of the consideration which the South enjoys abroad, and especially in England, is due to the fact, that, in the South, a governing class is recognized, which corresponds to the governing classes wherever an aristocracy or monarchism exists. By a community of ideas, the South commands the sympathy, and enjoys the confidence and secret support, of the enemies of democracy the world over. Through the political and pecuniary support which the public men of that section have derived from slavery, they have been able to take and maintain social positions at Washington, which, by circumstances, were denied to much the larger number of Northern representatives; and thus they have influenced the politics of this country and the opinions of other nations. Consider by how many sympathies and interests England is bound to encourage the policy and promote the fortunes of the South. There is the sympathy of the governing class in England for the governing class in the South, even though they are slaveholders; there is the hostility of the ignorant operatives in their manufacturing towns, who, through exterior influences, have been led to believe that whatever hardships they are brought to endure are caused by the desire of the North to subjugate the South; there is the purpose of English merchants and manufacturers to cripple, or, if possible, to destroy the manufactures and commerce of the North; and, finally, there is the hope of all classes, that, by the alienation or separation of the two sections, England will derive additional commercial advantages, and that the scheme of here establishing a continental republic will be abandoned, never to be again revived. There is, moreover, a reasonable expectation founded in the nature of things, and possibly already supported by positive promises and pledges, that England is to stand in the relation of protector to the Confederated States. Nor will she be disturbed in the least by the institution of slavery, if perchance that institution survives the struggle. If she can be secure in the monopoly of the best cotton lands on the globe; if she can be manufacturer and shopkeeper for the South; if she can deprive the North of one-half of its legitimate commerce; if she can obtain the control of the Gulf of Mexico, of the mouth of the Mississippi; if she can command the line of seacoast from Galveston to Fortress Monroe, or even to Charleston, and thus compel us to make our way to the Pacific by the passes of the Rocky Mountains exclusively,—there is no sacrifice of men or of money or of principle or of justice that would be deemed too great by the English people and government. But what then? Are we to make war upon England because her sympathies and interests run thus with the South? Is it not wiser to consider why it is that the South is sustained by the interests and sympathies of England? If slavery for fifty years had been unknown among us, could there be found a hundred men, within the limits of the United States, who would accept a British protectorate under any circumstances or for any purpose whatever? And is it not therein manifest that our foreign and domestic perils are alike due to slavery? And shall we not have dealt successfully with all our foreign difficulties, when we shall have established the jurisdiction of the United States over the territory claimed by the rebels? But, until that happy day arrives, we shall not be relieved for an instant from the danger of a foreign war; and, if the rebellion last six months longer, there is no reason to suppose that a foreign war can be averted. When we offer so tempting a prize to nations that wish us ill, can we expect them to put aside the opportunity which we have not the courage and ability to master? We have observed the hot haste of England to recognize the rebels as belligerents; we have seen the flimsy covering of neutrality that she has thrown over the illegitimate commerce that her citizens have carried on with the South; and from the time, manner, and nature of her demand for the release of Mason and Slidell, we are forced to infer that she will seize every opportunity to bring about an open rupture with the United States. And, though Mr. Seward has carried the country successfully through the difficulty of the "Trent," we ought to expect the presentation of demands which we cannot so readily and justly meet. Indeed, enough is known of the Mexican question to suggest the most serious apprehensions of foreign war on that account.

The necessity for speedily crushing the rebellion is as strong as it was at the moment when Lord Lyons made the demand for the release of the persons taken from the deck of the "Trent."

Is there any reason, even the slightest, to suppose, that, by military and naval means alone, the rebellion can be crushed by the 19th of April next?

Yet every day's delay gives the Confederate States additional strength, and renders them, in the estimation of mankind, more and more worthy of recognition and independent government. Their recognition will be followed by treaties of friendship and alliance; and those treaties will give strength to the rebels, and increase the embarrassments of our own government. It is the necessity of our national life that the settlement of this question should not be much longer postponed.

By some means we must satisfy the world, and that speedily, that the rebellion is a failure. Nor can we much longer tender declarations of what we intend to do, or offer promises as to what we will do, in the face of the great fact, that, for eight months, the capital of the republic has been in a state of siege. If, in these circumstances of necessity and peril to us, the armies of the rebels be not speedily dispersed, and the leaders of the rebellion rendered desperate, will the government allow the earth to again receive seed from the hand of the slave under the dictation of the master, and for the support of the enemies of the Constitution and the Union? If there were any probability that the States would return to their allegiance, then, indeed, we might choose to add to our own burdens rather than interfere with their internal affairs. But there is no hope whatever that the seceded States will return voluntarily to the Union.

There could be no justifying cause for the emancipation of the slaves in time of peace by the action of the general government; and now it must be demanded and defended as the means by which the war is to be closed, and a permanent peace secured. If, before the return of seed-time, the emancipation of the slaves in several or in all of the disloyal States be declared as a military necessity, and the blacks be invited to the seacoast where we have and may have possession, they will raise supplies for themselves, and the rebellion will come to an ignominious end, through the inability of the masters, when deprived of the services of their slaves, to procure the means of carrying on the war.

TREASON THE FRUIT OF SLAVERY.

A SPEECH DELIVERED AT A MASS MEETING HELD IN THE CAPITOL GROUNDS, WASHINGTON, JULY, 1862.

GENTLEMEN, — I am a stranger to you, and I do not know any good reason why your committee of arrangements should have undertaken to introduce an acquaintance between us. I am sure you, upon your part, will regret it, however I may regard it. I may as well tell you where I am from, — from Massachusetts. What we propose in that State is to carry on this war, in sunshine and storm, against all odds, on this side of the water or the other. We rally under the national banner, not for this generation alone or for this century, but for all generations and for all centuries. And, for ourselves, we mean to offer the last man, the last dollar, and the last hour's labor of the last citizen of our Commonwealth, ere these rebels, with treason on their lips and treason in their hearts, shall accomplish that which they have undertaken. If to-night there shall come news of disaster, I know, that, in the Commonwealth to which I belong, every heart will be nerved for renewed efforts in the cause of liberty and humanity. My friend, Mr. Chittenden, says he proposes to ferret out traitors. I propose to go one step further, and ask you why there is treason, as, without treason, there could be no traitors. Speaking for the first time in the free, open air in the city of Washington, which bears the name of the Father of my Country, I will pronounce the words: If it had not been for slavery, there would have been no treason; and, when slavery shall cease to exist, there will be no traitors. That is the beginning and the end of this war, — slavery in the beginning, freedom in the end. There is no other solution of the difficulty; and as an American citizen, with all the responsibilities resting upon me, treasuring as I do the memories and traditions of the past, I proclaim here that there can be no peace, until, from the length and breadth of this republic, the cry shall go up, "Slavery, slavery, has ceased." How and when? These are questions that we submit to the President, in whom we confide, and his Cabinet; but I believe this, — that the faster he and they march on towards the conclusion when slavery shall have ceased to exist, just to that extent they will merit the reward and gratitude of their countrymen and all mankind.

My friends, I see here laborers, — men who with their bones and sinews are to carry on this war. I have heard that in the city of Brooklyn, day before yesterday, there was a riot between the free white laborers and the colored men; so also there have been conflicts in Cincinnati and elsewhere through the North. What is the solution of this difficulty between the white and colored races of the North? Freedom to the blacks. Then will they go from the North to the free Territories of the South, to which by nature they belong. You should have made South Carolina and Florida free; and I would praise God with gratitude, such as has never swelled my heart, if to-night I could hear, by the President's proclamation, that South Carolina and Florida were free, and dedicated to the black population of this country. Then competition with the white laborers of the North would cease. The negroes would go to the cotton-fields and the rice-plantations of the South that invite them, leaving to the white people of the North entire freedom from competition in labor. But, on the other hand, there are some who say, reconstruct the old Union, with the eleven seceded States introduced anew, without the abolition of slavery. What, think you, would then happen? Will the slaves remain in the South? No; but they will escape by hundreds and millions to the North, and come into competition with the free laborers there. You cannot doubt this. Will you return them to their masters? Certainly not. Humanity is against it; justice is against it; expediency is against it.

I have been in Cairo, Ill., where I was told that the people were nearly all secessionists six months ago. Negroes ran away, and came there, and the secessionists and authorities and citizens could not carry those people back. You have then to take the choice,—abolish slavery in these seceded States, give the negroes a home there, and carry them out of the North by the mild power of persuasion, or else allow the North to be overrun by escaped fugitives from the South. Give them a home on territory which they and you have fought for, in the coast region of the South, and give us the North for the free white population of the North. Therefore I say, my friends, that this doctrine of emancipation in the eleven seceded States — immediate, unconditional, universal — is the solution of the difficulty of the war, and consequently the conclusion of peace. What I have said has been based upon the wise and just proposition of the President, that, in the loyal States, compensation shall be made to loyal masters. I would go still further. If in these eleven seceded States you can find men, slave-owners, who have done, under the circumstances, all that could be reasonably expected, I would compensate them also. But never, with my consent, shall the treasury of this country be opened to compensate rebels for the loss of their slaves.

I wish to leave with you in the end the words offered in the beginning. They are these: Without slavery, there would have been no treason; and, without treason, there would have been no traitors, no war. Upon slavery the responsibility lies for this enormous waste and outlay of men and money. Over the whole North, there are mourning homes and desolate hearth-stones, aged parents stricken down with sorrow, grief penetrating young hearts. All is chargeable to this foul and infamous institution of human slavery; and, if there be a God in heaven, and if he be just, as we believe, we cannot imagine, with the instincts and perceptions we have, that he should ever look with favor upon a people twenty million strong, struggling, in their first faith, to compel five million of rebel slaveholders and their associates in the South to be true to the flag and Constitution, and, at the same time, struggling to compel four million of slaves to be true to their rebel masters. It is a greater work than you can accomplish. There is no power upon earth equal to the undertaking. These men of the South, instigators of the rebellion, controlling this country through the administrations of Franklin Pierce and James Buchanan for eight years, did not abandon the government until the government was shown to be inadequate to maintain the institution of slavery. They stood by the government as long as the government was strong enough to maintain this institution. What do the people of the North propose to have this administration do? Put down the rebellion, of course. Either slavery must die, or the government is at an end. The time has come when men of all minds and conditions must take their choice whether these United States shall be sustained and slavery driven out, or otherwise. Slavery will last as long as the war, and the war as long as slavery. It is your duty to take slavery by the throat, and destroy it.

One word more. I belonged to the old Democratic party. It was a party of courage, from the time of General Jackson to the administration of Franklin Pierce; and the country should now borrow a lesson of courage from that party. Let the truth be declared with courage and determination, and slavery shall then cease, and this war shall end. Let the war-cry be, "Slavery shall cease, slavery shall cease!"

GENERAL WADSWORTH AND THE NEW-YORK ELECTION OF 1862.

SPEECH DELIVERED IN WASHINGTON CITY, SEPT. 27, 1862, AT A MEETING CALLED TO RESPOND TO THE NOMINATION OF GENERAL WADSWORTH FOR GOVERNOR OF NEW YORK.

I MEET you to-night, gentlemen, that I may, with you, express the satisfaction which we feel that the great State of New York, in the nomination she has made of General Wadsworth for the highest office in her gift, has already indicated her purpose to maintain the Constitution, and to re-establish the authority of this government over the States which to-day deny it. I come, too, that I may express my belief, founded on an acquaintance somewhat intimate, though of short duration, that he whom the people of New York are to elect to the chief-magistracy is a man worthy in all respects of the suffrages of the people of that great State, and of the confidence of the country.

This is a time, gentlemen, when neither in civil life nor in the conduct of armies in the field is it safe to trust to men who lack earnestness in the discharge of the duties to which they are called. It is the duty of all men who participate in the administration of public affairs — and its performance is due to themselves, to their country, and to Heaven — to abandon the positions they hold, if they do not believe, earnestly, fully, and without wavering, in the great cause to which the people of this country are devoted. That cause is the maintenance, on this soil, of the principles of freedom, regardless of color or country or race. We acknowledge in the government which we set up, and in the rights which we recognize in all men, that he who has been created by his Maker in the image of his Maker is entitled to equal rights as a man and a citizen. It is the denial of the great right of human equality before the law that has compelled us to taste of this cup of humiliation. Yea, it is that denial which forces us to drink of the cup to the very dregs; and it is only through this humiliation that we can pass to that triumphant glory, as a people, when it shall be declared in the face of despots, on this continent and on the other, that all whom God has created are free, are equal before the law.

There is a belief in some quarters that republican institutions on this continent have failed. The despots of Europe are elated with the hope that that which they have prophesied is to be fulfilled in the failure of republican institutions in America.

Gentlemen, republican institutions have not failed. They are, indeed, put to a severe trial in these days; but they have not failed. There has been, however, a failure on this continent and in our affairs; and we may wisely consider how and in what we have failed. Simply in this, — in the attempt, not made by the framers of the government, but by men thirty and forty years ago, who had then already abandoned the principles of freedom, to set up and perpetuate a government half slave and half free. That attempt has failed. Washington, Jefferson, Madison, and their associates had no faith in such a government; and the government which they set up was not of that character. They knew that slavery existed; but they did not believe that a government founded on slavery and freedom could stand, and they made no attempt to found such a government.

What was their belief? It was this: that slavery was an evil, that it was temporary, that it was passing away. They believed that freedom was permanent, that freedom was aggressive, that it was to so continue; and, if this belief had controlled the heart and minds of the people of the South, slavery would have passed away, the rebellion would not have come, and the war and its scenes would have been omitted in the history of this republic; but, thirty or forty years since, there appeared a class of men in the South who attempted to set up the opposite doctrine, — that freedom was temporary, that it was limited, and that it was to disappear. They maintained, that slavery was a good, that slavery was permanent, that it was to be aggressive, and that finally, on this continent and in this government, it would be supreme. The failure is in the attempt of men who had already abandoned the doctrines of republicanism, to establish, within the forms of the Constitution, a theory to which the fathers of the republic never assented, in which they never believed, — that it was safe or possible to establish a government which should continue half slave and half free. That attempt, made by Calhoun, Jefferson Davis, and the other supporters of the rebellion, has failed; but republican institutions have not failed. These are strong to-day, and they will be strengthened by the war.

Out of this bitter humiliation, this terrible experience in the life of the nation, they will come forth improved and purified, so that future generations will believe in this as the revolution in behalf of freedom, — freedom for the human race. As the revolution of 1776 was a revolution for the freedom of nations, and inasmuch as the life of the man, the life of the race, is more worthy of preservation than the life merely of a nation, so shall this revolution shine prominent upon the pages of history as peer with any other revolution, not in the character of its origin, but in the fact that twenty million of people united, and, with one heart, with one mind, placed their sacrifices of blood and treasure upon the altar of the country for the maintenance of republican institutions on this continent.

Gentlemen, this war has continued for a year and a half; great sacrifices have been made. No man can tell how long it will continue; but I can predict what must occur before it closes. The race of slaveholders on this continent must be exterminated. Not the people of the South, but the race of slaveholders on this continent, must be exterminated, before this war can end.

On the 23d of this month, the first great step was taken towards the extermination of the race of slaveholders, by the declaration of the President of the republic, that in ninety days, if the rebellion shall not then have ceased, slavery in the eleven rebellious States shall be overthrown. When that declaration shall have been made a practical fact, as it will be, then the dawn of the day of peace will have appeared.

We must gird ourselves anew for the contest; and I have already indicated that the principle of the men in the council and in the field should be earnestness of purpose and fidelity to the cause of the country. When such men shall lead armies, when such men shall give direction to public affairs everywhere, in low places as well as in high, then the day of triumph will begin.

Further in regard to the State of New York. No calamity to the country could be greater than the indication, if it were possible that the indication could be given, — the indication, by the great State of New York, that she falters in this contest. That indication will not be given; but, if the great State of New York should fail to give its vote for him whom we here honor to-night, that failure would be taken as an indication by the North, by the South, by all Europe, that the State of New York falters in her devotion to this cause.

I cast no imputation upon the men who oppose us in the canvass in that State. I do not know what their opinions are; but I do know what the opinion of the world would be, if any other man than General Wadsworth should be elected to the chief-magistracy of that State. It would be simply this, that New York faltered in her devotion to this cause; and the result of it would be that every rebel heart throughout the eleven seceded States would be cheered by the announcement that New York had faltered. Such a result, however, my friends, will not happen. It cannot happen.

But I suggest its possibility, as indicating the interest which the country and all mankind has in the result of the contest which is soon to be commenced in that State. And the city of New York, the emporium of all our foreign and domestic commerce, with three-quarters of a million of people already within her limits, destined long before the close of this century, if the North triumph, as the North must triumph, in this contest, to be the centre of the whole civilized world, — the city of New York has in this contest that at stake which cannot be overestimated. Is it for that city to falter in the contributions which she makes, either of opinions, of money, or of men, when, by the success of the scheme of the Southern conspirators, the Southern portion of this republic would be separated from the Northern? Can the city of New York afford the sacrifice that she would be called upon to make if secession should accomplish what has been undertaken?

Gentlemen, one word more. I say the race of slaveholders in the South is to be exterminated. What follows? Seneca said of the Roman, "Wherever the Roman conquers, he inhabits." Wherever the American conquers, he inhabits. And from the millions of our countrymen from the North whom we are sending into the field I bid the South take warning; for we shall pour over the border, during the next ten years, a quarter or a half a million of people, who will regenerate the whole State of Virginia, so that she shall be, when in the embrace of freedom, what she could never be while lying under the power of slavery, — the first State in all industrial resources, not only of this continent, but of the world.

With her climate, her fertile soil, her inland navigation, her resources in iron, gold, and other minerals, Virginia will be the first State of the republic. And we, who to-night proclaim and advocate the extermination of the race of slaveholders, do it in behalf of the people of the North, of Ireland, of Germany, and in behalf of the oppressed over all Europe, because we open to them new fields of industry, of wealth, of domestic prosperity, and happiness. We, the people of the North, who carry on this war for the maintenance of the nation, do it in behalf of the human race. It will be the reproach of England, that, in the hour of our adversity, she looked upon us with hostility; that she was unwilling that a great and free republic should be established and maintained on this continent. Yet England is to derive from this revolution, next to ourselves, the largest amount of advantage; for the time will come when, upon Southern soil, the free labor of the North and the free black labor of the South will increase the production of cotton twofold, threefold, fourfold; and, without cotton, England's prosperity must wane and disappear.

What is the fact to-day? That the whole production of cotton is not equal to seventy cents, when manufactured, for each inhabitant of the globe; and slavery and slaveholders on this continent, by the monopoly of the best cotton lands of the world, have produced cotton in limited quantities only, and sold it to the manufacturers of the world at famine prices. When we have emancipated the slaves, when we have inspired them with sentiments of self-protection and with hopes of prosperity, we may increase the product of cotton from four million to eight million, and from eight to sixteen million of bales, before the end of this century; and that product is in behalf of civilization, for the benefit of the whole world, but not more for the interest of any country than for England. I say again that it will be the reproach of England upon the page of history, that, in the hour of our adversity, she looked with hostility upon us.

But we shall come out of this war a better, wiser, and more powerful people, with a debt, no doubt, of five or ten hundred million of dollars, possibly fifteen hundred million of dollars, but with credit unimpaired: and, gentlemen, many of you will live to see the day when that debt shall have been paid; for we have in this country elements of wealth which are denied to any other country on the globe. Every acre of the South which we are to redeem from slavery, every acre of land in the far West, when it shall have been occupied by a free laborer, is at once security for this debt, and the means by which it is to be paid. We have, first, pecuniary resources sufficient to carry on this war; but, secondly, the people have a right to demand of every man who has the control of time and money, that it be used so as to produce the greatest possible results to the cause in which we are engaged.

The public credit can be maintained; the public credit will be maintained; armies will be raised; navies will be created; men will appear capable of guiding our armies, of controlling our navies; and we shall be successful ultimately. Let no man have any doubts in regard to this. The more we are tried, and the longer foreign countries, by refusing to recognize the right, continue this war by giving encouragement to the rebellion, then in that proportion will our power be magnified when the rebellion ceases. I believe, that, when this war is ended, and England shall see that we are able, upon a moment's notice, to put half a million of fighting men, trained veterans, into the field; when we have an iron-clad navy, manned by seamen who have trodden the waves during all their boyhood and manhood, — she will regret, when her day of trial comes, that she hesitated to do that which was right and just in the beginning, which was to have said to these rebellious States and these traitors, "You will receive no countenance or encouragement from us." If England had made this declaration on the 20th of April, 1861, the rebellion would have had no power further to harm her or to harm mankind.

SUGGESTIONS CONCERNING THE FURTHER PROSECUTION OF THE WAR.

[This article was prepared as early as January, 1863; and portions of it were printed in the Washington "Chronicle" in February and March of that year: but it was thought to be inexpedient to publish the portion which suggests a plan of operations against Richmond. The editors also declined to print the paragraphs relating to the office of General-in-chief of the army.]

THERE are differences of opinion among loyal men concerning the objects for which the present war should be prosecuted by the people and the government of the United States. There are a few persons who are prepared to propose or to accept dishonorable conditions of peace, either upon the basis of a restoration of the Union, or a permanent separation; but the great majority of American citizens are determined to re-establish the authority of the national government over all the territory which was within the limits of the Union previous to the outbreak of the present rebellion. The peaceful existence of two governments between the lines of the Mississippi, the Atlantic, the great lakes, and the Gulf of Mexico, is an impossibility. The hope or the expectation of such a condition of things is a delusion. The war in which the nation is now involved can have but one solution,— the establishment of a common government over the region now rent and devastated by civil strife.

The men who propose peace propose that which is impossible. If the rebellion be not overthrown, its triumph will not be limited to the establishment of an independent government; but, gradually and by steps clearly foreseen, it will subjugate to itself the territory of the North, as well as occupy and possess the States of the South. But, in the nature of things, the rebellion cannot succeed. Many events may occur to strengthen it, to delay, to encourage; but the end is to be the subjugation of the rebels, and the seizure and occupation of the rebel States. Offers of mediation, foreign interference, foreign war, may embarrass and cripple the North; but, after all and always, the necessity and the duty will continue. The rebellion is to be crushed, the rebels are to be subjugated, the power of the old government is to be re-established over all the seceding States. There is not only no interest in the North that can accept peace upon any other basis, but there is not even a man who can afford to share its disaster and its dishonor.

Those who suppose, be they of the North or of the South, that no more men will be furnished, labor under a serious error. When one army has disappeared, another will appear. If there be no statesmanship in council, if there be no genius or capacity in the field, we still have numbers and courage, to be wrought finally into desperation; and arithmetic will do the rest. We can, in even battles, or with odds of losses against us, exterminate the fighting population of the South; and there will then remain millions of fighting men, millions of laboring men, in the North, with freedom for the whole continent, and a career of prosperity and power open before us as a nation.

But we have statesmanship and genius and capacity; and, though these characteristics have not been developed rapidly, they exist in our rulers, leaders, and people. We have made great mistakes, neglected favorable opportunities; but all nations have done the same. The rebels, with years of preparation for leadership, have not exhibited high qualities in any branch of their service.

During the twenty months of actual war, the North has made acquisitions of territory and gained many strategic points, none of which have been retaken by the rebels. The enemies of the country have raised great armies, fought many battles, some of them successful battles; and yet they have been losing ground. Without assistance from abroad, their future experience will be the same; and assistance from abroad will only magnify the war, involve Europe in the contest, and put far off the day when the South will contribute to the comfort and progress of the human race. Foreign interference is not impossible; but it is less probable than it was in March, or even in December, 1862.

It is always to be assumed, that the ruling classes of Europe are hostile to this government, and that they welcome, and, as far as opportunity allows, they aid and encourage, the rebellion. In England, this hostile feeling is strong. It is exhibited by the press, in Parliament, and by the ministry. It has not yet dared to defy the sentiment of the masses, and to ally itself openly with the rebels. Any movement by France will be dictated by a desire to occupy the North, and perhaps England, so that her policy in Mexico and Central America may be prosecuted without open opposition by her two rivals in commerce and war. If, by an alliance with England and mediation in American affairs, yet so managed as not to come to open hostilities, Napoleon can secure a footing in Mexico or Central America, and establish a channel of communication with the Pacific, he will have succeeded, in connection with the canal across the Isthmus of Suez, in putting a girdle around the globe, and in securing commercial and military advantages of the most signal importance. His policy, it may be, looks only to the employment of the United States and Great Britain during the ensuing two years, that he may successfully advance these schemes of a comprehensive ambition, not unworthy a great ruler of any age or country.

The influence of the cotton famine is more likely to be diminished than increased. It is not improbable that one-half of the ordinary crop of American cotton will be accounted for by the increased production of other countries. In 1863, there will be no deficiency, except what may arise from the growing demand for cotton manufactures. As, however, the high price of cotton has led to the more common use of wool and flax as substitutes, we may reasonably anticipate a gradual reduction in the price of cotton, tested by the standard of gold. Especially will this be the case should there be obtained from the American States a quantity exceeding two hundred thousand bales during the next ninety days.

It is also to be noted, that the Proclamation of

Emancipation disarms the masses of Europe of any sympathy they might have had with the South. This fact may not only be declared by the friends of emancipation: it must be admitted by its opponents. Hence it follows that war cannot now be safely inaugurated by any country of Europe, except upon issues distinct from those connected with the controversy in the United States. These issues may be formed by England or France, if the motives be sufficiently strong. The hostility of England is due to her institutions, to the distresses of her people, and to her history and traditions in connection with America. Now that the North, in its dealings with the South, is put unequivocally on the side of freedom, it will not be easy for the British Government to give open aid or official recognition to the rebellion.

France is not our enemy; Napoleon is not our enemy. If his policy is now openly or covertly hostile to the United States, he is not likely to be drawn so far as to develop that policy into actual war. He may annoy us; he may counsel mediation; he may seek to involve England in hostilities: but the positive, armed interference of Napoleon cannot reasonably be anticipated.

It may, then, be assumed safely, as the basis of our domestic policy, that there is before us a period of time during which we shall be free from the active, or at least from the open, interference of other governments. If Russia is our friend, as we have reason to believe, every thing in honor should be done to preserve her as our friend. Her friendship for us is security against the hostility of England. The British possessions on the north, in case of war against England by Russia and America as allies, would almost inevitably be transferred and partitioned. At any rate, England will be slow to assume so great a risk.

But it is to be observed, and it should never be forgotten by people or rulers, that, in periods of strife, when human passions are excited, and when individual and national ambitions are distempered and feverish, no security can be taken, not even for a month or for a day, that the waywardness of the multitude, or the caprices of a monarch or a minister, may not involve nations in controversies and war. So, then, if, by processes of reasoning upon facts as they are known, we relieve ourselves measurably of anxiety concerning foreign interference, we should act nevertheless as though such interference were impending. Hence we should increase and strengthen our navy for defensive and offensive war, whether against the rebels or their possible allies. No reasoning upon this point is needed. The people will only be satisfied when every power of the country that can be turned into this channel is sought out and used to exhaustion.

If, among the calamities in store for this nation, foreign war be one, and if when that calamity comes it shall appear that the government has neglected to do what might have been done for the defence of the coast, for the protection of our commerce on the ocean, and for the assault of our enemies in their strongholds, the current of popular indignation will break down all the barriers of office, and overwhelm minister and administration. Not considering at all what has been done (and much has been done) to increase and strengthen the navy, no delays should be permitted, no economy of mere money should be tolerated; but every appropriate power of the nation should be devoted to the task of strengthening the maritime force of the United States. Each week that the war continues beyond the time when by possible exertions it could have been closed, will, in its cost, be equivalent to the sum needed to build and equip an iron-clad fleet which would bid defiance to the fortifications of Vicksburg, Mobile, Fort Darling, or Charleston. So vast are the proportions of this war, that relatively there is no economy worth considering but the economy of time. Days pass, expenses are necessarily incurred, debts inevitably accumulate. There should be a careful supervision of public expenses, a rigid system of accountability, due punishment should be administered to all who are guilty of fraud; but, however faithfully these things may be done, the savings will be insignificant when compared, or rather when contrasted, with our monthly or even weekly expenditures. The use or the waste of a day, as it shortens or protracts the war, is the great economy or the great extravagance of the nation. Hence not unwisely were the people instinctively restive when disciplined armies wasted precious weeks and months in unexplained delays. The sacrifice of human life incident to war is not so much dependent upon the losses in battle as upon the diseases of the camp. Therefore, in war, economy of life is to be attained by activity. In war, as in all the other undertakings of men, there is security in vigor, there is safety in courage. It is not alone that, by the exhibition of these qualities, the enemy is harassed and weakened: they who possess these qualities are themselves encouraged and strengthened. The economy of time is at once the economy of money and the economy of human life.

But this economy is the fruit of capacity, of discipline, of system; and it cannot be secured in any other way.

The capacity of the loyal States for the business of war was, in the beginning, entirely unorganized, and only in an inconsiderable degree developed. The experience of the nation in Mexico, Utah, and on the frontiers inured to the benefit of the rebel States, as the result of a policy long since adopted and steadily pursued. Yet, among men of the first and second rank in our army, there is no lack of capacity. There are many, no doubt, who occupy places for which they are not fitted. Such officers should be removed from positions of trust, whether the unfitness they exhibit is due to actual incapacity or to a lack of earnestness in the war. Mere professional service, which has no higher purpose than to preserve one's honor untarnished, is altogether unworthy the life of a true soldier of the republic; and, whenever such men are discovered, whatever their rank or reputation, they should be relieved summarily from duty.

Next, all regiments numbering less than four hundred men should be consolidated, and the most incapable officers discharged from the service; and the same rule should be applied to companies and company officers. By this means, the efficiency of the army would become at once a fourth greater than it now is; and especially in the fact that officers would be anxious to preserve their men from death and desertion, while they would be stimulated to secure a character which would avail them in case of consolidation. At present, officers of regiments boast of the small number of men fit for duty, as though this fact were evidence of courage and worth! No amount of care on the part of officers can save men from death; but the faithful performance of duty would sensibly diminish the losses of the army.

The work of consolidating the broken regiments of the army cannot with safety or propriety be longer delayed.

In a civil war, it is a great error to depend exclusively, or even chiefly, upon professional soldiers for leaders. In such wars, the passions are the masters; and hence those who are indifferent to the questions at issue are uniformly unsuccessful. War is not different from other pursuits; and in no other pursuit is success attained by the performance of mere professional duty. There must be an exhibition of will,—a determination to accomplish what is undertaken. In this war, there is no place for the mere professional soldier. In this war, a General must believe in the nation's cause, or he cannot fight successfully the nation's battles. The nation's cause is freedom; the rebels' cause is slavery. He who believes in slavery cannot succeed as the defender of freedom. Hence it follows that a military education alone does not qualify a man to take a leading part in this contest.

The rebels have intrusted but few commands to persons who are not representatives of the cause for which they contend. A military education or a military experience renders the services of a leader proportionately valuable; but it is wiser to confide in a representative of the opinion, who has but a small share of military knowledge, than to trust a professional soldier who has no fixed opinions in favor of the principle involved.

But it is not safe to confide implicitly in the common aphorism that war is a science. If it be a science at all, it is a science only as agriculture, manufactures, and commerce are sciences. In strictness, this cannot be said of these pursuits; but it is rather only true, that, for their development and progress, we are indebted to the sciences. It does not follow that a statistician or geographer will make a successful merchant; that an astronomer will best navigate a vessel; that a chemist, therefrom and thereby, is a good farmer; that a school-teacher can administer a system of education; or that the student of the laws of force and of motion will acquire wealth and distinction as a manufacturer. Indeed, human experience teaches the opposite. The successful merchant is he who, having adequate ability, and a determination to succeed, summons to his aid all the contributions which science has made, and so applies these contributions as to render his undertakings successful. This is the law of success in war, as well as in the vocations of peace.

While a military training is not to be set aside, its greatest value relatively will be observed among subordinates and men of common capacities; nor has it happened, nor will it ever happen, that it can be said of any truly great commander, that he would have been otherwise than a great commander if he had not received a military education. What a man has done, rather than what has been done for him, should be the test of his ability to serve the country in the present crisis.

Without discipline in an army, there can be no security for success; and there can be no discipline without power in commanders to try subalterns and soldiers for offences prejudicial to good order, and to inflict immediate punishment, whether such punishment be the dishonorable discharge of officers, or the penalty of death upon soldiers or officers. These proceedings should be summary, and without appeal to the President. Military rules are necessarily severe, — military discipline is necessarily harsh; and it is never safe for men in civil life to revise the judgments of commanders in the field, who realize daily the necessity of exact and unrelenting proceedings. War is a stern teacher; and any attempt to smooth its pathway only swells the aggregate of losses and horrors. The failure of an officer or soldier to discharge his whole duty, or his neglect to prepare and hold himself ready for service, should receive severe punishment as the means whereby losses and disasters are avoided. An army can never pay too much for the virtue of discipline: the losses that follow disorganization cannot be foreseen, but in anticipation they can never be exaggerated.

Intemperance is an evil in the army, and chiefly

an evil among officers. It is not only because intemperance is a vice that the rules should be rigidly enforced against all who are guilty, even in a single instance, but chiefly as a means of securing the country against losses by surprises on the part of our enemies, and incompetency on our own part, which yield successive harvests of defeats, disasters, and humiliations. An officer who is guilty of intemperance should be instantly, and in dishonor, dismissed from the service.

There can be no trustworthy discipline in the army until officers and men are held to the most rigid accountability for their good conduct; and especially is it true that there can be no discipline until desertion, the greatest crime of the soldier next to treason, is punishable and punished by the death of the offender. Outside of the War Department, rumor is the only authority for our losses through this channel; and it is doubtful whether the records of the Department contain accurate and complete information upon the subject. But enough is known in the streets to warrant the statement, that, since the first of December last, all the recruits obtained will not make good the losses by desertion. The license given to soldiers in this particular, by law and by neglect, must weaken and ultimately destroy the armies of the republic.

In this particular, as in all things connected with military affairs, authority and its rigorous exercise are the only securities for the public welfare. The first requisite of the army is discipline, — discipline at any cost. The second requisite of the army is action. For activity in the administration of public affairs, military and civil, there is usually a necessity; and, if there be no necessity, there is always justification or plausible excuse. For inaction there is never a necessity, and seldom a justification.

And the time has come when the country, when the President, should consider whether the office of General-in-chief of the Army is not, in the nature of things, necessarily calculated to divide responsibility; to diminish public confidence; to weaken the power of the President as the Commander-in-chief of the army; to embarrass the administration of the War Department, to which the nation ought to look and must look for the means of prosecuting the war efficiently, systematically, and triumphantly. It may be necessary, and in times of public peril it is no doubt wise, for the President to seek and to accept the counsels of experienced and competent persons; but such are the limitations to the capacities of men, such the accidents and mistakes incident to human conduct, and such is the authority of nature in the elements and in the unforeseen obstacles which they often interpose, that military operations in the field must be left *exclusively* to commanders in the field. Any exercise of authority, or any tender of suggestion even, is always a hazard, and, if obeyed or accepted, is usually a disaster. All the military operations and doings of a government in time of war should fall under one or another of three heads: —

1. A general plan of the campaign.

2. The appointment of officers to be assigned to active service in the field.

3. Timely and sufficient supplies.

To what extent can a General-in-chief, resident at the capital, render valuable services in either of these three particulars? If he be the most competent man in the country, then he should be placed at the head of the War Department, and made the constitutional adviser of the President. Upon the present basis, there is a divided jurisdiction; and, in the nature of the case, neither the General-in-chief nor the Secretary of War can, at any moment, be in possession of all the information relating to the army that is essential to the safe exercise of the best judgment. There should be one man in authority under the President who should be administratively in possession of all the military information which is or can be known to the government. There can be but one such man. What should be his office, what his relation to the President? He can only be in possession of the necessary information by virtue of his office as the head of the War Department; for it is there that all military information naturally centres. If the channels of information are divided, some trending towards the War Department, and others towards the office of General-in-chief, neither will be able to give safe advice. Nor is it easy to estimate the importance of securing to the head of a department every item of information, however valueless it may seem, when considered as an isolated fact. We can have but one Department of War, which must have a head who should be responsible to the President and to the country. He should be the recipient of all information touching the fortunes of the army in the field; and if, by the creation of the office of General-in-chief, the Secretary of War is deprived of any information to which otherwise he would be entitled, he is necessarily made accountable for doings of which he can have no knowledge. Hence come disasters inevitably.

These observations are addressed to the question of the expediency of continuing the office of General-in-chief, and are made without reference to the eminent soldiers who have filled the exalted and influential position.

From the commencement of the war, there has been a universal opinion that the Mississippi River should be opened. As yet, the government has failed to accomplish this great undertaking. Such are now the fortunes of the country, and the dangers impending, that delay in the prosecution of this work is full of peril. It is hoped and generally believed that the present season will realize the expectations of the country in the fall of Vicksburg and Port Hudson.

There should, however, be no uncertainty. It is in our power to concentrate so vast a force upon the Upper Mississippi that it will be impossible for the rebels to maintain their present position. Indeed, it is in our power to transfer the war to the West, where the river would be the base of our operations from New Orleans to Memphis. Such an opportunity should not be overlooked. If we succeed in this effort, every thing else will follow. Mobile will fall. The separation of Texas and Arkansas will diminish the supplies of the rebel armies, and enable the government to devote the resources of those great States to the cause of the Constitution and Union. Moreover, the acquisition of these extensive cotton-growing regions will furnish at once a supply of one-fourth of a million of bales of previous crops; and it will so stimulate industry, that, in 1864, the product will be twice what it has been in former years. When we can export five hundred thousand bales of cotton, our resources and credit will be wonderfully augmented. As far as our own government is concerned, the war should be transferred to the valley of the Mississippi. The rebels must accept battle there, and submit the waning fortunes of the Confederacy to the arbitrament of arms where the advantages of position and supplies are with us. Let there be no delay in the adoption of a policy which will give the government these manifest advantages. All thoughts of a movement upon Richmond may well be postponed for the present. It is, indeed, to be assumed, upon any sound theory of future movements, that an attack upon Richmond is to be incidental, while the chief object should be to secure the control of the Mississippi River; and, in this attempt, the troops of the East, and especially of New England, should be employed. By such a movement, the soldiers of the Atlantic would be made acquainted with the characteristics, ideas, and necessities of the West; while the people of the great valley might be better satisfied than heretofore of the fidelity of the East to the interests of the whole country. It is too plain for argument, that, with our resources, and with our communication with the Mississippi at its mouth, and our exclusive command of its waters above

Memphis, we can carry on the war upon its banks with great advantages on our side. We should first cut the railway communications westward from Vicksburg; then cut the railroad communications between Vicksburg and the country eastward. These things were done previous to, and in anticipation of, the recent attack upon that post. The force aggregated should be so vast as to render defeat quite impossible. The rebels must concentrate their forces at Vicksburg. In the end, the town must fall. Nothing else can happen; and in proportion to the magnitude of the force employed by the rebels, and the vigor and pertinacity of the defence, will be the magnitude of the success when it comes. River communications are cheaper and safer than railway communications. If a vessel or even a fleet of transports should be destroyed upon the Mississippi, the great highway remains. It cannot be removed or obstructed.

The success of the Union armies is to be achieved by transferring the war to the Mississippi. As this noble river is the bond which cannot be broken; so upon its bosom are to be borne the brave men of the West and the East, who, on its banks, will illustrate the courage of the country, and achieve the great, the crowning, victories of the republic.

It may be, that, at this moment, our preparations are adequate for the reduction of the rebel strongholds upon the Mississippi: but this may well be doubted; and, in any view of probabilities, it is the part of wisdom to make the most formidable demonstration that our resources permit. Vicksburg is more important to the rebels than Richmond: its subjugation is more important to us; its capture is an undertaking which can hardly fail of success; and, for this undertaking, the most sturdy and comprehensive plans should be organized and prosecuted without delay.

Shall Washington be left without protection? Certainly not. The season protects Washington against all attacks by the Upper Potomac until the first of May. The approaches by Arlington Heights are easily defended. The Lower Potomac is impassable. Leave Virginia, between the Potomac and the Shenandoah, to the care and mercy of whomsoever may desire to lament over, or rejoice in, the devastation which the rebellion has produced.

This course will enable the government to reduce the Army of the Potomac materially. Of the force thus relieved, fifty thousand may be sent to the West; and a force of at least fifty thousand more should be landed upon the right bank of the James River as near Richmond as practicable, and, if possible, above the mouth of the Appomattox. These troops should be supported by gunboats in the river. There are points within the limits indicated — that is, between the Appomattox and Richmond — so strong by nature, and so easily strengthened by art, that the whole rebel army may be defied. This done, and the second important point in the rebellious States is menaced, and can never be relieved so long as we command the James River. Under these circumstances, Richmond cannot be abandoned. With fifty thousand troops in Washington, who can be transported in a few hours to the Upper James, where, in combination with the army of observation, a hundred thousand men might in any week be precipitated upon the rebel capital, nearly the whole of Lee's army would be retained for its defence. If it should happen otherwise, then the armies of the republic combined, by a rapid movement from Washington, Fortress Monroe, and Suffolk, would attack the city with the best prospects of success.

There may be those who are reluctant to divide the Army of the Potomac, which is endeared to the country by its great deeds as well as by its unparalleled sacrifices and sufferings. Let all such consider that there is not the remotest chance of a successful movement upon Richmond by the way of Gordonsville or Fredericksburg, or by any other interior route. The distance is great; the country is destitute of subsistence for men or cattle; there are numerous streams, rivers, and ridges, to be crossed. All these are difficulties, barriers, obstacles in our way; and they all constitute defences for the enemy. This only further can be hoped of the Army of the Potomac during the next three months, if left to operate from its present base,—that it may interrupt the communications between Richmond and Fredericksburg, and compel the forces in the latter place to fight or capitulate. But, inasmuch as Fredericksburg is of no considerable importance to the rebels, any movement promising success would lead to the evacuation of that city, and the retreat of the rebel army towards Richmond. A pursuit must end in disaster. Therefore not one day should be spent upon the Rappahannock more than may be necessary for the proper withdrawal of the army.

The advantages of a position upon the James River, and especially of a position above the mouth of the Appomattox, deserve consideration. It threatens three vital points of the enemy,—Petersburg, Fort Darling, and Richmond. Our army would be within a triangle, of which the longer leg—the James River, between Richmond and the Appomattox—would be the base of our operations; the other sides being the Appomattox below Petersburg, and the railway between Petersburg and Richmond. This railway is distant from the James River from five to twenty miles. It is well known that this railway is defended by fortifications of an important character; but the length of the line is so great that it cannot be successfully maintained against such attacks as could be made from the river. We should be able by a night's march to cut it at one or many points, and thus interrupt the connections between the cities. Moreover, an advance might be threatened or made towards or upon Richmond upon either side of the river.

With all these manifest advantages, we should occupy the attention of an army larger than our own, while we rested in comparative safety; always menacing, and as opportunity offered attacking, the stronghold of the enemy. With the fall of Vicksburg, there could be a concentration of forces below Richmond, and upon the side from whence the city is finally to be taken. Whenever an army of one hundred thousand men is encamped upon the triangle between the two rivers, the rebels will be called to evacuate Richmond, and attempt the defence of a lower line toward the cotton States, or to abandon Petersburg and trust Richmond to the integrity of the railway communications to the West and South-west. In either case, Richmond is weakened. When is this to be done? Not until other important preliminary undertakings are accomplished.

The order might be this: First, menace Richmond by the transfer of an army of observation to the James; withdraw from the Rappahannock as circumstances may dictate; then strengthen the Army of the West, and mass such a force upon the Mississippi that the rebels will yield the river. This is not only possible,—it is practicable: it is not only practicable, but it is certain; and, being at once possible, practicable, and certain, the necessities of the country may well demand its attempt upon a scale proportionate to its importance to the cause of the Union, rather than to the real difficulties of the undertaking itself. We should no longer attempt to maintain positions which are not important in a strategic point of view. We should no longer strive to protect loyal men or loyal districts in the rebel States. We should mass forces upon strategic points still in the possession of the enemy; attempt first the reduction of those places which are vulnerable to a combined attack by the army and the navy; and henceforth, without fear or apprehension, we should admit to ourselves, and in our official intercourse with foreign nations we should declare, that, while the end of the rebellion cannot be foreseen, the war for the Union will be prosecuted until the power of the government is re-established.

In time, — we cannot foresay how long the time, — the river will be opened to commerce, and for the purposes of war; Texas and Arkansas will be separated from the Confederacy; Mobile, Charleston, and Wilmington will be taken; the blockade will become more and more effectual; and the world, including traitors in the North and jealous enemies in Europe, will admit that the rebellion is thenceforward without hope. Industry and finance will be relieved; cotton will find its way to greedy and well-paying markets; the country west of the Mississippi will be opened to all trade, except in articles contraband of war; and the national credit will be restored at home and abroad. The end of the war may not be reached even then. Richmond may continue as the rebel capital. It may even be wise to postpone the active siege of that city until the Confederacy is severed by a second line from Mobile to East Tennessee. During the present year, we ought to be satisfied with nothing less than the possession of the Mississippi and the capture of the cities of Charleston, Wilmington, and Mobile; and, with these results attained, enough will have been done to render the future reasonably secure.

The successes of the year 1862 were not less important in character, nor less difficult in accomplishment; and it may therefore be anticipated reasonably, that, in the year 1863, the rebellion will be pressed back upon the interior of the cotton region east of the Mississippi River.

In assigning the entire year to the work of opening the river and securing the Atlantic coast, it is not assumed that so much time is to be used in these several enterprises; but there will certainly be no ground for apprehension if the year should be so required.

Although our previous attempts upon Richmond have been unsuccessful, no just inference can be drawn from these failures as to the strength of the place, or our fortunes in the future concerning its capture. The city is strong in its isolation, and the character of the country on the north and northwest affords reasonable security against attacks from the land side; but, from its position at the head of a navigable river, it is exposed necessarily to capture from the sea. Whenever its railway connections with the South and West are permanently interrupted, it will be at the mercy of the besiegers. Again, river fortifications are quite generally staked upon the fortunes of a field-fight. In the absence of Fort Darling and other fortifications upon the James, our gunboats might ascend to Richmond without engaging the enemy upon land. We shall be compelled to flank the fort by land, and the enemy will have no resource but to engage us in the open country. If we have the power to take Richmond in the absence of Fort Darling, its existence can only work delay.

With an army in the angle between the rivers, supported by gunboats (which need not be ironclad), we are in the most secure position possible. A successful defence ought to be made against an army numerically twice as strong as our own. A defeat could only result from cowardice, incapacity, or treason. When the position shall have been sagaciously chosen and taken, we may wait the progress of events at Richmond, and elsewhere along the theatre of war, or we may advance immediately to the conquest of the city. It is assumed that the position indicated should be taken at once, inasmuch as the rebels will then be compelled to strengthen Richmond by the withdrawal of forces from the line of the Rappahannock, and even from the Gulf coast, or they will abandon Richmond at once. It would seem that an army of fifty thousand men at the point indicated, supported from the river, would be proof against any successful attack; yet the presence of such a force at a position so near the capital of the rebel States would compel the rebel leaders to hold in reserve at Richmond, or its immediate vicinity, at least one hundred thousand men. By this we gain in numerical strength; and the facility with which we could transport troops from the Chesapeake, the Potomac, and Fortress Monroe would fill the enemies of the republic with the most serious and overpressing apprehensions.

It would seem, then, to be a military necessity that such naval force as may be required should at once appear in the James River upon the line indicated, that the rebels may be kept from occupying strategic points essential to the execution of the plan suggested. It would not follow, nor ought it to follow,—unless the rebel force in Richmond was greatly reduced, so as to invite and assure the success of an attack,—that an attempt would be made immediately upon the rebel capital. Delay would be advantageous in some respects. We compel the rebels to concentrate for the defence of Richmond, we use the season for the capture of the Southern ports; and, succeeding in these undertakings, we render the occupation of Richmond by June or July next the most probable event of the future.

If, after the capture of the cities of the Gulf and the consequent breaking of the lines of railway, we are to fail in reducing Richmond, then it is assuredly true that a winter and spring campaign upon that city would also prove a failure. If we contest for the Mississippi River, for Mobile, for Charleston, for Wilmington, it is not in the nature of things that we should fail everywhere. Indeed, the probability of success is so great that we may feel assured of the accomplishment of all these undertakings during the first half of the present year.

These things successfully accomplished, and it might be wise to delay the attack upon Richmond even beyond the year 1863. The railways through the South should be cut and destroyed for long distances; the iron removed or rendered useless; every bridge that can be reached should be burned, or otherwise destroyed; the navigable rivers should be traversed by armed boats; and East Tennessee occupied, and its railway communications with Richmond broken up. The capture of Charleston and the other ports of the Atlantic, together with the opening of the Mississippi River, will satisfy the country and the army that the campaign has been successful; while foreign nations will be compelled to admit in their policy, if not in words, that the restoration of the Union is an accomplished fact. Time, decision, energy, and the capacity to use circumstances aright, to foresee events that in the laws of reason and of human logic are inevitable, will do the rest. If, moreover, we capture Mobile and Wilmington, who will ask whether Richmond can be taken? Richmond can only capitulate, and the rebel leaders can only choose between capture and flight. It might, indeed, happen that the attempt to advance this policy would lead the rebels, under the influence of despair and hope, to abandon Richmond; or, withdrawing the body of the army southward, to trust the defence of their capital to fortresses, intrenchments, and the soldiers within the fortifications. This policy would still leave us the advantage, as, by falling upon the railways in the rear of their army, we could separate Richmond from the Confederacy. Upon the basis laid down, it would seem incredible to history that the spring and early summer should have passed away, and the rebel authority continue as it is at this moment.

The policy, then, to which these suggestions lead, embodied in propositions, may be stated thus: —

I. Open the Mississippi River.

II. Menace Richmond with a formidable naval force upon the James River, and a formidable land force upon the angle between the James and the Appomattox; and be prepared to support this force from the Potomac and other points, should it be deemed necessary for defence, or to advance upon Richmond if the rebel army in that city should be materially diminished.

III. The capture of the ports named by sudden attacks of large forces on land and water; regarding the capture of Richmond as a thing to be desired and attempted should circumstances so invite, but not to be pursued as an object of the war, nor as in any considerable degree essential to the ultimate success of the national arms.

IV. The abandonment of the attempt to protect loyal men in the rebel States. Nor should any effort be made to induce such to identify themselves with the government until our successes and the experience of the rebel population shall have made it safe for loyal people to announce and defend their opinions without the active protection of the national government. When the rebel power shall have been broken, the opportunity for the free expression of opinion will gradually return to the people. Then such free expression will not be attended with personal danger; but, until that time arrives, it is wise for our government to direct its military operations without regard to the existence of loyal men, discountenancing expressions of loyalty in the rebel districts rather than giving encouragement to them. The rebel territory is so vast that it is simply impossible to give personal or even local protection to the people. We should attempt—(1) To occupy so much rebel territory as is essential to the protection of the loyal States, and nothing more; (2) To seize such strategic points as may be necessary for present or future operations; (3) To penetrate the rebel territory for the purpose of breaking and destroying lines of communication. When these things shall have been successfully accomplished, the rebel army will be separated into parts; its sources of supply cut off; its ultimate annihilation certain.

THE POWER OF THE GOVERNMENT TO SUPPRESS THE REBELLION.

SPEECH DELIVERED BEFORE THE NATIONAL UNION LEAGUE ASSOCIATION, WASHINGTON, D.C., JUNE 16, 1863.

IT would be unkind in me, ladies and gentlemen, if I were to-night, under the circumstances both of the climate and of public affairs, to make a long speech, even to indulgent hearers.

Since the rebellion opened, I have followed but one line of conduct in regard to whatever I have thought, done, or said in reference to public affairs. I do not propose any departure from that course to-night. It is simply this: to give that advice and counsel which the exigencies of the country demand, without regard to its effect upon myself or upon the opinions, purposes, principles, or feelings of other men.

The crisis is too important to allow any man to deviate from that course of conduct; and what I have said and done, and what I shall say or do, all turns upon one idea, and has in the end but one purpose; and that is, the extinction of the institution of slavery, as the means by which the rebellion is to be quelled, the Union restored, and civil war for ever after prevented. Believing this to be the necessary and inevitable consequence of the overthrow of that institution, and educated as I have been in the traditions and histories of our country, — having observed to some extent, with such faculties as I could command, the greatness of the republic, and conceived to some extent its nature, grandeur, and power, — if I believed in the system of slavery, I should yet feel called upon to surrender it, and to aid in its destruction, in order that the republic might live. If two years ago it were not admitted that this was a contest of life or death in which we are engaged, no sane man can to-day have any doubt upon that point.

But there can be no concession, there can be no compromise, there can be no arrangement, there can be no treaty, nor can there be any return of Jefferson Davis and his allies, or of the slaveholders, as slaveholders, into this Union.

The government has not been framed which can sustain a struggle such as inevitably must result from the existence within its limits of any considerable number of men who entertain the ideas which these men entertain. The war that is now desolating our land, is not the result of the preaching of anybody, North or South. It is not the result of what has been done in Congress, or of what Congress has failed to do; and, if you will search the records of time, you will find that this rebellion in which we are engaged, this war which we are prosecuting hand to hand with the enemies of the republic, is the most logical and most inevitable of which history gives us any account. It is not spasmodic nor exceptional. It is necessary, because we founded a government upon antagonistic and hostile ideas. You might as well hope to establish an harmonious and enduring church upon the Koran and the Bible, as to expect to maintain, through successive ages, institutions and forms of government based in part upon the equality of man, and in part upon the subjugation of man to tyranny. In saying this, I make no reflections upon the men who framed this government. If, on the one hand, the men of the North had believed that slavery would be extended and perpetuated, they never would have put their hands to the compact; and, if the men of the South at that day had believed in the institution of slavery, they had too much respect for the truth to have asked their friends in the North to form an alliance with them. The men of the North and South, with few exceptions, believed that slavery was temporary, transitory, and even then passing away; and that liberty was permanent and universal in its application to all men.

Some of those whom I address remember the memorable event of the presence of the Hungarian exile, Kossuth, in our country. It was my fortune to introduce him in Fanueil Hall, in Massachusetts; and I recall to-night the opening passage of his speech, not in language, but in meaning. Said he: "You err in speaking of 'American liberty.' You should say, 'Liberty in America.' There can be no such thing as American liberty. God is God: liberty is liberty."

Now, then, reviewing the past, I can but come to the conclusion, that one great source of our failure is, that we have undertaken to establish here, upon this continent, American liberty, and have confined its application to men of a particular color, and have, acting upon that idea, disregarded entirely the rights of one-eighth of the people occupying the territory of the United States. Believing, as I do, in an overruling Providence, I cannot doubt, that the suffering through which we are called to pass, is, in some way or other, a punishment upon the nation for its great sin in this respect. Therefore, if I am either a patriot or a Christian, it is my duty to declare that there can be no peace until the institution of slavery is exterminated.

Thus much, then, for the cause of the war and the means by which we are to secure peace and permanent prosperity.

I doubt not we are to-day passing through the crisis of the war. This great contest was not to be settled by a battle or a campaign; but it required battles, campaigns, time, and exhaustion. We have had exhaustion, battles, and campaigns. Time will bring us to the end of the war by the subjugation of the rebels. Whether they be in Pennsylvania or Maryland or Virginia, our determination is still the same, — to press upon them with undiminished power, and compel them finally, as finally they must, to yield to right, to justice, to the Constitution, and to the establishment of the principles of liberty as the birthright of every man.

It has been a prominent feature of the political contest arising out of the rebellion to complain of the administration of public affairs.

I do not doubt that we have made many mistakes and committed many acts which it would have been well to have avoided, and that we have omitted to do many things that should have been done. But these are comparatively incidental, and do not affect the main result.

On the other hand, the rebels have been disappointed. They have failed again and again to accomplish what they had expected. When, in February, 1861, Breckinridge, in the House of Representatives, as Vice-President of the United States, declared Abraham Lincoln President, he surrendered the cause of the rebels, with which he had been identified, betraying at once his associate traitors and the country which had honored him. When he announced Abraham Lincoln as President of the United States, he gave up the contest, with reference to the result; for it made the war constitutional and for the Union, and himself and his associates traitors. They are to-day dying under the effect of the declaration Breckinridge then made; for he then and there acknowledged that Abraham Lincoln was President of the United States according to the Constitution.

The rebels have been deceived by a few men in the North, as to the purposes of the North. They were led to expect that the controversy would be settled without a resort to arms.

I was a member of the Peace Congress, and I well recollect what they desired. It was that the radical men, as they were called, should give a pledge that there should be no war, let come what else might. Mr. Seddon, now a member of Davis's Cabinet, spoke fifteen minutes in an imploring speech, asking for a declaration, that, whatever else might happen, there should be no war. For one, I left them in no doubt as to what my ideas were, by declaring, that, if they persisted in secession, one of two things would happen, — either the armies of the North would march to the Gulf of Mexico, or the armies of the South would march to the great lakes. The former has been accomplished, and the rebels are now attempting the latter. They will be again disappointed.

They have been deceived, also, in the course England has taken, not because there was lacking in the British Government and aristocracy a disposition to favor the South, but because neither they nor the British Government took into consideration, that the President of the United States, on the first day of January, 1863, would pronounce emancipation in the seceding States.

That proclamation has, I doubt not, changed the public sentiment of England, giving encouragement to the men and the cause that favored the Union. Thus, too, has the proclamation prevented the British Government from entering into any open alliance with the rebels. This proclamation is, in a certain sense, our security with the world; and, if the world will allow us to carry on this contest in our own way and in our own time, there is no doubt of the result. Great Britain, I doubt not, is now considering what, in case of war with this country, she could do? If she should capture New York and destroy the cities along the coast, still there is capacity to navigate the ocean, to carry on the business of privateering, so that the four million tons of British shipping shall disappear. It will be in our power, in case of war, to shut up the British people upon the British isles, and dictate to them, the thirty million there, the *per-diem* allowance of bread they shall eat. This power is good security for peace. I am not for war: I am for peace. I believe, however, that Great Britain has pursued an unjust policy in our affairs, which, if it be not in some way or other, and that speedily, atoned for, will result in war. I ask whether it is in the nature of a nation, with a people twenty million strong,—supposing that the South has parted from us for ever,—soon to be thirty and ere long to be fifty million, to carry in remembrance, and unatoned for, the circumstances, that Great Britain allowed vessels, built by and according to the rules of naval architecture, to depart from one British port, seamen to depart from another, ammunition and guns on British isles to be placed upon these vessels, and thus British ships, manned by British subjects, to be clandestinely brought out of British ports; and then to submit silently to the claims before the world that that government has no responsibility for these things, for the depredations committed by these vessels. It is not necessary to know what the laws of nations are or are not. I know perfectly well that if I sell a man burglarious weapons by day, and harbor him at night, and he robs and steals, some responsibility rests upon me.

Resuming the consideration of domestic affairs, let me call your attention to one possible difficulty before us. That possible difficulty is the return of the seceded States to this Union *as slave States.* I have looked with interest towards Louisiana, at the indications there made that the loyal people of that State are about to frame a new constitution and ask for admission into the Union. The policy of allowing these eleven seceded States to return to the Union with the institution of slavery upon them, after all the experience we have had, after all the sacrifices we have made in men and treasure, is to receive into the Union the cause of all our woes. I do not desire to see the return of these States to the Union, unless they return with republican forms of government. I trust that the time will come when the highest tribunal of this country can be sufficiently bold to declare that where the institution of slavery exists, there a republican form of government cannot be. Such an opinion would be a glory to the age. It would be a triumph worthy of the sacrifices we have made, if these eleven States can return one by one into the Union as free and redeemed under the Constitution. That instrument was framed to secure freedom, justice, and equality among men. But what a calamity it would be to us, what a sin, if we were to receive these eleven States, with all their crimes upon them, to be again the source of innumerable woes to future generations! Consider, also, my friends, that after what you have done, if you in any way countenance the reconstruction of the Union with slavery existing in these States, you will become responsible, not only for the civil wars, but for the servile wars, which inevitably must follow. Do you think that when you have trained the colored men in the arts of war, and given them muskets, arrayed them against their masters, that they are to be bound in chains? No, no, no. If there be a man here, or in the North, who is ready to accept Virginia or South Carolina with the institution of slavery, then, here and now in advance of that crime, I charge that he, after the measure of his capacity and influence, is responsible for the civil and servile wars that shall follow.

I am for the restoration of the government as a government of peace, and as a government of equal and sovereign States, and as a government under which those rights that are named in the Declaration of Independence shall be secured to all the people. Until we have such a Union, there can be no peace. But I expect something, my friends, from those in the North who, even now, resist the policy of the administration, and denounce the conduct of the war. The test to which Northern men of the Democratic party are now put, in the fact that the capital of the great State of Pennsylvania is menaced, will bring forth their patriotism, possibly in some degree latent hitherto. The test will develop, I doubt not, the spirit of patriotism among those whom we have been led to regard as the friends and allies of the South. If there are men in the North who, under the banner of the so-called Democracy, have given their hands against the administration, there must be many who, in this exigency, will rally under the old banner of the country. To such we have a right to appeal, under all circumstances, to support the administration. In the prosecution of the war, let them say, to-day, whether they will sacrifice the Union that their party may have a party existence, or save the Union first, and then afterwards identify themselves with parties, according to opinions and principles?

Hence it becomes those men in the North who are for the Union to openly declare and maintain their opinions.

I, for one, was opposed to the election of Mr. Seymour, Governor of New York; but I hope and believe that he will not be found wanting in this hour, this emergency. I hope and believe that he will rally the immense powers of the Empire State to the support of the Union, without regard to the question whether the administration is or is not an administration of his choice.

In approaching the conclusion of my remarks, I invite you to consider the aspect of affairs, in their relation to the past, and with reference to the future.

And, first, is not the government, in its military power and in its finances, to be exhausted by the prosecution of the war? If a great rebellion like this shall be crushed in three or five or seven years, it will be the most marked event in military annals. Yet, with many reverses, such has been our success, upon the whole, that there are sufficient reasons for believing, that, in the first three years of this administration, the rebellion will have been effectually overthrown. But, it may be asked, can we endure such delays, and sacrifices of labor and life, and expenditures of money, as the next twelve months will require? Most assuredly we can, and years more of such sacrifices and expenditures, if the spirit of the people be not broken by maleadministration of civil or military affairs. With success, there will come the restoration of national credit at home; with success, there will be opportunity to negotiate loans abroad; with success, immigration will increase, so that our agriculture and manufactures will enjoy their accustomed prosperity; with success, if it be only by securing the navigation of the Mississippi River, there will follow a supply of one-half to one million bales of cotton; with success, there will be an opportunity to reduce the army in the field, or to recruit from a class whose services to the country are less valuable as producers than the services of the men now engaged in military life.

There should be no hesitation about employing colored men as soldiers; indeed, it is now certain, that, for a few months, the army will fall largely below its present force, if such persons are not received. The chief opposition to the policy of enrolling black men comes from those who sympathize with the rebels. Their opposition admits of a ready solution. As slavery was the cause which led the slaveholders to inaugurate the rebellion, so the unpaid labor of slaves is the chief support of the rebel armies in the field. Emancipation strikes at the overthrow of the rebellion by depriving the rebels of the benefits of slave labor. If the government goes onward one step, and enlists these emancipated men, the rebels are not only deprived of the support heretofore derived from slave labor, but they are destined to meet these very slaves in fair fight, where slave and master for once are on terms of equality. This war is to go on. The North cannot arrest it without yielding to the demands of the rebels; and mothers, fathers, wives, and sisters have only to say that they are willing that two hundred thousand colored men shall bare their bosoms to the deadly blast, or, on the other hand, that they prefer the unnecessary sacrifice of their own husbands, sons, and brothers. It is the demand of humanity and justice that the colored men should participate in this great struggle. They are four million. They are a race. They are Americans by birth. They have a future on this continent. They are men. It is at once a duty and a right that they participate in a struggle which promises so much of good or evil to them and their descendants. If the country is to be free, they share most largely in that freedom. If slavery ceases, the colored race advances to a new dignity among the peoples of the earth. If the slaveholder is to be exterminated, who more than the slave should share in the dispensation of a divine justice due to the master as the oppressor of the black man, and as the author of an attempt to overthrow a government which for nearly a century has vindicated its right to be classed among the best governments of any age or country?

If the colored men participate in the great struggle, and by their deeds establish their right to freedom, they bind the country to them with bands which cannot be severed. It does not follow that political rights are to be conceded to these people. The future will settle every question of that sort; but they should have the opportunity on the field to assert their manhood and their right to a place on this continent. The enemies of freedom in the North have zealously asserted that the free States would be cursed by the immigration of the colored people. The continuance of slavery is the only means by which this irrational prophecy can be fulfilled. Hence the desire of the enemies of freedom that slavery shall continue; hence their hostility to the President's emancipation policy; and hence their earnest purpose to prevent the enrolment of colored men in the armies of the republic. In justice to the colored race, the work of enrolment should go on; as a wise expediency on the part of the government, the work of enrolment should go on. The new enrolment of citizens will yield but few trained soldiers before August or September. During the summer and early autumn, it may be difficult to obtain a sufficient number of volunteers. After the returned soldiers shall have had an opportunity to rest and to visit their friends, and after the harvest of the summer is over, there will be no lack of men to meet the wants of the country, without estimating those who may be raised under the recent act of Congress.

But the chasm of three to six months must be bridged. The summer campaign upon the lower Mississippi and upon the Gulf coast should not be left for white soldiers exclusively, or even chiefly. The nation cannot afford in a life-contest to risk a campaign, or to sacrifice in pestilential regions thousands of valuable lives to the prejudices of fanatics and traitors, who seem to desire no success for the Union, unless it is equally advantageous to slavery.

As slavery is the enemy of the Union, and has ever been its enemy from the beginning, so now when it has attempted by war to effect its destruction, the supporters of slavery, whether they are of the North or of the South, are necessarily the enemies of the Union. Such prefer its sacrifice, if it can be saved only by the emancipation of the slave and by his services in the field.

The mode of raising and organizing colored troops is not unimportant. A certain number of thousands can be raised in the North; and the plan of their organization may be essential to the entire undertaking. As regiments, there can be no doubt of their value. They are, for the most part, men of intelligence and courage. Of those who were recently in slavery, this cannot with safety be assumed generally. It is practicable, and it may be wise, to organize skeleton regiments in the North, of one hundred or two hundred men each, including non-commissioned officers. Such regiments can be formed speedily, and subjected to drill and discipline. They may then be sent South to recruit from those of their brethren who have come, or who may hereafter come, within our lines.

If we organize a force of one hundred thousand from the colored race, will it not be wise to distribute among the whole mass those who may be enlisted in the North? Will it not happen that the men from the North will be able to inspire their colored brethren with confidence in the purposes of the government? Will not the slaves, fresh from the grasp of the slaveholders, be more rapidly educated to the performance of their duties as soldiers and men, when constantly in contact with those who have enjoyed the advantages which freedom in the North secures even to the negro race?

And will there not be security that the whole force will perform the service required in a more efficient manner?

There is no reason, in the nature of things, why the negro should not become a good soldier, and there is no reason why he should not be employed.

If there are men who expect to heal the division between the rebels and the old government, they are deluded; if they do not so believe, and yet represent that this may be done, then they are traitors and villains. The issue is a plain one. The rebels must be conquered, subjugated, destroyed, or driven out of the country, or they will subjugate the North to the purposes of the rebellion. There is no room for compromise, for arrangement. The question is one of power. When the rebellion is crushed, when the rebel leaders are exterminated or driven out of the country, there will be no reason why the States now controlled by traitors may not return to their places in the Union, with all the rights of sovereign States. Thus will the old Union be restored. If the phrase, "the restoration of the Union as it was," means the return of Mississippi under the lead of traitors who now represent her in the rebel government, then there neither can nor ought to be any restoration of the Union; but, when Mississippi is controlled by loyal men, there will remain no reason why she should not enjoy the rights and privileges of a sovereign State.

It is a singular coincidence, that the enemies of the Union in the North and the rebels in the South propose to construct a single government, with the exception of New England; or to construct a Southern confederacy and a Northern confederacy, in league with each other, — New England to be excluded. All these suggestions are the suggestions of traitors. The policy of these men is to change the government in its character through the agencies of separation, war, anarchy, and exhaustion, by which they may be prepared for a despotic system, under which the poorer white men and the negroes of the South and the laboring classes of the North can be subjected to the domination of tyrants. The security of the government, and of the free people of the North, is in the vigorous, determined, unyielding prosecution of the war. If we are prosperous, let there be no disposition to make terms, except such as have been made with the States of Maryland and Missouri.

If we are unsuccessful, then apply new energy, raise more men, and by our persistency demonstrate the possibility of accomplishing what we have undertaken. In the line of this policy there can be no failure.

Next to the military operations, the condition and management of the finances deserve the most anxious consideration. The ways and means of raising money upon public credit belong to the head of the Treasury and to Congress; but it may not be amiss to suggest the sources of payment which the country can command. Whatever may be said to the contrary, there is not the least reason for believing that the continuance of the war upon the present gigantic scale will swell the public debt to two thousand million of dollars until we are far advanced into the last half of the year 1864.

If we estimate the sum relatively, and consider the increased numbers, wealth, and productive power of the people, our indebtedness will be less in 1864 or 1865 than it was at the close of the Revolution or at the close of the war of 1812. Measured by numbers, it is only equal to a debt of two hundred million in 1783, and to a debt of four or five hundred million in 1815. It is also true that the capacity of the same population to produce real wealth, not money in dollars, whether gold or paper, but articles of subsistence and common utility, is twice as great in 1863 as it was in 1815. Upon the restoration of the Union and the return of peace, our annual revenues from present sources alone will rise to three hundred million dollars. If we allow one hundred million for current expenses, and one hundred and twenty million for interest, there will remain eighty million for the payment of the principal, which will insure the liquidation of the public debt in less than twenty years.

If, as the result of the war, cotton shall be produced hereafter by free labor, we can monopolize the markets of the world, increase our product in twenty years to ten million bales per annum, subject the crop, whether for domestic or foreign use, to a tax of from two to four cents per pound, and defy competition. Here is a source of revenue as yet untouched, which will yield, in the first year of peaceful labor, from thirty to fifty million of dollars, to be augmented in less than twenty years at least one hundred per cent.

No human power can anticipate the productive

wealth of the mines of gold and silver; but it is not unreasonable to predict that the annual returns will reach four hundred million by the year 1875. This wealth may not in any considerable degree inure directly to the advantage of the treasury; but so vast an increase of the precious metals will at once depreciate the currency of the country and the world, and diminish public and private indebtedness, by allowing the debtor to meet a given liability with a less outlay of labor. This increase and depreciation enables the laborers and capitalists to meet their taxes with less inconvenience. It only remains, then, for those charged with the financial affairs of the government to provide means of raising money upon the public credit. We offer better security for our indebtedness than was ever before offered by this or any other nation. We have a large industrious population; we have vast resources in nature in the old States; we have millions of acres of fertile land; we have mines of gold and silver which will verify the traditions of the ages of fable, and make real the visions of romance; we have a monopoly of the best cotton-growing lands of the world. A debt of two thousand million of dollars is less for the United States than is a debt of one thousand million of dollars for Great Britain. This would be true in an almost equal degree if the effort to re-establish the Union were to prove a failure. There is, therefore, no real ground for discouragement in our military or financial affairs. We must, however, be firm, persistent, unyielding in our efforts. We are stronger than ever before: the South is weaker than ever before. It only remains for us to do those things which a wise forecast dictates.

We must not think of a peace as the price of separation or as the result of a treaty. Let the war be prosecuted with all the power which the people can command, until the right of this nation to exist is fully vindicated. Let the war be prosecuted until the rebellion is overthrown. Let the war be prosecuted until the Constitution is recognized in the rebel States as the supreme law of the land. The object of the war has not been changed, nor can it be changed. That object must ever be the restoration of the Union; for when the rebellion is overthrown, when the rebel States are controlled by loyal people, and the administration of public affairs is intrusted to loyal-minded men, they will return to the Union upon those conditions, and those only, which are imposed by the existing Constitution.

The government must employ all the means at its command for the suppression of the rebellion. It is, therefore, a duty to augment our own power to the largest possible degree, and to do all that civilization justifies to weaken the resources and diminish the capacity of the public enemy.

Hence come the right and the duty to declare, that, in the eye of the nation, slavery no longer exists; hence emancipation is not pronounced as the end or the object of the war, but as the means by which it is to be brought to a speedy termination. Hence emancipation is a military necessity, and not a mere public policy.

If slavery were profitable or advantageous in any

way to slave-masters in time of peace, slavery is profitable or advantageous to the slave-masters in time of war. By emancipation, the war power of the South loses that profit or advantage, whatever it may have been, and the capacities of the rebellion are to the same extent diminished.

The emancipation of the colored race and the enlistment of the colored men are measures already justified by the necessary and universal rule of war. By emancipation, we diminish the resources of the public enemy; by the enlistment and service of loyal men, whether black or white, we augment our own.

The friends of the country must support the government, — not without criticism, where criticism is believed to be demanded; nor even without condemnation, where condemnation is deserved. But whoever counsels resistance to the measures of the government, or foments public distrust, is an ally of the rebels, and the enemy of the Union. The President is not above law nor beyond the sphere of accountability. In all that he does, he takes the responsibility at his peril; but, as President, he must be obeyed. He acts constantly in the presence of the great power of impeachment. In what he does and in what he neglects to do, he is responsible, in the most solemn forms, to the representatives of the people and the States; but until impeached, and removed from office, he is still President and must be obeyed, as well in reference to those acts about which men differ as in regard to those concerning which there is a substantial agreement. As the President is the head of the government, and the first officer of the nation; as it is his duty to see that the laws are executed; as he is, or should be, consequently and necessarily in possession of all information concerning the domestic and foreign affairs and relations of the country; as his power to act constantly and immediately never ceases; as his capacity to act is not dependent upon terms or sessions of tribunals or bodies; and as there is, except the President, no assembly, tribunal, judge, or magistrate in the land, that has at all times the necessary information under the Constitution concerning the public welfare, and the necessary continuing constitutional capacity to do what the public safety may demand, — so in the President alone is vested the great authority, in the name and for the protection of the people, to suspend the writ of *habeas corpus* whenever the "public safety may require it." The President takes this responsibility at his peril. If he acts for the people, and in defence of their rights and institutions, then is he honored and vindicated; if for party or personal purposes, then will he be condemned and disgraced. For the security of the people against treason, against rebellion, against invasion, vast powers have been confided to the President: for the security of the people against the improper and tyrannical use of these powers, their representatives are clothed with authority to arraign and try the President, and condemn and sentence him if he be found guilty.

But the act by which the writ of *habeas corpus* is suspended is necessarily binding for the time being, and in the nature of the case it cannot be revised or annulled by any tribunal or magistrate. If it can be so revised, then a judge having no official knowledge of the foreign or domestic political affairs of the nation is competent to annul the act of the President in a matter relating to the public safety. This claim is too absurd to be refuted, and too monstrous to be defended. The President is the commander-in-chief of the army and the navy. In the hands of an unscrupulous man, this power could be made to include the power to annul rather than to suspend the writ of *habeas corpus;* and hence the denial of the right in the President to suspend the writ, is only calculated to diminish the power of a conscientious and capable magistrate to protect the rights of the people, while the power of a bad President to oppress the country remains undiminished in his authority as the commander-in-chief of the army and the navy.

The right to suspend the writ of *habeas corpus*, as a constitutional right vested in the President, gives to a bad man no power to harass the people, which, as commander-in-chief of the army and navy, he could not at any moment assume; while the denial of the right deprives a patriotic and trustworthy magistrate of a chief means of preserving the public liberties in time of public peril.

A reasonable apprehension of tyranny is no doubt wise; but there is no wisdom in the denial by a free people of those powers which are essential to the public welfare.

There should be faith in rulers and faith in the people. The nation has all the capacities which come from six centuries of progress in England and

America. If any thing good shall be overthrown in the present convulsions, it will re-appear when peace returns. The evil that is crushed, the tyranny that is removed, will never again disturb the peace or retard the progress of the land. The people will hate tyranny more than ever before: their love of liberty will be purer and holier.

Libertas a Deo est et perire non potest.

CONFISCATION OF REBEL PROPERTY.

SPEECH DELIVERED IN THE HOUSE OF REPRESENTATIVES, JAN. 19, 1864, UPON THE JOINT RESOLUTION TO AMEND A JOINT RESOLUTION, EXPLANATORY OF "AN ACT TO SUPPRESS INSURRECTION, TO PUNISH TREASON AND REBELLION, TO SEIZE AND CONFISCATE THE PROPERTY OF REBELS, AND FOR OTHER PURPOSES," APPROVED JULY 17, 1862.

THE subject before the House, uninteresting as a matter of debate, is already a good deal hackneyed. Having assented in the committee to this report, it may not be amiss for me to state, with such clearness and brevity as I can command, the grounds on which my assent was given.

It was suggested by the gentleman from New York [Mr. Kernan], who spoke early in this debate, that, while he doubted the constitutional authority of Congress to confiscate the real estate of traitors absolutely, even if he were convinced of that authority, he should doubt the wisdom of such a public policy. I submit to that gentleman, and to those who sympathize with him upon this point, that, if it be clearly shown that such a power exists, then it was granted by the framers of the Constitution for some purpose, anticipating or apprehending an exigency in the fortunes of the country when it might be expedient and proper to put that power in full force.

If the power is found in the Constitution, I ask the gentleman from New York whether he is of opinion that the men who framed the Constitution could have anticipated any condition of public affairs in which the exigency would be more urgent than that which exists at the present time? It is well enough for nations to be merciful, but justice is a higher attribute than mercy. If the power exists, I submit that the exigency for its extreme exercise exists also. It is a very different thing to men engaged in this treason, whether they hold their lands by authority of law, or whether they hold them at the pleasure and by the favor of the government against which they have rebelled. In this condition of things, I maintain that it is the duty of the country and government to seek for a true interpretation of the Constitution, to ascertain as exactly as possible the limits of Congressional authority, and march boldly in the organization of a system of justice and penalties to the very limits of that authority, wherever they may be found; and, then, let the amnesty come, so that we can distinguish between great offenders, who, of their own motion in violation of the Constitution,—in violation of the rights, not only of their country, but of all mankind, not only of this age, but of all coming ages,—rebelled against the government, and those who have been duped, misled, seduced from their public duty. On these we will have compassion; and gentlemen on the other side will come to understand, that the majority here and in the country will execute justice, and remember mercy also.

I am not sure, sir, that there is any material difference between the report of the committee, and the amendment proposed by the chairman of the Committee of Ways and Means, in the effect to be produced on such rebels as may be made amenable to the statute of July 17, 1862. I understand the joint resolution now before the House to be of such a character, that, if adopted, it will be the duty of the courts of the country to administer the penalties prescribed in the law, to the full limits of constitutional authority. If by repealing the joint resolution of July 17, 1862, and putting into operation the law unrestricted, or if by enacting another and more stringent statute, we transcend the Constitution, it will be the duty of the courts to limit the statute within constitutional authority. Therefore, practically, I do not see that there is a difference between the joint resolution, and the amendment proposed by the gentleman from Pennsylvania [Mr. Stevens].

Mr. Stevens. — The resolution of the committee restricts all the forfeitures under the Confiscation Act to what they are already in the case of attainder for treason in the Constitution. Now, the act itself has no reference to the section of the Constitution referred to; but there are confiscations outside of that entirely, not for treason, but as the property of alien enemies. Therefore the resolution of the committee confines the operation of the act of 1862 much more than the original resolution did. If the gentleman will modify the resolution so as to make it read that the act of 1862 shall produce no forfeiture beyond the limits of the Constitution, I am content.

Mr. Boutwell. — I understand that to be the object of the joint resolution. But I will say, by way of answer to the first suggestion of the gentleman from Pennsylvania, that when we find in the Constitution, as in that part relating to treason, distinct and definite authority given to the government in the way of punishment, we cannot look to any other provision of the Constitution, or to any general principle, for the purpose of getting authority to inflict other and different penalties. The authority is to be found in that provision of the Constitution, or it is not to be found anywhere.

Something has been said in the course of this debate in regard to the act of July, 1862, and something is found in the President's message touching the authority of the government to proceed *in rem*, as it is called, under the fifth section of this act, — the allegation being that such proceedings are not by due process of law, as required by the Constitution. An analogy has been drawn in some quarters from the authority of the Government in prize courts. It does not follow, necessarily, that, because the Government may proceed *in rem* against enemies' property found on the ocean, it may therefore proceed against other property found in other and different positions. The principle, as I understand, of the law on which proceedings *in rem* are justified in prize cases is this: enemies' property being found *in transitu* on the ocean, a presumption at once arises, that either that property or the proceeds of it, in one way or another, are to inure to the benefit of the public enemy, and no inquiry can be instituted in court as to whether the individual owner is an enemy or a friend. It is sufficient that he is *de facto* under the jurisdiction of the belligerent,—that he is an inhabitant of the territory against the people of which we are waging war.

Property on land is not subject to seizure or confiscation, because there is no presumption existing generally that it is to be used for the benefit of the enemy. It may be taken for the necessities of the army; but it cannot be proceeded against *in rem*, as property taken upon the sea may be.

It is necessary, when we propose a new measure, to find authority in one of two conditions of things,—either in a principle not heretofore established, or else in a principle heretofore recognized, but not extended in its application so as to sustain the proposed measure.

I submit to the House, as justifying the seizures provided for in the fifth section of the act of July 17, 1862, that while the condition of property belonging to rebels does not create the presumption, in and of itself, that it is to be used in support of the rebellion, still the law itself requires proof, equivalent to the evidence on which presumption is to be based in the case of enemies' property taken on the ocean. By the fifth and sixth sections of the act, the government is to show that the owner of this rebel property is an officer of the army or navy, or in the civil service of rebels in arms against the Government of the United States.

And, when we have established that fact, is it not equal to the presumption that arises when enemies' property is taken *in transitu* on the water? Upon such proof, it is a fair presumption that the property belonging to a rebel officer, in arms against the United States, is either designed of itself to be for the benefit of the rebels, or else that it is to be converted into other property which is to inure to the benefit of the rebellion. Therefore it follows, that the same principles which justify proceedings *in rem* in prize cases justify similar proceedings against the property of the various persons specified in the fifth section of the act of July 17, 1862. And therefore I feel satisfied, for one, that upon this view of the subject the difficulty is substantially removed.

I come next — for I do not mean to occupy the attention of the House a great while — to the particular authority granted by the Constitution for doing what we propose shall be done; and I commend to the gentlemen on the other side of the House a reflection which must be common to us all who have had some experience in public or in professional life. The authority of a statute, or the scope of a constitutional provision, can never be fairly considered or discussed as a measure, until there is an actual case arising; and nothing is more common than for the courts of the various States, whenever a call is made on them for an opinion on a matter in reference to which no case has actually arisen, — and such calls are occasionally made by the executive or legislative branches of State governments, — either to decline to give an opinion, or, if an opinion is given, to submit it with the distinct understanding that the court is not bound by it. It is only when a case is before a court, and arguments are submitted, that a true construction can be attained.

I do not agree at all with the gentleman who last addressed the House [Mr. Bliss], as to the effect of Mr. Madison's commentary upon this provision of the Constitution. That, however, I shall have occasion to consider hereafter.

A word in passing in regard to Judge Story's authority. I dare say, from the nature of the language used by him in his Commentaries, that he understood this provision of the Constitution as it is interpreted by gentlemen on the other side of the House.

I would not disparage Judge Story as a lawyer; but as a great man, as a man of capacious and grasping intellect, he must be placed in the second class of the great men which this country has produced. When he wrote he had no case before him. He has merely followed English law. What he has written in his Commentaries is a reproduction of what he had read in the English books.

I will refer also to the language of Mr. Madison. Our fathers, when they framed the Constitution, intended manifestly to guard against two things: first, the forfeiture of estates by proceedings instituted subsequently to the death of the offender; and, secondly, the attainting or corruption of blood by which the heirs of the offender should become incapable, either to enjoy the estates which had not been forfeited, or which might descend to them from the progenitors of the offender, and subsequently to his death. The Constitution has sufficiently guarded Congress upon these points, and the language of Mr. Madison relates to the limitations upon the powers of Congress.

I call attention to a very singular circumstance,

in connection with this provision of the Constitution. I find, in examining it as printed in the Manual, that it is without punctuation after "blood" and after "forfeiture." In the copy of the Constitution prefixed to the statutes, as printed by Little & Brown, there is a comma after "blood" and another after "forfeiture." These circumstances led me to look at the original instrument in the office of the Secretary of State; and I find that there is a comma after "blood," but none after "forfeiture." The Secretary of State was so thoroughly convinced that such was the reading of the Constitution, that I have an official certificate from him to that effect. It will be said very likely, that punctuation is never regarded in the construction of statutes. That is the legal declaration; but I never knew a person so entirely insensible to the influence of facts, that he could discuss and consider and decide upon a statute regardless of punctuation. In such an instrument as the Constitution, framed with care, and signed by men who were responsible for it to the country and to future ages, it is to be presumed that every thing, even to the punctuation, was deemed a matter of importance. Punctuation, even in a statute hastily and loosely drawn, decides its interpretation whenever the language is equivocal or ambiguous.[1]

[1] In the original report of the Constitution by the Committee of Detail, the clause reads thus: "No attainder of treason shall work corruption of blood, *nor* forfeiture, except during the life of the person attainted." (Elliot's Debates, vol. 5, p. 379.) The change of *nor* to *or*, and the omission of the comma after forfeiture, seem to conclude the question as to the intention of the framers of the Constitution.

It is worthy of observation, that that portion of the Constitution which sets forth the evidence necessary to a conviction for the crime of treason is drawn substantially from an English statute passed in the 7th and 8th of William III., showing that our ancestors were familiar with the English law bearing upon the subject.[1] But we need not even a single piece of testimony on this point; for we know very well, that they were versed in the English law, and in every thing relating to the feudal system, as no other body of men ever were in Great Britain or in this country.

I think it not out of place to refer to a work not much known, and hardly ever read. I speak of the correspondence between the provincial House of Representatives of Massachusetts and the provincial Governors of Massachusetts from 1765 to 1774; and in which the whole feudal system is discussed with clearness, power, and precision, such as are exhibited in no other work I have ever seen. It relieves our revolutionary contest from that historic fable, that we instituted a war for independence upon the subordinate issue of a tax of threepence a pound upon tea. Our ancestors, in their legal

[1] By the statute of 7th and 8th William III., it was provided as follows: "And be it further enacted, that from and after the said five and twentieth day of March, in the year of our Lord 1696, no person or persons whatsoever shall be indicted, tried, or attainted of high treason, whereby any corruption of blood may or shall be made to any such offender or offenders, or to any heir or heirs of any such offender or offenders, or of misprision of such treason, *but by and upon the oaths and testimony of two lawful witnesses, either both of them to the same overt act*, or one of them to one, and the other of them to another overt act of the same treason; unless the party indicted, and arraigned, or tried, shall willingly, without violence, *in open court confess the same*," &c.

and solid and responsible arguments, never put the contest upon that basis. It might have been a ground of appeal to the people: but, through the feudal system, they traced our rights to the king; and maintained with great clearness, that they were no more amenable to the Parliament of Great Britain than the Parliament of Great Britain was to the legislatures of the several colonies in this country. They maintained that the people of the colonies and the people of Great Britain were independent of each other. The argument of this correspondence throws light upon one of the allegations in the Declaration of Independence.

The colonists rebelled against George III., not because he was not the legitimate king, but because he combined with the Parliament to deprive the people of this country of their liberties. Our ancestors well knew the legal history of Great Britain in reference to treason and forfeiture. Blackstone refers us to a provision of the statutes against treason, passed in the reign of Elizabeth; and he uses this phrase in regard to the forfeiture as limiting the power of the courts, "save only for the life of the offender." If our ancestors intended that forfeiture should be only for the life of the offender in all cases, how has it happened, that, when they went to the statute of William III. for the language used in stating the evidence necessary to a conviction for treason, they should have used language in reference to the penalty which rendered their meaning uncertain? During the reign of Elizabeth, it was provided by statute, that persons convicted of treason should forfeit all their goods and chattels, and the use of their lands, tenements, and hereditaments, during their natural lives only. This statute remained in force until about the time of the union of Scotland and England.[1]

When we consider that the men who framed the Constitution had this language before them, that they extracted a certain portion of the Constitution from the statute of William III., is it to be presumed that they should have neglected to make this point clear by using the words of the statute of William, if they had such a purpose as is contended for by the gentlemen on the other side of the House? So far from their having had any such purpose, I think it the plainer, more natural, as well as necessary construction of the Constitution, that the contrary is the case. I believe that gentlemen will see as they go on in this debate, or in their practical experience of the operation of the law, that it is a reflection upon the judgment of our ancestors to maintain that they intended to do that which gentlemen on the other side of the House say they have done.

We are to look upon this question as a question of public policy also, to a certain extent. Suppose a man is convicted of treason, and is proceeded

[1] By the statute of 5th Elizabeth, c. 11, the crime of clipping and washing coins was declared treason; and it was provided that the offender should suffer the pains of death, and lose and forfeit all his goods and chattels, and also lose and forfeit all his lands, tenements, and hereditaments, during his natural life only. By the statute 1st Elizabeth, c. 5, certain offences were made high treason, being, as enumerated, the highest crimes known to the law; and it was provided that the offender should forfeit to the Queen all his goods and chattels and the profits of his lands, during his life.

against, and the law is held as gentlemen on the other side of the House allege that it should be held. The offender is to be executed in forty days. You forfeit his life-estate in his land. He has a remainder, which he can sell to a brother traitor not yet convicted, and perhaps not yet suspected; and his property, thus converted into money, is made serviceable to the rebellion. Was it not the intention of the framers of the Constitution, that forfeiture of estate should not only deprive the offender of its use, and thereby be a penalty upon him; but that the cause with which he was identified should be deprived to that extent of the means of support? Gentlemen construe the Constitution in such a manner, that, when we have forfeited the estate during life, the offender may then put the remainder into money, — which, in such a case, would be the chief value of the estate, — and turn it into the treasury of the rebels.

I have said, that by the Constitution our fathers intended to do two things; and a true interpretation of this clause, according to the punctuation, shows that their ends were accomplished. Congress has power to declare the punishment of treason, — but no attainder of treason can work corruption of blood. Here are two propositions. Congress has power to declare the punishment of treason; that is, the full, supreme, unlimited power, except as it may be controlled by the two clauses following: "But no attainder of treason shall work corruption of blood." That is an absolute prohibition upon the power exercised by the British Parliament to work corruption of blood through attainder of treason. If the construction contended for by the gentlemen upon the other side of the House prevails, I do not see why the Constitution must not be read to this effect: "that no attainder of treason shall work corruption of blood, except during the life of the person attainted."

But who does not see the absurdity of thus working corruption of blood during the life of the person attainted? Under the Constitution, we can do to the person convicted all those things, which by the corruption of blood could have been worked by the common law of England upon him. We can make him an outlaw; and, therefore, to say that we have authority, under the Constitution, to work corruption of blood during the lifetime of the offender is simply an absurdity. It does not give us any power which we could not exercise without that provision. "But no attainder of treason shall work corruption of blood," — thus securing one object they had in view, — "or forfeiture except during the life of the person attainted."

I do not feel any apprehension as to what the judgment of the House may be upon the meaning of the word "except," whether it is regarded as the equivalent of "unless" or not. But I think it clear, from a reference already made, that two centuries ago "except" had for a synonyme "unless." The gentleman from Ohio [Mr. Cox] remarked, that the judge of the Eastern District of Virginia had said that "except" did not mean "except," but meant something else. The judge, I apprehend, said no such thing. He said that "unless" was the synonyme of "except;" and that our fathers often used the word "except," where "unless" might be used by us. One quotation has been made which I commend to gentlemen on the other side, in connection with this bill, and also with the peculiar sympathy which they seem to show to their deluded brethren of the South, — I do not know as they regard it as authority, — "Except *ye* repent, *ye* shall all likewise perish." But I accept "except," exactly as they desire to have it understood in the Constitution. Gentlemen in this House and elsewhere have made a distinction which nowhere exists in the Constitution.

The word "forfeiture" has not a particular reference to real estate more than to goods and chattels. "Forfeiture!" Forfeiture of what? Of that which the offender possesses. Gentlemen say, "Life estate is the estate intended." And here again we see how we have been misled by British institutions. Before the Constitution was framed, entail and primogeniture were comparatively unknown in this country. It is possible there were a few entailed estates in some of the States of the Union, or estates entailed for a limited period of time. Now, knowing as we do that our fathers were opposed to the whole system of entail and primogeniture, is it to be supposed they intended, when they were decreeing pains and penalties for the crime of treason, to introduce the doctrine of entail, and separate estates of fee-tail and remainder?

They intended, when they used the word "forfeiture," that the party convicted should be deprived of that which he possessed, neither more nor less. Where the estate is a life-estate, the Constitution forfeits the life-estate; and where the estate is in fee, the forfeiture must apply to the whole estate.

The laws of the States generally do not recognize any such estate as a life-estate, except in particular cases.

Here is a grave question, — one which possibly may be satisfactorily answered, but how I do not see. All the laws relating to the tenure of estates are framed by the several States, and in most of them there is no separate estate known as a life-estate. Whoever owns the fee has the whole estate. What, I ask, upon the construction claimed by gentlemen upon the other side, is to be the effect of the interpretation of the constitution for which they contend?

I hold, as a matter of constitutional law, that Congress has no power to create a life-estate in Massachusetts, even for the purpose of wresting it from a traitor, if there be one there. The Congress of the United States, and the laws of the United States, in reference to the forfeiture of the property of traitors, must take that property exactly as it is declared and defined by the law of the State in which the property of the criminal is found. Mr. Clay said in 1839, upon another and a very different subject, that "that is property which the law recognizes as property." We have no such division of property recognized by the laws of the States, except in particular cases, as a life-estate. If, then, you find a traitor in Massachusetts, if you arraign and convict him, and inflict a penalty upon him, you must forfeit his property, whether lands or chattels, exactly as it exists under the laws of the State. You cannot create a life-estate, and forfeit it, and give the remainder to somebody else.

Upon all these facts, Mr. Speaker, I can come but to the conclusion, that the framers of the Constitution intended to guard against two evils in the British system: first, the forfeiture of the estate by proceedings instituted after the death of the offender; and, secondly, the corruption of blood so as to disable the heirs of an offender from inheriting through him. The construction I have given to the Constitution secures these two objects, and it must be observed that it gives full force and effect to every word in the instrument relating to treason; and, when we have found a satisfactory use for every word, it is unnecessary to look further, and especially when the interpretation given is consistent with the general policy and ideas of the country. I have, then, no hesitation, for one, in sustaining a measure, be it this joint resolution or any other, which shall provide for the forfeiture of the estates of persons convicted of treason, whether those estates be in goods and chattels, or lands held by fee-simple titles, or in land in which the offender has a life-estate. If he has a life-estate merely, he forfeits that; if he owns the fee, he forfeits the fee; if he owns goods and chattels, he forfeits his goods and chattels. We thus inflict a necessary and just punishment upon the offender, and take security that his property will not by some indirection be used in behalf of the rebellion.

THE CONDUCT OF THE WAR.

[FROM THE "NATIONAL REPUBLICAN," FEB. 5, 1864.]

WE have heretofore expressed the opinion, that the energies of the government should be directed to the work of strengthening ourselves on the Mississippi, and crippling the rebellion at its extremities in Tennessee and Louisiana; and that, in the mean while, no serious effort should be made against Richmond. Our south-western lines may now be considered secure, although it is in the highest degree probable that a vigorous effort will be made to drive our forces from Knoxville and Chattanooga, by a formidable movement across the Tennessee River between those points, or at a point west of the latter town.

The attempt will be a desperate one; and the preparation on our part should correspond to the exigency in which the rebel leaders are placed. While a success by the rebels would be temporary in its results, it cannot be denied that any thing less than the complete overthrow of the plan would be a disgrace to our arms. We are greatly superior in numbers; our soldiers are animated by the recollection of recent victories, and inspired with confidence in the speedy and successful termination of the war. The veterans have re-enlisted generally;

and the numbers of the army are augmented weekly by the addition of several thousand recruits, many of whom have seen service heretofore.

There ought to be no cause for apprehension, although we cannot overlook the fact that it is possible for the rebels to combine the greater part of their available force upon a single position. As the rebel lines are contracted by our successes, their ability to concentrate their army at a given point is increased. Hence our necessity for large armies was never greater than at the present time; and there is no doubt that our available force on the first of March next will equal, if it do not exceed, that of any previous period of the war.

Richmond is again the point of chief interest. It is the only base for rebel movements upon Maryland, Pennsylvania, and West Virginia. Once in our possession, and these States are secure, while the rebel forces would soon be compelled to abandon North Carolina. Following this, and without delay, they would retire from East Tennessee, and concentrate their forces in South Carolina, Georgia, and Alabama. These States are quite unable to sustain an army of one hundred thousand to two hundred thousand men, for even sixty days, in addition to the present population, swollen beyond that of any former time by the influx of whites and blacks from the northern rebel States. Hence, if we can maintain our positions at Knoxville and Chattanooga, the capture of Richmond is, in effect and in fact, the end of the war.

It is therefore quite unnecessary, if not gravely impolitic, for us to assume the offensive in the

West. The army in that quarter should be treated as an army of observation, occupying such positions as will best guard the approaches to Tennessee and Kentucky, while it is prepared to take advantage of any weakness of position or force on the part of our opponents. We ought, then, to struggle for the overthrow of the rebel army in Virginia.

How is this to be done? or, rather, how is it to be attempted with a reasonable hope of success? The campaigns of 1861 and 1862 were failures. Yet the Army of the Potomac is composed of good materials, — not inferior to any other army of the republic. The Eleventh Army Corps, when transferred to the West, at once achieved a position not less honorable than that accorded to the veteran heroes of Shiloh and Vicksburg. There is no reason to suppose that the other corps of the Potomac Army are in any degree inferior.

It has been led by able and brave men. Of the six Generals who have successively had command, one or more at least would be approved as a good officer by every citizen and military critic in the country. Why, then, have we failed to capture Richmond? Some may say that our misfortunes are due to the interference of the government at Washington; but there are those who know that this suggestion has no foundation in fact. In the nature of things, the government must be responsible for the general plan of a campaign; but the details of its execution are necessarily left to the judgment of the commander in the field.

It is probably true, that neither suggestions, nor the absence of suggestions, on the part of officials in Washington, could have changed materially the result of the several campaigns in Northern and Eastern Virginia. We have there encountered the best army of the rebels, led by their ablest officers, while acting under the advice of Davis and others at Richmond, and inspired by the belief that the existence of the Confederacy was indissolubly connected with the fate of that city. These were facts amounting to serious difficulties, if not obstacles in our way; to which were superadded the physical features of the country in which military operations have been conducted.

The region between the Potomac and the James Rivers is traversed by numerous and nearly parallel streams and rivers, and ranges of hills and highlands. These, considered singly, are barriers to the movements of an army; and, collectively, they become an insuperable obstacle when viewed in connection with the fact, that an advance to Richmond does not relieve us from our dependence upon the Potomac as a base of supplies, unless we seek our way through the swamps of the Chickahominy. These are the natural and unavoidable obstacles which have impeded our progress. It may be true that it was well during these three years to contest for supremacy with the rebels between the Potomac and the Rappahannock. The rebellion could not have been overthrown by strategy, by bloodless victories, by advantages of position merely.

It was necessary that battles should be fought, that sacrifices should be made, that thousands should be slain, that the capacity of each side should be fully tested. This has been done; and no one can say that it was not as well for the cause of the republic that these sacrifices should have been made within sight of the capital as elsewhere. However this may be, there was always a controlling consideration which does, and will, fully justify the administration in the policy it has pursued, since the memorable disaster of the Peninsular campaign of 1862, under the lead of McClellan, and in deference to his views. We have combated the enemy in front of Washington, where he has been crippled and the capital of the country at the same time defended.

There has never been a moment until the present when it was safe to trust Washington to its fortifications and the men within them; but we believe that our strength is so great, and the capacity of the enemy for offensive movements so much weakened, that the safety of the capital should not be the occasion of distrust with reference to future operations. Moreover, the plan we suggest does not so remove the Army of the Potomac as to deprive the city of succor in case of danger.

Our successes in the West are due, in a good degree, to the existence of navigable rivers, and the use we have made of them. The ascent of the Cumberland and Tennessee Rivers was followed by the victories of Fort Henry and Fort Donelson. Columbus, Ky., being thus flanked, and assailable from the land side, was abandoned. Memphis followed. Nashville fell into our hands. The possession of the river, and the presence of a small naval force, saved the honor of our arms at Shiloh.

Our operations on the Mississippi are well known.

The navigation of the Tennessee is the security for Chattanooga, as it was the means of our success in its capture.

The rebels are without a navy and without capacity to man and use ships if they possessed them. Our advantage on the rivers is undisputed. Communication upon water is safer than upon railways even, always more economical, and for transporting sustenance for a large army it is more effective. Hence a river is the most advantageous base of supplies; and our experience proves that an army, protected by gunboats, even though beaten in the field, is safe from serious disaster.

With this experience and these views, considered in connection with the changed relative condition of the combatants, we do not hesitate to advise the use of the James River as the route to Richmond. It is at once safe, certain, and economical. It is navigable to the city; and there are, as far as is known, no fortifications of a formidable character below Fort Darling. If our forces ascend the river to a point above the mouth of the Appomattox, and effect a landing there, it is impossible that they should fail to maintain themselves, if supported, as they would be supported, by gunboats in the river. This being accomplished, the railway from Petersburg to Richmond is at our mercy.

Next, there would be no serious difficulty in cutting the railway beyond, which leads from Richmond to Danville; and thus would the Confederate capital be separated from the South, except by the route through Gordonsville and the mountains at Lynchburg, and through East Tennessee. This circuitous and exposed line would soon be broken. Indeed, so desperate are the fortunes of the rebels, and so inexorable are their necessities, that the occupation of the south bank of the James River in force will be followed by the evacuation of Richmond without delay.

In any event nothing worse could happen than an effort on the part of the enemy to dislodge us. This, as we have demonstrated, would be impossible; and, if we chose to trust to the arbitrament of arms in the open field, we could select our own positions with more certainty than in the country between the Potomac and the Rapidan.

The army can be supplied and reinforced as easily upon the James as upon the Potomac; while the withdrawal of the rebels for the purpose of strengthening Johnston or Longstreet would enable us to take possession of the city, relieve the Army of the Potomac, and place it in hand for service elsewhere.

The spring campaign should be commenced early; and it should be prosecuted with the purpose, and in the expectation, of overthrowing the rebellion before midsummer. This is the reasonable demand of the country, and, without exaggeration, we may say that it is the necessity of the country. There can be no doubt that the rebellion is in its final struggle. Its friends do not expect it to survive the frosts of the next autumn.

It will die with the annual death of its long-adored, greatly magnified, but now powerless King Cotton. This will happen by the force of compression and the influence of time, without further active effort on our part. This course is to be shunned, however; for it gives the enemies of the republic, North and South, an opportunity to embarrass the country politically, and to jeopard the election of a Union man to the Presidency.

If the rebellion be not suppressed by August or September, it is not improbable that Davis will abdicate; that the rebel Congress will place supreme power in the hands of Lee, who is not embarrassed, as are the politicians of the South, by pledges or declarations upon political subjects; and that he will issue a proclamation offering to lay down his arms, to surrender all public property, transfer the guns and munitions of war in the hands of the rebels to the United States, upon condition, that the leaders, as well as the masses, are pardoned, and that the States resume their places in the Union without terms as to their domestic institutions. In extremity, they will not hesitate to adopt this or a corresponding policy.

While the friends of the Union could not accept these or any similar terms, it is foreseen that the opposition would rally with hope and with increased confidence of success. The safety of the country requires a policy which shall secure peace without terms. There must be no negotiation; there must be no treaty; there must be no haggling about conditions. Hence there is an overpowering necessity for a wise and vigorous policy in the conduct of the war.

If the rebellion be not crushed, substantially, by the first of August next, the nation will be involved in new difficulties.

The country has furnished men, it has furnished money; and the most convincing reasons exist for the belief that the staggering rebellion will soon be destroyed.

SALE OF GOLD.

DEBATE ON THE BILL AUTHORIZING THE SECRETARY OF THE TREASURY TO SELL GOLD, MARCH 14, 1864.

MR. BOUTWELL. — I agree with my colleague who addressed the House this morning [Mr. Alley], that the passage of the joint resolution, as it comes from the Senate, will have some effect upon the price of gold; but I believe that the effect will be temporary only. The condition of this country, its necessities, and its fortunes, justify an attempt, at least, to put its financial affairs upon a broader basis than is contemplated by this resolution, either as it went from the House or with the amendment introduced by the Senate.

It is a peculiar circumstance, that, thus far, the Secretary of the Treasury is not publicly committed in favor of the passage of this measure. My opposition to granting authority to the Secretary to sell gold does not proceed from the apprehension that he will exercise the authority unfaithfully, or intentionally to the prejudice of the public interest; but I am opposed to granting this power, because, in the first place, I think we have no right to grant it. I do not speak of *right* in the sense of power, but I mean to say that we have no moral right to grant the authority. In the next place, if I were satisfied that we had the right, I should still think it unwise, in the highest degree, to exercise it.

It has been observed, that, when this resolution passed the House and went to the Senate, gold advanced from three to five per cent in the markets of New York. On Saturday, it declined six or seven per cent below the highest rate previously attained. I trust that no man will be influenced in his vote by a fact of this character; for it can be explained in several ways. It may be explained by supposing that the men who deal in gold, having the opinion — the honest opinion, very likely — that the passage of this measure will produce a temporary depreciation in the price, prepared themselves for that event; or the rise in price may have been a device on their part to secure a grant of authority to the Secretary to make the proposed sales. But it does not follow that the passage of this resolution in either shape — the shape in which it passed the House or that in which it passed the Senate — is calculated to affect permanently the price of gold. We are to judge the measure with reference to its effect upon the country generally, and through a long period of time. In what I say, I address myself to a condition of war. If we soon obtain peace, — as I trust we may by the success of our arms, — the character of our financial measures will be comparatively unimportant. Considering the resources of the country, the capacity of its people, and its productive power in a time of peace, we feel assured that the nation can rise superior to the effects of unfortunate or even unwise legislation; but, in discussing this measure, I address myself to the probable condition of the country, should the war continue, not only during the year 1864, but also during the year 1865.

If the war shall thus continue, what is to be the condition of the country in reference to the supply and use of coin? In the financial year of 1864–65, there is to be a demand for coin to the extent of $85,000,000. The Secretary of the Treasury has estimated the receipts from the custom-houses, for the same period of time, at $70,000,000, showing a deficit of $15,000,000.

Sir, I never heard of this bill until the morning when it was called up for consideration by the Committee of Ways and Means, and on which I submitted my amendment to the House. When the resolution was presented, my mind went back to certain thoughts I had had, touching our finances; one of which was, that the time was coming when it would be difficult for the government to secure specie enough to meet its liabilities. I had suggested privately to my colleague who is upon the Committee of Ways and Means [Mr. Hooper] the propriety of imposing a tax on cotton, to be paid in specie. I thought that such a tax might give us from twenty to forty million dollars, which might be appropriated to the payment, in coin, of the interest on the public debt. In this connection, and naturally, I was led to reflect on the measure proposed by the Committee of Ways and Means. I supposed, that, instead of a surplus of coin in the next sixteen months, there would be a deficiency. Speculators, who are not responsible for the financial condition of the country, may give advice, either wise or unwise, without care or thought; but I feel bound to submit, that, in accordance with the doctrines of the Constitution and the principles of liberty which we have inherited from our ancestors on the other side of the Atlantic, the responsibility for the financial condition of the country rests upon this House; and I submit, deferentially, that whoever upon this floor takes into consideration the financial condition of the country until July next only, and omits the year that is to follow, fails to comprehend the great facts upon which the safety of the republic rests. We must look to the next year, as well as to this. Sir, I was bred to business, and early instructed in the principle or rule of commercial safety, that a merchant who has a surplus of funds which he does not need for the purpose of meeting his immediate liabilities, but who has issued paper maturing the next month or the month after, instead of going into the market and loaning his temporary surplus to his neighbor, or investing it in stocks or real estate, should go to his creditors and anticipate his indebtedness, and thus provide for his liabilities and sustain his credit.

Is not the government to-day in the position of a debtor who has more money than he needs at the moment, but who will be called upon in the next four, six, or twelve months to pay an amount which he cannot obtain in the ordinary course of business during the months when the indebtedness is to mature?

The purpose of this resolution, as adopted by the House, is to relieve the Treasury of a temporary surplus, which, it is alleged by the Committee of Ways and Means, — and the force of their statement I did not fail to see, — is affecting unfavorably the business of the country. It was my purpose, by anticipating the payment of the interest coupons, from time to time, to carry the temporary surplus of the present financial year over to the year 1864–65, when, according to the estimates of the Secretary, there will be a deficiency. I thought it a wise proposition. I submit, deferentially, to the House, that the facts have not changed. A member of the Committee of Ways and Means [Mr. Hooper], whom I honor as my colleague, stated to the House, in the original debate, that there would be a surplus of from ten to twelve million dollars on the first of July next. This surplus of $12,000,000, added to the estimated receipts for the year 1864–65, makes an aggregate of $82,000,000. You will be called to pay, during the year 1864–65, $85,000,000; so that, if these estimates are correct, there will still be a deficit of $3,000,000.

And now the proposition submitted to the House and the country is, that, instead of applying this temporary surplus of ten or twelve million to the payment of coupons that are to be paid in coin unless the government intends to repudiate, the Secretary of the Treasury shall go into the market and sell this coin. One of two things must then happen, if these estimates are true, and if the war continues, — and all that I say is on that assumption, — you will either refuse, in the year 1864–65, to pay your interest in coin, or you will go into the market and buy coin for the purpose at the cheapest price at which you can get it. The government is in the condition in regard to money in which it would be in reference to bread for the army, if there was a short crop of grain, and the government, having control of a quantity necessary for the maintenance of the army, and more than could be used within the next three months, but not having a surplus beyond the requirements of the next twelve months, should, in order to force down the price, sell that which it had in store, put it into the hands of speculators ready to buy it, and then trust to the tender mercies of greedy men when the exigencies of the country should demand bread for the army at any cost.

We have, temporarily, a surplus of money. And what is the proposition? To take ten or twelve million, a temporary surplus, put it into the markets of New York, sell it to the speculators who will make a ring large enough to buy it (they can hold it for six months for two and a half or three per cent), and when your exigencies come, when the day of your distress is upon you, as it will be if the estimates of the Secretary of the Treasury are right, you will be in the power of these men. I ask whether the representatives of the people are prepared to authorize a measure so fruitful of disaster, if the war shall continue twelve or eighteen months longer.

It is said that the Secretary of the Treasury is not likely to act under your authority. There is no man on this floor whose confidence in the Secretary of the Treasury exceeds mine. I have known him personally; I have known him somewhat intimately; and I believe, that no public officer, from the establishment of the government till now, has exercised his high trusts with a more sincere and conscientious regard for the interests of the country. But it is not the officer that is to be clothed with this authority: it is the office. I am free to say that I do not mean to vote to intrust any public officer with authority, except on the ground of necessity; and while I do not hesitate to give my vote for all necessary authority to enable the executive to carry on this war, while I am not troubled by the suspension of the writ of *habeas corpus*, while I have no apprehension that the liberties of the people of the country are to be wrested from them, I yet maintain that it is no time, when we are conferring great and unexampled powers on executive officers that are necessary to be conferred, to confer upon them also powers that are unnecessary. This is the time, if ever, to withhold authority not absolutely indispensable, in order, that, if it should happen that there should be an attempt to abuse any of the powers which, in good faith, we have granted, we may still have in our hands the means of reclaiming those abused powers from unfaithful public servants.

Mr. Alley. — I desire to ask my colleague if he knows any thing more necessary than to protect the currency of the country in the present emergency, and whether he does not believe, as we do, that the possession, by the Secretary of the Treasury, of the powers that we propose to give him would, to some extent at least, protect the currency.

Mr. Boutwell. — I will say to my colleague, in all frankness, that, if I had no more faith in the efficacy of this measure than was expressed by him in his remarks to-day, I certainly should not vote for it. I do not think this measure necessary to protect the currency. It will prove a palliative, not a remedy.

Mr. ALLEY. — Will my colleague answer me further? Does he not believe, if the Secretary of the Treasury should not exercise that power, the fact of his possessing that power will prevent, to a considerable extent, speculation in gold?

Mr. BOUTWELL. — The chief element which enters into speculation everywhere is uncertainty. Uncertainty is the basis of speculation. This measure, as it comes from the Senate, introduces into the business of the country a new element of uncertainty; to wit, the will of the Secretary of the Treasury.

Mr. HIGBY. — Would not our finances be in a firmer condition by the passage of the House bill, without the Senate amendments, than its passage with those amendments, and be a greater check upon speculation in the public credits? When a surplus of gold had accumulated, would not the anticipation of payment, and making payment in amount as paper should demand, be far more powerful in controlling the market than to allow the purchase of government paper at the lowest price it could be obtained at in market?

Mr. BOUTWELL. — I give an affirmative answer to the questions, as far as I understand them.

Mr. Speaker, I was saying, when interrupted, that one of the chief elements of speculation is uncertainty. We know very well, that the premiums on maritime risks, in time of war, are not based upon actual losses from privateers, but upon the apprehensions and fears of the underwriters of what those losses may possibly be. If you give to the Secretary of the Treasury the power to sell gold, in addition to the power he now has to buy gold, it will always be an element of uncertainty in the gold market, in addition to those elements which exist at present; and a merchant or speculator, buying gold or selling gold, will always take into account the fact, that the Secretary of the Treasury may go into the market and buy or sell gold, and force it temporarily above or below the price at which it was held on the day of the sale or purchase.

There is yet another objection to giving the Secretary of the Treasury this power. We do not know whether he will exercise it or not; and this House ought not to confer power unless it believes that an exigency will exist when he ought to exercise it. I believe, no such exigency can exist while the law of 1862 remains upon the statute-book. On the 25th of February, 1862, the Congress of the United States passed a loan bill, asking the country and the world to furnish $500,000,000 to enable us to carry on the war. In that bill, we introduced two pledges. The first was, that nothing but coin should be received in payment of custom-house duties; secondly, that this coin should be appropriated, first, to the payment of the interest on the public debt, and, secondly, that a sinking fund should be created by the use of the coin in purchase of bonds, equal to one per cent of the whole public debt. The balance, if any, was to go into the general treasury. What is the proposition which comes to us from the Senate? It contains, to be sure, a promise to secure the payment of the interest on the public debt; but no attention is given to the second great pledge, — the establishment of a sinking fund, — which each year should be increased in an amount equal to one per cent of the public debt. The redemption of this pledge will require, for the years 1863–64 and 1864–65, not less than $15,000,000. I ask gentlemen, in all sincerity, how they are to defend themselves to their constituents and to the world, if they disregard this solemn obligation. Is there any defence? I know of none.

A gentleman, in endeavoring to satisfy me that this bill ought to pass, assures me that the world does not know that we have made this pledge. I cannot say whether the world knows it or not. I know it. This is sufficient for me. I know that this pledge was made, and therefore, so long as I have power, I intend to keep it. I will attempt to keep it, though the Committee of Ways and Means make no provision therefor. I ask, What defence, what excuse, what justification, is offered? Is it said that the government intends to secure this gold at a cheaper rate by and by? I ask my colleague on the Committee of Ways and Means, if to-morrow I were to give him a bond under seal that I would convey to him in fee, in one year, a certain estate, and the next day he should hear that I had conveyed it by warranty deed to a third person, would he not feel, that, at that very moment, I had violated my faith?

Mr. STEVENS. — Suppose the piece of property was to be conveyed a year hence, and he concluded to sell it to somebody else, have I a right to say any thing before the year comes round, and before I see whether or not he has then any thing to pay with?

Mr. BOUTWELL. — The gentleman will observe that that is a different case entirely from this, because here the law says that "from and after the first of July, 1862," the government will do so and so. The day of performance has already passed. Nearly two years have transpired, and you have not yet taken the first step towards the creation of this sinking fund. And now, when you say you have twelve or twenty million of gold, and that you do not need it for paying interest, I turn to the statute, and ask you why you do not establish the sinking fund which you have agreed to establish.

Mr. HOOPER. — Will the gentleman yield a moment?

Mr. BOUTWELL. — I wish to say one word more to my colleague upon the committee before I yield. Would not my colleague [Mr. Hooper], whenever he found that I had conveyed away the estate by warranty deed to a third person, say I had already violated my obligation, although he would have no legal right to call upon me for a performance of the condition of my bond before the year transpired? If, incidentally, he should mention the matter to me, and I should say, "I am a rich man, but I happened to be a little embarrassed, and thought it convenient to get some money more economically than by borrowing, and hence sold this estate in the market; but, in a year, I shall be in funds, and then I will repurchase this property and convey it to you, and so comply with the conditions of my bond," would he not have a right to complain? Who does not see that it might be out of my power to comply with my obligations? If to-day I could repurchase the property, it does not follow that the party owning the property will not change his mind. Or he may die, and his heirs or trustees may be the parties with whom I should have to deal, and my colleague might be compelled to go into court and seek damages for the loss of the land which I had promised him.

Mr. Hooper. — I rise to answer the question. I should say, if I heard he had made the transaction such as he represented, knowing him so well, I should not believe it, unless I had it from his own lips.

Mr. Boutwell. — You surely ought to have as much confidence in the faith of your country as in mine.

Mr. Hooper. — But I desire to ask my colleague how he proposes to put this amount into the sinking fund in gold. I want to know the mode and manner of doing it. I ask him, as a man of business, if he were the Secretary of the Treasury, how he would do it.

Mr. Boutwell. — I have thought of the mode. The law is not explicit; but I suppose the intention to be, that the Secretary of the Treasury should take the surplus of gold, and, after paying the interest on the public debt, buy bonds in the market and set them aside, stamp them as belonging to the sinking fund, pay the interest each six months, and invest the interest and the annual one per cent of the capital of the debt in additional bonds, to be treated in the same manner each six months afterwards. I do not know whether it would be competent for the Secretary of the Treasury to purchase the United-States notes with the gold, and then with the notes purchase the government bonds. I say, I do not know whether the Secretary would be authorized to do this. What I do know is, that he would have the right to take the gold and buy the bonds. Whether he has a right to take the intermediate steps is not so clear.

Another objection I have to granting this power is, that, while I have the utmost confidence in the Secretary of the Treasury, I know very well he could not personally execute this trust. He must employ agents. I do not know whether those agents will be trustworthy or not, though I know he would adopt every safeguard in his power. On the other hand, I know all the markets of speculation would be agitated to their very depths, in order to ascertain what the purposes of the Secretary were.

Mr. Stevens. — Does not the Secretary now employ agents to keep all this gold?

Mr. Boutwell. — Do not misunderstand me. I say, that, when he purposes to make a sale of gold, he must employ somebody to do it. He cannot do it himself, and therefore the information that gold is to be sold must be communicated to at least one person; and, when it is communicated to one person, we do not know how many other persons may get the information.

This is a matter which affects not only the price of gold, but also all the business relations of the country. It is not possible to affect the price of gold permanently, unless you first or simultaneously affect the price of exchange. Our exports, during the last year, amounted to nearly $332,000,000, including foreign merchandise exported, estimated in the currency of the country. Our imports were over $252,000,000, estimated in the gold currency of other countries. There was a balance against us, which was met by the export of specie, to the amount of $54,000,000. If a merchant has exchange which is payable in gold in Great Britain, he can command gold there; and, if he cannot buy gold here as cheaply as he can get it there, he will get it there. Therefore, I submit the proposition, based upon all the experience of this country and of the world, that gold cannot rule higher permanently than exchange. The price of exchange is based upon the exports and imports of the country. Whenever your exports are greater than your imports, you can bring down the price of gold, and you cannot permanently reduce it by any other means. A sale of State or national bonds abroad will yield exchange, and reduce the price of gold.

Now, sir, even if this war goes on, there will be a changed and more favorable condition in our financial affairs. We have information that the receipts of cotton from the South amount to about eight thousand bales a week. The necessities of the country, at the present moment, do not exceed four thousand bales. We shall soon be exporting cotton at the rate of three or four thousand bales a week, which will yield us seven or eight hundred thousand dollars in exchange. In the next place, we have been importing a great quantity of linen and woollen goods and wool, on all of which duties have been paid, and for which our exports have been sent abroad. We shall gradually diminish these imports when our mills begin to run, and the use of cotton is restored to what it was previous to the opening of the war. These facts tend to show, that, hereafter, the exchange will be in our favor; that the price of gold will be gradually reduced; that our imports will be diminished; that the revenue derived from the custom-houses will be reduced, and thereby the means of the government to pay the interest on the public debt in coin will be lessened also. In these facts we find a reason why we should not throw the millions of surplus coin we now have into the market. I regard this measure, then, as a temporary expedient, but as one not calculated to produce beneficial results during a long period of time.

I come next, Mr. Speaker, to a statement with reference to measures of public policy, which seem important, and which, I think, will gradually and ultimately furnish us some relief. The first is *economy*. I do not care to dwell upon this topic, but it is in this House that economy, in regard to national expenditures, must be practised, if it is practised anywhere.

The second point is taxation. If the Committee of Ways and Means shall report a bill embracing, in some degree, the principle contained in the resolution offered by the gentleman from New York [Mr. Freeman Clark] a few days ago, by which the revenue shall be increased to two or three hundred million dollars a year, we shall have taken a great and important step toward the restoration of our finances.

Next, it is a pressing necessity — I do not know how the difficulty is to be met and overcome, but it is a pressing necessity — that the circulation of paper be reduced. When the war opened, the circulation of paper was hardly more than two hundred million dollars, issued by the State banks of the country. The last report brings up the issue by these banks to $238,000,000. We have issued something like four hundred million of United-States notes. We have also in circulation certificates of indebtedness and five-per-cent scrip, redeemable in one and two years. These pass from hand to hand, and enter into the currency of the country. The latter are taken up by the banks because they bear interest, and the banks then put into circulation the non-bearing-interest legal-tender United-States notes, which they have heretofore retained for the purpose of redeeming their circulation. To the extent of the issue of this paper, the currency of the country has been increased. In addition to that, we are now inaugurating what I believe to be in itself a wise system, and one which ought to be maintained, but which (I am speaking of the national-bank system) will ultimately increase the circulation of the country $300,000,000.

It is not a matter of surprise, that, under such circumstances, the currency of the country appears to be, and is in fact, depreciating. In regard to the gold speculators, I believe, that, in the run of six months, gold is neither higher nor lower on account of what they can do. They work on a certain basis, which is the value of exchange. They may, for a few days, force gold above the price of exchange; but, ultimately, the price of gold in the market depends on the price of exchange, which is equivalent to gold; and the rate of exchange depends upon the relation between the exports and imports.

The country needs about $1,000,000 of exchange per day, while the demand for gold is only about one-fourth as much; or, considered together, the demand for foreign exchange and for gold is about one and one-fourth million dollars per day. The supply and demand for exchange must therefore fix the price of gold. Hence, until you can do something to decrease the rates of exchange, you can do but little to diminish the price of gold.

I wish to make one suggestion, and I do it with great deference. It is, whether it would not be wise, under existing circumstances, for the government to authorize a loan, principal and interest payable in foreign countries, either in London, Hamburg, or Frankfort, to run for a long time, — say twenty, thirty, or forty years, — because it may be twenty, thirty, or forty years before the government can pay the entire debt, even under the most favorable circumstances. This loan should be put at a low rate of interest, say four per cent, which would be a cheap rate for the government. The bonds should not be sold in the outset, because if you sell the government securities in foreign countries for a given sum, and draw against those securities and sell the exchange in the market, you force down the rate of exchange, and the government is a loser; but if you can make a special deposit of these bonds, drawing against them to a certain amount, with the right to sell the bonds whenever you please, and then put the exchange into the market, the effect of it will be to force down the price of exchange. Exchange being forced down, gold will follow, because the exchange can be converted into gold; and thus you do something to strengthen the government, and restore a better relation between the price of paper and the price of gold.

I made this suggestion to a banker, and his reply was this: "The bonds might as well be sold on this side of the Atlantic." I say no. There is a very material difference; it is this: we are bound to look, not only at the immediate effects upon business by the loans we are creating, but we are bound to look at their ultimate and permanent effects. In the beginning of the war, it would not have been wise to borrow money abroad; but circumstances have changed, and it may be now expedient to do that which, in the beginning, it was not expedient to do. It is for our interest that all money borrowed abroad should be borrowed on securities that cannot be readily sold in the United States.

My reason for the opinion is this: if our present bonds were negotiated abroad upon a basis of gold at sixty per cent premium, and if gold should fall to twenty-five per cent premium, as we hope it will during the present summer, should we have military successes, the bonds would be sent back to this country, and would pay a large profit to those who had bought them abroad. The return of these bonds would create a demand for gold and exchange, force up prices, and re-inaugurate the evils against which we are now contending. I think, the better way is to place a certain amount of the loan on the other side of the Atlantic for the sake of the exchange, by which we can force down the price of gold, and yet put that loan on such terms that it cannot be negotiated in this country. That can be done by making interest and principal payable abroad, and putting the interest at a rate below the current rates at home, so that people here would be reluctant to buy it. My suggestion is, that, if we can create a four-per-cent loan of one or two hundred million for a long period of time, place it abroad, draw against it, force down the price of exchange and the price of gold, we can ultimately sell these bonds at par.

And now, in conclusion, I ask the House to consider which of the two measures before us is best calculated to strengthen the credit of the country.

Mr. Speaker, I am one of those who believe that this nation is able to carry a debt of two, three, or four thousand million dollars, pay the interest regularly, and ultimately pay the principal. I believe it can be done by adhering to sound principles, and that moral as well as financial considerations must enter into our policy. If we have pledged the nation's faith even to our own hurt, I say we should keep it. If other nations, to say nothing of the people of this country, in looking at our legislation in order to ascertain what security they have for their claims upon our treasury, see that we do not hesitate, when an exigency not very great is upon us, to take some portion of this coin which we have pledged to a particular use and devote it to another use, will it not weaken our credit abroad? Will not the people of other nations justly say, "There is no dependence to be placed upon the credit of the United-States government: without any special exigency, they have already taken a portion of the money they had pledged to us, and appropriated it to another use; and how can we tell, that, in some exigency that may arise, they will not take the remainder, and leave us to receive the principal and interest of the debt they owe us in irredeemable paper currency?"

But if, on the contrary, these nations, in looking at our legislation, see that we pay our interest in coin, as we agreed, and, having an amount of coin on hand larger than is required to pay the interest on our public debt, we devote it to a sinking fund, with which we lay a foundation for the redemption of the principal of that debt; if they see, that in the midst of a war the magnitude of which is such as the world never saw before, with a public debt of ten or twelve hundred million, we not only adhere to our obligations to pay the interest in coin, but we anticipate that interest, — it will strengthen our credit at home and abroad, and enable us to negotiate loans upon favorable terms.

Mr. Speaker, is there any man who can compare the results which will be likely to follow, and which, it seems to me, will certainly follow a line of policy such as I have marked out, with the results that will follow the act of throwing some ten or twelve million dollars into the gambling-shops of New York, with the expectation that it will reduce the price of gold there four or five per cent, and hesitate as to the course he ought to pursue? If these men in future should have the government in their power, they will wring the last drachma of your possessions from you. Who, in comparing these results, can hesitate in deciding which course will be most beneficial to the government?

PERSONAL EQUALITY AND PUBLIC PROSPERITY.

SPEECH DELIVERED AT BALTIMORE, APRIL 1, 1864.

THIS is the first time, gentlemen, that I have had the opportunity to speak in a slave State upon the subject of slavery. Indeed, in a pretty long public experience, I have spoken in a slave State but once before in my life; and, as I come from a Commonwealth which has not within these last three years made that rapid progress in opinion upon the subject of slavery which you have made, it is possible that I may seem to be a conservative man.

I introduce what I have to say with an observation perhaps as radical and possibly, if it be offensive at all, as offensive as any that I shall make. A statesman of Virginia more than fifty years ago, declared that the institution of slavery converted every slaveholder into a tyrant. I judge from the tabular statements which I have seen published, setting forth the distribution of political power in this Commonwealth, that not only has here every slaveholder been a petty tyrant, but that the institution of slavery has been a vast system of political despotism to the white people of this State, as well as a system of personal despotism to the black people.

I congratulate you on the great movement for which you are indebted to the traitors of the South and the traitors among you who inaugurated this rebellion, demonstrating again, in the history of nations and of peoples, that Divine Providence sometimes chooses vile instruments to work out its beneficent designs. To these men are you indebted for the opportunity to strike at once from yourselves the shackles of political despotism in which you have been bound, and to strike from your fellow-beings, I do not hesitate to call them your brethren (Jefferson, the apostle of Democracy, did not hesitate to call the Africans residing in Virginia his brethren, and I think you are not better than Jefferson), — to strike from your brethren the personal shackles in which they have been bound.

This is an unusual opportunity, such as does not often come to a people; and I suppose it is true here, as it is true everywhere and in all ages of the world, that to the mass of the people, the hard-handed men, to that class known in British life and British history as the yeomanry, is the country to be indebted for its redemption from the great curse of slavery. Gentlemen, if you are not prepared to work for emancipation upon the ground of its exact justice, upon the ground of its conformity to the natural rights of man and to the laws of God, then you had better withhold your hands until you are satisfied that it is just to the black man that he should be emancipated. If you do not so believe, you are unfit to put your hands to this great work, which means the equality of all men before the laws.

My friend, Mr. Davis, has spoken, in passing, of the charge made against him and against those associated with him, that they favor the equality of the black man with the white man. I am not for the equality of the black man with the white man, nor for the equality of the white man with the black man. I do not suppose they are equal. I am not for the equality of any two among you, because I do not believe you are equal. I do not recognize my friend, Mr. Davis, as my equal: I do not claim that I am his equal. We differ in a great many things; we probably are not exactly alike in any thing: but that declaration, that great fundamental truth uttered by Jefferson in the Declaration of Independence, that "all men are created equal," is the ideal truth towards which you must work in the struggle for emancipation. All men are created equal; not that they are equal in height, not that they are equal in strength, not that they are equal in moral qualities or intellectual powers. Such equality is not according to the law of Providence, as we understand it. The Declaration of Independence means exactly this,—that no man is created under any political subordination to any other man; and the ballot is the evidence, the symbol, the pledge, by which we recognize that every other man is politically our equal, that he has a right to take a share in the government. That is what a popular government means. Do you not understand, that, if you lay down a rule by which you exclude any portion of the people from a participation in public affairs, in that rule you have recognized a principle which may be carried still further, and which may ultimately exclude you?

This doctrine of exclusion is the doctrine of king-craft; it is the doctrine of despotism. If you may exclude some men from political power because they are not as wise, or because they are not as learned, or because they are not as strong, or because they are not as wealthy, the principle, generally applied, results ultimately in this, — that he who is the wisest, or the most learned, or the strongest, or the bravest, or the wealthiest, is to rule all the rest; and that is despotism. It is the rule of democracy, that each man, without regard to any other qualification or condition or circumstance, has a right to participate in public affairs. But in this State, owing to the existence of the institution of slavery, which creates a common interest among a class of men who, according to the ancient Virginia doctrine, are tyrants from the very fact that they are slaveholders, the slaveholding class have so organized your political system that one man in one county has the political power of two men or three men in another county.

I do not know how you feel in Maryland, but in Massachusetts we would not recognize such a doctrine for a day. We would move that old Commonwealth from shore to mountain, and every voice should be raised and every arm nerved to strike down a system so disorganizing in its character and contrary to the principles of justice, though not only eighty thousand slaves should be emancipated, but the fourteen thousand slaveholders should be trampled in the dust. Your system is a tyranny to the whites in the free section of the State.

Gentlemen, it has come to this, that you, free white men, if you think it any privilege or any good fortune that you are free white men, are compelled in self-defence to decide whether you will strike down an institution which is subversive of human rights, the rights of white men and the rights of black men. If you liberate these eighty-seven thousand colored people, I do not know what they will do: I do not think you, in discussing this question, have any right to inquire. If there is a man who is apprehensive that by some means or other the negro will come to be his equal, then I apprehend that that man instinctively—and instinct very often is God teaching through the human heart—feels that he is pretty near the level of the negro, and that very soon the negro will rise to his level.

A man who has confidence in his own capacity is not troubled about other people, as to whether they are getting along well in the world or not; but those who just make a shamble through life and never take one firm step on God's solid earth, not having confidence in themselves, are continually laboring under the fear, that, by some means or other, they are soon to be upset.

I hope the laboring people will ponder this question well. Occasionally in my own State and in my own district there have been appeals to the laboring people, that, if slavery were abolished, the negroes would all go North, and would there come in competition with the laboring men in the cities and large towns, and that finally there would be a dearth of labor, a scarcity of the means of living, and great evils would ensue. I went into the city of Lowell just on the eve of the last congressional election. That rumor had been circulated. I said to them, "Gentlemen, I think the case is just this: The negro hereafter will not live in a slave State;" and that is exactly what I would like to say to the slaveholders of Maryland, — the negroes will not live in slave States any longer, they are to live in free States.

And I said to the people in Massachusetts, "The question is just here: If you give your votes in such a way as to secure freedom in the Southern States, where the homes of the slaves are, the slaves will stay there, and the few who are here will return." I also put this question to them, and I would ask the slaveholders the same question, — if they ever heard of the negro running away from hot weather, if they ever heard of the negro running away from the miasma of a swamp, if they ever heard of his deserting his home or leaving the place where he was born, for any reason except one, that he was in slavery.

As an answer to those who demand compensation, I would say this: Slavery does not exist in the North; it never shall, by the grace of God and the firm will of the people of this country, exist again in the eleven rebellious States.

We are to have a free zone on the South, from the Potomac to the Rio Grande, where there shall everywhere be unfurled the flag of freedom.

Now, then, slaveholders of Maryland, what is before you? Your negroes, if you continue to maintain the institution of slavery, will not stay in Maryland: they will either go to Virginia, where there will be freedom, or they will go North; and, although there is in the Constitution a provision that fugitives shall be delivered up, you will find after this that there will be nobody North, and that there will be nobody South, to deliver them up; and you will find it also very difficult to make the Constitution work without somebody to enforce it. We are determined not to enforce it. You may just as well understand it as not. Slaveholders, no more negroes are to be caught anywhere.

Under these circumstances, what are your negroes worth? With Pennsylvania and Virginia free, the North star inviting them in one direction, and the Southern cross in the other, what are your negroes worth? Who will catch them when they run away? Nobody. Then, if you are to be compensated at all, you are to be compensated according to the value of them. Get your jury; see what they are worth: they are worth nothing to you to-day. If they have any shoes on their feet, their shoes are worth more to the master than the body that stands above them. There is no just demand; there is no equity; there is no claim. It is the misfortune of this particular kind of property. A very peculiar institution it turns out to be now,—they always said it was "peculiar,"—it turns out to be peculiar. It has no defenders anywhere. The day of "Northern men with Southern principles" is over. It has gone, and never will return.

I have also to say that it is not only due to the Southern men who have been engaged in this rebellion, that this war, with all its sacrifices, is upon us; but it is due very largely to the men of the border States, and to Maryland among them. It was my fortune to be a member of the Peace Congress of 1861; and when the records of that Congress are published, and the speeches given to the world, you will find that Maryland, by her delegates, contributed something to bring on this rebellion. If she, with the other border States, had stood firm under the flag, and said to the seceding and then rebellious States, "If you persist in the course on which you have entered, we will make war, we will establish the authority of the government, we will maintain the integrity of the Union," even then, in the month of February, 1861, they could have arrested the rebellion.

They did not do it; they pandered to treason. Instead of going home to their own people in the border slave States and telling them the truth, they asked us of the North to go home to our people and tell them a lie. We refused to do it. In that Convention I declared three things; I will repeat them here. The first was, that I abhorred the institution of slavery; the second was, that if, to save the Union, it was necessary to make further concessions to the institution of slavery, I would have no part in saving the Union; and the third was, — and I say, if there had been a response to this third statement by the slaveholders of the border States and the conservative men of the free States, the rebellion might have been arrested, — I said to those gentlemen, standing face to face with Rives and Seddon, of Virginia and other men from North Carolina, and from Tennessee, and from Missouri, "If you persist in this rebellion, we shall march our armies to the Gulf of

Mexico, or you will march your armies to the great lakes." In that great crisis in the country's history, nothing but firmness, decision, a declaration that the Union should never be severed without war, would have arrested the rebellion. Jefferson Davis and his allies now engaged in this rebellion are not more guilty, in my judgment, before the country for the horrors and outrages of this unexampled conflict than are those timid, time-serving, conciliating, compromising men of the North, who in that day did not dare to declare for the people the truth that was in the people's hearts, that this Union should never be severed.

How is it, then, that these men, slaveholders, generally the allies and confederates of the conspirators of the South, ask you, the bone and sinew of Maryland, to contribute of your labor to compensate them for the eighty-seven thousand, more or less, of slaves that they hold in violation of the law of God, and with no better authentic record of the right they assert than the statute, if there be a statute, framed by themselves or their ancestors, declaring their title to that which never by the law of God was recognized as property?

While looking at this question of emancipation in Maryland merely as a pecuniary or industrial question, I should say it were cheap for Maryland to buy all these slaves at three hundred dollars apiece; still I would never counsel as a friend, nor consent if I were an inhabitant of Maryland, that one dollar should be paid, even though it would be cheap to buy them at three hundred dollars or five hundred dollars a head. Justice is above all price; and, when justice is done, the heavens do not fall, but they bend and accept the homage of man. Now is the time when the people of Maryland should, in the reconstruction of their government, found it on the principle of justice. Go to the Declaration of Independence, — "all men are created equal," — and found your State upon that great doctrine.

Will you allow me to allude to Massachusetts? We founded our government in 1780 upon the doctrine that all men are created free and equal; and, although previous to that time there were a few slaves, the first judge that ever sat upon the bench when the question came up of the right of property in slaves, looked at our Bill of Rights, and said, "Here it is declared that all men are created free and equal; and you have no right, under this declaration of rights, to hold this human being. He is free." Thus, without any legislation whatever, but by the declaration of rights in our Constitution, and the decision of an upright judge, slavery was stricken down.

Thus plant your system of government in your Constitution, recognizing the equality of man, and strike down the institution without compensation to the slaveholder. I cannot doubt, that, when you have made Maryland a free State, you will see her take new and rapid strides in industry, in wealth, in the development of your resources. I do not like to compare Maryland to my own State in natural advantages; and yet Maryland, in soil, in extent of territory, in mineral resources, is incomparably superior to Massachusetts. In Massachusetts, we have persistently, through two hundred years, kept one thing steadily in view, — the education, elevation, and protection of the individual man. We are constantly educating in our public schools, at the public expense, a quarter of a million of children.

We have a hundred institutions of learning scattered over the State, endowed by the public will, maintained by universal taxation, in which the child of the poorest man can get a better education to-day than the son of the richest man could obtain in any institution in America when the Revolutionary War opened. By developing, educating, perfecting the individual man, we add to individual and public wealth. The statistics show (I hope you will not consider me aggressive in my remarks) that an individual man in Massachusetts, in his productive power, is equal to two and a half men in Maryland, on an average.

This is due to the fact that we believe that the brain and the moral faculties educated and developed are the basis of individual and public prosperity. We do not believe in ignorance; we do not believe in degradation: but we believe in the elevation of every individual, however humble he may be in his origin or in his surroundings.

The few black people that we have among us we attempt to elevate; and, though prejudices exist among us against the colored race, we still have done this. In one of our normal schools for the education of young ladies as teachers, I have seen a colored girl with seventy-five or eighty or one hundred young ladies of white complexion, sitting at the same desk, pursuing the same studies, nothing ever occurring which indicated that the white ladies in the school regarded her other than as a sister.

At the graduation of the class to which she belonged, by the vote of her associates of the class she was elected to write and deliver the closing poem. I saw her afterwards a teacher. She is now at Port Royal, off South Carolina.

I do not mean to say that the colored race can equal the white race: but I say that for two centuries and more you have held them in chains; for two centuries and more you have depraved them; for two centuries and more you have deprived them of their just rights before God; and now the time has come when you have at once before you the opportunity and the duty to "loose the bonds, and let the oppressed go free."

Let them do that which they have the opportunity and the capacity for doing. Establish public schools; educate them; improve them; give them an opportunity: do for them what it was thought of sufficient importance by Dr. Adams, of Boston, when he delivered a eulogy, after the death of Mr. Choate, upon that illustrious man, to mention in his sermon, as characteristic of the person whom he eulogized. He said that Mr. Choate, walking across the fields one day, saw a bug on its back. With his cane he turned it over, and said, "Get on your legs, and take a fair start in the world." What I ask for the black race is that you put them on their feet, and give them a fair start in the world. If they distance you, it will be because they have some capacity which you have not. My judgment is, that you will keep sufficiently far ahead not to be disturbed by them; but, if they get ahead of you, they will leave the road behind.

There is another consideration. You cannot just now — I do not know what may be the condition of things fifty or one hundred years hence — but you of Maryland cannot just now afford to part with the black people. They are capable of performing a great deal of labor. You need them to cultivate your lands, to develop your resources; and you cannot, without loss, pursue a policy which drives them from your State. If you continue as a slave State, with a free region South and a free region North, the negroes will escape, and you will be left with a greatly reduced laboring population. While you continue as a slave State, the free laborers of the North and of Europe will not come here. Any man who is not driven into exile as it were, who has a home in a free State, and is obliged to labor with his hands for the means of subsistence, does not migrate to a slave State. In a free State, — I speak of my own State, because there I know more of the people than I know of the people in any other State, — labor is not only rewarded, but it is honored. The dignity of labor is taught in every public school; it is instilled by the example of every father and of every mother; it is the belief of the churches; it is the universal public sentiment, that a laboring man is "a man for a' that." But in a slave State, where slavery is the controlling power, — I suppose it is not so in the city of Baltimore, where there is a large predominance of free population, and a public sentiment controlled by free opinion, — but in a slave State, and in a slaveholding community, labor is considered degrading, and a laboring man is not regarded as a respectable man. Therefore a man trained in a free State, and dependent upon his own hands for his means of subsistence, does not go into a slave State.

If, then, you continue the institution of slavery, your present laborers will escape, and new ones will not come, and your nine thousand square miles of territory will be comparatively a waste; your mines will not be developed; your water-power will not be improved. On the other hand, if you abolish slavery, and proceed to educate your children, black and white, make labor respectable, you not only retain the productive power of this people, but you bring other laborers to you, and you build up a great commonwealth upon this central shore of the Atlantic. I saw, the other day, a statement that you had by estimate six thousand million of tons of coal underlying the surface of Maryland. Six thousand million of tons, at a dollar per ton, will pay the present debt of the United States twice over. I do not know but that we shall come here to get the coal at twenty-five cents a ton to pay our debt.

When I look at your natural facilities, your advantages, I am astonished that you have not more fully developed them in the past; and I can attribute the neglect only to the institution of slavery. While in my own State, on Cape Cod, on the elbow which extends from Barnstable all the way round to Provincetown (as every one who looks at the map sees), fifty or sixty miles, there is not a foot of fruitful land; and yet along this narrow cape you find people not only in the possession of a competency, but living in luxury. On this cape there is a fact which has no parallel on the continent, — a garden, the soil of which was imported from Oporto. When we thrive on sand, and import the soil in which we raise our vegetables, what ought you to do here?

RIGHTS OF THE REBEL STATES.

SPEECH UPON THE "BILL TO GUARANTEE TO CERTAIN STATES, WHOSE GOVERNMENTS HAVE BEEN USURPED OR OVERTHROWN, A REPUBLICAN FORM OF GOVERNMENT," DELIVERED IN THE HOUSE OF REPRESENTATIVES, MAY 4, 1864.

MR. SPEAKER, — Before any steps can be safely taken for the organization of local governments, either by or for the people inhabiting the territory included within the eleven once-existing States, but now rebellious districts, of the Union, it is necessary for Congress and the country to come to an understanding of the legal and constitutional relations subsisting between those people and the Government of the United States.

It is my chief purpose — indeed, I may say that it is my only purpose — to contribute something, if happily I may, to the attainment of that common understanding; but, before I proceed to a discussion of the questions involved in the bill now under consideration, I beg the indulgence of the House while I allude briefly to the remarks made by the gentleman from Ohio, my colleague upon the committee that reported this bill [Mr. Ashley], in reference to the policy of the President in Louisiana and Arkansas, and to the conduct of General Banks, in his administration of the Department of the Gulf.

It ought to attract observation, that, since this rebellion opened, the Thirty-seventh Congress commenced its existence, and ceased to exist; that this Congress is now closing the fifth month of its first session; and that up to this time no efficient, indeed no legislative steps whatever, have been taken by which the executive is to be guided in the affairs of the people occupying the territory that has been reclaimed from rebel domination. Under these circumstances, I think it due to the country that this House, at least, should do nothing which conveys any reflection upon his policy, unless that policy be clearly and manifestly in contravention of the Constitution, or of the well-ascertained and admitted principles of the government.

When the Mississippi River was opened to navigation; when the subordinates of the rebel government were separated from the capital of the so-called Confederacy; when the populous parts of Louisiana were torn from rebel dominion, and the State of Arkansas, in various ways, indicated that there was an existing opinion among the people in favor of a return to the allegiance which was due from them to this government,—the executive had but one of three courses before him: either to be silent, to be inactive; to govern by military authority alone; or to establish a civil government, or at least to take initiatory steps for the establishment of such a government. It was unquestionably his right and duty, in the absence of all legislative action, to govern these districts of country by military power as fast and as far as they were reclaimed.

I agree with what has been so often said upon this

floor, that, as far as practicable, we should avoid the exercise of military authority in the civil affairs of the people. I do not know that any thing has been done in Arkansas and Louisiana in the re-establishment of civil authority, that is in contravention of the known principles of our government. The President has initiated steps for the organization of civil authority; and, in the absence of legislative action, I hold it to have been his duty to take steps in that direction. Whatever may be our opinion of the President on certain points, — and I do not stand here or anywhere as his defender, — but admitting that he has marked peculiarities, and admitting also a lack of executive control over those intrusted with the performance of administrative duties, I yet think we ought to have confidence in a statesman who from the year 1858, when he carried on the memorable contest in Illinois with Douglas, until now, has been true to the principles of human liberty and true to the application of those principles under the Constitution to the people of the country, both white and black.

A life of devotion to principle, a life of service,— and I make this remark, not only with reference to the President, but to his subordinate who is charged with the administration of affairs in Louisiana,— a life of service and a life indicating capacity, should not be set aside even in the presence of errors or of temporary disasters. Therefore, though the President may have made mistakes in the affairs of Louisiana and Arkansas, it ill becomes any man, who believes in the principles of human liberty, and that they are destined to control this continent, to arraign the executive. He should stand justified when he has acted in good faith, with loyalty to the Constitution, and with just regard to the rights and liberties of this great people. These remarks are also alike applicable to my friend who is charged with the conduct of affairs in Louisiana. For twenty years and more I have known General Banks. I have known him to be a man of capacity, struggling against adverse influences and adverse fortune, almost from the moment he crossed the threshold of manhood to the present time. He has often been frowned on by circumstances; but he has, in all the emergencies of his life, risen superior to the attacks of enemies, and even sustained himself against the assaults of fortune. Whatever other men may think, it is my firm belief, even in the presence of what seems to be a temporary disaster in military operations in Louisiana, that General Banks will do his duty to the country, and redeem the territory west of the Mississippi River from the thraldom of the rebellion.

Still further, without entering into an examination of particular things done in Louisiana, I assert that, from the moment New Orleans was wrested from the grasp of the rebels until now, there has been no part of our territory reclaimed from their control in which the rights of the citizens have been as well protected as in Louisiana, or where there has been so little of personal trouble and suffering, especially among the black race. To be sure, wages have been fixed for them; but they have been saved from the lash of the taskmaster; they have been free; they have been at liberty to choose their own places of labor; and Louisiana is to-day relieved from the institution of slavery. And further, upon information received from many sources, I say that Louisiana is not only free from slavery through the President's proclamation, but she is to be free permanently, through the fact, that her people are being identified, day by day and week by week, with the institutions and principles of freedom. On many of the plantations, schools have been opened, under the direction of General Banks, for the education of children. Thus freedom is becoming the public policy in Louisiana, not through proclamations, not through legislation, not through the Constitution alone, but through the settled conviction of the people, that slavery is wrong, and that freedom is right.

And now I come to what I purpose to present in the way of argument in favor of the passage of this bill. It is necessary in the beginning that we understand the legal and constitutional relations subsisting between the people of the rebel districts of the country and the national government. Nobody denies that we are in a war which taxes our capacity and resources. The question is asked, and it has been often discussed, Who is responsible for this war? The time will come when the question will be of no consequence. I am not sure that the time has not come already. I think that the responsibility for the war is in the institution of slavery, in its intrinsic incompatibility with freedom everywhere and always. It was incompatible in the beginning; and it was accepted as an existing fact in the States of the country, merely because our fathers saw no way of escaping from its malign influence, and also because they labored under the hope, which has proved thus far a delusion, that slavery was temporary, and would gradually disappear; that freedom was permanent, and would become universal.

Slavery has increased and strengthened in this country under the influence of two considerations: first, the apparent pecuniary advantages to be derived from it. The slaveholder and the slaveholding communities were deceived. The result is seen in the great fact, that the slave States, with a more inviting climate, with a more fertile soil, have less accumulated wealth than is possessed by the free States as the products of the labor of one or two hundred years. There are no two slave States in this Union that Massachusetts could not have purchased in the open market when the rebellion commenced. In this remark I exclude the idea of property in human beings. The greater wealth of the free States is due to the circumstance, that slavery, instead of being a profitable, was an impoverishing institution. But men rested in the belief that it was profitable, and therefore they sought to maintain and extend it.

The other reason for fostering and extending slavery in this country is found in the circumstance that the politicians, South and North, gained power by it. Chiefly, indeed exclusively as far as the North is concerned, are they who sit on the other side of the house, and their political predecessors, responsible for this unholy alliance.

The spur of this rebellion was in the census of 1860. It is a memorable fact, which has been noted often, that in 1820, when the census disclosed the truth as to the growing power of the North, as compared with that of the South, and again in 1830, and again in 1850, we were on the brink of a revolution. At these several epochs, this great fact appeared with full force, and Southern leaders were aroused for the moment in the hope that they could strike down in some way or other the power of freedom upon this continent. In 1860, they saw it was impossible for them to continue in the ascendant, and therefore they sought a separation.

But, Mr. Speaker, the South has been guided by men of sense and capacity. They did not enter upon this revolution without counting its cost. They estimated the cost upon the basis of facts which were in their possession, and the evidence which was in their possession tended to this result: that there would be no war; that separation could be effected without a contest of blood on their soil. In the Peace Congress, it was the constant cry of the secessionists, "Give us the assurance, radical men of the North, that there shall be no war." And it was there, and at that moment, that Northern men failed to assert the great truth which was in the hearts of the people, that, if these men persisted in the attempt to secure secession, there would be war. I believe, if Northern men and men from the border States had been faithful to truth and duty, the calamity of secession would have been averted. Mr. Seddon, the present Secretary of War for the rebellious States, occupied fifteen minutes of the time of the convention, after a motion was made to adjourn *sine die*, in imploring the members of that Congress to give them the assurance that there should be no war. The South believed that there would be no war. How came they to entertain that belief? They knew that we had two and a half men for every one at the South. They knew that we were vastly their superiors in all the material resources of war. How came they to believe that we would not exercise the powers which we had? I can explain it only upon one ground, the ground disclosed in the letter of Franklin Pierce, the ground disclosed in the message of James Buchanan of December, 1860, that, if there was war, it would be in the North.

I will take the responsibility of reading an extract from a speech made in the Peace Congress by a Northern man, — Mr. Stockton, of New Jersey. I have copied it from the notes prepared by Mr. Chittenden, and they correspond with my own minutes made at the time, and with my recollection of the remarks made by Mr. Stockton. He said: —

> "I know that this Union cannot be dissolved without a struggle. Will you hasten the time when we shall begin to shed each other's blood? Force fifteen States! Why, you cannot force New Jersey alone. Force the South! Why, they won't stop to count forces. Neither side can be frightened. Don't think of it. You cannot frighten the North any more than you can a Roman soldier. You cannot frighten the South. You cannot frighten either any easier than the chieftain whom the Roman poet has immortalized.
>
> "When men meet to save their country, they must be prepared to offer up every thing, to sacrifice their lives, if neeessary. How can men stop for platforms which will destroy their country?

"I appeal to the brotherhood, the fraternity, of the North. My friends, peace or war is in your hands. You hold the keys of peace or ruin. You tell us not to hasten this matter. Well, you don't realize the facts, the consequences. No one does. Do you talk here about regiments for invasion, for coercion? You, gentlemen of the North, you know better. I know better. For every regiment raised there for coercion, there will be another regiment raised for resistance to coercion. If no other State will raise them, remember New Jersey.

"Pause, gentlemen. Stop where you are. You will bring strife to your own doors, to your very hearthstones, — bloody, desperate strife. The war will be in your own homes, among your own families. Under ordinary circumstances, you would hesitate. If the question was about the tariff, you would hesitate, and look at the awful consequences."

It was, as I verily believe, such declarations as this which led the South to engage in a mad crusade for the destruction of the government. They naturally supposed, that, after a very short period of commotion, the North would accept what they demanded, — a separation of the Union. They failed: the North could not afford to see this Union dissolved. It had not the power to submit to its dissolution. Gentlemen upon this floor and elsewhere, I apprehend, make a great mistake when they suppose that the Union depends on the Constitution. The Constitution, in its preamble, declares that the object for which it was framed was "to form a more perfect Union," implying a previous existence as a Union; and we know that the articles of confederation implied also the existence of a Union. The Declaration of Independence, in its first sentence, sets forth the doctrine of the unity of the colonies: "When in the course of human events, it becomes necessary for one people to dissolve the political bands which have connected them with another, and to assume among the powers of the earth the separate and equal station to which the laws of nature and of nature's God entitle them," &c.; thus assuming in 1776 the doctrine of the unity of the colonies, of the unity of the continent. That unity cannot be broken. It is now disturbed; it cannot be destroyed.

The only question, then, in which we have any voice, is, whether we shall pursue a policy by which the Union may be restored on the basis of freedom, or whether, like cowards, we are to lie down and suffer the ruthless hand of despotism to triumph over us. Either a republican government under the Constitution of the United States, or a despotism guided by Jefferson Davis and his successors, is to be the rule of public life on this continent. Sir, whatever differences of opinion we may have as to the policy which has governed the administration in the conduct of the war, it cannot be doubted that, at the present time, as in the beginning of this controversy, the chief hope of the rebels is drawn from the assurances given by men belonging to the Democratic party. The confidence of the South to-day is not so much in the armies which they control, as in the possible ascendency of a party in the North by whose success agreements, conditions, and arrangements may be made, and their independence recognized.

Gentlemen upon the other side of the house indicate that they do not accept this as true. I make here a qualification. The gentleman from New York, from the fifth district [Mr. Fernando Wood], whom I do not now see in his seat, says that there can be no such thing as a war Democrat. I do not agree with him. There are war Democrats in this House, and thousands of thêm in the country. What I do say is, that there can be no such party as a Democratic party in favor of the prosecution of the war. It is illogical that there should be a Democratic party in favor of the war. The administration, the Union party, is in favor of its prosecution. Whenever a logical issue is made against that party, it must be made upon the ground that the war is not to be prosecuted. How can a man in this crisis of the country's life, who regards the salvation of the Union as of more consequence than any thing else, differ from those who support the administration in the prosecution of the war? They only have a logical ground of difference who believe that the war is wrong, and that it ought at once to cease. Therefore it follows, that gentlemen on the other side of the house who believe that the war ought to be prosecuted, can, in the nature of things, find no efficient means for carrying out their views, except in allying themselves with those who also believe that the war should be prosecuted. The men in any party who have logic can control that party; and therefore, without going into any inquiry whether the gentlemen who are for peace upon that side of the house have more capacity than the gentlemen who are for war, I still predict that the gentlemen who are for peace will control. They have a logical foundation on which to stand, and they will guide the Democratic party. There may be war Democrats; but a Democratic party in favor of the prosecution of the war, cannot be maintained permanently.

It is necessary further, as it seems to me, that we should understand the relations subsisting between the States and the national government. I cannot discuss this subject at length. It is apparent from an examination of the Constitution, that the States are supreme in certain things, the general government is supreme in certain other things, and finally that there are in the Constitution two tests, at least, which establish the supremacy and sovereignty of the nation over the States. One of these tests is in that provision by which the general government guarantees to every State a republican form of government. There is no corresponding guarantee by the States to the Union. The States have not undertaken to guarantee to the nation a republican form of government; showing that the national government is supreme, and that it is assumed to be able to maintain its own institutions and authority. There is also another provision, requiring every officer of each State to take an oath to support the Constitution of the United States; and the Constitution of the United States is made the supreme law of the land, any thing in any State constitution or any law to the contrary notwithstanding. In these two particulars, as in many others, the Constitution of the United States is supreme. The States are sovereign in their spheres, but they are not supreme;

and the power of the general government is defined in the Constitution itself.

I could not but be amused at the gentleman from New York [Mr. Fernando Wood], who examined the meaning of the words "compact" and "federal" for the purpose of giving the House information as to what the Constitution of the United States means. It so happens that neither of these words is used in the Constitution of the United States, and therefore, whatever may be their meaning, they throw no light on the Constitution itself. But, in order to ascertain what the powers conferred on this government are, we must go to the Constitution. Calling it a compact does not make it any more or less strong than if you call it a constitution or a league or an agreement. Thomas Hobbes has said, "Words are wise men's counters, they do but reckon with them; but they are the money of fools."

I now proceed to consider the condition of the rebellious States with reference to the general government. Gentlemen on the other side of the house assert that the States still exist; that all that is necessary is that officers shall be elected to fill the offices, and then these States are at once in the Union.

The gentleman from Pennsylvania [Mr. Stevens] maintains, as I understand, that these States are out of the Union, that their territory is alien territory, and that we are making war against alien enemies. I do not admit either of these positions to be true. I feel quite sure that these eleven once-existing States are no longer States of the Union. The evidence on which I rely in support of this position is found, first, in the declaration made by the authorities of those States, that they no longer exist as States of the American Union. Next, we find that for three years and more they have been resisting the authority of the government, and have been carrying on a war against it. It is absurd to say that States or people are a part of the government under the Constitution, and entitled to constitutional rights and privileges, when they have been thus carrying on war against the government.

Next apply the tests of the Constitution. The Constitution provides that no State shall raise armies. These eleven States — if they are States in the American Union — have been for three years engaged in raising armies. The Constitution declares that the States shall not enter into any treaty, alliance, or confederation with each other. These eleven States are, as is notorious, in alliance and confederation with each other against this government, and have been so confederated together for three years. The Constitution requires that the officers of each State shall take an oath to support the Constitution of the United States; while it is notorious that every officer exercising authority or jurisdiction has taken an oath absolving himself, as far as he could do so be an oath, from all allegiance to this government. Therefore, applying these constitutional tests to the eleven once-existing States, we find that there is no response tending to show that they are States in the American Union.

Nor do I admit that the people in the rebellious States are aliens. They are not of any other country, they are not of any other legal jurisdiction, but they are within the jurisdiction of the Union. Three years ago, as all admit, they were a portion of the Union; and, although they have been carrying on a war, that war has not thus far been successful, their independence has not been acknowledged by us, nor has it been recognized by any other nation. They therefore are not aliens. They are, to be sure, public enemies; but they are not alien enemies.

Then what is the condition of the people occupying the territory once included in these eleven States? As I believe, and as I attempted to set forth in certain resolutions which I submitted to the House a few weeks ago, these States as political organizations which this government can recognize, have by their own will ceased to exist. I then submitted the views which I entertain upon that point, to the effect that the existence of a State is a fact within the control of the people themselves, and cannot be influenced by any extraneous power whatever, and that therefore these States, by the will of the people thereof, have ceased to exist as political organizations forming or constituting a part of the American Union.

What, then, remains? Unquestionably, it remains true, that the Government of the United States has legal jurisdiction over this territory and over the people who occupy it; but, admitting that fact, it is an absurdity to say that these States still exist, and that the people thereof may, without our consent, elect officers and send representatives to this body, and senators to the other branch of Congress. I refer, in this connection, to a remark quoted in the "Federalist," from Montesquieu: "Greece was undone as soon as the King of Macedon obtained a seat among the Amphictyons."

Gentlemen upon the other side of the house propose that our enemies may come into this hall and into that of the other branch of Congress, and take their seats. What happened to Greece when the King of Macedon obtained a seat in the Amphictyonic Council will surely happen to us as a nation when we concede any portion of this government to our enemies. Yet that is the proposition of gentlemen on the other side of the House, if their position has any force whatever.

I suppose it will not be denied, that we have the right to fix rules and regulations for the admission of new States. It certainly cannot be denied on this side of the House. It would be a monstrous proposition, that the people of a Territory — I speak now of Territories acknowledging their allegiance to this government, as Nevada or Nebraska — can frame a constitution such as pleases them, and secure, as an absolute right, their admission into the Union as a State, without any judgment being passed upon that question by Congress. The fact that no State was ever admitted into the Union, except by a vote of Congress, implies that, for any reason that may be satisfactory to Congress, such admission could be refused.

If then, the application of a Territory to be admitted into the Union as a State may be refused, it may be refused for any reason which, in the judgment of Congress, may be deemed sufficient. The reason rests in the mind of Congress. Congress will naturally consider the constitution, the institutions, of the proposed State, its extent of territory, and any other circumstances which may properly come within their view, and then decide whether the Territory shall be received as a State into the Union.

If this be true in reference to a Territory, and if it be also true, as I believe it is, that these States as States have ceased to exist, they can only be restored to this Union as States upon the occurrence of two events. The people of the proposed State, a majority of them, as is required by this bill, must apply for admission into the Union as a State, having first declared their loyalty to the Union and to the Constitution of the United States. When a State shall so apply for admission, with a proposed constitution for a State government that shall conform to the Constitution of the United States, it will then be competent for Congress to say whether it shall be admitted or not. Congress exercises this discretion according to its best judgment, and from its decision there can be no appeal.

This bill fixes three unalterable conditions precedent to such application, without a compliance with which no one of these once-existing States can re-appear in the Union.

It is asserted on the other side of the House, that we have no right to make such conditions precedent to the organization of a State government, there being a provision in the Constitution that the United States shall guarantee to each State a republican form of government; and State governments having existed and been recognized as republican in form by Congress, in which the institution of slavery existed, we have no right to change our opinion as to what a republican form of government is. It is at that point exactly where we differ. I say that the question as to what constitutes a republican form of government is under the Constitution always open to the judgment of Congress. I do not mean to say that Congress can appoint a committee of inspection or scrutiny in reference to the Constitution of Kentucky, for example. Kentucky having been admitted to the Union, the question for the time being was decided, and her Constitution and form of government are recognized as republican. But suppose a controversy should arise in Kentucky, as in Rhode Island two and twenty years ago, and a party by a majority should establish another government, frame another constitution, and exercise authority under that constitution, and there should be a conflict, then the question would be brought before Congress to investigate the matter whether either or both were republican in form. Certainly not whether the old constitution or new is republican in form according to the judgment of our ancestors, not whether it is republican according to the writings of any commentator; but if, in the opinion of Congress, it should appear that one of these is republican and the other is not, then Congress would set up the republican government, even though the old government should be destroyed thereby.

While I do not claim for Congress the right of scrutiny of the governments of existing States, yet, if the question is forced upon Congress in such a manner that it cannot be avoided, then a decision is to be made. From that decision there is no appeal. The Supreme Court, in the Rhode-Island case, held, that, when Congress decided the question of the character of the State government, whether it was republican in form or not, that decision could not be investigated, could not be examined, could not be controlled by any other department or tribunal. We mean by this bill to give notice to the people occupying the territory of the eleven once-existing States, that, if they shall frame new constitutions, they must come here with governments republican in form, according to our ideas.

Gentlemen on the other side have taunted us with the charge that we have changed our policy in reference to the object of this war; that it is no longer for the preservation of the Union, but for the emancipation of the slave. I deny this; but, if the policy of the war has been changed, it is not the first time in the history of human affairs that similar changes have taken place. I remember that it is the undeviating testimony of history, that from the opening of the colonial controversy in 1764 to the month of September, 1774, less than eight months prior to the massacre of Lexington, there was not a paper, there was not a public man, there was not a representative assembly, that did not declare that it was the settled purpose of the people of these colonies to maintain the union with Great Britain. Our ancestors denied again and again the charge made that they contemplated independence. But on the 4th of July, 1776, they declared their independence of the mother country. Events had changed opinions, and opinions had changed the public policy. While we have not changed our policy in regard to prosecuting the war for the purpose of restoring the Union, we do mean, that, when it is restored, it shall be restored on republican principles, and that there shall be no new State admitted into the Union from the unoccupied western territory, or from Mexico, or by the re-establishment of regular governments in the eleven rebellious States, that is not republican in form, according to our ideas. The "Federalist" says: —

> "There are two methods of curing the mischiefs of faction: the one, by removing its causes; the other, by controlling its effects.
>
> "There are, again, two methods of removing the causes of faction: the one by destroying the liberty which is essential to its existence; the other, by giving to every citizen the same opinions, the same passions, and the same interests."

We purpose to cure the evil of this faction by removing its cause, — slavery; and to give to every citizen of the republic "the same opinions, the same passions, and the same interests," in reference to human freedom.

And we are to maintain the doctrine on this continent, I trust, that, wherever slavery exists, there republicanism is not; that, wherever slavery exists, there a republican form of government, under the Constitution, cannot be. Hence we give notice in this bill to all the inhabitants of those revolted districts, that they may form State governments, and be admitted into this Union, upon certain conditions, the chief of which is that involuntary servitude shall cease to exist.

The argument upon this bill, as far as it depends upon me, is now concluded; and we approach the moment when the judgment of this House is to be expressed. The discussion in which we have been engaged has not elicited marked attention in this hall, nor has it attracted in an unusual degree the notice of the country. Yet in this measure lie the germs of a new civilization for one-half of a continent. The area of the eleven rebellious States, for whose guidance we now establish a fundamental law, is twice as great as the area of the thirteen colonies; and it is nearly equal to that of England, France, Spain, and the empire of Austria, combined.

If our arms shall be successful, — and of this I cannot doubt, unless Divine Providence shall reverse the order of things for purposes inscrutable to mortal eyes, — this vast territory is by this great act dedicated to freedom for ever. With freedom, there will come a new civilization. This new civilization will be marked by an interpretation and preaching of the Holy Scriptures uninfluenced by the lusts and ambitions and designs of a slaveholding aristocracy; and it will be illustrated by a system of free schools for the education of the children of all the people, whether black or white. Under the new civilization, labor will be honored and rewarded; the immense landed estates will be broken up; and the children of poverty hitherto, whether white or black, will be endowed by the law and by the fruits of their own industry with a portion of the soil; and thus they will become the supporters and defenders of the country, contributing to its enrichment and power.

There is one feature of the bill which does not receive my approval, and to which I assent only in deference to what I suppose is the present judgment of this House and of the country. I speak of the limitation of the elective franchise to white male citizens. The right of suffrage is not a natural right, but it is the highest among political rights. No community which denies the right of suffrage to any considerable number of its adult male inhabitants can ever be safe from intestine commotion; for, wherever this right is so denied, the people cannot be safe or even free from oppression. And, even if a community in which the right of suffrage is thus limited should be free from actual oppression, still the government could not escape the suspicions and charges which result from an unjust distribution of political power. In free countries, the rights of the people are frequently acquired, and they are generally preserved, by the ballot. When the ballot fails, the resort is to the sword. When you deny the ballot to one-third or one-half of the people of the vast territory covered by the provisions of this bill, what do you leave for them, or offer to them, but a resort to the sword as the means of removing or redressing the grievances of which they are already the foredoomed victims?

I had indulged the hope, until recently, that this House would recognize the political rights of the colored race, by securing the elective franchise to certain classes, or at least to a single class of those who hereafter should enjoy the protection of the Constitution. The vote upon the amendment of the Senate to the bill establishing the Territory of Montana dissipated at once, and for the present, this hope. The country will speedily revise our proceedings in this particular. Mark the progress of events! It is not yet two years since you were willing to contribute to the cause of the Union by the emancipation of the negro. I do not now speak of gentlemen on the other side of the House. I address myself to the friends of the administration.

But now the President's proclamation of emancipation is accepted with signal unanimity by the people of the country. It has already received the considerate judgment of mankind; and may we not also reverently believe that it receives the constant favor of Almighty God? I am aware that gentlemen on the other side of the house still utter their accustomed denunciations of the measure; but their words are like the wonderful missile of the South-Sea Islander, which cuts the air fiercely, and then falls harmlessly at the feet of him from whose hand the weapon was hurled.

The people accept the freedom of the negro; having recognized his right to freedom, they bid him to do service for the country. When he has served the country in the field, the justice of the nation will guarantee to him the power to maintain his rights in civil life. At first, you remanded the fugitive negro to his rebel master. Then, and reluctantly, you accepted the services of the negro upon the condition that he should dig in the trenches, and thus relieve the white soldier of the most arduous portion of his labors. Then, if he could still be classed as a laborer, you would allow him to perform the duty of a soldier in garrison and in pestilential regions; but at last you have recognized his manhood and given expression to a public sense of justice by allowing him the position, pay, and emoluments of a soldier of the republic.

Thus are events our masters; and thus does the country hesitate, even in the presence of these events, to perform those acts of justice which are due to one race, and necessary for the salvation of the other. When, and by what means, and for what period of time, do you expect to set up and maintain loyal governments in the rebellious districts of the Union, unless you confer the elective franchise upon the negro? The military power must at some moment not remote be withdrawn. The remnant of the dominant class will be powerful for a generation. There is a large number of poor whites, unaccustomed to independent thought or to independent action. The colored people are loyal, and in many States they are almost the only people who are trustworthy supporters of the Union. Will you reject them? I ask whether you will reject the civil and political power of the colored people in South Carolina, for example. If I could direct the force of public sentiment and the policy of this government, South Carolina, as a State with her ancient name, should never re-appear in this Union. Georgia deserves a like fate. When the Constitution was formed, she united herself with South Carolina, and forced the recognition of the institution of slavery. They are the two States that are responsible for the continuance of this institution. I appeal to gentlemen who have examined our colonial records, for the proof of the assertion I make, that in North Carolina, in Virginia, Maryland, and in every one of the now free States then existing, declaration after declaration was made against the institution of slavery. It was condemned in Maryland, in Virginia, and in North Carolina. South Carolina and Georgia breathed into it the breath of life; and, if I had the power, neither of those States should re-appear in the Union. Florida does not deserve a name in this Union. What then? Let these three States be set apart as the home of the negro. Invite him there, by giving to him local political power. Give him the right of suffrage in those States, and the colored population, as rapidly as it can be spared from the industrial pursuits of the North, will aggregate upon the shores of the Atlantic and the Gulf of Mexico. Give them local self-government, and let them defend themselves as a portion of this republic.

[Here the hammer fell.]

Mr. Ashley. — I ask that, by unanimous consent, the gentleman's time shall be extended for ten minutes.

No objection was made.

Mr. Boutwell. — I do not, in my place here, ask that in Kentucky or Maryland, or in any one of the northern loyal States where a negro population exists, the right of suffrage shall be given to them; but in the rebel districts, and especially in South

Carolina, Georgia, and Florida, I would provide for the right of suffrage to colored persons. They have earned it by their services in the field; and there is a degree of injustice in asking a man to peril his life in the cause of the country and in defence of institutions in the creation and conduct of which he has no voice whatever. There is an injustice in this. It cannot stand the test of time nor the scrutiny of civilization.

Sir, great misrepresentations have been made, not only with reference to the negroes in this country, but with reference to the experiment of emancipation in the British West Indies. I will read a few statistics, which, in their results, show what has been accomplished by the black population of the West Indies emancipated by the British Government less than thirty years ago. I venture to anticipate what I have to say by expressing my belief, that, with the exception of Greece, there are no people on the face of the earth who have made more progress than the emancipated slaves in some of the British West Indies. What have they done? Take, for example, Barbadoes. They have opened schools; and, out of a population of 140,000, 7,000 children are in the schools, and they have over 3,000 landholders. In Antigua, with a population of 35,000, they have more than 10,000 children in the day and Sunday schools, and 5,000 landholders among those who were formerly slaves. In Tobago there are 2,500 landholders, in a population of 15,000. In St. Lucia, with 25,000 inhabitants, there are more than 2,000 land-owners. And even in Jamaica, which is an exception to the West-

India islands in the matter of prosperity since emancipation, in a population of 400,000 they have 50,000 freeholders. These returns are for 1860.

So, then, if you test that people who came from slavery and barbarism in 1834 by the two tests of primary civilization, the cultivation of the soil and the education of children, they have made great progress. But it is worth while to remember that Barbadoes is one of the most populous portions of the globe. Of the one hundred and six thousand acres of land, one hundred thousand are under cultivation; and the price of the cultivated land is from four to five hundred dollars an acre.

If it is shown in a single instance that emancipated slaves have been able to take care of themselves and make progress, though there may be twenty instances of failure, still the one instance of success demonstrates their capacity, and the failures are to be attributed to misfortune and the influence of circumstances.

The dependencies of Guiana, Trinidad, Barbadoes, and Antigua, previous to emancipation, produced 187,000,000 pounds of sugar, and in 1856–57 they produced annually 265,000,000, showing a gain of nearly 78,000,000 pounds a year; and their imports went up from $8,840,000 to $14,600,000 a year.

Mr. Hincks, the late Governor-General of the Windward Islands, states, from his own knowledge and observation, that, on an estate in Barbadoes, ninety blacks perform the work formerly done by two hundred and thirty slaves; and that the produce of each laborer during slavery was 1,043 pounds of sugar, and the produce of each laborer since emancipation is 3,660 pounds. He also states that the cost per hogshead under slavery was £10 sterling, while in 1858 it was produced at a cost of £4 sterling. In Antigua, with a population of 35,000, they contribute equal to £1 sterling each by taxation, for the support of religious, charitable, and educational institutions. I assert that the experience of the British West Indies has demonstrated the capacity of the negro race.

I ask for this people justice. In the presence of these great events; in this exigency when the life of the nation is in peril, and when every reflecting person must see that the cause of that peril is injustice to the negro, — I ask that we shall now do justice to his race. They are four million. They will remain on this continent. They cannot be expatriated. They await the order of Providence. Their home is here. It is our duty to elevate them, to provide for their civilization, for their enlightenment, that they may enjoy the fruits of their labor and their capacity. The nation which is not just shall finally

> "Stand
> Childless and crownless in her voiceless woe,
> An empty urn within her withered hand."

NOTE. — The following resolutions, referred to in the foregoing speech, were presented to the House of Representatives on the sixteenth day of February, 1864: —

"*Resolved,* That the Committee on the Rebellious States be instructed to consider and report upon the expediency of recommending to this House the adoption of the following

"*Declaration of Opinions:*

"In view of the present condition of the country, and especially in view of the recent signal successes of the national arms promising a speedy overthrow of the rebellion, this House makes the following declaration of opinions concerning the institution of slavery in the States and parts of States engaged in the rebellion, and embraced in the proclamation of emancipation issued by the President on the first day of January, A.D. 1863; and also concerning the relations now subsisting between the people of such States and parts of States on the one side, and the American Union on the other.

"*It is therefore declared* (as the opinion of the House of Representatives), that the institution of slavery was the cause of the present rebellion, and that the destruction of slavery in the rebellious States is an efficient means of weakening the power of the rebels; that the President's proclamation, whereby all persons heretofore held as slaves in such States and parts of States have been declared free, has had the effect to increase the power of the Union, and to diminish the power of its enemies; that the freedom of such persons was desirable and just in itself, and an efficient means by which the government was to be maintained, and its authority re-established in all the territory and over all the people within the legal jurisdiction of the United States; that it is the duty of the government and of loyal men everywhere to do what may be practicable for the enforcement of the proclamation, in order to secure in fact, as well as by the forms of law, the extinction of slavery in such States and parts of States; and, finally, that it is the paramount duty of the government and of all loyal men to labor for the restoration of the American Union upon the basis of freedom.

"*And this House does further declare,* That a State can exist or cease to exist only by the will of the people within its limits, and that it cannot be created or destroyed by the external force or opinion of other States, or even by the judgment or action of the nation itself; that a State, when created by the will of its people, can become a member of the American Union only by its own organized action and the concurrent action of the existing national government; that, when a State has been admitted to the Union, no vote, resolution, ordinance, or proceeding on its part, however formal in character or vigorously sustained, can deprive the national government of the legal jurisdiction and sovereignty over the territory and people of such State which existed previous to the act of admission, or which were acquired thereby; that the effect of the so-called acts, resolutions, and ordinances of secession adopted by the eleven States engaged in the present rebellion is, and can only be, to destroy those political organizations as States, while the legal and constitutional jurisdiction and authority of the national government over the people and territory remain unimpaired; that these several communities can be organized into States only by the will of the loyal people, expressed freely and in the absence of all coercion; that States so organized can become States of the American Union only when they shall have applied for admission, and their admission shall have been authorized by the existing national government; that, when a people have organized a State upon the basis of allegiance to the Union and applied for admission, the character of the institutions of such proposed State may constitute a sufficient justification for granting or rejecting such application; and, inasmuch as experience has shown that the existence of human slavery is incompatible with a republican form of government in the several States or in the United States, and inconsistent with the peace, prosperity, and unity of the nation, it is the duty of the people, and of all men in authority, to resist the admission of slave States wherever organized within the jurisdiction of the national government."

THE ENROLMENT OF TROOPS AND THE PROCLAMATION OF EMANCIPATION.

DEBATE IN THE HOUSE OF REPRESENTATIVES, JUNE 25, 1864.

MR. BOUTWELL. — My chief purpose in desiring to obtain the floor is to state to the House the reasons by which I have been controlled thus far in refusing to vote for the proposition to repeal the commutation clause of the Enrolment Act. In the first place, I have given the vote in deference to what I suppose to be the public sentiment of the country. I understand that substantially — not exactly, perhaps, but substantially — the calls for troops by the President have been met. I thought, to be sure, from the observations of the gentleman from Ohio [Mr. Garfield], made this morning, that he supposed that because the Representatives on this floor from Massachusetts had refused to support the repeal of the commutation clause, as recommended by the Military Committee, they were prepared to indorse the observation which that gentleman made on the previous day, when this subject was under discussion, — an observation which I thought unfortunate; an observation which I thought calculated to alarm the country; an observation which I thought calculated to give strength, courage, and confidence to its enemies; an observation which, if my memory served me, to the very last words and the very last letter used, I would not repeat here or elsewhere, even in the way of quotation. I thought, also, when he was referring to Massachusetts, that he supposed, inasmuch as we took the responsibility of differing from the judgment of the Military Committee, that therefore we were prepared to abandon this war, to sacrifice the country, and to involve it in irretrievable ruin. If it was his intention to suggest to the House and the country, that Massachusetts, or a man of hers who has a right to speak on her behalf, here or elsewhere, had come to any such conclusion, then he misunderstood, if he did not intentionally misrepresent, that State.

Mr. Garfield. — Do the gentleman's remarks apply to me?

Mr. Boutwell. — To no other man upon this floor.

Mr. Garfield. — I wish to say that I have made no reference whatever to Massachusetts; have never in my life intimated, by any word I have uttered, that Massachusetts was derelict of duty, for, if I love any State in the Union better than my own, it is Massachusetts; and I trust the gentleman from Massachusetts will not do me the wrong of intimating that I intentionally or unintentionally said any thing upon this floor disrespectful to that State. What I said in my closing remarks before the House, when this subject was last up, and which have been referred to this morning and criticised, I believe to be true. The same thing has been declared in higher places than mine, and we have got to meet it. It is courageous to meet it, and cowardly not to meet it.

Mr. BOUTWELL. — I judge no man, but I was able to connect the observations made upon one occasion with those made upon another. The gentleman recollects the remark made the previous day, which was an expression of his opinion of the effect of a certain vote given, in which vote the delegation from Massachusetts participated; and I recollect that to-day he called the special attention of this House and of the country to the previous history of Massachusetts, and to her Conscription Act of 1693. I may have erred in the inference to be drawn from those remarks; and, if I have so erred, I have done injustice to the gentleman; if not, the remark I made is but just.

Now, sir, the position of Massachusetts, as I understand it, is this: she does not desire a rigid conscription either of her own citizens or of the people of the country, so long as the war can be prosecuted vigorously and with reasonable hope of success by other means. What we say, and what we present to the House and the country, is the great fact, that thus far we have substantially complied with the requisitions of the President for men and money. If there has been no failure under such circumstances as to indicate, as a consequence of that failure, our inability to prosecute the war, then we ought not to inaugurate a policy which gives offence even to one man. Not merely should we hesitate to inaugurate the policy proposed, in deference to opinion upon this side of the House, but we are bound to consider the sentiments even of those who differ with us upon matters of public policy, but who are in favor of prosecuting the war. When the country is no longer able to carry on the war without a rigid conscription, we shall not hesitate to accept the necessity as the means of restoring the Union and preserving the national life. But, at the same time, I say here, what I have already said to many of my constituents,—and it is a declaration by which I mean to be bound so long as I have a voice either as a citizen or a representative,—that nothing in men or money or means shall be withheld from the government: all shall be yielded according to the necessity existing.

Sir, if the gentleman from Ohio [Mr. Garfield] had read the whole history of Massachusetts, he would have known that, in the Indian war of 1675 and 1676, we sacrificed one-twentieth of our inhabitants, and that every twentieth building in the colonies of New Plymouth and Massachusetts was laid in ashes. Be it ever remembered that that war ended without a treaty of peace. It is the only war on this continent that was ever brought to a conclusion without such a treaty. The children of the men who made these sacrifices for the defence of their homes will make equal sacrifices for the defence of the nationality of the country, looking to a termination of this war when there shall be no treaty of peace. When I say there shall be no treaty of peace, I do not wish to be understood that this is a war of extermination either of the blacks or whites. I believe that only one thing is necessary on the part of the Southern people, and that is that they shall abandon the institution of slavery. When they shall have laid down their arms and abandoned that institution, which, as I believe, was the source and is the support of the war, then we shall yield to them their positions in the Union, accord to them all their local and State rights, and maintain their position and rights in the Union as we maintain our own. But, sir, until this war is ended, there can be no compromise, no arrangement, no treaty.

I am not disposed to despair at all of the republic, or of the power of the government to maintain itself. The gentleman from Kentucky [Mr. Mallory] said this morning that the whole policy of the country was changed by the proclamation of the President; and he attributed that proclamation to the meeting of the Governors of certain States at Altoona. I am not here to be put upon the witness-stand; but it so happens that I have the means of knowing that the proclamation of September, 1862, was entirely independent of, and antecedent to, the meeting of the Governors at Altoona. The meeting of the Governors had no connection with the proclamation. The gentleman from Kentucky should remember, that, prior to the issuing of that proclamation, we had met with but few successes, and that we had endured many, many reverses. Lee had battled for four days under the fortifications of the capital, and had finally crossed the Potomac into Maryland. It was not until the country put itself on the side of justice that it had a right to expect the favor of Divine Providence, or any of those successes which have rendered this war glorious in the cause of freedom, truth, and justice.

Mr. Mallory. — Will the gentleman state when that convention of Governors assembled at Altoona?

Mr. BOUTWELL. — I think it assembled at Altoona previous to the 22d of September; but I assert, as within my own knowledge, that the issuing of the proclamation was determined upon previous to the meeting at Altoona.

Mr. MALLORY. — Can the gentleman inform me when the issuing of that proclamation was determined upon?

Mr. BOUTWELL. — I cannot go far in this matter. I assert distinctly the fact which is within my own knowledge, that the President, previous to the meeting of the Governors at Altoona, had decided, in a certain contingency, which happened upon the Wednesday preceding the 22d of September, to issue the proclamation; and therefore the inference I draw is in contravention of the declaration of the gentleman from Kentucky, that that proclamation was the result of the meeting of the Governors at Altoona.

Mr. MALLORY. — Will the gentleman tell us the contingency on the happening of which that proclamation was to be issued?

Mr. BOUTWELL. — I said, Mr. Speaker, when I mentioned this fact, that I was not to be put upon the stand as a witness. I have made a statement as of a fact within my own knowledge, and history will confirm the statement.

Mr. MALLORY. — If the gentleman from Massachusetts does not wish to answer the question, or to state the fact, I will not insist.

Mr. BOUTWELL. — I have done nothing more than this, — to put my statement of a fact, which I assert to be within my own knowledge, against the declaration of the gentleman from Kentucky, that the proclamation of emancipation, or the monitory proclamation of emancipation, was issued in consequence of the meeting of Governors at Altoona.

Mr. MALLORY. — We know that the President himself stated, on the 13th of that month, that he had no idea of issuing such a proclamation, and that he argued against issuing it. I want to know from the gentleman from Massachusetts whether it was between the 13th and 22d, and if so, at what point between these two periods the President had prepared the proclamation, and had determined to issue it upon a certain contingency. I would also like to know what that contingency was.

Mr. BOUTWELL. — The gentleman from Kentucky is good at questioning, but I have to keep myself within the limits which I stated.

Mr. DAWES. — Courtesy is an exchangeable commodity.

Mr. BOUTWELL. — I trust I shall lose nothing by my courtesy.

Mr. MALLORY. — Of course not. I decline to ask any more questions.

Mr. BOUTWELL. — The gentleman from Kentucky has made some observations in disparagement of negro troops. I have entertained the opinion in relation to this whole question of emancipating the negroes, and putting them into the service of the government, that it was a legitimate means of diminishing the power of the enemy and of augmenting our own. I have never thought it necessary to inquire how far the loss of a negro slave diminished the power of the rebels to carry on this war. I dare say the gentleman from Kentucky has been called upon seriously to contemplate that question. I have only felt that in some degree, I cannot say how great, it diminished the power of the rebels to continue the contest. Therefore I said, dismissing entirely the question of justice and humanity, if you please, that it is properly within the policy of the government to emancipate the slaves as a means of diminishing the power of the rebels. When the question arose as to using the emancipated negro in the service of the country, I said again, it is not possible that a negro, who has contributed to the support of the South, should be unable to do something for the enlargement of the powers and for the augmentation of the resources of this government.

I am therefore in favor of his going into the service to dig trenches, to garrison forts, to shoulder the musket, and to serve the country in the ranks as a soldier, and to do more whenever and wherever there shall be an opportunity, and he shall exhibit the capacity, for doing more.

The gentleman from Kentucky made some observations to prove that the negro did not fight well. There are many specific facts to the contrary. I happen to have a letter, written by a captain who belongs to the Twenty-second Regiment, United States colored troops, which was in the fight before Petersburg, on the 15th of this month. He says, "My second sergeant was killed in the first charge, just before we reached the rebel works; and altogether the regiment lost one hundred and thirty-three killed and wounded;" showing conclusively that the colored troops did not hesitate to put themselves in exposed positions, and to maintain themselves in those positions.

Mr. PENDLETON. — Will the gentleman allow me to ask him one question before he passes from the subject he is now discussing?

Mr. BOUTWELL. — Certainly.

Mr. PENDLETON. — I desire to ask the gentleman whether he knows when the proclamation of the President was finally agreed upon; not when it was issued, for we all know that; but I have no doubt the gentleman knows when it was decided upon.

Mr. BOUTWELL. — The gentleman from Ohio ascribes to me a knowledge which I have never claimed.

Mr. PENDLETON. — He has given the House and the country to understand that it was agreed upon before the time it was issued.

Mr. BOUTWELL. — I have not given the House or the country to understand that it was *agreed* upon at any time.

Mr. PENDLETON. — When the gentleman says that it was agreed upon or determined upon that it should be issued before a certain time, as I certainly understood him to say, — knows it was determined upon, or that the President desired to issue it prior to the Wednesday before the 22d of September, when it was issued, — and that its being issued depended upon a contingency which was expected to happen, and did happen, upon that Wednesday, I desire him to answer, if he is at liberty to answer, and, if he is not, to say so, what that contingency was.

Mr. BOUTWELL. — I gave notice in the outset that

I did not mean to be drawn into any explanation beyond the statement which I made.

Mr. Pendleton. —I desire to know, then, whether it was the gentleman's purpose, when he made the announcement that he would not be put upon the witness-stand, to simply state to the House such parts of a transaction, which he says was within his own knowledge, as he may see fit, and that he will not be induced to state any thing beyond?

Mr. Boutwell. — Exactly.

Mr. Pendleton. — The gentleman then knows when it was intended to be issued, but declines to state it to the House.

Mr. Blaine. — I hope, Mr. Speaker, that the gentleman from Massachusetts who holds the floor [Mr. Boutwell] will consent to be interrupted long enough to permit me to address an inquiry to the gentleman from Kentucky [Mr. Mallory] who has just addressed the House. I understood that gentleman to assert, and to reiterate with great emphasis, that the emancipation proclamation was issued in consequence of the pressure brought to bear upon the President, by the meeting of the Governors at Altoona, in the autumn of 1862.

Mr. Mallory. — I said it was issued in consequence of the pressure brought to bear upon him by these Governors.

Mr. Blaine. — Will the gentleman state at what date the President's proclamation was issued?

Mr. Mallory. — On the 22d of September.

Mr. Blaine. — Will the gentleman state further at what time the meeting of the Governors took place at Altoona?

Mr. MALLORY. — Some days before.

Mr. BLAINE. — Not at all, sir; that meeting was on the 24th of September, two days after the proclamation was issued.

Mr. MALLORY. — Oh, no!

Mr. BLAINE. — Yes, sir, I am correct. I had a personal recollection of the date; and I have further certified it by documentary evidence, which I sent for, and now hold in my hand.

Mr. MALLORY. — It makes no difference what was the date of their meeting: they were here in Washington days before, and brought such a pressure to bear upon the President as induced him to issue such a proclamation.

Mr. BLAINE. — It will not do for the gentleman to escape in that way. The distinct allegation was, that the meeting of the Governors at Altoona applied the pressure which forced the President to issue the emancipation proclamation.

Mr. MALLORY. — These governors were here, as we all know, before the meeting at Altoona. The matter was talked about all over the country. The President himself, in his interview with the border-State men, spoke of the pressure that was being brought to bear upon him by Greeley and these other men, and begged us, for God's sake, to save him from that pressure.

Mr. BLAINE. — I think the gentleman is mistaken about the Governors of the loyal States being here before they went to Altoona. I know that at that time the Governors of all the loyal States were doubly pressed with duties in their own executive chambers. I know that Governor Washburne, of my own State, with the greatest difficulty was able to leave to attend that meeting at all. I recollect particularly this circumstance, because the Governor invited me to accompany him on the excursion, which invitation I was obliged to decline. And many of the other Governors found very great difficulty in leaving their own States to attend that convention; and the gentleman may be sure that they did not come on to Washington hobnobbing and holding consultations here for a week in advance. They arrived at Altoona after the President had issued his proclamation; and it is simply impossible, therefore, that their meeting could have brought to bear upon him a pressure which induced him to issue it. The anachronism into which my friend has been led, and which I have thus pointed out, is quite as conclusive in the premises as Mr. Weller hoped the *alibi* would prove in the celebrated Pickwickian trial.

Mr. PENDLETON. — One more question.

Mr. STEVENS. — The gentleman from Massachusetts says he will not be cross-examined, and I do not see any advantage to be gained by keeping him longer on the witness-stand.

Mr. PENDLETON. — I desire, when the gentleman from Massachusetts says that an event occurred on Wednesday, on the contingency of which the proclamation was or was not to be issued, to know what that contingency was.

Mr. STEVENS. — Before the gentleman from Massachusetts answers that, I want to make a motion.

Mr. PENDLETON. — I beg that the gentleman will wait until this matter is settled.

Mr. STEVENS. — But the gentleman from Massachusetts persists in saying that he will not be examined, and all the gentleman's questions, therefore, will avail nothing. What I desire to propose is, that this evening's session be set apart for the discussion of this subject. There are several gentlemen, I believe, on that side of the House, who have speeches they desire to make. I know of some instances in which superfetation has taken place already [laughter], and serious consequences may occur if opportunity is not afforded to get them off. Nobody, of course, will be obliged to come to hear them; and I therefore propose that this evening shall be set apart for debate, and that no business shall be done.

The SPEAKER. — Is there objection to this evening being set apart for debate?

Mr. ASHLEY. — I object.

[Mr. CRESWELL moved to dispense with the evening session for this evening.

The House divided; and there were, ayes eighty-three, noes not counted.

So the motion was agreed to.]

Mr. PENDLETON. — I desire to ask the gentleman from Massachusetts upon what event, happening on a certain Wednesday, the issuing of the President's emancipation message was contingent?

Mr. BOUTWELL. — The wisdom of the remark with which I prefaced my first statement is more and more manifest as I proceed. The questions put to me are not founded upon any thing I have said. The gentleman's question states that the event was to happen on Wednesday.

Mr. PENDLETON. — It did happen on Wednesday.

Mr. BOUTWELL. — I have already stated to my friends on that side of the House that I do not intend to answer that question. With all due respect to them, I do not intend to answer that question. I stated just exactly what I wanted to say, for the purpose of repelling, so far as I could, the imputation that the President was controlled in issuing his emancipation proclamation by any assembly of men anywhere. If what the gentleman from Kentucky [Mr. Mallory] has asserted be true, of which I have no knowledge, then so much higher is my opinion of the President's wisdom, that he abandoned a policy which had brought nothing but disaster upon the country, and raised himself to the contemplation of the supreme truth, that justice to the enslaved was involved in this contest; and that neither he nor the country could hope for the blessing of God until they saw the injustice of slavery, and determined by one supreme decree to strike down slavery and slaveholders.

Mr. PENDLETON. — Will the gentlemen yield to me?

Mr. BOUTWELL. — Certainly.

Mr. PENDLETON. — I ask the gentleman whether the issuing of that proclamation did not depend upon a victory being obtained by the Union forces? I will be satisfied with any answer, but I want an answer.

Mr. BOUTWELL. — In regard to these questions, I have already said I would not answer.

The SPEAKER. — Whenever the gentleman declines to yield, the Chair will protect him in his right to the floor.

Mr. Pendleton. — The gentleman yielded to me to put the question, and he declines to answer it.

Mr. Boutwell. — I made the declaration in the beginning, that I would not be put upon the stand as a witness in reference to any particular statement I made; that I intended to make a statement, and leave it there for what it was worth. I have yielded to the gentleman many times, — an excess of courtesy which has borne heavily upon the patience of the House; and yet he still persists in putting the same question to me.

Mr. Pendleton. — I understood the gentleman to say that that proclamation did not depend on the meeting of any set of men. Do I understand the gentleman to say that in its broadest and fullest extent?

Mr. Boutwell. — Having met the inquiries and declarations of the gentleman from Kentucky in reference to the Governors at Altoona, with the consent of the Chair, this business of interruption is at an end.

Mr. Pendleton. — Certainly I will not persist in my interruptions, if not agreeable to the gentleman.

Mr. Boutwell. — To gentlemen on that side of the House, and especially to the gentleman from Kentucky, and those who have been engaged with him in this hopeless struggle to perpetuate the institution of slavery, I submit for their consideration, in this hour of their grief, that we have not only had the preliminary proclamation of September, 1862, but also the great charter of liberty upon this continent, the proclamation of 1863; and whether there be peace or whether there be war, whether there be victory or whether there be defeat, whether there be union or disunion, that decree is eternal for this continent; and the gentlemen from Kentucky who still hope to resuscitate the institution of slavery, whether they give a timid and uncertain support to patriots struggling for the preservation of the Union, or whether they attempt to withhold from the government the physical and moral power of the slave element upon this continent, are still doomed to disappointment, and to disgrace, permit me to say, without personal reference to any man. It will stand upon the page of history as a foul blot, that the fairest portion of the North-American continent, that Kentucky, blessed with a soil rich and a climate inviting, a State of all the States which should have buckled on the armor, and, with the ancient warlike energy of her people, rallied to the support of the government in the hour of its trial, — that she, I say, deliberately bowed the knee to slavery, and rendered the issue of the contest for a time uncertain. Devastation has already wasted her land, and she will yet be an object of pity to the people of this continent and of the world. And I now offer my sympathy in anticipation of the inglorious future which awaits that State, if her present policy be pursued, tendered with some hope that she may —

Mr. Mallory. — We scorn and despise your sympathy. [Loud cries of "Order!"]

Mr. Boutwell. — With the hope that she may yet redeem her honor.

[Mr. Mallory made some remark amid tumultuous cries of "Order!"]

Mr. Boutwell. — But I anathematize her no

longer. Kentucky has upon this floor some men true to liberty; and, if my voice could pass beyond these walls and reach those other sons of hers, misguided, unfortunate, but not yet lost to the Constitution and the Union, I would invite them, in common with the people of this country, to abandon the institution of slavery, to rally to the support of the Union and the Constitution, and thus help to make this continent the home of the free, where there shall be neither slave nor master any more.

CHICAGO CONVENTION OF 1864.

SPEECH AT FANEUIL HALL, SEPT. 6, 1864.

FELLOW-CITIZENS,—It depends very much upon what we believe as to the future of this country and the rights of the people, whether we rejoice or mourn in consequence of the events in Mobile Bay and before Atlanta. If it was true on the 30th day of last month that the people of this country ought to take immediate efforts for the cessation of hostilities, then, gentlemen, we have cause to mourn rather than to rejoice. I understand that there were people in this country who before the 30th of August, since this war opened, had not, as an aggregate body of men, expressed their opinions in reference to this war, who then at Chicago declared that it ought to cease. I noticed, recently, two observations in the leading opposition newspaper of this city. First, a fear was expressed that hard names would be used; and, secondly, an apprehension was manifested that this meeting would have a political aspect or influence. I thought it likely enough that it would exert a political influence; for I observed in other newspapers that it was called to express congratulations over the events which have taken place in Mobile Bay and before Atlanta, and I thought that those events had had a political effect. I did not see exactly how it was possible that men should assemble together to rejoice over events having a political aspect, without the meeting and the rejoicing having a political aspect also. Gentlemen, I have come here with the design, that, so far as I am concerned, the meeting shall have a political aspect. These times are too serious for the acceptance of any suggestion that hard names are not to be called, if hard names are deserved. The question is, not whether the meeting shall have a political influence, but whether it is really necessary to the salvation of the country that it shall have a political influence. I observed certain indications, while the person who last occupied the platform was speaking, which I thought were a slight deviation from that much-talked-of right of free speech. Now, then, I am about to read a resolution adopted at the Chicago Convention. I shall make two propositions in reference to it. I shall then ask whether this assembly assents to or rejects those propositions. If there be any man in this hall who denies or doubts the propositions, if I have the consent of the honored chairman of this meeting to ten minutes of time in which I can engage the ear of the assembly, I surrender it to that man, that he may have an opportunity upon this platform to refute, if he can, the propositions which I lay down. The second resolution of the Chicago platform is in these words: —

[At this point, there was considerable disturbance in the rear of the hall, created by one individual, and several voices cried out, "Free speech!" "Out with him!"]

He will be more useful to the country if he

remains here. If he goes away, there is no chance for his conversion to the truth: if he remains here, he may be saved.

> "While the lamp holds out to burn,
> The vilest sinner may return."

I hope gentlemen who favor free speech will listen attentively to this resolution: —

"*Resolved,* That this convention does explicitly declare as the sense of the American people, that, after four years of failure to restore the Union by the experiment of war, — during which, under pretence of military necessity, or war-power higher than the Constitution, the Constitution has been disregarded in every part, and public liberty and private rights alike trodden down, and the material prosperity of the country essentially impaired, — justice, humanity, liberty, and the public welfare demand that immediate efforts be made for a cessation of hostilities with a view to an ultimate convention of all the States, or other peaceable means, to the end, that, at the earliest practicable moment, peace may be restored on the basis of the Federal Union of the States."

[The resolution was greeted with a feeble clapping of hands, a slight attempt at cheers in the rear of the hall, and a storm of hisses.]

If there be gentlemen here who approve this resolution, I hope they will have the opportunity to cheer. [About half a dozen persons commenced to cheer, but abandoned it on hearing their own voices. The speaker proceeded:] Gentlemen, the two propositions which I lay down are these; and, if any one of those gentlemen who indulged in the luxury of a cheer just now chooses to come upon the platform, I fulfil my pledge. The first is, that this resolution, as far as known, meets the approval of the rebels in arms against this government. The second is, that this resolution meets the approval of all the men in the North who sympathize with the cause of the rebellion, and desire its success. If any person denies the truth of these propositions, let him, with the leave of the chair, take ten minutes upon this platform. [No one appeared.] If there is nobody to refute these propositions, I take it for granted that they meet the general assent of this vast assembly; and, if so, is this the time, when a great convention professing to represent a portion of the American people in a period of war, not having spoken since hostilities commenced, should frame a leading resolution so as to meet the assent and approval of the enemies of the republic? And is not this the time, when such things are done, for men who have a faith in the country, and a belief in its right to exist, to declare the reasons for that belief? I propose to discuss the resolution. First, it demands a cessation of hostilities. I have heard the word "armistice" mentioned to-night. The declaration of that resolution is not for an armistice. An armistice, according to its general acceptation and use, implies a suspension of hostilities upon the expectation and condition that the war is to be resumed. Not in this resolution, nor in the whole series of resolutions to which this one belongs, is there an intimation, that, when a cessation of hostilities has been effected, the war is ever to be resumed; and, if the war is not to be resumed, then a cessation of hostilities is an abandonment of the government. It is treason. I declare here that the proposition for a cessation of hostilities is moral and political treason; and, further, every man who knowingly and after investigation, and upon his judgment, favors a cessation of hostilities, is a traitor. The issue, gentlemen, is no longer upon the tented field. The soldiers are true to the flag; and they will fight on and march on until the last rebel has fallen to the dust or laid down his arms. The soldiers are true; but the cause of the Union is in peril at home, where secret organizations are mustering their forces and gathering in material for which there can be no possible use except to revolutionize this country through the fearful experience of civil war. Oh, how I long for a more complete knowledge of the English language, that I may select a word or a phrase which shall fully express the enormity of this treason!

The rebels of the South have a cause. They believe in the institution of slavery; they have been educated under its influence. They thought it in peril. They made war with a fair pretence on their part; but what excuse, what palliation, is there for those men in the North who, regardless of liberty, of justice, and of humanity, ally themselves, openly some and secretly others, with the enemies of the republic? Spare, spare your anathemas, gentlemen. Do not longer employ the harsh language which you can command in denunciation of Southern traitors. They of the North who give aid and comfort to the enemy deserve to monopolize in the application all the harsh words and phrases of the English language. Cessation of hostilities: what follows? Dissolution of the Union inevitably. Will not Jefferson Davis and his associates understand that when we have ceased to make war, when our armies become demoralized, public sentiment relaxed, when they have had opportunity to gather up the materials for prosecuting this contest, that we cannot renew it with any reasonable hope of success. Therefore, if you abandon the contest now, it is separation: that is what is meant, and nothing else can follow. But suppose that what some gentlemen profess to desire could be accomplished, — a reconstruction of the Union by diplomatic relations inaugurated between this government and Jefferson Davis, and suppose the South should return, — what follows? When you have permitted Jefferson Davis and his associates to come back and take their places in the government of the country, do you not see that with the help of a small number of representatives from the North, whose services they are sure to command, they will assume the war debt of the South? Gentlemen of the North even say that the war is equally unjust on our part. If it be equally unjust on our part, why should not the government, when restored, assume the debt of the South as well as pay that incurred by the North? Therefore, the first step to your final destruction is the assumption of the war debt of the South. When you have assumed that debt, and taken the obligation to pay it, these men of the South will treat the obligation lightly, and, upon the first pretext, they will renew secession and march out of the Union; and you, with your embarrassed finances, will find yourselves unable to institute military proceedings for their subjugation. Therefore I say, that, by the plan of reconstruction which some men desire, you render secession certain, bankruptcy throughout the North certain. The repudiation of the public debt is not a matter of expectation or fear, it is a matter of certainty, if you assent to any reconstruction of this Union through the instrumentality of Jefferson Davis and his associates. You must either drive them into exile or exterminate them. You must break down the military power of the rebellion, exterminate or exile the leaders, and bring up men at the South who are in favor of the Union, and who are opposed to the assumption of the rebel war debt. There is no other way of security to yourselves. Are you prepared to cease hostilities, with the expectation of negotiations with Jefferson Davis for the dissolution of the Union or for its restoration? Either course is alike fatal to you; for the war must go on until peace is conquered. The friends of immediate peace offer you as negotiators Franklin Pierce and A. H. Stephens; one of the Seymours, either of Connecticut or New York; Wise, of Virginia; Vallandigham, of Ohio; and Soulé, of Louisiana. The only negotiators, gentlemen, to be trusted, as long as the war continues or there is a rebel in arms, — the only negotiators are Grant upon one line, and Sherman upon the other.

What further does the cessation of hostilities mean? It means that the blockade is to be removed, and the South to be allowed to furnish itself with material and munitions of war. What does it mean on the land? What does it mean on the sea? That you are to furl your flag at Fortress Monroe on the Petersburg line; that you are to remove your gunboats from the Mississippi River; that you are to abandon Fort Jackson and Fort St. Philip at its mouth; that you are to undo the work of the gallant Farragut in Mobile Bay; and so along the coast and upon the line from the Atlantic to the western bank of the Mississippi River. You, people of the North, who have been victorious, upon the whole, through three years of war,—you are to disgrace your ancestry, you are to render yourselves infamous in all future time, by furling your flag, and submitting anew to rebel authority upon this continent. Are you prepared for it? I ask these men here who cheered the resolution adopted at Chicago, whether they, men of Massachusetts, and in Faneuil Hall, will say, one of them, with his face to the portraits of the patriots of the Revolution, that he asks for peace through any craven spirit that is in him? Is there a man among them all, from whatsoever quarter of this city, renowned in history,—is there a man of them all who will stand here and say he is for a cessation of hostilities? If so, let him speak, and let him, if he dare, come upon this platform and face his patriotic fellow-citizens. [A call was made for cheers for McClellan in the rear of the hall, but nobody seemed disposed to respond. The speaker continued:] I am willing a cheer should be given for any man who has been in the service of his country, however little he may have done. Is there a man in Faneuil Hall for peace? [Voices: "No!"] I intended, as far as was in my power, to give to this meeting a political aspect in favor of the country and against traitors. If there be no peace men in this assembly, then that object, as far as we are concerned, is accomplished.

ABRAHAM LINCOLN.

EULOGY DELIVERED BEFORE THE CITY COUNCIL AND CITIZENS OF LOWELL, AT HUNTINGTON HALL, APRIL 19, 1865.

THE nation is bowed down to-day under the weight of a solemn and appalling sorrow, such as never before rested upon a great people. It is not the presence of death merely: with that we have become familiar. It is not the loss of a leader only that we mourn, nor of a statesman who had exhibited wisdom in great trials, in vast enterprises of war, and in delicate negotiations for the preservation of peace with foreign countries; but of a twice-chosen and twice-ordained ruler, in whom these great qualities were found, and to which were added the personal courage of the soldier and the moral heroism of the Christian.

Judged by this generation in other lands, and by other generations in future times, Abraham Lincoln will be esteemed as the wisest of rulers and the most fortunate of men. To him and to his fame, the manner of his death is nothing; to the country and to the whole civilized family of man, it is the most appalling of tragical events. The rising sun of the day following that night of unexampled crime revealed to us the nation's loss; but, stunned by the shock, the people were unable to comprehend the magnitude of the calamity. As the last rays of the setting sun glided into the calm twilight of evening, the continent was stilled into silence by its horror of the crime, and its sense of the greatness of the loss sustained.

If we believe reverently that God guided his chosen people in ancient times, that he was with our fathers in their struggle for independence, we are likely also to believe, that, in the events transpiring in this country, the Ruler of all the earth makes his ways known to men in an unusual manner, and to an unusual extent. If God rules, then are not all men, even in their imperfections and sins, in some mysterious way and under peculiar circumstances the doers of his will? To the human eye, Abraham Lincoln seems to have been specially designated by Divine Providence for the performance of a great work. His origin was humble, his means of education stinted. He was without wealth, and he did not enjoy the support of influential friends. Much the larger part of his life was spent in private pursuits, and he never exhibited even the common human desire for public employment, leadership, and fame. His ambition concerning the great office that he held was fully satisfied; and the triumph of his moderate and reasonable expectations was not even marred by the untimely and bloody hand of the assassin. During the canvass of 1864, and with the modesty of a child, he said, "I cannot say that I wish to perform the duties of President for four years more; but I should be gratified by the approval of the people of what I have done." This he received; and, however precious it may have been to him, it is a more precious memory to the people themselves.

His public life was embraced in the period of

about six years. This statement does not include his brief service in the Legislature of the State of Illinois, nor his service as a subordinate officer in one of the frontier Indian wars, nor his single term of service in the House of Representatives of the United States nearly twenty years ago. In none of these places did he attract the attention of the country, nor did the experience acquired fit him specially for the great duties to which he was called finally. He was nearly fifty years of age when he entered upon the contest, henceforth historical, for a seat in the Senate from the State of Illinois. This was the commencement of his public life, and from that time forward he gained and grew in the estimation of his countrymen. At the moment of his death, he enjoyed the confidence of all loyal men, including those even who did not openly give him their support; and there were many, possibly in them it was a sin, who came at last to regard him as a divinely appointed leader of the people. The speeches which he delivered in that contest are faithful exponents of his character, his principles, and his capacity. His statements of opinion are clear and unequivocal; his reasoning was logical and harmonious; and his principles, as then expressed, were consonant with the declaration subsequently made, "that each man has the right by nature to be the equal politically of any other man." He was then, as ever, chary of predictions concerning the future; but it was in his opening speech that he declared his conviction, which was in truth a prophecy, that this nation could not remain permanently half slave and half free.

In that long and arduous contest with one of the foremost men of the country, Mr. Lincoln made no remark which he was unable to defend, nor could he, by any force of argument, be driven from a position that he had taken. It was then that those who heard or read the debate observed the richness of his nature in mirth and wit which charmed his friends without wounding his opponents, and which he used with wonderful sagacity in illustrating his own arguments, or in weakening, or even at times in overthrowing, the arguments of his antagonist. And yet it cannot be doubted, that for many years, if not from his very youth, Mr. Lincoln was a melancholy man. He seemed to bear about with him the weight of coming cares, and to sit in gloom as though his path of life was darkened by an unwelcome shadow. His fondness for story and love for mirth were the compensation which nature gave.

In the midst of overburdening cares, these characteristics were a daily relief; and yet it is but just to say that he often used an appropriate story as a means of foiling a too inquisitive visitor, or of changing or ending a conversation which he did not desire to pursue.

During the first French revolution, when the streets of Paris were stained with human blood, the inhabitants, women and men, flocked to places of amusement. To the mass of mankind, and especially to the inexperienced, this conduct appears frivolous, or as the exhibition of a criminal indifference to the miseries of individuals and the calamities of the public. But such are the horrors of war, the pressure of responsibility, that men often seek refuge and relief in amusements, from which in ordinary times they would turn aside.

In Mr. Lincoln's speeches of 1858 there are passages which suggest to the mind the classic models of ancient days, although they do not in any proper sense rise to an equality with them. His style of writing was as simple as were his own habits and manners; and no person ever excelled him in clearness of expression. Hence he was understood and appreciated by all classes. The Proclamation of Emancipation, his address at the dedication of the cemetery at Gettysburg, and his touching letter to the widowed mother who had given five sons to the country, are memorable as evidences of his intellectual and moral greatness.

His speeches of 1858 are marked for the precision with which he stated his own positions, and for the firmness exhibited whenever his opponent endeavored to worry him from his chosen ground, or, by artifice or argument or persuasion, to induce him to advance a step beyond.

His administration, as far as he himself was concerned, was inaugurated upon the doctrines and principles of the great debate. He recognized the obligation to return fugitives from slavery, and it was no part of his purpose to interfere with slavery in the States where it existed. It must remain for the historian and the biographer, who may have access to private and personal sources of knowledge, to inform the country and the world how far Mr. Lincoln, when he entered upon his duties as President, comprehended the magnitude of the struggle in which the nation was about to engage.

The circumstance that his first call for volunteers was for seventy-five thousand men only is not valuable as evidence one way or the other. The number was quite equal to our supply of arms and materials of war, and altogether too vast for the experience of the men then at the head of military affairs. The number was sufficient to show his purpose,— the purpose to which he adhered through all the trials and vicissitudes of this eventful contest. His purpose was the suppression of the rebellion, both as a civil organization and as an armed military force, and the re-establishment of the authority of the United States over the territory of the Union. There yet remain, in the minds of men who were acquainted with Mr. Lincoln in the spring and summer of 1861, the recollection of expressions made by him which indicate that there were then vague thoughts in his mind that it might be his lot under Providence to bring the slaves of the country out of their bondage. But, however this may have been, he never deviated from his purpose to suppress the rebellion; and he conscientiously applied the means at his command to the attainment of that end. Thus, step by step, he advanced, until in his own judgment, in the judgment of the country, and of the best portion of mankind in other civilized nations, the emancipation of the slaves was a necessary means for the successful prosecution of the war. Mr. Lincoln was not insensible to the justice of emancipation; he saw its wisdom as a measure of public policy: but he delayed the proclamation until he was fully convinced that it offered the only chance of averting a foreign war, suppressing the rebellion, and restoring the Union of the States.

In the great struggle of 1862, Mr. Lincoln exhibited a twofold character. He was personally the enemy of slavery, and he ardently desired its abolition; but he also regarded his oath of office, and steadily refused to recognize the existence of any right to proclaim emancipation while other means of saving the republic remained. He sought the path of duty, and he walked fearlessly in it. Until he was satisfied of the necessity of emancipation, no earthly power could have led him to issue the proclamation; and, after its issue, no earthly power could have induced him to retract or to qualify it. When an effort was made to persuade him to qualify the proclamation, he said, in reference to the blacks, "My word is out to these people, and I can't take it back."

It has been common, in representative governments, for men to be advanced to great positions without any sufficient evidence existing of their ability to perform the corresponding duties, and it has often happened that the occupant has not been elevated, while the office has been sadly degraded. It was observed by those who visited Mr. Lincoln on the day following his nomination at Chicago in June, 1860, that he would prove, in the event of his election, either a great success or a great failure.

This prediction was based upon the single fact that he was different from ordinary men, and it did not contain, as an element of the opinion, any knowledge of his peculiar characteristics. History will accept the first branch of the alternative opinion, and pronounce his administration a great success. To this success Mr. Lincoln most largely contributed, and this in spite of peculiarities which appeared to amount to defects in a great ruler in troublous times.

Never were words uttered which contained less truth than those which fell from the lips of the assassin,—"*Sic semper tyrannis*,"—as he passed, in the presence of an excited and bewildered crowd, from the spot where he had committed the foulest of murders to the stage of the theatre from whence he made his escape.

Mr. Lincoln exercised power with positive reluctance and unfeigned distaste. He shrank from the exhibition of any authority that was oppressive, harsh, or even disagreeable, to a human being. He passed an entire night in anxious thought and prayerful deliberation, before he could sanction the execution of Gordon, the slave-dealer, although he had been tried, found guilty, and sentenced to death. There is but little doubt, such was the kindness of Mr. Lincoln's nature, that he desired to close the war, and restore the Union, without exacting the forfeit of a single life as a punishment for the great crime of which the leaders in this rebellion are guilty.

Could this liberal policy have been carried out, it would have been the theme of perpetual eulogy, and its author would have received the acclamation of all races and classes of men.

Mr. Lincoln had not in his nature, or in the habits of his life, any element or feature of tyranny.

He had no love of power for the sake of power. He preferred that every man should act as might seem to him best; and when, in the discharge of his duties, he was called to enforce penalties, or even to remove men from place, he suffered more usually than did the subjects of his authority. It is easy to understand that this peculiarity was sometimes an obstacle to the vigorous administration of affairs. But on the other hand, it must have happened occasionally that these delays led to a better judgment in the end.

Mr. Lincoln was, in the best sense of the expression, an industrious man. Whatever he examined, he examined carefully and thoroughly. His patience was unlimited. He listened attentively to advice, though it is probable that he seldom asked it. For nearly fifty years before he entered upon the duties of President, he had relied upon himself; and it is said, that, in the practice of his profession, he never sought opinions or suggestions from his brethren, except as they were associated with him in particular causes. He had the acuteness of the lawyer and the fairness of the judge. The case must be intricate indeed which he did not easily analyze, so as to distinguish and estimate whatever was meritorious or otherwise in it. He saw also through the motives of men. He easily fathomed those around him, and acted in the end as though he understood their dispositions towards himself.

He appeared to possess an intuitive knowledge of the opinions and purposes of the people. His sense of justice was exact; and, if he ever failed to be guided by it, the departure was due to the kindness of his nature, which always prompted him to look with the compassion of a parent upon the unfortunate, — the guilty as well as the innocent. He was cautious in forming opinions, and disinclined to disclose his purposes until the moment of action arrived. He examined every subject of importance with conscientious care; his conclusions were formed under a solemn sense of duty; and, while that sense of duty remained, he was firm in resisting all counter influences. In unimportant matters, not involving principles or the character of his public policy, he yielded readily to the wishes of those around him; and thus they who knew him or heard of him in these relations only were misled as to his true character.

No magistrate or ruler ever labored more zealously to place his measures and policy upon the sure foundation of right; and no magistrate or ruler ever adhered to his measures and policy with more firmness as long as he felt sure of the foundation. His last public address is a memorable illustration of these traits of character.

The charmed cord by which he attached all to him who enjoyed his acquaintance, even in the slightest degree, was the absence of all pretension in manners, conversation, or personal appearance. This was not humility, either real or assumed; but it was due to an innate and ever-present consciousness of the equality of men. He accorded to every one who approached him, whatever his business or station in life, such hearing and attention as circumstances permitted. For himself he asked nothing of the nature of personal consideration. In the multiplicity of his cares, in his daily attention to cases touching the reputation and rights of humble and unknown men, in the patience with which he listened to the narratives of heart-broken women whose husbands or sons or brothers had fallen under arrest or into disgrace in the military or naval service of the country, he was indeed the servant and the friend of all.

The inexorable rules of military discipline were sometimes disregarded by him; he sought to make an open way for justice through the forms and technicalities of courts-martial, bureaus, and departments; and it is not unlikely that the public service may have received detriment occasionally by the too free use of the power to pardon and to restore. But the nation could well afford the indulgence of his over-kind nature in these particulars; for by this kindness of nature he drew the people to him, and thus opinions were harmonized, the republic was strengthened, and the power of its enemies sensibly diminished.

Mr. Lincoln never despaired of the republic. During the dark days of July, August, and September, 1862, he was not dismayed by the disasters which befell our arms. His confidence was not in our military strength alone: he looked to the Lord of hosts for the final delivery of the people.

Following this attempt to analyze Mr. Lincoln's intellectual and moral character, it remains to be said, that neither this analysis, nor the statements with which it is connected, furnish any just idea of the man. He was more, he was greater, he was wiser, he was better, than the ideal man which we should be authorized to create from the qualities disclosed by the analysis. And so, possibly, there will ever remain an apparent dissimilitude between the appreciable individual qualities of the man and the man himself.

Mr. Lincoln was a wise man; but he had not the wisdom of the ancient philosophers, who declared it to be the knowledge of things both divine and human, together with the causes on which they depend; but he was rather an illustration of the proverb of Solomon,—"The fear of the Lord is the instruction of wisdom."

Mr. Lincoln must ever be named among the great personages of history. He will be contrasted rather than compared with those with whom he is thus to be associated; and, when compared with any, he is most likely to be compared with the Father of his Country. If this be so, then his rank is already fixed and secure. In many particulars, he differs from other great men. When his important public services began, he was more than fifty years of age; while Cromwell was only forty years old when called from retirement, and most eminent men in civil and military life have been distinguished at an earlier age. He had no military experience or military fame. He was taken from private life, and advanced to the Presidency, upon a pure question or declaration of public policy,—the non-extension of slavery. He entered upon his great office in the presence of assassins and traitors; and, from that day to the day of his death, he dwelt in their presence, and faithfully performed his duties. He conducted the affairs of the republic in the most perilous of times. In the short period of four years, he called three millions of men into the military service of his country. During his administration, a rebellion, in which eleven States and six millions of people were involved, was effectually overthrown. But the great act which secures to his name all the immortality which earth can bestow is the Proclamation of Emancipation. The knowledge of that deed can never die. On this continent it will be associated with the Declaration of Independence, and with that alone. One made a nation independent: the other made a race free.

There are four million of people in this country who now regard Abraham Lincoln as their deliverer from bondage, and whose posterity, through all the coming centuries, will render tribute of praise to his name and memory. But his fame in connection with the Proclamation of Emancipation will not be left to the care of those who have been the recipients of the boon of freedom. The white people of the South will yet rejoice in the knowledge of their own deliverance through this gift to the now-despised colored man. And finally, the people of the United States, of the American continent, together with the whole family of civilized man, shall join in honors to the memory of him who freed a race and saved a nation.

What fame that is human merely can be more secure? What glory that is of earth can be more enduring? What deed for good can be more widespread?

The knowledge and influence of the great act of

his life will extend to every continent and to all races. It will advance with civilization into Africa; it will shake and finally overthrow slavery in the dominions of Spain, and in the empire of Brazil; and at last, in that it saved a republic and perpetuated a free representative government as an example and model for mankind, it will undermine the monarchical, aristocratic, and despotic institutions of Europe and Asia.

What fame that is human merely *can be more secure?* What glory that is of earth *can be more enduring?* What deed for good *can be more widespread?*

Yet this great act of his life rested on a foundation on which all may stand. In the place where he was, he did that which, in his judgment, duty to his country and to his God required. This is, indeed, his highest praise, and the only eulogy that his life demands.

That he had greater opportunities than other men was his responsibility and burden: that he used his great opportunities for the preservation of his country and the relief of the oppressed is his own glory.

Had Mr. Lincoln been permitted to reach the age attained by Jefferson or Adams, his death would have produced a profound impression upon his countrymen.

Had he now, in the opening months of his second administration, fallen by accident or yielded to disease, the nation would have been bowed down in inexpressible grief. Every loyal heart would have been burdened with a weight of sorrow, and every loyal household would have felt as though a place had been made vacant at its own hearth-stone.

That he has now fallen by the hand of an assassin is in itself a horror too appalling for contemplation. Had the deed been committed in ancient Greece or Rome, we could not now read the historian's record without a shudder and a tear. All those qualities in the illustrious victim which we cherish were spurs, ever goading the conspirators on to the consummation of their crime.

His love of country and of liberty, his devotion to duty, his firmness and persistency in the right, his kindness of heart and his spirit of mercy were all reasons or inducements influencing the purposes of the conspirators. Neither greatness nor goodness was a shield. Had he been greater and better and wiser than he was, his fate would have been the same.

In this hour of calamity, let not the thirst for vengeance take possession of our souls. But justice should be done. The circle of conspirators is already broken and entered by the officers of the law, and mankind will finally be permitted to see who were the authors, and who the perpetrators, of this great crime. For the members of this circle, whether it be small or large, and whomsoever it may include, there should be neither compassion nor mercy, but justice, and only justice. Judged as men judge, this crime is too great for pardon. The criminals can find no protection or harbor in any civilized country. Let the government pursue them with its full power until the last one disappears from earth. Vex every sea, visit every island, traverse every continent, let there be no abiding-place for these criminals between the Arctic seas and the Antarctic pole.

This, Justice demands as she sits in judgment upon this unparalleled crime.

One duty and one consolation remain. He who destroyed slavery was himself by slavery destroyed. Whoever the assassin, and however numerous the conspirators, love of slavery was the evil spirit which had entered into these men and taken possession of them. Slavery is the source and fountain of the crime, and all they who have given their support to slavery are in some degree responsible for the awful deed. Let, then, the nation purify itself from this the foulest of sins. And this is our duty.

In the providence of God, Mr. Lincoln was permitted to do more than any other man of this century for his country, for liberty, and for mankind. Mr. Lincoln is dead; but the nation lives, and the providence of God ever continues. No single life was ever yet essential to the life of a nation. This is our consolation and ground for confidence in the future.

RECONSTRUCTION: ITS TRUE BASIS.

SPEECH DELIVERED AT WEYMOUTH, MASS., JULY 4, 1865.

THE series of events of the last four years, ending in the overthrow of the rebellion, impose upon us obligations and duties more important and solemn than have rested upon the American people at any previous period in their history. We are able, however, for the first time to rejoice in the complete, or, at least, in the near, fulfilment of the great truths contained in the second paragraph of the Declaration of Independence. Our ancestors said: "We hold these truths to be self-evident,—that all men are created equal, and that they are endowed by their Creator with certain natural, essential, and unalienable rights, among which are life, liberty, and the pursuit of happiness." They believed these cardinal truths; and Mr. Jefferson, in the original draft of the Declaration of Independence, charged the King of Great Britain, in addition to many other allegations, with the pre-eminent crime of having countenanced the African slave-trade, and opposed all measures for its overthrow or restriction. We have passed through a great struggle, which was a necessary incident of our national life, due to the fact, which now we can comprehend, and which it is neither disgrace to our fathers, nor dishonor to us, to confess, that our national system contained a fundamental error; namely, that it was possible to set up and maintain permanently a government based in part upon the principle that "all men are created equal," and in part upon the principle that a certain portion of mankind have the right to hold a certain other portion in bondage. This was the experiment in government tried here by the adoption of the Constitution of 1789, and the experiment has failed. The government which was then set up, founded in part upon the principles of freedom and in part upon the principles of slavery, has failed; it has gone down in blood, amid horrors such as have not often been witnessed in Christian countries. There has been no failure of republican institutions; nothing has occurred to diminish our confidence in the capacity of the people to govern themselves; but, on the other hand, their conduct in relation to the questions and issues of the times is the sublimest event of history, and furnishes conclusive evidence that just governments are strong, and democratic governments are wise. The question before us is, whether out of this struggle there shall come a nation purified and glorious and permanent in its institutions and in its policy, or not.

Thus far, under Providence, the Union and the cause of justice have triumphed. We look upon the past with satisfaction, marred in two particulars only: first, that so many of the brave men of the republic have fallen in defence of its principles and of its integrity; and, secondly, that he who was the moderate, consistent, and trusted leader of the people finally became the great martyr to republican institutions, to the right of this nation to be free.

I congratulate myself, and I congratulate you, that, in the course of remark on which I purpose to enter to-day, I follow the lead of that great man, — who, intellectually and morally, will stand among the foremost men of this country, of this age, and of the world, — in reference to the rights of the negro race as citizens of this country, and inhabitants of this continent. We know now, from the record exposed since his death, that it was one of the objects which he had near to his heart, to secure to the negro population the right of suffrage, without which, I shall, as I think, be able to show you, there can, in this country, and under republican institutions, be no security for any other right whatever.

We have come out of the war triumphantly. We entered upon it, four years ago, reluctantly, uncertain as to the issue. There were those then who, seeing beyond the present moment, were assured that the people who occupied the continent, the descendants of the men who, in the first paragraph of the Declaration of Independence, before the Constitution was formed, or the Union, in terms, had an existence, declared that these then united colonies constituted one people, would never give up their right to be the inhabitants of a country indivisible and perpetual. That expectation, gentlemen, has not only been realized, but we have also subjugated those who, more than thirty years ago, treasonably conspired for the overthrow of this government, for the destruction of republican institutions on this continent, and for the suppression of the hopes of liberty and of freemen throughout the world. They are subjugated; and the question remaining for you, citizen soldiers, for you, citizens of the republic, to decide, is, whether, in the reconstruction of the government, those men, and they who, like them in principle, are like them also in purposes, shall re-appear to guide, control, disturb, and finally ruin the republic, or whether you will reconstruct the nation upon the eternal principle of the Declaration of Independence, that "all men are created equal." Justice, *justice*, is the only foundation for statesmanship, the only security for national life; and our fathers, in departing from the principle of justice in the original construction of this government, left to their posterity the woes through which we have passed. Believing, as I do, that these horrors and sacrifices and sufferings are a just judgment of Heaven upon this nation, for its great sin in reference to the institution of slavery, which is but one form of injustice, so here and everywhere during these four years I do pledge and have pledged myself to resist the re-establishment of this government upon the principle of injustice. If there be those, few or many, who, in their anxiety to reconstruct their government speedily and according to its ancient forms, choose to forego the securities which ought to be taken, I have no lot or part with them. I prefer to stand alone, upon the principle of justice, as the only foundation on which the government can securely rest. And if there be those who choose to take the responsibility of becoming, in the eyes of posterity, the agents for the repetition of the woes which we have endured, let the responsibility be upon them. I feel assured, however, that whatever may be the prejudices of some, whatever may be the influence of tradition upon others, whatever may be the distinctions of race or color that exist among us, the people of this country are finally to re-establish the government upon the distinct enunciation of the doctrine that "all men are created equal." Building upon that foundation, the nation will withstand the storms and the floods of time: but if you build upon injustice, upon wrong, upon distinctions of race, of color, or upon caste, you build upon the sand; and when the storms come, and the winds blow, and the rains fall, then will the structure that you have reared be brought down in ruin upon your heads.

Nor is the triumph of the day limited to the restoration of the Union as a result, and the overthrow of slavery as an incident, of the war. We have placed the United States, as a nation, in the front rank of the nations of the earth. We have had no war with England or with France, and we trust that the time is far distant when there shall be any rupture of the relations of amity that now exist. This nation is for peace, as it ever has been; but, in the subjugation of the rebels of the South, we have conquered both England and France, as well as the enemies of republican institutions the world over. If you were to ask an Englishman whether France or the United States is the first naval and military power of the world, he would answer at once, the United States. If you were to ask a Frenchman whether England or the United States is the first naval and military power, he would also answer, the United States. If you were to put the question to a Russian whether England or France or the United States is the chief military and naval power of the world, he would at once answer, the United States. As Themistocles acquired the reputation of being the first general of Greece, by the circumstance that all his rivals recognized him as the second in merit, each claiming to be first himself; so we, by the judgment of the people of all those nations, are to-day accorded the chief rank among the naval and military powers of the earth.

I hope you will pardon me, my friends, if now, before I proceed to the purpose which I have in view on this occasion, I refer to the circumstance of my invitation to speak here to-day, that there may be no misunderstanding on the part of any. Your committee, when thus honoring me, received the statement that I preferred not then to accept it, but rather desired that they should communicate to their associates of the committee, and to the public possibly to some extent, the fact, that, if I accepted the invitation, I must do it with the distinct understanding, that I was to discuss those topics, and those only, which concern the fortunes of the country. The time has long since passed when I had the ambition to speak for the purpose of speaking; and, during this war, I have invariably declared what I believed to be the truth without regard to any consequences personal to myself.

I wish, also, thus early to state my views of

the policy now pursued by the administration in reference to the great subject of reconstruction, because it is quite likely there may be some present who will draw inferences from what I shall offer. If I understand President Johnson, he does not object to negro suffrage. It is, however, his desire that the right should be extended to the negroes of the once-existing eleven States, recently in rebellion, by the white people of those States, who were authorized to vote when the rebellion commenced. If negro suffrage can be secured in that way, I shall, for one, readily accept the result without any inquiry as to the means. But if, on the other hand, as I expect, the attempt to secure negro suffrage, through the white people of the eleven rebel States, shall fail, I then expect that President Johnson, and those who are co-operating with him, will accept the judgment of the country, — if it shall prove to be the judgment of the country, — that negro suffrage must be secured by some other means. Therefore, while I am content that these efforts should be made, and while I shall welcome the result if it be favorable, I look upon the efforts as experiments, not binding upon President Johnson or upon his administration or on the country; and, as was the fact in 1861 and '62 in reference to the expediency of emancipation and the enrolment of colored soldiers in the army of the republic, I now expect that the people will take this matter into their own hands. I believe with reference to President Johnson, as in 1861 and '62 I believed in reference to President Lincoln, that he will accept the judgment of the country, if, upon the whole, the public opinion shall be that negro suffrage is essential to the security of the Union, as well as to the protection of the negroes themselves. Therefore I counsel discussion, argument, on the part of those who believe in negro suffrage; patience, that those in authority may have an opportunity to make this effort to secure the reconstruction of the government according to the ideas that have first presented themselves to them; that no one be committed to any particular line of policy, but all look to the grand result, — the reconstruction of the goverment upon the principle of the equality of men.

But such is my confidence in the justice of the policy which we maintain, such my conviction of its necessity, that I am assured it does not only not need the support which we now attempt to render, but that its success is not even dependent upon the power of office or the wisdom of leaders.

There was a divine policy in our affairs which made emancipation a necessity; and we are now so subject to circumstances that all plans for the reconstruction of the government which do not recognize the political rights of the negro are sure to fail. The white men of the North must recognize the political rights of the black men of the South, or surrender their own equality in the government of the country. They must decree political freedom for the blacks, or accept political inferiority for themselves. Hence I well know in the beginning what their conduct will be. Nor do I underestimate the apparent difficulties in our way. There is, first, the wide-spread and plausible error, which I shall attempt now to refute, that, if we deny the existence of the eleven States as States, we admit the heresy of secession; there is next the prejudice against the negro race, coupled with a sad misapprehension as to his capacity to take care of himself, and to serve the country; and, finally, there is the difficulty, amounting to an obstacle in the estimation of some, that certain of the loyal States do even now deny to the negro the right of franchise. But all these are errors, misfortunes, and wrongs, rather than serious difficulties in our way. When slavery existed, citizenship was of course denied to the slave class in all the slave States. It was also natural in States where slavery did not exist, but where its ideas were carried by immigrants, or where its social and business influences prevailed, or, possibly, by mere comity in some cases, that the public policy should be fashioned upon the theory, that slavery, or at least a condition of political inferiority, was the proper fortune of the black man. It is likely that the overthrow of slavery will be followed by a revision of this policy; but, in any event, the argument in favor of negro suffrage in the rebellious districts is as valid when addressed to Illinois or Indiana as when addressed to New York or Massachusetts.

The war for freedom and the Union has been carried on by the whites and negroes born on this continent, by the Irish and the Germans; and, indeed, by representatives of every European race. With this fresh experience, we ought to make it a part of the organic government, that no State shall make any distinction in the enjoyment of the elective franchise on account of race or color.

Asking you to bear with me while I proceed further in the discussion of this subject, I desire to call your attention to the question of the power of the national government over the eleven States that have been engaged in this rebellion; to the question of power with reference to the result we seek, — the right of the negro to vote in the State where he happens to be. There are those who believe that these eleven States are States in the Union, precisely as they were in 1860; or, rather, there are those who use language which would lead us to believe that they are of opinion that the eleven rebellious States are still States in the Union. The fact, however, is, that the government, during these four years, has proceeded upon the idea that they were not States. President Johnson himself, in the declarations he makes to the provisional Governors whom he is just now appointing, says, that, in order that the representatives of those States may be recognized by the Senate and House, they must abolish the institution of slavery, and ratify the amendment to the Constitution, prohibiting slavery in the United States. Would he address that language to New York or Ohio or Massachusetts? In the very fact that provisional Governors are appointed; in the very fact that terms are made with those provisional Governors, and, through them, with the people, — we have evidence abundant that the President does not recognize these States as States in the Union, with the powers of the old States. They are in a different condition, confessedly. Will any one even pretend that South Carolina has the same immediate, unquestionable, indisputable right of representation in the Senate and House that is enjoyed by New York and the other loyal States? In the House of Representatives, for example, although the Constitution of the United States says that a majority of the House shall be a quorum for doing business, and it would require one hundred and eighteen at least to make a majority of all the members of the House of Representatives, including Representatives from the eleven disloyal States, we still have been acting — laws have been passed, armies have been raised, public debt has been incurred, bonds have been issued — upon the principle that a quorum was a majority of the representatives from the loyal States. Ninety-four, instead of one hundred and eighteen, has been the recognized quorum of the Thirty-Eighth Congress. We have acted upon the principle that those who were not present, who were voluntarily absent, were not to be considered or consulted at all; and in the same manner, gentlemen, we shall be obliged to act finally in reference to the amendment to the Constitution. There are twenty-five loyal States of the Union: there are eleven disloyal States, that have not been represented in either branch of Congress for four years, that have had neither governor nor judge nor legislator within their limits sworn to support the Constitution of the United States; but, on the other hand, all their State and local officers have taken an oath, abjuring the Constitution of the United States. I wish, in the beginning, to assail the doctrine that these States, because they were once States in this Union, are still States in this Union. We assert that they have ceased to exist, and I think I can show you how they have ceased to exist. Consider, first, how a State is created. It is created, as you all know, by the will of the people within its limits. How was Massachusetts created? By an assembly of the representatives of the people of the State forming a Constitution, submitting it to the people, and, when that Constitution was ratified, by the election of officers under it. They did not yield to external power or external authority. A State, as a political organization, is the product, the political product, of the people within its limits; it cannot be created, it never has been created, by any external force whatever. But what follows? I am, as far as this doctrine is concerned, a State-rights man; not one who believes in the sovereignty of the State over the nation, not one who believes in the right of the smallest State — as Delaware, for example — to decide whether this republic has a right to exist or not; but I am of those who believe that State rights are a necessary and essential fact in the political organization and constitution of this country; and, while subject to the supreme authority of the nation, the States are powerful instruments to protect public liberty, promote the general welfare, and secure the blessings of freedom to ourselves and our posterity.

Can a State be destroyed? I answer, it can. That is to say, its political existence, including its organic law, can be destroyed, — eradicated. By whom? By the people who created it. Do you say they have no right to destroy it? I answer, in concurrence, they have no *right* to destroy it; but we must look at the fact, and not at theories, nor even at the mere declaration of the law. The declaration of the law, both human and divine, is, that no man has a right to take his own life; but it is possible for a man to take his life, and, when he has taken his life, it is useless, it is visionary, it is insane, for men to stand up and say, "This thing cannot be done: God's law is against it." It *is* done: the dead body is before you. And so it is useless to say that the people of a State cannot destroy the State, because they have no legal right so to do. It is not a question of legal right: it is a question of fact.

Now, what are the facts? Take South Carolina, for example. Is she a State of the American Union? Did she not, in the most solemn manner known to human proceedings, in December, 1860, declare that she ceased to exist as a State of the American Union? Did she not proceed, in conformity with that declaration, to annul all her relations to the national government, and to create new relations with another government, foreign and hostile to the government of the United States? and has she not, during these four years, sturdily refused to elect any man to office who was known to be in favor of the government of the United States? and, after all this, do you say that South Carolina is still a State of the American Union?

What else did she do? She preserved her State organization; but she transferred her allegiance to the so-called Confederate States. Hence, as a political organization, as a body or corporation or State which the government of the United States could recognize, she, by her own act, ceased to exist. What followed? By the success of our arms, we have destroyed the State of South Carolina, that professed to owe allegiance to the so-called Confederate States, and the old State of South Carolina has not been reproduced; and therefore there is no State of South Carolina, as a political organization, which can be recognized. All men, I think, when put to the test, will admit it. If Mr. Rhett, or any other man from South Carolina, were to come to the Senate of the United States, and say, "South Carolina is a State in this nation, I have been duly elected by the legislature of that State, I ask for my seat," would he not be rejected?—and for this reason, that South Carolina, at the present moment, in the judgment of everybody, has not that immediate and distinct and unquestioned and unquestionable right to be represented in Congress, that appertains to New York or Pennsylvania or Ohio. What I ask of the country is to accept the fact, that the political organization known as South Carolina has ceased to exist by the will of the people who at the first created, and who from the first until 1860 sustained, that organization as one of the States of the American Union. What follows? That South Carolina, the people and territory, are out of the Union? that they have seceded? By no means. The jurisdiction and authority which the national government originally had over the territory and people of South Carolina remain; and we shall exercise that jurisdiction and authority just as far and as fast as we can. But the result is, that, for the purposes of government to-day, South Carolina is a blank piece of paper, on which may be written a new form of government, on which a new form of government must be written by the people of South Carolina, and can be written by nobody else. What next? What is the authority of the general government? A State may exist by the will of its own people; but it cannot exist, primarily and originally, as a State of the American Union, and, indeed, it cannot exist at all as a State of the American Union, except by the consent of the representatives of the existing government. Therefore, when South Carolina has formed her government, and asks for the admission of her Senators and Representatives into Congress, it is then for the representatives of the existing States and of the people of the Union to say whether they shall be admitted or not. At this stage in the proceedings, there is a legal and constitutional opportunity to examine their principles of government, and decide whether they are in general correspondence with the settled policy of the country.

If you assent to what I have said thus far, then I ask you confidently to accept without argument the proposition, which I should be ashamed to argue to any of my countrymen, that a Constitution which disfranchises more than half the people of a State is not a "republican form of government," in the eye of the Constitution of the United States, and which we are bound to protect a people in maintaining and enjoying. It is just at this point that we have the power over the people of all the rebel

States with reference to the constitutions or forms of government which they may set up.

With your leave, gentlemen, I will read a statement, as succinct and direct as I could prepare upon this point, which was framed more than a year since, and which I have no disposition to alter in the least degree. It is this: that a State can exist or cease to exist only by the will of the people within its limits, and it cannot be created or destroyed by the external force or opinion of other States, or even by the judgment or action of the nation itself; a State, when created by the will of its people, can become a member of the American Union only by its own organized action and the concurrent action of the existing national government; when a State has been admitted to the Union, no vote, resolution, ordinance, or proceeding on its part, however formal in character or vigorously sustained, can deprive the national government of the legal jurisdiction and sovereignty over the territory and people of such State which existed previous to the act of admission, or which were acquired thereby; that the effect of the so-called acts, resolutions, and ordinances of secession adopted by the eleven States engaged in the present rebellion is, and can only be, to destroy those political organizations as States, while the legal and constitutional jurisdiction and authority of the national government over the people and territory remain unimpaired; that these several communities can be organized into States only by the will of the loyal people, expressed freely and in the absence of all coercion; that States so organized can become

States of the American Union only when they shall have applied for admission, and their admission shall have been authorized by the existing national government; that when a people have organized a State upon the basis of allegiance to the Union, and applied for admission, the character of the institutions of such proposed State may constitute a sufficient justification for granting or rejecting such application.

But, if there be those among you who still doubt the authority of the national government over the people and territory of the eleven rebellious States, I ask them to consider the fact that the Supreme Court has decided that we have been engaged in a territorial war, and that, with reference to the territory and people in antagonism to the Government of the United States, we have all the rights of a belligerent power. We have carried on the war to a successful termination; we have subjugated the rebellious people; we have overthrown their military power; we have acquired jurisdiction over the territory; and consequently we have a right to demand as much as we should, if, in a war with Mexico, we had acquired Chihuahua or Sonora, — that, when these once-existing States are reconstructed and admitted to the Union, they shall come with institutions which are in substantial harmony with the settled policy of the nation. And therefore, upon either of these theories, — upon the theory of the power of the people of the rebel States, or upon the theory of the war power of the government, — we find sufficient reason and justification for what we propose. And I implore you not to allow your minds to be diverted from the conclusion which we have thus reached, nor your judgments to be biased by the expectation or apprehension that it is my purpose, upon this foundation, to demand justice for the negro race. I assume not too much, when I say that you all, and, indeed, all my countrymen of the loyal States who entertain loyal purposes, would accept these conclusions without hesitation, if it were understood that the exercise of this just power of the nation were demanded to prevent the establishment of the office of Governor in a single family perpetually, or to prevent in any applicant State the constitution of an order of nobility, in which the government of the State should be vested permanently. If, then, this assumption be true, your objection is not to the claim that the general government has this power of scrutiny and exclusion, but to the subject-matter or the manner of its exercise. It remains for me to satisfy you, if I may be able, that the exercise of this power in the interest of universal suffrage in the South is more important to the nation than would be its exercise for the exclusion of the principle of hereditary right in public office in any or all of the applicant States.

In passing, permit me to say that there are four methods or forms of government which might be established in the rebellious States: first, military governments, responsible to the executive of the country; secondly, territorial governments, in which a law of Congress should define and pre scribe the rights of the people in reference to suffrage, with the power lodged in the President and Senate to appoint the Governor, Secretary of State, District-Attorney, and perhaps some other officers; thirdly, to recognize these States as States in the American nation, and this without any inquiry and with their old constitutions; and, fourthly, by treating the people of these eleven States as within the jurisdiction of the general government, but without institutions of any sort, permit them to frame governments and apply for admission to the Union. A military government, being irresponsible, expensive, and, for the most part, tyrannical, is unacceptable to the American people. It can be continued for a short period of time only, but ere long it would be compelled to give place to another form. Probably, with reference to some of the States, as South Carolina and Florida, a territorial government would be best adapted to the existing condition of things. In Arkansas, Tennessee, and Louisiana, there is possibly so large a loyal sentiment, that, if the colored people were allowed the right of suffrage, those States might be safely restored to their ancient relations to the Union. It therefore follows, as the practical result, that it will be necessary to adopt different lines of policy for different States.

But I wish you to consider with me the effect of permitting these eleven States to act as though they were still States within the Union. I believe there is one consideration which will control all classes of men in this country, without regard to their opinions concerning the negro; one consideration which will finally control in resisting the recognition of those States except upon the basis of universal suffrage. I refer to the subject of representation in the lower House of Congress. I have observed, within a few days, that a leading New-York journal has made the remark that the friends of negro suffrage were too fast in conceding to the rebellious States the right of representation for the four million of colored people. Gentlemen, the fact is, we are neither too fast nor too slow. We have nothing to do with the question. The Constitution of the United States, in its first article, second section, and third paragraph, has settled this matter. The words are these: —

> "Representatives and direct taxes shall be apportioned among the several States which may be included within this Union, according to their respective numbers, which shall be determined by adding to the whole number of free persons, including those bound to service for a term of years and excluding Indians not taxed, three-fifths of all other persons."

If the Proclamation of Emancipation is to stand, these four million of heretofore slaves are to be free. They reside in the fifteen old slave States. These States are to have political power in Congress, not only according to the number of *white* persons within their limits, but according to the number of *free* persons, black as well as white. What is the result? To-day, upon the census of 1860, under the three-fifths rule, there are nineteen seats in the House of Representatives which may be filled by men whose constituency, if they were voters, would be negroes of the South. In 1870, there will be a new census, and a new apportionment of political power. The South will take political power in the House of Representatives according to its combined white and colored population. I have made an estimate, which is probably not far from what will prove to be true in 1870. There will be about four and a half million of colored people in the old slave States; there will be about nine million of white people in the old slave States; and there will be about twenty-two million of people in the free States,—making thirty-five and a half million in all. Upon the constitutional basis, political power will be apportioned, in 1870, in this wise: To the four and a half million of negroes in the South, thirty Representatives; to the nine million white people in the South, sixty Representatives,—ninety Representatives from the South. To the twenty-two million of people in the North, one hundred and forty-four Representatives in Congress. Now, what is the inevitable result of the doctrine that these eleven rebellious States are States in the Union, and have a right to be represented as States? It is this: that the nine million of white people in the South are to do all the voting in the fifteen old slave States; and when you consider that the war in the South has proved pretty nearly a war of extermination of all the men between twenty and forty-five years of age, and that the proportion of women and children is vastly greater than the natural proportion of women and children to adult males in any community that has not been ravaged by the fires of war, you will understand that the number of voters among those nine million of people will be but a small proportion of the whole. These white voters of the South are to elect ninety Representatives to Congress. And who are the white men of the South? They are the men who have been in arms against the republic and against the soldiers of the republic. They are of a race which through two centuries has been contaminated by the vilest crime, the crime of slavery, until the whole public sentiment of the South has become debauched, until it has given birth to conspiracies, for the perpetration of the crimes of arson, of murder, of treason, of assassination, in all their hideous and unnamable forms,—such crimes as could not have been committed, or even contemplated, in any other country, or by any other people. It is out of the institution of slavery that there came the infamous decree by which sixty thousand of the soldiers of the republic were starved in the prisons and pens of the South; and will the people of this country, if they have a prejudice against the negro race such as human beings never felt toward any of the animate creation, from the foundation of the world until now,—will the people of this country, if they have such a prejudice even, exclude the negroes from the ballot-box, and allow it to be controlled by these nine million, or the representatives of these nine million, of white people in the South? Under all circumstances, a majority, a confessed majority of the white people of the South, have shown themselves the enemies of this country; the loyalists among them, the men who have stood by the old flag, have been few, "like angel visits." On the other hand, the black man, despised, down-trodden, with no reason to cheer or bless the flag of the republic, which to him, from the foundation of the government until the signal shot upon Fort Sumter, had been only the ensign of oppression, with no reminiscences or traditions in its behalf, has proved true to the country, has led and guided and cheered the soldier, has enlisted in the armies of the republic, has fought for the integrity of the nation and the safety of freedom; and can it be, *can it be*, in the heart of any man of the twenty million of inhabitants in the North, with an ingratitude unexampled save in the instance of Judas Iscariot, now to consign these people, their race, and their posterity to the tender mercies of the men who instituted Libby Prison and Andersonville, who sent to the islands of the ocean for the pestilence with which they hoped to blast the cities of the North, who instituted arson as a plan, and finally closed their career of systematic and organized crime by the assassination of the President of the republic? Do you propose to allow these people to send ninety Representatives into the Congress of the United States, when, according to numbers, they would be entitled to but sixty? Upon the basis of thirty-five and a half million of people, a constituency would consist of one hundred and fifty thousand inhabitants; and, the number of members of the House being limited by law to two hundred and thirty-four, the white voters of the South would take sixty members in their own right, and thirty more upon the basis of the negro population,—giving them ninety votes. They would then lack but twenty-eight votes of a majority in the House of Representatives, — twenty-eight votes which New York alone could give, which two or three other States in a moment of disaffection might give. And what is the result, or at least the possible danger? The government of this country is in the hands of rebels. Will not the men interested in public securities look to it that no such exigency arise? We have issued two and a half thousand million of public securities, the value of which depends entirely upon the good faith of the people of this country. If you put the power into the hands of these rebels, one of two things is sure to happen, — either that the rebel debt will be foisted upon the national government, or the national debt will be repudiated. And more than that: if these nine million of people in the South are to elect ninety Representatives, they will elect one for every one hundred thousand white persons represented by the voting population; while, in the North, it will take one hundred and fifty thousand persons to constitute the basis of representation; that is, two voters in the South will have equal power in the government of the country with three voters in the North. I submit that the people of the North, unless they are infatuated, so that there is no hope of their being able to comprehend the means necessary for their own salvation, will reject — once, twice, thrice, continually reject — every proposition which recognizes those States as States of the American Union. One of two things must happen, — either that the negro shall be allowed to vote, or that, by an amendment to the

Constitution, the representative power shall be based upon voters; and if, as is contended by those who oppose negro suffrage, these eleven States are States in the Union, as it requires three-fourths of the States to make an amendment to the Constitution, and as the eleven States are more than one-fourth, and are interested in the maintenance of the present condition of things, there is no hope of an amendment of the Constitution. Therefore, fellow-citizens and countrymen, you have but one path before you, and, thank God! it is the path of justice, and in it you must walk; and that path leads you to contend for and to secure to the negro the right of suffrage in this country.

We are told that the negroes will vote with their masters. I do not know whether they will or not; but it is no excuse for us, in denying them their rights, to say that they will vote in a particular way. If they have the right to vote, we are not to trample that right under our feet, because we infer that they will hereafter exercise it in some way disagreeable to us. But the same persons told us, in 1861 and 1862, that, if we put arms in the hands of the negroes, they would fight on the side of their masters. Was that prediction verified? By no means. And neither will this prediction be verified, unless the spirit of the masters is changed, and they vote on the side of this government.

It is well enough, also, for us to consider the subject of voting with reference to the negroes of the South. We have a constitutional provision in Massachusetts, that no man shall vote unless he can read the Constitution, and write his own name, — a very proper provision; but consider that it was instituted with reference to men about whose loyalty there was no question, but only this question existed, as to whether they were competent to judge of the administration of public affairs. In the ordinary course of things, it is necessary that men should be able to read and write, in order to decide intelligently upon questions of public policy. We do not, to-day, ask suffrage for the negroes because they are competent to judge of questions of public policy; but we ask for suffrage for them because they are in favor of this government, and the white people of the South are against it. That is an issue already made up. Parties have taken their stand. The whites, by a majority, are on one side; the blacks, unanimously, are on the other. They understand that question, and that is the vital question to us. It is not whether, in South Carolina, judges shall be elected by the people or appointed by the Governor: that question very likely would be better solved by men who could read and write. But the question in which we are concerned is not a question of internal policy, not a question of local or of State administration; but the question is, "Shall this government exist?" We know that the negro is in favor of its existence, and therefore, for all the purposes of voting, whether he can read and write or not, he is a safe depositary of power; and therefore I am in favor of allowing him to vote, without going into any inquiry whether he can read and write, because his power at the ballot-box is now essential to us, just exactly as his power in the field with the bayonet was essential to us during the war. In this country, there are but two means of exercising power. One is by the bayonet, in time of war; the other is by the ballot, in time of peace. We have taken the bayonêt, in time of war, out of the hands of our rebel enemies. What are we invited to do? To put the ballot, which is the instrument of power in time of peace, into the hands of our enemies, and deprive our friends of the privilege of exercising that power. Was there ever any infatuation equal to this? If these four million who have been loyal to the flag and to the Union had been Germans in the South, instead of negroes, not a man would have raised the question whether these loyal Germans, upon the restoration of the government, should be allowed to vote. Every man, with one voice, with one acclaim, would have said, "They, of course, are to vote. The only question remaining is, whether the rebels who have been in arms against this government are to be permitted to vote or not." You thus see, my friends, how far the country has been drawn aside from the true question at issue by that ancient prejudice, originating in slavery, and which has been fostered, imbittered, and spread by the influence of slavery throughout this country. You are not willing to allow to a patriot under a black skin that which you would readily concede to a patriot under a white skin. Are the people of this country more disposed to put power into the hands of rebels because they are white, than into the hands of patriots who happen to be black?

There are some over-sensitive persons who are

rather reluctant to give suffrage to the negroes, because they fear it will irritate the white people of the South. Well, my friends, I am for conciliation. I see already that very few men in the South are to be punished. Nobody among the whites is to be disfranchised. Of all the men who are suffered to live and to remain in the South,—white people, I mean,—all will enjoy the elective franchise; and I have already reached the conclusion, that there are but two men who are in any danger of suffering the penalty of the law for the crime of treason. They are Davis and Lee. I may turn aside for a single moment to say here, what I think will find a response in the judgment of the country, that those two men, above all others, deserve to pay the highest forfeit ever exacted by human tribunals from those who have violated human law. There were many leaders in the rebellion. The guilt of those men is inconceivable, and of course inexpressible. But Davis and Lee, by a peculiar supremacy, were the leaders. One was at the head of the military and the other at the head of the civil and military power of the so-called Confederacy. If we select these and execute them, it will be a warning to all men, in all time, that it is not safe to be the leaders of a rebellion against this government. Therefore, by their execution, you take all the security for the future which you can take. If you go beyond these two men, I know not where you are to stop. There are ten, twenty, fifty, one hundred, perhaps one thousand, other men who are equally guilty, each with the other. Inasmuch as no country can afford to exact blood, to any considerable extent, for political crimes, we should do that which will be justified upon the page of history, and which will lead to all the practical benefits which can result from the punishment of any number of traitors. By a peculiar pre-eminence, these two men are responsible to the country for the slow murder of our soldiers in prison. At any moment, Davis or Lee could have put an end to this cruel torture and murder of men, through months and almost years of suffering. It cannot be said, perhaps, of any other man engaged in the rebellion, that it was in his power to have suppressed this systêmatic murder; and therefore they are peculiarly responsible to the army of the republic, to the country, and to mankind, for this great crime. It is only second in turpitude to that of Mithridates, King of Pontus, who seized a Roman proconsul, carried him to the city of Pergamus, and ordered melted gold to be poured down his throat. At the same time, he sent a letter to all the cities and provinces of his kingdom, directing his officers to seize all persons owing allegiance to Rome, and execute them on a day named. Under this order, a hundred and fifty thousand men, women, and children were murdered.

Cicero referred to this crime, after the lapse of more than twenty years, in his speech, — the greatest, perhaps, of his speeches, — his speech for the Manilian law, in which he urged the appointment of Pompey to the supreme command of the army as the only means by which this crime and offence to Rome might be avenged, in common with other crimes and wrongs which the state had suffered at the hands of its enemies.

But, however heinous the crime of the rebels in the treatment of prisoners, and however responsible the Southern people are for the war and its woes, there will be no condign punishment except what is inflicted upon these two men; possibly even they may escape: but there is one punishment which we can carry home to every rebel in the South. He has been afraid of negro equality. The ballot is, in a certain sense, the symbol of equality. The Declaration of Independence does not mean that "all men are created equal" in every respect, but that no man is, by nature, in a state of political subserviency to any other man. All are equal, none supreme. I know of no punishment which would be so universally efficacious throughout the rebel States as to put into the hand of the negro the ballot, that at the ballot-box once a year, or once in two years, or once in four years, he may stand the equal of his former master. This is a punishment that will go home to every rebel in the eleven rebellious States.

By the emancipation proclamation, we have taken the initiatory steps towards the freedom of the negro; but how are liberties secured? Are there laboring men here to-day? What security have they for the integrity of their families? What security have they for the benefit of the writ of *habeas corpus?* What security have they for the education of their children at the public expense? What security have they that their testimony shall be taken in a court of justice? Their security is in the ballot. We say that men possess certain "natural, essential, and unalienable rights." How are those rights to be defended? Either by the bayonet or by the ballot. If the negroes are to protect themselves in their rights, it is for the country to give them the means, by giving them the ballot. And it is not less in favor of the South than of the whole country that we advocate negro suffrage. We of Massachusetts remember the difficulties in Rhode Island, less than a quarter of a century ago, when men of our own race, having the political power of the State in their own hands exclusively, refused to recognize the rights of other men of the same race, the same blood, equally qualified with themselves, until the concession was extorted from them by revolution; and do you expect that the white men of the South, if you allow them to institute governments with political power in their own hands exclusively, will ever concede it to the negroes, until the negroes extort it from them at the point of the bayonet? These negroes are four million to-day. They will increase through decades and centuries until they are eight, ten, twenty million; and, if you do not give them the right of suffrage now, at some future time they or their posterity will demand it, and secure it by force. Instead, therefore, of being the enemies of the South, when we demand negro suffrage, we are its real friends, because we take security in their behalf, at this early day, that hereafter they shall be saved from intestine commotion, from civil and social wars.

Perversion and misrepresentation are powerless, and argument thus far has not been heard, in behalf of the monstrous proposition that the North should consent to such a reconstruction of this government as will guarantee perpetually to two white men in the South the political power that is accorded to three white men in the North. Who are they, and what are they, if they exist at all within the limits of the loyal States, who are prepared to maintain the doctrine that Virginia, South Carolina, Florida, and Texas have the same immediate and indisputable right of representation as is enjoyed by New York, Illinois, Pennsylvania, and California? That they have not this right, is conceded by all, or by nearly all, among us. No one is prepared to accept South Carolina with her old constitution. The veriest stickler for State rights demands some alteration. This demand, however slight it may seem in its practical application, is the equivalent in principle of the demand I make. South Carolina is in the Union with her Constitution of 1860, or, as a political organization known as a State, she is not in the Union at all; and, if she is not in the Union as a State, her application for admission may be rejected until she appears with a frame of government in substantial harmony with the policy of the nation. You must be just to the negro. When you invited him to assume the uniform of the army of the republic, when you put the musket into his hand, when you asked him to jeopard, and, if need be, to sacrifice, his life in defence of the country, you did in fact, if not in terms, agree, that, if the cause — his cause as well as your own — was successful, he should have the same part in the government as yourselves; and therefore you cannot, without the basest ingratitude, now reject him. I am compelled to declare to you, my friends, in all sincerity, heinous as are the crimes of these Southern men, infamous as they will be upon the page of history, that if the people of the North, now that they have acquired liberty for themselves, now that they have secured the restoration of the Union by the services and sacrifices of the negro in common with their own services and their own sacrifices, should surrender him, bound hand and foot, as he will be if he does not enjoy the right of suffrage, into the custody of his enemies, made doubly ferocious by the events of this war, and into the custody of your enemies also, your position upon the page of history, and in the judgment of posterity, will be only less infamous than theirs. I know of no excuse that we can offer to ourselves, I know of no excuse that we can offer to this generation in other countries, I know of no excuse that we can offer to mankind in the coming ages, if, after having accepted the services and the blood of these men in defence of the flag, of liberty, and of the Union, we turn and conspire with these their ancient oppressors, and trample our faithful allies in the dust. Let it not be that this infamy is reserved for the people of this country. Of all the woes of which we have drunk through these four years, of all the instances of degradation which have been treasured up in the long annals of mankind, I know of none which will compare with the woe and the degradation of a free people, who, having secured their own liberties by the blood of their fellow-men, with base ingratitude offered their allies to the common enemy,—to the enemy of the country, of liberty, and of mankind.

I have thus, gentlemen, attempted to demonstrate the existence of sufficient and constitutional power in the government to enable Congress to hold the people of the rebellious districts under the jurisdiction of the national authority, while they are excluded from any voice in the public councils, until they frame State governments which are truly republican in form, and until evidence is furnished that the public sentiment of each proposed State is so far loyal as to justify the expectation that its general policy will accord with the general policy of the country; and this without claiming to interfere, and without interfering, with the institutions of a State.

I have also sought to demonstrate that the exercise of this power is necessary for the security of the loyal people, the preservation of the public credit, as it is connected with and dependent upon a constant exhibition of good faith, by the people and the public authorities. Moreover, you cannot fail to be influenced by the plain statement, that, under the Constitution, you must secure the elective franchise to the negro, or surrender your own equal right in the government of the country; and, finally, you are not insensible to the obligations resting upon you to secure to all men the means of protecting those rights of person and property which are the evidences of freedom and its constant support. This policy furnishes at once security to the country, equality to the whites of all sections, justice to the negro, universal punishment of the rebels, the only efficient means of stimulating the industry and developing the resources of the South, and, at last, adequate and permanent protection against civil and social feuds and wars in all portions of the country where the two races are nearly equal in numbers or strength.

I have assumed also that the instances of pardon of rebels by the President will be increased, and that in peace we shall abandon the policy which was inaugurated in time of war, and adapted to a time of war, of confiscating the property of rebels who are not distinguished by any special criminality from their associates in treason. Whether you indict and try persons or confiscate their property, the number of the guilty is so great, that many necessarily escape. During the war, we seized the property of individual enemies, as a means of diminishing the power of those in arms against us. The reason no longer remains, and it will probably be thought wise to modify our legislation so as to relieve the mass of Southern people from all apprehension. So, too, we can have no security for the loyalty of a State, until a clear majority of its population are known to be worthy of trust. Whenever a State is restored to the Union, the loyal sentiment should be sufficiently powerful to permit those who have been disloyal to exercise the elective franchise; otherwise you nourish alienation, and encourage the elements of treason and war. Our policy towards the mass of our enemies must be liberal. Restore to them, with as little delay as possible, all the personal, civil, and political rights which they enjoyed previous to the rebellion.

With such an exhibition of magnanimity towards those who have been our enemies, not even they can justly complain when we demand the elective franchise for those who have been our friends. Thus does this policy appear to be wise and conservative as a national policy; thus is it necessary to ourselves; thus is it just to our friends; thus is it magnanimous to our enemies.

EQUAL SUFFRAGE.

SPEECH DELIVERED BEFORE THE NATIONAL EQUAL SUFFRAGE ASSOCIATION OF WASHINGTON, DECEMBER, 1865.

I HOPE, ladies and gentlemen, not to trouble you at great length; at least, to leave you time and patience to listen to what will be said by our friend who will speak after I have closed.

I understand that to-day there has been a vote taken in this city, but I know not whether in the neighboring city of Georgetown, on the question whether the colored people shall enjoy the right of suffrage in this district. I am always disposed to listen to the will of the people, to consult their judgments; and, even in matters of grave legislation, I would to some extent be guided by their prejudices. I think, however, it should be borne in mind by those who dwell here permanently or for temporary purposes, that this district was set apart as the seat of government, and made by the Constitution subject to the exclusive control of the Congress of the United States. Whether or not all men shall vote is a question which does not even as much concern those who live in this city as it does those whom I immediately represent; and that, in its decision, those who represent the country are very likely to act upon the opinions which they understand are entertained by the country. Furthermore, the opinions expressed here are no guide, or even counsel or suggestion, to those who are intrusted with the administration of public affairs. The people hold, first of all, in concluding the contest we have carried on for four years at such great sacrifice, that the only proper consummation would be the recognition of the equality of all men before the law. It is here, at the capital of the nation, that the example should be set of that just recognition of all races of men, which is set forth in our Declaration of Independence, as well as in that great charter of human rights on which Christian civilization for eighteen hundred years has depended.

I mean to-night to speak rather generally of the right of suffrage.

If I shall occupy as much time as I anticipate on that question, I cannot even apply the propositions, I shall attempt to lay down, to the existing affairs of the country.

It is said that the right of suffrage is not a natural right.

Possibly you will think, on consideration, it is of very little importance whether it is a natural right or not.

If it is not a natural right, then I take it that it is not in any sense more the right of a white man than of a black man. And if it is a natural right, then it is equally the right of the black man as of the white man.

To the argument it is entirely immaterial whether it is a natural right or not.

If we consider merely those natural rights which are personal, they are hardly more than the right to breathe, the right to exist, the right of locomotion; but there are other rights which may not be natural, — personal rights, which are not less important than those which are called natural rights. The right of suffrage may not be a natural right in the sense of a personal right, but I think it is a natural social right the moment that society exists; and the existence of society is in obedience to natural law, from which no portion of the human race, not even barbarous nations, not even wandering tribes, not even nomads of the desert, have ever been able to escape. I think you must agree, on reflection, that, whether the right of suffrage be a natural right or not, it is a right which no man who has once enjoyed it will ever willingly yield up. He will rather sacrifice his own life, he will sacrifice his property, he will sacrifice possibly every thing he holds dear except the existence of his family; and, if this right be such to us who have enjoyed it, it is only on the gravest considerations, and for the most urgent reasons, we are justified in withholding it from others. I think, if you will consider society, you must agree, that it is not the individual man, not the woman, not the child, that is the element or unit of society; but it is the family.

I start, then, with the proposition that the family is the element of society, the unit of the State, and not the man, or the woman, or the child. When you consider the existence of the family, and when you consider the existence of more families than one, you have then a guide for the personal rights, not merely of the head of the family, but of all the members of the family. Consider society in any aspect you please, and it is perfectly plain, if the family be an element of society, that, in all the circumstances which concern the fortune and welfare of society, the family has the right of judgment and expression; and that this right is not due to the condition of the members, whether they are of one race, of one color, or of one class: it is the common right of humanity, wherever society exists. Wherever the family relation is known and recognized, then, on all questions which affect the fortunes of individuals, on all questions which affect the fortunes of the family, the family has the right of judgment and the right to express that judgment.

When I say the element of society and the unit of the State is the family, and that the family has the right of judgment, and the right of expressing that judgment, I have laid the foundation for the exercise of the right of suffrage; for every thing to which suffrage tends, which its power guards, which its authority creates, has reference to the protection of individuals and of families, in their relations, in their property, in their rights, in their liberties of every sort. There must be an expression, and a mode for the expression, of the opinion of the family. And here, possibly, I may come upon delicate ground. Nor should I approach this particular part of the discussion, if it were not often said, if you allow negroes to vote, of course women and children ought to vote also. Well, in this matter of voting, I accept the logic of truth, to whatever results it may lead. I think I can offer, or at least I shall offer the reasons which are satisfactory to myself, why both women and children should not vote.

First, as regards children: there is in nature — and nature teaches us the truth in all these matters — a law which no people can overcome, — that, in the existence of the human being, there is a period of infancy, of minority, of incapacity to guard and control affairs; but there is a period also when this minority is overcome by years, by discretion, by the attainment of majority as we call it, — that is, the period of life when, according to the ordinary course of human events, the individual is able to judge for himself of those matters which concern him personally, and, consequently, in reference to matters which concern his fellow-men. As to the period when minority ceases, the law must necessarily be arbitrary. In some Grecian States, it was sixteen; with us, it is twenty-one. It is immaterial where the limit is fixed, so you admit there is in nature a period of minority.

As regards women, the policy of the law, accepting the teachings of experience, is this: that in the house, in the family, there is but one opinion. Such is the general fact. It is not the opinion of the father, of the husband, merely; it is not merely the opinion of the wife and mother; it is not the opinion of the children: but it is the result reached by the influence of the domestic life of the family. It is a result reached by the experience, the judgment, and observation of all.

Now, then, you may say — I know the exceptions exist — that there is even in the family a difference of opinion on public matters. Very well; be it so. These are exceptional cases. The wisdom of the law, doubtless, is this: that so sacred is the home, so to be respected by the law is the family, that, wherever a difference of opinion exists, there should be no means for the expression of that opinion. It is wise policy in the law so to decree.

If there be but one opinion in the family as a general thing, it is the wise policy of the law, as the result of the experience of all ages, that, where a difference of opinion exists, it is better for the family that there should be no mode of expressing that difference. Then the question arises, By whom shall the opinion of the family be expressed? I think nature again teaches us, that the man who, by the law of nature which no community has ever been able to overcome, is the defender of the family, whose life is to be jeoparded in its behalf if circumstances require it, is that member of the family who is to give expression to the judgment of the family. If there be but one opinion in the family, inasmuch as the object of voting is to ascertain its judgment, the multiplication of votes, by allowing women and children to exercise the right of suffrage, adds nothing to the political power of the State, any more than it would in taxation, if, instead of assessing the tax of the family upon the father, you assessed the same aggregate upon the individual members. So, if there be but one judgment in the family, it needs but one voice to express it.

Next, what logical results follow from this? It would happen, and very properly happen, if we accept the logic, that, where the woman is left as head of the family, she should have a voice in expressing the opinion of the family on public affairs. That was the case in Hungary during some portion of the existence of that nation, and certainly there can be no objection to it.

Another thing would happen: those men who are without families would be kept from the ballot-box. My only solution of this difficulty is, that there is a reasonable presumption, that, at some time or other, they are to become the heads of families, and that therefore they should be properly attending to their political duties beforehand.

There are two other classes of persons excluded, — paupers and criminals; and you see at once the reason for their exclusion.

When you have proceeded thus far, if you accept the argument which I have submitted, I think you see that it is difficult to go beyond, and say for what reason you shall exclude the head of a family from expressing the judgment of the family on public affairs. We have in this country, as you know, excluded four million of people who are colored and of African descent. They have been absolutely excluded in the slave States, where they were held in slavery, and very generally excluded in the free States. I should like to have any person, just at this point, offer a good reason, why, now that this people are free, are made a part of society, are to be protected in their personal rights, they should be deprived of the privilege of participating in the government. Is color a reason why a man should not participate in the government of his country? Is race a reason? We have received from abroad thousands and tens of thousands of men; and after they have remained here, according to the judgment of the law, a sufficient time to justify the inference that they intend to make this country their home, to support and defend it, we accept them as citizens, with the rights of citizens.

Now, when we have amongst us three or four million of persons native born, are we to exclude them from all participation in this government on account of color alone, — for no reason except color? I suppose those who object to their enjoyment of the elective franchise would say, No, it is not on account of color; but, because these men are colored men, we infer their incapacity to exercise properly the elective franchise. But what inference is to be drawn from that fact? A pretty large part of the human race are colored people. The Chinese, the inhabitants of the islands of the East Indies are not white, the ancient Scythians, all the people who lived in the north of Africa and upon the coast of the Mediterranean, were colored people.

The Phœnicians, who not only navigated the Arabian Sea, but in the ante-historical ages passed round the Cape of Good Hope into the Indian Ocean and the islands of the Indian Sea, — men who probably visited this continent, — were not white people. Therefore you can infer nothing from the fact that a man is colored, as to his capacity.

As regards the three or four million of colored people on this continent, when we consider that they have been in servitude during many generations, that they have been deprived of all privileges, even the privilege of self-education, nothing whatever is to be inferred from the fact of their color. I have observed that the people who are most strenuous in resisting the advancement of other persons are those who apprehend, indistinctly, that, if those other persons are permitted opportunities to make progress, they will come into competition with themselves. I think the white race of this country, if they are that superior race they claim to be, ought certainly to be willing to accept the contest on equal terms. If we are beaten, if the negroes make more rapid advancement than we are able to make, I think we ought gracefully to yield the superiority to them. The suggestion is an imputation upon the white race; and that man who fears the elevation of the colored race, lest they come to an equality with the white man, I apprehend instinctively feels he is not that superior being he would have other men think he is.

But the exercise of the elective franchise is no evidence of the equality of men, — not the least. It is not evidence of equality, more than is the service which men perform as jurors. You look at twelve men in the panel, and do you infer, because they happen to be together, that they are all equal? When you see witness after witness called upon the stand, occupying the same place, to give testimony of what they know severally of the matter in issue, do you infer that those witnesses are all equal? You infer nothing of the kind. You only infer that their services, in that particular capacity, are essential to the administration of the law. When you give all men the right to vote, there is no ground for inferring that they are equal to each other in any particular, but only that the services of these men at the ballot-box are essential to the proper administration of the law. The right to vote is not a right merely, it is a duty. When a man has a place in society; when, by the constitution of the government under which he lives, authority is derived from the consent of the governed, — it is his duty, as well as his right and privilege, to go to the ballot-box, and express his opinion on public affairs.

The essential difference between our government and the aristocratical and monarchical governments of Europe is in the fact, that by theory, if not yet in practice, our government is a popular government, while theirs are in a greater or less degree exclusive. Therefore for what reason are we to exclude any portion of our citizens from the enjoyment of the elective franchise? Whenever we do it, whether it be in a large or small degree, we admit that our theory of government is wrong, and that theirs is right. Our theory is, that the whole people are better and wiser and stronger than a minority, however large. The theory of their governments is, that the whole people are not to be trusted with the administration of affairs; that some, for one reason or another, are to be excluded. Do you not see, if you are to exclude men for any reason except crime or dependence on the public for support, — if you are to exclude men for any other reason, — there is no line upon which you can stop? Is it not the old organic theory of monarchical governments, inasmuch as the mass of the people were not to be trusted, power must be put into the hands of the wisest or bravest to be found amongst them?

I come to my own State of Massachusetts. It is not often Massachusetts is called, in any particular, to aid those who are for limiting the rights of man: generally her distinction has been that she has advanced as far and as fast as possible upon the road which leads to the amelioration and elevation of the whole human race. But in our State, it is true, we have a provision in the Constitution, adopted ten years since, by which persons under sixty years of age, who come to the ballot-box, must be able to read the Constitution and to write. There are, indeed, many reasons for a provision of this sort; but I think, upon careful examination, they are reasons which will not bear the test of scrutiny. The effect, undoubtedly, of such a provision would be to induce persons, who might otherwise have remained in ignorance, to acquire a knowledge of reading and writing. I will say here, for I do not mean to be misunderstood, I do not particularly object to such a provision; but I ask you as friends of the country, that every man, without regard to qualification or condition, shall be admitted to the ballot-box. And what I ask is, that, when you make a provision which limits the right of anybody to exercise the elective franchise, it shall be a provision which applies equally and alike to all men and to every race.

If it be true, as I suppose it is, that there are thousands and tens of thousands of white men in the eleven States recently in rebellion who cannot read and write, I cannot understand how they are qualified to go to the ballot-box and vote for Representatives to Congress and for Electors of President and Vice-President, while those men who are black men, and who are no more ignorant than their white brothers, are denied the privilege upon the ground of incapacity. That is political logic which I cannot understand; but I think you will find on examination that the absence of ability to read and write, is not a reason for excluding a man from the polls. What we want is representation based upon public judgment. It is better that men should be learned, it is better that men should be wise, it is better that they should be honest. It is the duty of the government and of individuals to do whatever may be done to promote these things; but, after all, when you say that A shall not vote because he does not know as much as B, on the next occasion B may be excluded because he does not know as much as C, and so on to the end of the alphabet, when you will have placed all power in one man because he is wiser than others. That is the essence of aristocracy, of monarchy, of governments opposed to democracy. It is not pretended that men are equally wise or learned or honest, but only that the wisest and best government is obtained by taking the judgment of all men, wise and ignorant, learned and unlearned, and accepting the results.

This war has demonstrated two propositions which we all shall do well, I think, to bear in mind, that this government is wiser and stronger than any other. The wisdom of the government was first and chiefly, I say with due respect to those who have administered public affairs in legislative and executive departments, — the wisdom of this government, in this great crisis, was primarily the wisdom of the people. They anticipated the necessities of the case. They saw more clearly in States remote from the theatre of war what was necessary than even they who were intrusted with the administration of public affairs here.

It was true as early as November, 1860, before the result of the presidential election had been obtained or the election itself had taken place, that men in the various and remote sections of the country anticipated distinctly the events upon which the country was about to enter. I hope it may be recorded and remembered to the courage of the people of the country, that they anticipated the necessity of the proclamation of emancipation long before any voice went out from this capital. And so I say now, while we who are intrusted with public affairs may stand here and deliberate and move cautiously, first in one direction and then in another, the great body of the people are moving with a step precise and irresistible to the result which they see is the necessity of the condition in which the country is placed, — the granting of the right of manhood, the right of suffrage, to four million of colored people, who have already been emancipated.

I say this government has proved stronger than any other. The great mass of the people in the North, from the fact that they and their fathers through generations had had a part in the government, that it was their government, volunteered for the defence of the Union. Do you suppose that in England, in France, or in Austria, or anywhere else within the limits of the civilized countries of the earth, two or three million of men would have volunteered in defence of their country? By no means; but the old men and the young men of this country rallied to the support of the Union because they felt it was their government, because they felt it was their work which was threatened by traitors and rebels; and therefore they perilled their lives for its defence.

And it was chiefly due to the fact, that universal suffrage existed in the North, and that it did not exist in the South, that we are indebted for the triumphant conclusion of the war. If there had been no restriction upon suffrage, if these four million of black people in the eleven or fifteen Southern States of this Union had been free and endowed with the elective franchise, had possessed power, had had part in the government of the South, and had entered with their masters into this contest against the Union and integrity of the republic, they would have succeeded. Our power was in the universal right of the people to participate in the government of the country. Their weakness was in the fact that they had denied to one-third of their people the right to participate in the government. Therefore I say a popular government is stronger than any other. It is founded in the rights and affections of the people, and it will be upheld and defended by their lives. And, if there be any such thing as immortality for a State, it must be in the fact, that the State itself is founded in the immortal rights and aspirations of the people, — the right of each individual to his own life and his own liberty to a participation in the government under which he lives, and which he is bound to defend.

I do not say what the country chooses to do. I do not know what its opinions are on this question, of suffrage. I know inferences are drawn from certain events, from elections which have taken place, that the people are opposed to negro suffrage in the South; but I know, as well as I can know any thing of the future, that the people of this country are ultimately, and at a time not far distant, to reach the conclusion that they have no safety except in demanding and securing for the colored people of the South equal rights with the white people of the South.

In 1856, I was going from this city homewards. When in the State of Delaware, the train was thrown from the track. It was in the month of August. Nobody was injured, and, as usual, nobody was to blame. The passengers gathered in little squads, and, as it was before the election, they began to talk of political matters. I fell in with a company of gentlemen, chiefly from the South, — one from Georgia, and one, I think, from Texas. The pending election was the topic of conversation. Some were for Mr. Fillmore, who, you will recollect, was a candidate; and some were for Mr. Buchanan, of pleasant memory. The discussion went on, but I took no part in it. After a time, they proposed a canvass to see how the gentlemen gathered in this little knot would vote. Some voted for Mr. Fillmore, some for Mr. Buchanan; and, when they came to me, I said quietly I would vote for Fremont. That produced a little stir among these gentlemen, and, unluckily for the country, it so interrupted the canvass that we do not know to this day how it stood.

The gentleman from Georgia seemed very much disposed to press the conversation, and especially upon the public sentiment of the North, to know how we were. I saw the sort of people I had to deal with, and thought I would not move forward in the expression of my opinion rapidly; but, after a time, I said quietly, We are to beat you by and by; I do not know when. Said this gentleman, How do you come to that conclusion? I replied, You may assume any opinion you please; you may assume that the people of the North are all for Mr. Buchanan or all for Mr. Fillmore; still the result in the near future is, that we shall vote against the institution of slavery, and I come to that conclusion from these premises: The clergy and churches of the North are very generally against slavery. The schools, although they do not teach politics, are all in favor of human liberty. Last and chiefly, the women of the North are against negro slavery. To-day I say the same thing. The same influences are at work in the North in favor of justice, — justice to the black man, as well as to the white man. There are persons, I doubt not, in the North who have never claimed, and who would not perhaps to their friends admit, that they were controlled by these opinions and sentiments, yet who earnestly and reverently believe that this war, with all its sacrifices, is a just punishment, sent by Heaven upon this people for the great sin of slavery, which is but one form of injustice, and who mean, now that they have waded through blood, have seen their sons and brothers fall beneath the power of the rebellion and by the hands of treason, to clean the garments of the country from the foul stain of injustice of every form which can be ascribed to the nation in its political character. It needs no eye of prophecy, this being the case, to penetrate the future, and to see what is before us. It will turn out, whatever men may advise, whatever doctrines they may entertain in their hearts, that any arrangement or compromise or apparent settlement of this business upon any other foundation than that of justice will not stand.

I ask you, gentlemen, and I ask the country, whether four million of people are to be held as unworthy to participate in this government. I ask whether we are now to adopt a policy by which rebellion and insurrection, war and bloodshed, throughout the slave States, will be rendered certain in the future. Does any man suppose that these four million of people, one hundred thousand or a hundred and fifty thousand of whom have been in arms for the defence of this government and this country, who have been taught the arts of war, who know the power of organization, who know their rights and the means by which they are to be defended,— does any one in his senses suppose that these four million of people are quietly to submit to any arrangement, to be made here, by which they are to be deprived of their rights as men? Doubling in population as they do in every twenty-three years, soon to be eight, and soon after to be sixteen million, does any one suppose there are means by which they can be made loyal to the government of the country, except by a free, just, and generous concession to them of their rights at once? Those who ask us to pursue a policy by which these people are to be deprived of all share in the government of the country, ask us to consign these eleven States to civil and social war for an indefinite period of time. There can be no security for life, there can be no security for property, among them. The path of justice is the path of safety.

I have spoken longer, perhaps, than is well; only one thought remains which I care to present. It has been said that this is a white man's country. You will remember that the President himself, in a speech to the colored people a few months ago, repudiated that idea; and I think there will and can be nothing in his life, or the life of any man of which posterity will be more proud, than the fact, that the President of the country, at this time, gave no countenance or support to so unjust a doctrine as that. I remember when Kossuth visited the country, and for the first time addressed the people of Massachusetts at Faneuil Hall, that he told those who had assembled in the Cradle of Liberty to listen to him, that they should not say American liberty, but liberty in America. Said he, "Liberty is Liberty, as God is God."

So I say this is not the white man's country, it is not the black man's country, it is not the red man's country: it is a country which by Divine Providence has been preserved during centuries, with all its fertility and resources, where men might create and build homes and government founded upon Christian civilization. This is a country — for so it was willed — to which should come all people whom God has chosen to place upon the earth. That man is, in some form or other, an enemy to the human race, who claims this as the white man's country or the black man's country. It is the country of man, set apart and dedicated by the Supreme Ruler of the world. To call us, who are now expecting and are about to enter on the enjoyment of a restored Union, for the first time to announce that this is the white man's country, is the basest ingratitude. If such was our opinion, we should, two years and more ago, before we invited men of another color to participate with us, to jeopard and sacrifice their lives in defence of the country, — we should then have declared, that when it was free and restored, it should be the white man's country. It does not lie in our mouths, after we have accepted the blood of these men; after they have stood in the ranks and upon the field of battle in the place of your fathers, husbands, sons, and brothers; now that they sleep the sleep of death, and their bones bleach upon the plains of the South, — to say that this is the white man's country. They have earned in the noblest manner, and with the largest sacrifices, the right to call this their country.

SUFFRAGE IN THE DISTRICT OF COLUMBIA.

SPEECH DELIVERED IN THE HOUSE OF REPRESENTATIVES, JAN. 18, 1866.

THE House having under consideration the bill extending the right of suffrage in the District of Columbia, —

Mr. BOUTWELL said: —

Mr. SPEAKER, — It is only recently that I entertained the purpose to speak upon this bill, and it was my expectation to avail myself of the kindness of the chairman of the Judiciary Committee to divide with him the time allotted to him by the rules of the House; but I accept the opportunity now presented, before the previous question is demanded, to state certain views I entertain on the subject.

I may say, in the beginning, that I am opposed to all dilatory motions upon this bill. I am opposed to the instructions moved by the gentleman from New York [Mr. Hale], because I see in them no advantage to anybody, and I apprehend from their adoption much evil to the country. It should be borne in mind, that, when we emancipated the black people, we not only relieved ourselves from the institution of slavery, we not only conferred upon them freedom, but we did more: we recognized their manhood, which, by the old Constitution and the general policy and usage of the country, had been, from the organization of the government until the emancipation proclamation, denied to all of the enslaved colored people. As a consequence of the recognition of their manhood, certain results follow, in accordance with the principles of the government; and they who believe in this government are, by necessity, forced to accept those results as a consequence of the policy of emancipation which they have inaugurated, and for which they are responsible.

But to say now, having given freedom to the blacks, that they shall not enjoy the essential rights and privileges of men, is to abandon the principle of the Proclamation of Emancipation, and tacitly to admit that the whole emancipation policy is erroneous.

It has been suggested, that it is premature to demand immediate action upon the question of negro suffrage in the District of Columbia. I am not personally responsible for the presence of the bill at this time; but I am responsible for the observation that there never has been a day during a session of Congress since the emancipation proclamation, — ay, since the negroes of this district were emancipated, — when it was not the duty of the government, which by the Constitution is intrusted with exclusive jurisdiction, to confer upon the men of this district, without distinction of race or color, the rights and privileges of men. And, therefore, there can be nothing premature in this measure, and I cannot see how any one who supports the Proclamation of Emancipation, which is a recognition of the manhood of the colored people of this country, can hesitate as to his duty; and, while I make no suggestion as to the duty of other men, I have a clear perception of my own. First, we are bound to treat the colored people in this district in regard to the matter of voting precisely as we treat white people. And I do not hesitate to express the opinion, that if the question here to-day were whether any qualification should be imposed upon white voters in this district, if they alone were concerned, this House would not consider — ay, not ten men upon this floor would consider — whether any qualifications should be imposed or not.

What are the qualifications suggested? They are three. First and most attractive, service in the army or navy of the United States. I shall have occasion to say, if I discuss, as I hope to discuss, the nature and origin of the right of voting, that there is not the least possible connection between service in the army and navy and the exercise of the elective franchise, — none whatever. These men have performed service, and I am for dealing justly with them because they have performed service. But I am more anxious to deal justly by them because they are men. And when it is remembered, that, for months and almost for years after the opening of the rebellion, we refused to accept the services of colored persons in the armies of the country, it is with an ill grace that we now decline to allow the vote of any man because he has not performed that service.

The second is the property qualification. I hope it is not necessary in this day and this hour of the republic to argue anywhere that a property qualification is not only unjust in itself, but that it is odious to the people of the country to a degree which cannot be expressed. Everywhere, I believe, for half a century, it has been repudiated by the people. Does anybody contemplate such a qualification to the exercise of the elective franchise, in the case of black people or white?

And, next, reading and writing, or reading, as a qualification, is demanded; and an appeal is made to the example of Massachusetts. I wish gentlemen who now appeal to Massachusetts would often appeal to her in other matters where I can more conscientiously approve her policy. But it is a different proposition in Massachusetts as a practical measure. When, ten years ago, this qualification was imposed upon the citizens of Massachusetts, it excluded no person who was then a voter. For two centuries, we have had in Massachusetts a system of public instruction, open to the children of the whole people without money and without price. Therefore all the people there had had opportunities for education. Why should the example of such a State be quoted to justify refusing suffrage to men who have been denied the privilege of education, and whom it has been a crime to teach? Is there no difference?

I suppose it will happen, even if you pass this reading amendment, that, between any two annual elections, any negro twenty-one years of age who is in this city, or who may come here, will acquire the ability to read. The requirement will not exclude many men. My objection is not that in this district it will exclude a great number from the exercise of the elective franchise; but I object to the measure upon principle. The right to vote is a higher and better right than can be derived from the simple fact that a man can read.

I have often elsewhere endeavored to trace the origin and nature of the right to vote. I believe that during this discussion the views I entertain have not been stated; and therefore, with such brevity as I can command, I will venture to offer the opinion I entertain of the nature and proper limitations of the elective franchise. While it may not be a natural right, like the right of locomotion, like the right to breathe, — a natural, personal right, — still I think I can offer suggestions, deduced from the law of nature — which will show that it is a natural social right. I accept, as the basis of what I have to say, the great law of nature supported by revelation, — the existence of the family, — from which no people, savage or civilized, has ever escaped. The family exists by divine authority. It is the first law of society, of the community; it is the element of all States, and it has generally one idea, one opinion, and one will, upon all questions affecting the fortunes of the family or of any of its members.

Thus the creation of man, and his doings after his creation, illustrate most conclusively two facts, — the existence of the family, and the unity of the will of the family. When we admit that the family is the element of the State, the unit of society, that it has but one will, what follows? That whenever more than one family is in existence, and the question arises what shall be done with reference to the community of families, then the families are to be consulted. Hence arises the doctrine that there can be no just government except by the consent of the governed.

What I maintain next is, that you have no right to exclude from this consultation any one of the families; for the moment you do so you violate the principle of government. Consequently, but one voice is needed for the expression of the one will of the family; and the question then arises, whose voice shall it be? Properly, the voice of that one who, if the government constituted by the agency and authority of the family be assailed, is to peril his life in its defence. Thus is demonstrated the priority of right by nature which gives to the man the expression of the voice of the family, rather than to the woman or the child.

Next, Mr. Speaker, is it not seen that, if these propositions be true, the right to vote exists independently of all human agency in the sense of law; and the doctrine that the right of voting is a conventional right is not sustained by reason or history? History shows only this, that the limitations upon the exercise of the right of voting are the results of conventions. The natural social right is the right of the family to speak in all matters which concern the welfare of the family as one family in the great society and family of man.

This demonstrates, I think, that the negro has everywhere the same right to vote as the white man.

And I maintain still further, that, when you proceed one step from this line, you admit that your government is a failure. What is the essential quality of monarchical and aristocratic government? Simply that by conventionalities, by arrangements of conventions, some persons have been deprived of the right of voting. We have attempted to set up and maintain a government upon the doctrine of the equality of man, the universal right of all men to participate in the government. In accordance with that theory, we must accept the ballot upon the principle of equality. It is enjoyed by the learned and the unlearned, the wise and the ignorant, the virtuous and the vicious.

The great experiment is going on. If, before the war, any man in this country was disposed to undervalue a government thus conducted, he should have learned by this time the wisdom and the strength of a government which embraces and embodies the judgment and the will of the whole people. If the negroes of the South, four million strong, had been endowed with the elective franchise, and had united with the white people of that region in the work of rebellion, your armies would have been powerless to subdue that rebellion, and you would to-day have seen your territory limited by the Potomac and the Ohio.

And if, in the North, suffrage had been limited, as it is in Great Britain, you could not have commanded two million six hundred thousand volunteers for the defence of the republic. The unity of sentiment in the loyal States was due to the fact that every man felt that the government was his own. This only illustrates how strong a government is when it is founded upon the judgment and the will of the whole people, and how weak it is when founded upon the judgment and the will of a part.

I advance still further. I have said that I consider this question as involving other issues than the mere matter of suffrage in the District of Columbia. I do not conceal my opinion from friend or opponent. I am of those who believe that any restoration of either of the eleven States lately engaged in the rebellion to political power in the government of this country, which is not coupled with or preceded by the condition that the negroes of the South are to vote, opens a way to the destruction of this government from which there is no escape. I declare, after the gravest deliberation and the calmest reflection,—and I say it with sorrow,—looking upon the country, rent by opposite opinions on this question, that, without such a measure as I suggest for the Southern States, this government cannot outlast those who are now in the vigor of manhood. Why and how will it fail?

It will fail and fall from the fact, that, by restoration without this all-essential guarantee, we put into the hands of our enemies in the South two weapons, the blows of which we shall be powerless to parry. One is the assumption by the government of a vast and overwhelming weight of indebtedness, to be followed by a foreign war. We see to-day how difficult it is to restrain and control the people of this country in their desire to take just vengeance for the wrongs inflicted upon them by England and

France. Assume the power of this government intrusted to the hands of the late slaveholders, the men recently engaged in rebellion: does any man believe that they are restored to their right mind, that they will give an ardent support to the government? All the testimony is that they are as alien and hostile to this government as ever, and that they only seek an opportunity to strike a deadly blow.

What opportunity do you give them? They are marshalling to-day in Virginia, in South Carolina, in Louisiana, their claims upon this government. They will demand $2,000,000,000 for slaves, untold hundreds of millions of dollars for depredations committed by our armies. An aggregate of thousands of millions of claims, or demands having the color of claims, will be marshalled against the government; and you invite sixty Representatives, united, bound together by the ties of interest and of ancient and unrelenting hostility, to enforce these claims. This Congress, no doubt, is incorruptible; but when there are claims against the government to the amount of $3,000,000,000, with the support that such representatives may afford, twenty-two in the Senate and sixty in this House, with all the influence of this immense demand against the government, do you expect to resist them? Do you expect to meet them with a paper blockade, constitutional amendments? If that is your expectation, your expectation will not be realized; and when they have involved the country in an indebtedness of four, five, or six thousand million dollars; when they have broken your credit so that in the markets of the world your paper will sell for fifty cents on the dollar, and, taking advantage of the just and natural hostility of the people against European aggression, they involve you in a foreign war,—what have they to do but to march out of the Union, and bid you defiance?

Mr. SMITH.—I ask the gentleman from Massachusetts whether the loyal man of Louisiana, or of any State of the South, who has never been in the rebellion, who has resisted it from the beginning and done all he could against it, is not entitled to damages, as any man from Massachusetts or any other loyal State of the government?

Mr. BOUTWELL.—I do not reply to that question, because it is not pertinent to the debate I am now engaged in. I only ask the House to notice how pregnant is the suggestion itself of argument in support of the view I am presenting of the dangers of restoration with the elective franchise in the hands of our enemies exclusively.

Mr. SMITH.—I do not know that it is pertinent to the result the gentleman proposes to come to, but it is to the position he has assumed, and the argument he has presented.

Mr. BOUTWELL.—Secondly, you leave the rebels in possession of a power which they will surely avail themselves of when they again undertake the destruction of the government,—the opportunity to bestow the elective franchise upon the negroes. If you fail to secure the black man in his rights, he will become in a degree alien and hostile to the national government. In this condition, he will be ready to accept the right of suffrage from the Southern leaders, and transfer his allegiance, sympathy, and support from you to them. Will you leave such a weapon in the power of your enemies, when, by a timely act of justice, you can secure the zealous and unwavering support of the black race in every generation? Throughout this contest, the blacks have exhibited the purest patriotism and the highest wisdom. Can any man name an act done by them that has been injurious to them as a race or prejudicial to the country? Or can any one suggest an omission that has been prejudicial to them or to the country? So will they exhibit wisdom hereafter. If we fail in our duty, we have no right to expect their support in the future.

It is not unreasonable to anticipate, that, in twelve or twenty-four months, several of the States recently in rebellion will confer the elective franchise upon their negroes. In Louisiana, one-eighth of the voting white population, I understand, are in favor of that measure. We know that this force must be augmented by accessions of loyal men, and for this reason, — every Union man in the South who wants protection for life, for property, and for his own political rights, is compelled by necessity to form an alliance with the negroes. They are his friends; and he must make common cause with his friends, whether they be white or black.

My chief objection to this proposed restriction is, that the rebel States are not likely to do any thing more for themselves than you do for the country when you pass judgment and establish your policy here. If you put a limitation or qualification upon the exercise of the elective franchise, who does not see that its enforcement is a question of administration? And herein there is a difference between Massachusetts and this district; there is a difference between Massachusetts and Louisiana. Our inspectors and examiners are in favor of suffrage, and they desire to give every man the elective franchise. Every doubt is given to the applicant. In South Carolina and Alabama, it is also a question of administration; and do you suppose the men who will preside, and decide this question, will come to the conclusion that a negro can read, when the result is that he must also vote? Will they accept testimony that he has been in the army, when they do not want his ballot brought to bear against them, as his bayonet frequently was during the war? Do you suppose they will tax him, when they know that taxation gives him the power to interfere in the government? More than that, I do not suppose that the colored men in this district would be safe in coming to the polls. I am pretty sure, that, in the old slave States, you would have to muster the entire black male population, so that they might go to the polls in safety.

I have thus given, with less preparation than I ought to have made for the discussion of so grave a question, the views I entertain upon this subject. But beyond this, when we proclaimed the emancipation of the slaves, and put their lives in peril for the defence of the country, we did in effect guarantee to them substantially the rights of American citizens; and a Christian posterity, and heathen countries also, will demand how we have kept our faith.

Mr. SHELLABARGER. — With the permission of the

gentleman from Massachusetts [Mr. Boutwell], I desire to make a single inquiry. It is this: I understand the bill, as reported from the Judiciary Committee, proposes to strike out the word "white" from all laws relating to the district, so that, according to the law, each citizen shall have the right to vote. Now, I wish to know whether the effect of the bill will be to submit to the officers holding the elections in this district the right to decide, under and in the light of the Dred-Scott decision, that no man can vote as a citizen who is of African descent, and whose ancestors were slaves.

Mr. Boutwell.—I suppose, Mr. Speaker, that it is settled by recent authorities that the word "citizen" embraces black persons as well as white.

Mr. Shellabarger.—The gentleman does not apprehend my inquiry. The authorities of this district, we all know, will regard the decision in the Dred-Scott case as law: and, if it is law, then no person of African descent, whose ancestors were slaves, will be permitted to vote under the provisions of this bill as reported by the committee.

Mr. Boutwell.—Very likely the gentleman is right. I am addressing myself to the expediency of putting a qualification to the exercise of the right of suffrage in this district; and but one thought further remains, on the discussion of which I was just entering when interrupted by the gentleman from Ohio.

Mr. Speaker, we are to answer for our treatment of the colored people of this country; and it will prove in the end impracticable to secure to men of color civil rights, unless the persons who claim those rights are fortified by the political right of voting. With the right of voting, every thing that a man ought to have or enjoy of civil rights comes to him. Without the right to vote, he is secure in nothing. I cannot consent, after all the guards and safeguards which may be prepared for the defence of the colored men, in the enjoyment of their rights, — I cannot consent that they shall be deprived of the right to protect themselves. One hundred and eighty-six thousand of them have been in the army of the United States. They have stood in the places of our sons and brothers and friends. Many of them have fallen in defence of the country. They have earned the right to share in the government; and, if you deny them the elective franchise, I know not how they are to be protected. Otherwise you furnish the protection which is given to the lamb when he is commended to the wolf.

There is an ancient history that a sparrow pursued by a hawk took refuge in the chief assembly of Athens, in the bosom of a member of that illustrious body, and that the senator in anger hurled it violently from him. It fell to the ground dead; and such was the horror and indignation of that ancient but not Christianized body, — men living in the light of nature, of reason, — that they immediately expelled the brutal Areopagite from his seat, and from the association of humane legislators.

What will be said of us, not by Christian, but by heathen nations even, if, after accepting the blood and sacrifices of these men, we hurl them from us, and allow them to become the victims of those who have tyrannized over them for centuries?

I know of no crime that exceeds this; I know of none that is its parallel; and, if this country is true to itself, it will rise in the majesty of its strength, and maintain a policy, here and everywhere, by which the rights of the colored people shall be secured through their own power, — in peace, the ballot; in war, the bayonet.

It is a maxim of another language, which we may well apply to ourselves, that, where the voting-register ends, the military roster of rebellion begins; and, if you leave these four million people to the care and custody of the men who have inaugurated and carried on this rebellion, then you treasure up, for untold years, the elements of social and civil war, which must not only desolate and paralyze the South, but shake this government to its very foundation.

ADMISSION OF TENNESSEE.

A REPORT TO THE HOUSE OF REPRESENTATIVES UPON THE ADMISSION OF TENNESSEE, SUBMITTED MARCH 6, 1866, AND SIGNED BY MR. WASHBURNE, OF ILLINOIS, AND MR. BOUTWELL, OF MASSACHUSETTS.

THE undersigned, members of the joint Committee on Reconstruction, dissenting from the report of the majority concerning Tennessee, respectfully submit the following statement: —

The last United-States census shows that rather more than one-fourth of the people of Tennessee are colored persons, and that less than three-fourths are white. The evidence submitted to the committee shows that the colored people are unanimously loyal to this government, and that about one-half of the white persons are disloyal. In East Tennessee, the number of loyal persons far exceeds the number of disloyal; while, in Central and West Tennessee, the loyal white population constitute only a minority of the whole.

The proposition of the committee contemplates the restoration of Tennessee to political power in the government of the United States, and that the elective franchise may be confined to the loyal white male citizens of the State for a period of about fifteen years; while no provision whatever is made for the exercise of the elective franchise by loyal colored people.

Previous to the rebellion, the voting population of the State, then limited to white persons, was about 120,000. Of the present voting population, not more than 62,000, and probably not more than 50,000, can be regarded as loyal. The result of the proposition of the committee is, that a State will be exercising power in the government of the United States, in which half its white people, numbering about 60,000, and all its colored population, numbering about 80,000 adult male citizens, will be excluded from participation in public affairs. Thus of about 200,000 adult male citizens of the State, not more than 60,000 will possess political power.

The exclusion for a limited period of time of the men who have participated in the rebellion, and as punishment for their offences, meets the approval of the undersigned, and cannot, by the parties excluded, be made properly the subject of complaint; but it is a very grave question, whether a State government can be set up and maintained, according to the theory of American institutions, in which seven-tenths of the adult citizens are deprived of a voice in its public affairs.

It appears conclusively, from the testimony of Major-General Thomas, Major-General Grierson, and others, that secret organizations exist in all the rebel States, whose purpose is to obtain representation in Congress, then to impair or destroy the credit of the national government, involve the country in a foreign war, and in the end avail themselves of the opportunity thus created to effect a dissolution of the Union and the establishment of a separate government. With a knowledge of these facts, it would seem to be of the first importance, in the reconstruction of the government, to secure in every State a loyal voting population. The statistics of Tennessee show, that it is entirely practicable, by the extension of the elective franchise universally, or by a qualification which will render it practicable ultimately, and within a reasonable time, for the adult male colored population to become voters, to place the government of that State irrevocably in the hands of loyal men.

In the exigency that exists, it would seem to be wise statesmanship to accept the services and political power of men who have shown themselves, under all circumstances, to be true friends of this nation. Moreover, the admission of the colored men to the exercise of the elective franchise would enable the loyal people of Tennessee to restore to the mass of their fellow-citizens who have been engaged in the rebellion, and who are not criminally or officially distinguished from their associates, to participate, without much delay, in the government of the State and of the country.

This measure, which cannot be safely adopted if the elective franchise is limited to the white people in Tennessee, will become entirely practicable by the extension of the elective franchise as suggested. The magnanimous character of such a proceeding could not fail to induce many of those who have been engaged in the rebellion to support the government in good faith. Moreover, the rule of excluding permanently, or for a long term of years, all those who have participated in the rebellion, if adopted in the case of Tennessee, must be extended to the other rebel States. In some of those States, not more than a tenth or a fifth of the people have been loyal; and in such States it would be impossible to set up a government, with any hope that it could be maintained permanently, in which the elective franchise should be limited to the loyal white people exclusively. Hence the country will be compelled to hold such States for a long period of time without representation in Congress, and subject to the authority of the national government.

This theory is contrary to the theory of our institutions, to the practice of the government, and cannot, for any considerable period of time, be pursued. In a few years, at furthest, such States, even those where the number of loyal white people is least, will be admitted to power in the government of the country, with the elective franchise in the hands of disloyal whites, who, by irresistible majorities, will control the policy of the States and the character of their representation in Congress.

Regarded as a national question, and as a subject affecting the peace and prosperity of the country, it is of prime importance to secure to each State a loyal basis for the maintenance of its government. It seems unwise to consider as of primary importance the political character of the representative who may offer himself for a seat in Congress. The right to be represented is the right of the people. No individual has a right to be a representative until he has been duly elected. While it is eminently proper for each branch of Congress to inquire into the loyalty of every claimant of a seat whose loyalty may be questioned, it still is vastly more important to ascertain the loyalty of the constituency he claims to represent. The official life of the representative, whether in the Senate or the House, is comparatively brief, while the constituency is enduring. If the constituency be loyal, the power of the representative for evil, even though he be a man of disloyal opinions, is relatively unimportant; but, if the constituency be disloyal, no limit can be assigned to its power to affect perniciously the public welfare.

It is also to be observed, that, technically considered, a man is loyal whose disloyalty cannot be proved. If a constituency is disloyal, it will always be in its power to select, as its representative, a man who is free from any personal participation in disloyal proceedings, and yet who will give his vote and influence in a manner to thwart, impair, and finally to destroy the government.

Nor can the undersigned be indifferent to the claim of the colored people of Tennessee to a participation in the government of that State and the country. By the laws of the land, they are citizens, and are entitled consequently to the rights and privileges of citizenship. Nor does it seem to be a compliance with the provisions of the Constitution by which the United States guarantees to every State a republican form of government, if we permit Tennessee to assume relations as a State while she excludes more than one-fourth of her people from the ballot-box, which is the only means of protection in time of peace.

It should be borne in mind also, that the colored people are to be taxed as other citizens, and that they are deprived of representation permanently by the existing laws of Tennessee. It is urged as an argument for admitting the rebel States immediately, that otherwise they are subject to taxation without representation, contrary to the theory of republican government. In the case of the rebel States, the deprivation of representative power for a brief time is the result of their own criminal folly; but what justification can be offered for recognizing a system of government in Tennessee which excludes permanently more than one-fourth of its inhabitants, while they are taxed equally with those who exercise political power?

The undersigned do not, on the present occasion, express any opinion as to the legal relation sustained by Tennessee to the Union, inasmuch as they consider it more important to secure her re-appearance as a State, clothed with full power, and in harmony with the general government, upon principles which guarantee at once loyalty to the Union and domestic peace within her own borders. They therefore recommend the following amendment to the conditions reported by the committee: "Said State shall make no distinction in the exercise of the elective franchise on account of race or color."

LOAN BILL AND CURRENCY.

REMARKS MADE IN THE HOUSE OF REPRESENTATIVES, MARCH 16, 1866.

MR. SPEAKER, — There are two facts connected with our financial experience which have not, as far as I have observed, been noticed, and which seem to me to contain all that is necessary for the solution of our difficulty. I am free to say, that, if I were to follow in this matter the dictates of my own judgment, I should not incline to any legislation, further than to remove from the mind of the Secretary of the Treasury the doubt which he entertains with reference to the authority conferred upon him by the last clause of the act of March 3, 1865, by which he is authorized to convert outstanding interest-bearing obligations into new interest-bonds. I would by law so construe that language as to allow him to sell new bonds, and with the proceeds reduce the outstanding interest-bearing obligations, such as compound-interest-bearing notes.

Mr. WILSON, of Iowa. — With the permission of the gentleman from Massachusetts, I desire to make a single inquiry. I understand that the Secretary of the Treasury has been engaged for some time in converting the outstanding interest-bearing indebtedness of the United States of various kinds into long bonds, bearing gold interest. Does the gentleman desire to be understood as saying that the Secretary of the Treasury doubts his power to do that which he has been doing for months, and is still doing?

Mr. BOUTWELL. — I am not able to speak from authority, and what I have heard may not be authentic; but I have heard that the Secretary of the Treasury had converted fifty millions, and, after that conversion, doubts arose in his mind. For myself, I think that the course which he pursued is entirely justified by the law, and that he would be justified in proceeding further in the same course. But if any doubts exist in his mind, or in the mind of any other intelligent person, I think it proper that such doubt should be removed by legislation. But inasmuch as the Committee of Ways and Means have thought proper to report a bill which goes further, I am, for myself, content to try the experiment — thinking it to be an experiment — of converting the interest-bearing obligations of the country into long bonds; but I am not disposed to go further. The first fact is, that, while there has been no reduction in the amount of the currency — the circulating medium of the country — since the close of active hostilities, there has been a considerable diminution in the market price of gold. The second fact which I think worthy of observation is this: that the merchandise of the country — by that I mean the portable property of the country — is to-day in gold worth more than the same articles of merchandise were in 1859 and 1860. The suspension of specie payment seems to me to result from one of two, or from the combination of two, causes, — a panic, or a panic followed by a decrease in the convertible property of the country; that is, a process of industrial exhaustion which probably results in a disproportion in the material; portable wealth in the one country as compared with the portable, convertible wealth of other countries. It is worthy of consideration, after the Napoleonic war, although Great Britain persistently, by legislation, attempted to effect a restoration of specie payments, it was not until after many years that she was able to accomplish that desirable result. I apprehend that our country is, at the present time, in an analogous condition. I attribute our inability to resume specie payments at the present time to this: that, as the result of war and the diversion of a large amount of individual force from the peaceful labors of life, we have to-day less of convertible property than we had when the war commenced. Let me illustrate our condition by a simple statement: If I owe my friend one hundred dollars, and have not the money or property with which to pay the debt, it is entirely useless for Congress to declare by law that I shall pay it, unless I am furnished with the means to do so; but if time be given, and I employ my capacities in some productive way, and earn a hundred dollars, if then disposed I can pay that one hundred dollars without the interposition of Congress. That is the condition of this country at the present time. We have less of iron, less of cotton, less of all other results of productive industry, than other nations have with which we are in commercial relations. We must wait until, by the application of productive power, the results of our industry agree more nearly with the results of the industry of other countries, and then our paper will come to be as valuable as gold; and if, by legislation, you then command the resumption of specie payments, it will be done without financial disturbance. I think it is wise policy for the country to allow things to go on without active interference. In the natural development of events, we shall resume specie payments as early as is consistent with the business interests of the country. I believe, myself, while we should not increase our circulation, that we should wait until another harvest has been gathered in, and until the results of that harvest have been made a part of the convertible property of the country, before we attempt any legislation in the way of enforcing specie payments. I do not know that I wish to extend my remarks. I have stated, very generally, to be sure, the views I entertain. First convert those bonds which will mature within the next two years into other bonds for a longer time, and also the interest-bearing treasury notes now in the banks, leaving the four hundred and fifty millions of currency in circulation. That amount I believe to be necessary for the wants of the country. Perhaps we have not considered that the operations of the internal-revenue department alone require from fifty to one hundred million to enable it to go on collecting, as it does, three or four hundred million of dollars a year. Then we have to consider that we have added four million of people — I mean the colored people — to the trading and consuming population of the country.

This new element creates a demand for a large amount of currency. We have also to consider that such has been the increase of the products of the mines of the world since 1860, that we can never expect a return to the old prices, and therefore it will require more of the circulating medium to transact business. The advance in prices in England, and upon the Continent of Europe, since 1860, is from fifteen to twenty-five per cent on all kinds of merchandise, while the advance in the price of land is considerable; indicating that the advance in this country, of which complaint is made, is due in part to a financial change which affects the entire commercial world.

REMARKS MADE IN THE HOUSE OF REPRESENTATIVES, MARCH 19, 1866.

MR. SPEAKER,—Nobody can be more reluctant than I am to oppose a measure of a committee of the House, or resist the policy of any department of the government; but I am inclined to maintain the position that under no circumstance ought this House to confide to any agent of the government authority to diminish the non-interest-bearing legal-tender notes. I am altogether opposed to endowing an agent to do that which we think ought not to be done. If this House will look at the condition of the country with regard to its finances, it seems to me it can reach but one conclusion; and that is, that the bill submitted by my colleague

[Mr. Hooper] is one which ought to receive the support of this House and of the country. And I have an observation to make to the gentlemen on this side of the House. After having passed through four years of the greatest peril, both in a military and financial point of view, I submit that now is not the time to accept gifts from the Greeks, and that it is now a matter of honor, as well as of right, that those who sit on this side of the House, and represent a majority of the loyal people of this country, should define and limit the financial policy of the administration. We have $450,000,000 of non-bearing-interest currency. We have $260,000,000 of national-bank currency, which may reach the maximum of $300,000,000, making $750,000,000 in all. We have, in addition to that, $180,000,000 of legal-tender notes, bearing interest, which, added to the currency, amount to something more than $900,000,000. Under this condition of things, gold is to-day quoted at 128⅝. Last Friday it was 130⅝. It was proposed on this side of the House, by those who object to the measure of the Committee of Ways and Means, that the currency of the country shall be reduced between now and the first day of December next, at the discretion of the Secretary of the Treasury, one hundred and eighty million dollars, or about twenty per cent of the existing currency of the country; and if, as gentlemen contend (a proposition which I do not admit), the price of gold follows the volume of the currency of the country, then gold should stand, with that reduction, at 105, when Congress re-assembles in December next. That, sir, is as much as the business of the country can bear; but if, in addition to that, a further reduction is made of one hundred million dollars, as is proposed, three-quarters of the manufactories of the central and northern portions of the country will be suspended.

Sir, it is not a question whether the laborers shall be able to earn a dollar and a half or a dollar a day, but it is a question of work and subsistence for eight thousand of my constituents residing in one of the cities of Massachusetts; therefore I should be false to my trust, if I hesitated to say that a limit should be fixed beyond which the Secretary of the Treasury shall not go in this condition of public affairs. We offer to fix it at $450,000,000 non-bearing-interest legal tenders, $300,000,000 national-bank currency; and, if that reduction be made, specie will approximate to par with paper next December, upon the theory to which I have before referred. The authority to reduce the currency without limit is a vast authority to confide to any man. It gives the Secretary the power to make every man in the country between the Rio Grande and the St. John's, weep or laugh any day at pleasure. I, for one, can consent to no such proposition; and yet I feel bound to say that there is no man whose general financial policy I would more heartily support than that of the Secretary of the Treasury; and I should look upon it as a calamity, if his place should be occupied by any other man whom it is my fortune to know. But, notwithstanding this feeling, and although we are all aware that the power is not to be exercised, yet, by confiding it to him, we give the people reason to apprehend, that, at some time, the power may be exercised by him, or by his successor, whoever he may be; and that apprehension will be a constant weight upon the business interests of the country. I appeal to the chairman of the Committee of Ways and Means to allow this bill to be recommitted to his committee without instructions, and take their judgment after this debate. If he will agree to allow the motion to recommit to be made, I think I may say that we will not object to the reconsideration; but, if the committee insist that there shall be no recommitment of the bill, then there is no course for us but to vote against the motion to reconsider the action of Friday last.

THE CONSTITUTIONAL AMENDMENT FOR EQUALIZING REPRESENTATION.

SPEECH DELIVERED IN THE HOUSE OF REPRESENTATIVES, MAY 9, 1866.

THE House having under consideration the joint resolution (H. R. No. 127) proposing an amendment to the Constitution of the United States, reported from the joint Committee on Reconstruction, —

Mr. BOUTWELL said: —

Mr. SPEAKER, — The gentleman from Wisconsin [Mr. Eldridge] has made some remarks in derogation of the Committee on Reconstruction. I do not purpose to reply at length to those remarks. He has said that the action of the committee is a failure. We knew very well from the beginning, that, as far as he and his friends were concerned, the labors of the committee would be a failure. He puts one question, however, in behalf, I suppose, of himself and his Democratic friends, which I feel bound to answer. He says, "The committee have not told us when our troubles" — meaning, I suppose, the troubles of himself and his Democratic friends — "will cease."

Mr. ELDRIDGE. — Oh, no! the gentleman certainly misunderstood me. I meant the troubles which the Republicans themselves were making.

Mr. Boutwell. — The troubles of the gentleman and his friends are very likely to increase.

But, Mr. Speaker, the chief object which I have now in view — and I trust, that, in seeking to attain that object, I shall not go beyond the line of parliamentary debate into the domain of partisan controversy — is to show how the proposition before us from that committee traverses the policy of the Democratic party with reference to the reconstruction of the government.

I admit that the policy of the Democratic party is a simple policy. It is a policy easily comprehended. It is a policy in which for ten years, within my observation, they have been consistent. It is a policy which they laid down as early as 1856, in the platform made at Cincinnati, wherein they declared substantially — for I cannot recite the precise language of the declaration, as it is many years since I read those resolutions — that it was the right of a Territory to be admitted into this Union with such institutions as it chose to establish, and not even by implication admitting that the representatives of the existing government have any right to canvass those institutions, or to consider the right of the Territory to be recognized as a State.

From that doctrine, which probably had its origin in the resolutions of 1798, the whole of their policy to this day has legitimately followed. First, we saw its results in the theories of Mr. Buchanan, announced in 1860, that, while the Constitution did not provide for or authorize the secession of a State from this Union, there was no power in the existing government to compel a State to remain in the

Union against its own judgment. Following that doctrine, they come legitimately to the conclusion of to-day, in which they are supported, as I understand, by the President of the United States upon the one side, and, as I know, by the testimony of Alexander H. Stephens, late Vice-President of the so-called Confederacy, upon the other. That doctrine is, that these eleven States, each for itself, have an existing, immediate, and unquestionable right of representation in the government of this country, and that it is a continuous right, which has not been interrupted by any of the events of the war.

This is a simple policy. It is a direct policy. It is a policy which can be comprehended. It is the policy of the Democratic party; and whether the President of the United States or the humblest citizen of the country accepts or avows it, he has no right whatever to call it his policy. It is the policy of the Democratic party.

I wish to lay before the House a proposition, and I beg the attention of Democratic gentlemen to it. I have written out the proposition with some care, and I think that I state exactly, and I hope not unfavorably, the position of the Democratic party on this question. The proposition is this: —

1. The Democratic party maintains that a State of the American Union cannot by its own acts separate itself from its associate States.

2. That the events of this war, including the individual, organized, and public acts of the people and governments of the eleven rebellious States, have not in any way changed the constitutional relations which, previous to the war, subsisted between

those people and States on the one hand and the national government on the other; and as a consequence, —

3. That those States respectively, and the people thereof, have an immediate and unquestionable right of representation; provided, always, that in each case the person elected now is, and heretofore has been, loyal to the government and a supporter of the Constitution of the country, of which fact each House is the sole judge on the question of the right of a claimant to a seat; and therefore, —

4. That no legislation or amendment of the Constitution is necessary, or even proper, as a prerequisite to the full exercise of the right of representation in the Congress of the United States by the people and States lately in insurrection.

Mr. Randall, of Pennsylvania. — If the gentleman will insert the words "the loyal people," I think he will state the position some Democratic gentlemen take.

Mr. Boutwell. — That is the difference between the gentleman from Pennsylvania and his friend, Mr. Stephens, of Georgia. Possibly there may be no difference. Stephens insists, that, if a man be loyal to-day, there shall be no inquiry into his previous character.

Mr. Randall, of Pennsylvania. — I do not know by what authority the gentleman classifies me with Mr. Stephens.

Mr. Boutwell. — I will not make any classification disagreeable to the gentleman. I wish to ask whether he means, by the word "loyal," a man who declares himself to be loyal now, or does he propose to ascertain whether the man has heretofore been loyal?

Mr. RANDALL, of Pennsylvania. — I mean to say, on the question of representation, that, when a man comes from a State, competent to be qualified as you and I have qualified, we should admit him.

Mr. BOUTWELL. — That is a proposition, and not an answer to the question.

Mr. RANDALL, of Pennsylvania. — The gentleman has urged the great consistency of the Democratic party. If he will allow me, I will send to the Clerk's desk, to be read, a portion of the Chicago platform. I would like to show the inconsistencies of his own party.

Mr. BOUTWELL. — I have no time for the inconsistencies of any party. When I have proved the consistency of the gentleman's own party, I think he ought to be satisfied. They have been consistent in wrong-doing as far as the interests of the country are concerned, and upon this point I make an observation which I desire to have considered in connection with the distinction with which I preface it.

I do not say that every man who supports the propositions which I have stated here to-day gave aid and comfort to the rebellion, and participated in treason; but the converse of this proposition is true, and the country ought to notice the fact. The instincts of men are higher than the reason of men; for, through the instincts, God teaches without the intervention of fallible logic and theories of reason. The instincts of men are right on all these matters. The affirmative proposition that I lay down is, that, as far as there is any testimony before the country, every traitor of the South, and every sympathizer with treason in the North, sustains the policy of the Democratic party and the President. That is an alarming fact. We traverse these propositions, and if there be any gentleman upon this floor not identified with the Democratic party who still sustains what he understands to be the executive policy, I will offer him five minutes of the brief time remaining to me to show to the House and country wherein the policy of the President differs from the ancient and consistent policy of the Democratic party.

Mr. Randall, of Pennsylvania. — I will show the gentleman.

Mr. Boutwell. — The gentleman is not called upon.

With all kindness, I desire to ask my friend who represents the sixth district of the city of New York [Mr. Raymond] whether he does not see that these propositions, which are sustained by the President and the Democrats throughout the country, if carried into effect portend the destruction of the government.

First, chiefly we traverse the Democratic propositions by a resolution now before this House in this particular. We demand equality of representation based upon the exercise of the elective franchise by the people. The proposition in the matter of suffrage falls short of what I desire; but, as far as it goes, it tends to the removal of the inequality at present existing: and, while I demand and shall continue to demand the franchise for all loyal male citizens of this country, I cannot but admit the possibility that ultimately those eleven States may be restored to representative power without the right to vote being conferred upon the colored people; and I should then feel myself doubly humiliated and disgraced, and criminal even, if I should neglect to do what is in my power in behalf of a proposition which equalizes representation.

Can any party or any man defend the Democratic proposition now before the country to allow the States lately in rebellion to come in with their power undiminished, so that two rebel soldiers, whose hands are dripping with the blood of our fellow-men, whose opinions as to the right of this government to exist are unchanged, shall exercise the political power of three loyal Union soldiers? Yet the gentlemen who support this proposition ask the country to accept these States with their representation undiminished. And those echoing the language of Alexander H. Stephens are unwilling that the Constitution shall be amended in this particular until the return of the eleven States, thereby rendering it absolutely impossible that there shall be any adjustment of these difficulties after the return of those States.

I can do no less than say that I believe that the man, of whatsoever party or State, who adopts this proposition, or uses his influence for its support by the people, is recreant to the cause of justice, of liberty, and of humanity, on this continent. And yet to that doctrine, so full of injustice and so flagrant in principle, the Democratic party is committed. And, in this hour of the nation's peril, it is our sad misfortune that we are compelled to admit that he who has received the suffrages of a generous people for the second office in the gift of the country accepts it as his doctrine.

The justification of all this is "once a State, always a State;" that there is no power in the general government to resist this policy; and that we who say that nothing shall be done in the way of restoration to political power to those States until this inequality is adjusted, are ourselves disturbers of the public peace, and advocates of disunion.

Well, sir, I am for a Union, but for that Union only in which there is substantial justice among the men and between the States composing it. I accept one fact, and no gentleman can escape the force of that fact; and that is, that these eleven States are not to-day represented in the Congress of this country, and with my consent they never shall be until this inequality is adjusted, or its adjustment provided for. That is the fact. How it has come to pass that they are not represented is not material to the business we have in hand. I accept the statement made by Mr. Lincoln in his last public address, that these States are out of their proper practical relations to the Union; and I assert, as a necessary and natural consequence, that they cannot get into their proper relations, except by our consent who represent the loyal States of this country. This is the material fact; and it is wholly unnecessary at the present time to inquire into the truth or falsity of the various theories which have been presented on the subject.

Some objection has been made by gentlemen on this side of the House, as well as the other, to the third section of the article reported by the committee. I freely confess that the adoption of the third section is not necessary to the subject-matter which we have in hand. My own views of reconstruction lead me in the opposite direction. I should prefer to include those who are our friends rather than exclude even those who are our enemies. But inasmuch as gentlemen on this floor are not prepared, as they say, to include those in the governing force of the country who have sustained the country, I see no safety for the present except in some sort of exclusion of those who are its enemies. We are to consider what sort of enemies these men are. We have defeated them in arms; but, in the proposition of the Democratic party, we invite them to the only field in which they have any chance of success in the contest in which they have been engaged.

They have been beaten; and what do you ask, and what do you offer? You ask them to come into the councils of the nation, where they have a chance of success, and where the only chance of success remains. Who are these men? They are the men who to-day are radically, honestly, persistently, and religiously opposed to this government, if this government exercises its functions. The gentleman from Wisconsin [Mr. Eldridge] may not have heard of what Mr. Stephens told the committee; and who is Mr. Stephens? Mr. Stephens was believed to be the most conservative, most Union-loving man in the whole Southern country; and, if the opinions to which I shall refer be his opinions, with how much stronger reason may we infer that they are the opinions of those to whom formerly he himself was somewhat opposed! What does he tell us? He tells us that in 1861 he protested against the action of the secessionists, not because he believed that they had not a constitutional basis upon which to stand, but because he thought secession bad policy, and he says that to-day his opinions are unchanged. That is to say, Mr. Stephens believes that this government has no right to exist, if the insignificant State of Florida, for instance, thinks it ought not to exist; and what Mr. Stephens believes, according to his own testimony, is believed by the great majority of the people whom he represents in Georgia, and in various portions of the South, and whose views he understands. These are the men that you are invited to receive into the government of the country, — men who deny the right of this government to exist.

It is said by gentlemen on the other side of the House, that, when they present a Representative here, he must be a loyal man. I need not say to gentlemen acquainted with the technicalities of the law, that a loyal man, for all purposes of representation, is a man whose disloyalty cannot be proved. When we open the doors of the Senate and of this House to representatives from that section of the country, they will be required only to present men who cannot be convicted of having participated actively and willingly in the work of treason; but they may send men here who represent treasonable and disunion opinions, and we shall have no power to protect ourselves against them. When ever was a more insidious idea presented to the people of this country than that there is any security in demanding merely loyal representatives? We are false to our duty if we do not go further, and require that in each of these States, before they are allowed representation, the masses of the people shall be loyal. The representative will reflect the views of the people. You cannot "gather grapes of thorns, or figs of thistles." You must wait, if it be necessary to wait, until there is a loyal controlling public sentiment in each one of these States. It is nothing to this country that Tennessee sends Mr. Maynard, a loyal man, here. We want to know what Tennessee is; and the circumstance that Mr. Maynard is himself a loyal man, if his State is not loyal, is a reason why he should neither ask to be received or we submit to his admission. And it is not sufficient that there be loyal districts in the State. A State is represented in the Senate and in the House as a State. There is no constitutional capacity for representation except through a State organization. Representatives in this House are apportioned by the Constitution among the several States, and the State is necessarily a unit for the election of Senators.

When we find that Tennessee is, as a whole, loyal to the government, then we may accept Representatives and Senators from Tennessee, and trust to the people to send loyal men here. But if we accept Representatives from Tennessee because they, individually, are loyal, while Tennessee herself is disloyal, she will soon thrust into this House, and into the government of the country, disloyal men. What does this policy portend? Mr. Stephens denies the constitutional efficacy of our amendment abolishing slavery. He says that slavery has been abolished by the States, implying thereby that it may be re-established by the States. He says that the law taxing the people of this country has no constitutional force, because the eleven States are not represented. Do you not see that his insidious and dangerous doctrines, which are responded to by the whole Democratic party of the country, portend the destruction of the public credit, the repudiation of the public debt, and the disorganization of society? We are the conservative, the order-seeking, the Union-loving, the loyal men of the country. They who oppose measures for the pacification of the country with reference to the rights of the States and the rights of individuals are the disorganizers, the disloyal and dangerous men of the republic.

Sir, it will be found that the Union party stands unitedly upon two propositions. The first is equality of representation, about which there is no difference of opinion. The second is, that there shall be a loyal people in each applicant State before any representative from that State is admitted into Congress. And there is a third: a vast majority of the Republican party, soon to be the controlling and entire force of that party, demand suffrage for our friends, for those who have stood by us in our days of tribulation. And for myself, with the right, of course, to change my opinion, I believe in the constitutional power of the government to-day to extend the elective franchise to every loyal male citizen of the republic.

EQUALITY OF THE NEGRO.

A SPEECH DELIVERED IN FANEUIL HALL, MAY 31, 1866.

GENTLEMEN, — I am in a good degree surprised by the kind reception you give me, and I think that for the moment you must have forgotten that I am a member of the central directory, an organization, as I understand, dangerous to the peace and liberties of this country. In connection with the organization of the Committee on Reconstruction is an event now historical, which I think was a chief means of public security and national life. I refer to the resolution adopted by the House of Representatives on the first day of its session, declaring that no Senator or Representative should be received into either branch of Congress, until the right of the State from which the person came had been recognized by Congress, with the concurrence of the President. It was in that act that we raised a bulwark against all the efforts that from that day to this have been made by the executive, by corrupt men, by parties, and by presses, to force the Congress of this country to deal with individuals, instead of dealing primarily and chiefly with the right of those eleven States respectively to be represented in Congress.

There are two questions, or two topics, as I observe from the responses given, in which you have a special interest. One is the punishment of the rebels, and the other is the recognition of the rights of the colored people of the South. As far as I can judge, you take but little interest in all the other topics presented to you. In regard to the first, the punishment of rebels, you may as well content yourselves with the belief that not a single rebel is to be in any manner punished as a criminal. The most that can be expected is a provision like that now pending for an amendment of the Constitution disqualifying certain persons from holding office, but beyond that the public expectation is to be disappointed. We have waited a year for the arraignment and trial of the leader of this great conspiracy; and apparently he is to-day no nearer a trial than he was a year since, although there is no legal obstacle whatever to his arraignment, trial, conviction, and sentence.

In regard to the other question, the rights of the men of the South who have been heretofore in slavery, there is more hope; and, for one, I believe that this government is never to be reconstructed until the full and equal rights of the colored people of the South are recognized as a governing force in the country. When I say that, I take into consideration all the incidents and the ultimate effect of that proposition. I do not expect merely a general declaration that the negro is to be equal to the white man before the law. That is an uncertain proposition. I do not know exactly what it means. I go further, and say that the negro is to exercise the highest privilege of the free man, — the ballot; and I expect, as a necessary consequence of the exercise of that privilege of a free man, that he is to be elected to office. There are those among us who would say that the negro is to enjoy equal privileges before the law. Others may say he shall exercise the elective franchise; but when we admit that he is to exercise the elective franchise, we must admit that he is to be eligible to office, and, if eligible to office, in the course of years he will be elected to office. Are you prepared for that? If you are not prepared for that result, you have not accepted the great principle on which this contest rests.

The last time that I stood upon this platform was after the fall of Atlanta, in the early autumn of 1864. This hall was then thronged; and before me was an assemblage, as I learned afterwards, composed of an organization called the McClellan Club of this city. Enrolled in that organization, as I saw from the faces before me and inferred from the responses given, were large numbers of Irishmen. The majority of them were natives of Ireland. I do not see many of them here to-day; but at this moment, when, from private information and public rumor, it is understood and believed that the Irishmen are engaged in some attempt, the exact nature of which we do not comprehend, for the redemption of their native land, I desire to make an observation to them. They never will succeed, they never ought to succeed, until they entertain more liberal views of the rights of men than they have manifested as citizens of this country. I think I have some right to make this observation, because in 1854 and 1855, when the entire sentiment of the State, or a vast proportion of the public sentiment of the State, was arrayed against them as a race and class, I took no part in the hostile movements. But I have not been an inattentive observer of passing events. They have hated despotism; but they have hated despotism, as I understand them, chiefly because they suffered from the despotic power of the tyrant, and not because they loved liberty. When the Irish people, and when our own people, have accepted the great truth, that it is not enough to hate the tyrant, but that it is necessary to love liberty for the sake of liberty, then we and they will have a just right to contend for liberty, and there will be good reason for believing in our success in the contests in which we are engaged.

I may as well in this connection make a further remark pertinent to Irishmen and to our own people also who entertain erroneous opinions concerning the negro. It is this: If I were to ask an Irishman why he left Ireland and came to this country, he could give but one answer. He would say that he left his native land on account of the oppression of England. The oppression of England has driven three million of Irishmen from Ireland to this continent. Many of them are in New England. They have come from a country vastly superior in all its natural resources to that in which they are dwelling. It has a better climate, a more fertile soil, vast mineral resources of every sort, water power sufficient to turn the entire machinery of Great Britain, fisheries, harbors, facilities for commerce, external and internal; and yet they have come from Ireland to New England,—

cold, dreary, cheerless New England. Here is only a barren soil, an uninviting climate. What, then, is to happen hereafter? We have been told and told, by high authority in times past, that, if we emancipated the negroes, they would come North. The real fact was, that, after the war had developed a sentiment of liberty in the negroes, there was no way of keeping them in the South except to emancipate them.

The people must now look at this fact in another of its relations. If you do not do justice, or see that justice is done, to the negro where he is, and where he chooses to remain, he will come where you are. Inasmuch as the attractions of Ireland could not keep Irishmen there, on account of the oppression of Great Britain; so, if you permit the oppression of the negro in Tennessee or Virginia or North Carolina or South Carolina, he will come here. Now, my friend from Ireland, you who believe it is the worst of things that the negro should vote lest he should be your equal, I have this to say to you. If you think it more pernicious to your welfare that the negro should vote for Mayor and Aldermen in Charleston, S.C., than that he should come upon the wharves and streets in this city, and compete with you for that labor with which you maintain your families, take your choice, and deprive him of the right to vote in Charleston, and he will come here; but, if you give him his rights where he is, you will retain whatever rights and privileges you now enjoy. Of all the disgraceful facts which have marked the annals of nations during the last century, there is nothing more to be reprobated, nothing which will be more severely and justly condemned by history, than the character and conduct of those of the Irish people who have come here to enjoy with us the liberties of this continent, and have allied themselves with the traitors and enemies of freedom, to some extent for the overthrow of the government and institutions of the country, and who now to-day lend willing aid to those who seek to deprive the negro of his just rights. While the redemption of Ireland from the oppression of Great Britain commends itself to the common sense and affections and sympathies of the people of this country, you of the Irish race can never expect to enlist our sympathies actively in your behalf, or engage our co-operation or secure our prayers, until you show yourselves, not the haters of tyranny merely, but the lovers of liberty as well,—ready to aid in securing for other men those rights which you seek for yourselves.

[At this point there was an interruption by a gentleman in the audience, who said, "I am an Irishman, and I am in favor of negro suffrage. I should like to ask if Irishmen have not fought bravely for the liberties of this country; if they have not been led on by brave men, Sheridan and Thomas Francis Meagher, and others, who, like themselves, were Irishmen."]

My young friend here says he is an Irishman, and in favor of negro suffrage. All the better for him. I have not complained of him, or of those who are like him, but of those of his countrymen who have here enjoyed those privileges which he enjoys, but who have not redeemed the pledge which in effect they made to the people of the country, to be true to freedom in this and every crisis. So far as they fought under Sheridan and others, all honor to them; but it is not enough that the war be carried on upon the battle-field only. The contest of arms is over; but we approach a greater contest, in which the men already subdued in arms seek to enter the citadel of the republic, and seize the power of the nation for the perversion of the institutions of the country and the overthrow of liberty. I complain, not that Irishmen did not go into the war and do duty on the battle-field, but that they now hesitate and allow themselves to be made the instruments of the ancient allies of traitors for the overthrow of the liberties of the people.

There are many topics of public concern, but I shall confine myself to the consideration of a single other subject. It is this: There are now pending in Congress certain propositions to amend the Constitution of the United States. Those propositions seek the public welfare in three directions: first, equality of representation; secondly, security for the future; thirdly, to some extent punishment of the rebels, by disqualifying them for a certain time from holding office. Many of you know, that, as far as I am myself concerned, I am not quite content with these propositions, because they omit to secure suffrage to the negro. I say here what I shall have occasion to say elsewhere, that the Republican party will not be committed to the admission of the rebel States upon the adoption by those

States of these proposed amendments to the Constitution. We shall demand something more, and in the enforcement of that demand we shall be resolute and uncompromising. We shall demand that those States severally, before they are admitted to representation on the floor of Congress, by their own fundamental law, shall provide for the enfranchisement of the negro. We shall accept nothing less. If the work of reconstruction is to be performed in disregard of the negro's rights, it is a work so unjust that I will not participate in it. If the people of this country, when they are appealed to in October and November next, insist on this work being done, they must provide other hands than mine for the doing of it. I am assured by testimony and by statements upon which I rely, that whenever Congress shall say that Tennessee, Arkansas, and North Carolina can be admitted if they provide for the exercise of the elective franchise by the negro, that that provision will be made. There are thousands and tens of thousands of Union men in those States who know perfectly well, that, if the negro does not vote, they will be powerless in the midst of rebels who control those States. They only desire that Congress shall say, You must do this before your State can be admitted, and they will proceed to argue with and induce their people to adopt a system of impartial franchise for black and white citizens. Thus the adoption of the proposed amendment to the Constitution is but part of the work. More remains to be done. And my chief desire has been to induce you and the people of the State to see to it, that no arrangement, no compromise, no system of reconstruction, is adopted or agreed to, which does not recognize the right of the negro as a citizen of the State where he is, and as a citizen of the country to which he belongs.

THE ADMISSION OF TENNESSEE.

SPEECH DELIVERED IN THE HOUSE OF REPRESENTATIVES, JULY 20, 1866.

THE House having under consideration the joint resolution providing for the admission of Senators and Representatives from Tennessee, —

Mr. BOUTWELL said: —

Mr. Speaker, — I am not ignorant of the fact that the votes of the House already taken foreshow conclusively its purpose to pass the pending joint resolution for the admission of Tennessee. I can see many reasons which operate on the minds of others, as they do upon my own mind, tending to such a course; but, after the most careful reflection during months and years, I am still as deeply convinced as ever of the dangerous nature of this proceeding. While I am conscious that my voice falls upon unwilling ears; that it is the fixed purpose of the House, in the presence of a great political struggle, to adopt this measure; and though I am the humblest of the members of this body, with less right than any other man to address the country, and with no hope whatever that my words will reach posterity, — I yet avail myself of the kindness of the gentleman who has charge of this resolution, and raise my voice here and now, and for the last time, against the consummation of this scheme.

This morning I offered an amendment, on which, however, the gentleman from Ohio [Mr. BINGHAM] declined to allow the House to vote, which embodies my opinions concerning the admission of Tennessee. If gentlemen observed the language of that amendment, they are aware that I have in some degree departed from my own settled convictions as to the right of all men to the enjoyment of the elective franchise, in deference to what I understand to be the judgment of the majority of this House, and possibly at this time to what is the judgment of the loyal people of the country. The resolution that I proposed provided for impartial suffrage in that State by the act of its own people, as a condition precedent to its admission to the exercise of power in the government. It secured justice to the colored people of Tennessee first, and then to the colored people of the revolted and still rebellious section of this country.

I am not troubled by the informalities apparent in the proceedings of the Tennessee Legislature upon the question of ratifying the constitutional amendment. It received the votes of a majority of the members of a full House; and, when the proper officers shall have made the customary certificate and filed it in the Department of State, it is not easy to see how any legal objection can be raised, even if two-thirds of the members were not present, and although that proportion is a quorum according to the Constitution of the State.

My objections are not technical, but vital and fundamental. First, the constitution which they submit here, and which by your preamble and by your vote you declare under the Constitution of the United States to be a republican form of government, is not, as it appears to me, such in fact. I have not time now, in these thirty minutes, to trace the history of the opinions entertained by the founders of the republic as to what constitutes a republican form of government. But, if they identified themselves with any opinion or idea upon this subject, it was this: that whenever powers were conferred by hereditary rules upon a class of men, or whenever by hereditary rules a class of men were excluded from all participation in the government, that government was necessarily anti-republican in form as well as in fact. I do not assert that it is necessary that every man should vote, and that a government in which terms and conditions are imposed is necessarily anti-republican: but the terms and conditions must be reasonable; they must be such as to render it not only possible, but probable, that the great majority will be able to meet the requirements of the law.

What is this House to-day, in the name of the people of this country and under the Constitution, declaring? That a State Constitution by which more than eighty thousand male citizens are for ever, for themselves and for their posterity, deprived of all part in the government of that State, is republican in form. Sir, that government is an aristocracy; it is an oligarchy; it is not republican; it is not democratic. Wherever a man and his posterity are for ever disfranchised from all participation in the government, that government is not republican in form.

Next, are we to question the existence of the power on our part to accomplish that which I now suggest ought to be accomplished, — the enfranchisement of the freedmen of Tennessee, — as the beginning of the great work of reconstruction upon a republican basis? We have positive power with reference to the States that have been in rebellion, which we have exercised by the passage of the act establishing and continuing the Freedmen's Bureau, and the passage of the Civil Rights Bill.

I do not now discuss the question whether we have the power directly to enfranchise the negroes of Tennessee and of the other States recently in rebellion. I have an opinion upon the question, but I offer no argument in its support at the present time. I believe that that power exists in Congress; but now I appeal to the negative authority of the government, that we may reject Tennessee, North Carolina, Arkansas, until they perform this act of justice for the country, for the negroes, for themselves. In thus requiring an additional act of justice on their part as a condition precedent to their return to the enjoyment of their former power in the country, we have the authority of President Lincoln, of President Johnson, and of numerous acts of this Congress and of the last Congress. We have exacted conditions precedent to the admission of those States to representative power in the government of the country. Through Presidents Lincoln and Johnson the country insisted upon the ratification of the amendment abolishing slavery, the repudiation of the rebel debt; and now we demand, even in the case of Tennessee, the ratification of the pending amendment to the Constitution equalizing representation, and all as conditions precedent to the exercise of power in the government. With equal, if not with more justice, we may demand an impartial system of suffrage.

Nor can it be maintained with propriety that this exaction shall not be made, because there are States, exercising their full functions as such, in which the negroes are excluded from the ballot-box. The injustice in those States is not of such magnitude as to endanger the peace and safety of the country; while, in the case of the rebellious States there seems only the alternative of equal suffrage through the demands of the government on the one hand, and civil or social war on the other. Hence, while we may condemn the exclusion of negroes from the ballot-box in States now represented in Congress, there may be no public necessity for an attempt to remedy the wrong by the action of the general government. Moreover, in the case of the loyal States, the general government cannot apply a remedy except by affirmative, positive action, for which the country is not prepared, and for which there is no controlling public necessity. In the case of the States lately in rebellion, we are not under the necessity of taking affirmative legislative action. The proceeding on our part is simply and wholly within the domain of the precedents cited and the authority of the Constitution. The abolition of slavery by the Constitution has given a new meaning to the phrase "republican government;" for it is now settled that a State in which slavery exists is not republican in form according to our Constitution, though previous to the ratification of the amendment the fact may have been otherwise. While slavery existed, it was generally true, however, that all free citizens were voters. To this rule there were some exceptions, but they were few and relatively unimportant.

I proceed now to consider the expediency of this measure. There are in Tennessee not less than two hundred thousand able-bodied adult male citizens; and you are consenting that the political power of that State shall be put into the hands of less than sixty thousand. By the Constitution of Tennessee, more than half the white male citizens of that State are disfranchised. Of this I do not complain; but, in addition thereto, eighty thousand male colored citizens of the State are also disfranchised, — making an aggregate of one hundred and forty thousand men who are excluded from participation in the government. The sixty thousand loyal white men come here, and ask to be accepted as a State; and you are solemnly resolving, in the presence of the country, in the light of history, and under the influence of the traditions of the republic, that the government is republican in form.

What do you invite and invoke in the future? Do you suppose that these sixty thousand rebels are to rest quiet under their exclusion from political power in the government of that State for any considerable number of years? Such an expectation, if entertained, will not be realized. On the other hand, this action invites and renders necessary a combination between the eighty thousand colored men and the sixty thousand rebels. The rebels, forgetting their past prejudices, and the loyal blacks, forgetting the disloyalty of the sixty thousand rebels, will join hands and overturn the government of the State. And what you are doing to-day for Tennessee you are to be invited hereafter to do for the other ten States of the South. There is only an alternative. It is in this: that the four million colored people shall escape from the tyranny which you authorize the Southern oligarchs to exercise over them. And I bid the people, the working people, of the North, the men who are struggling for subsistence, to beware of the day when the Southern freedmen shall swarm over the borders in quest of those rights which should be secured to them in their native States. A just policy on our part leaves the black man in the South, where he will soon become prosperous and happy. An unjust policy forces him from home, and into those States where his rights will be protected, to the injury of the black man and the white man both of the North and the South. Justice and expediency are united in indissoluble bonds; and the men of the North cannot be unjust to the former slaves, without themselves suffering the bitter penalty of transgression.

I ask of this House what the answer is to be, when the other ten States demand recognition and the admission of members. Do you say they shall not be admitted on the terms you now offer to Tennessee? What other terms will you exact of Arkansas, North Carolina, and South Carolina? You can exact none in addition to what you are now exacting, unless you demand for them what I now demand for the people of Tennessee, — impartial suffrage for all loyal adult male citizens. And, if you then hesitate to meet the question from which you now shrink, — the right of the negro to vote, — you will have no excuse for denying full political rights to the other ten States. Arkansas has complied with the conditions named in the preamble to the resolution; and you have no excuse for refusing to admit Arkansas, except the excuse I now offer for refusing to admit Tennessee. You will have again upon you that question which you so much dread, but which cannot be postponed and which must be met, whether the colored men of the South, once in slavery but now free, are to be endowed with the rights of citizens of this country. But if you say as you will say, unless the people rise in their majesty and demand justice for their suffering fellow-men, that these States may be admitted, as Tennessee is to-day to be admitted, then to what extremity of woe have you reduced the country! You have, as the result of your policy, four million discontented loyal persons made discontented by your action. You have in the States of the South more than five million discontented rebellious white people. You compel these classes, naturally enemies, to unite under the force of circumstances which now you may control for the good of the country; and if, as we believe, the white race is the dominant race, at least for the time being, in intellect and intelligence, you thus give to the rebel class of the South the moral, physical, and political power which can be derived from the influence they will exercise over the four million blacks. Does any one believe the blacks are to be exterminated? The old fable of Antæus is founded in the nature of man. They who labor on the soil never yet have been and probably they never can be exterminated. And consider, further, that the blacks are organized into churches; they are establishing everywhere schools; they are becoming the possessors of land; they have military knowledge. Do you expect that such a people, though yet in their infancy, are to be exterminated? They will continue to exist; they will thrive even under oppression; but the day may come, and I fear it may come soon if this policy be pursued, when they will assert by force, and by dangerous combinations, the natural rights with which they have been by God endowed.

And what do you offer to the loyal whites of the South? You offer them only submission, degradation, or expatriation. Do you suppose that, when you have established in the other Southern States governments like that of Tennessee, in which the disloyal whites are excluded, and the loyal blacks are also excluded, the loyal whites can withstand for a moment the surging waves of public sentiment which will rise and foam and rage, however unjust and foul their origin? If, on the other hand, the negroes are permitted to vote, even in small numbers only in the beginning, they naturally become the allies and friends of the loyal whites of the South; and especially will they be our friends in any future controversy involving the integrity of the Union. No country can afford to disregard the rights or the power of an eighth of its population;

and, above all, it is dangerous for this government to authorize or tolerate an unjust policy toward so large a proportion of its citizens.

There are in this country two great political public wrongs, one of which you have taken the proper means to remedy by an amendment to the Constitution, securing to a white man in the North equal political power with a white man in the South. We are agreed upon that. When a white man's rights are concerned, there is no difference of opinion upon this side of the House as to the necessity of protecting him. But there is another great wrong, for which you make no provision, offer no remedy, present no excuse; and that is the denial of the elective franchise to the black men of the South.

I must say for the gentlemen upon the other side of the House that they are consistent in this matter. They have never asserted the citizenship of the black man; they have denied it; they have never invited him into the army, nor called upon him to fight the battles of the republic. They have, as far as they had the power, refused his services; and, however wrong they may have been, they have been consistent in their course. But, upon this side of the House, it is otherwise. We have recently passed an amendment to the Constitution, to be submitted to the States, declaring that negroes are, under the Constitution, hereafter to be citizens; and now, when we have the power to secure for them the rights of citizens, we are silent. We have invited them into the armies of the republic, and now we abandon them to those who have been for years their enemies and oppressors. How are we to reconcile to ourselves, to our country, and to posterity this great inconsistency on our part?

I am as much attached to party as any man can be; but the jewel of the Republican party is its consistency, based upon justice, and now we abandon justice and accept inconsistency as our policy. Is not the history of this country full of warning? I will not mention names; but, from 1850 to the close of the rebellion, the pathway of ambition for parties and for men has been strewn right and left with the fragments of parties and the remains of politicians that have proved false to justice, to humanity, and to republican principles. Do you inquire whether these States are to be for ever excluded? By no means. We have assurances from North Carolina, Tennessee, Arkansas, and Texas, that, if this Congress will but demand impartial suffrage, the people of those States who are loyal to the Union will enter the contest, second the demand for impartial suffrage, contend for it, and ultimately, as they believe, they will secure it. I speak under the impression, the firm conviction, that we to-day here surrender up the cause of justice, the cause of the country, in the vain hope that the admission of Tennessee may work somewhat for the advantage of the party which has controlled the country during these last six years. We surrender the rights of four million people; we surrender the cause of justice; we imperil the peace and endanger the prosperity of the country; we degrade ourselves as a great party which has controlled the government in the most trying times in the history of the world. Fortunate will it be for us, for those whom we represent, and for the future of the country, if these apprehensions shall not be realized; and, humble though I be, but in the full conviction that they are not groundless, I enter my earnest protest against this proceeding. Believing it to be wrong, I declare my convictions in the presence of those who have the power to prevent the wrong; and I make the declaration with a sense of responsibility such as has never before rested upon me in any experience of my life.

THE USURPATION.

[FROM THE "ATLANTIC MONTHLY," OCTOBER, 1866.]

THERE are three passions to which public men are especially exposed, — fear, hatred, and ambition. Mr. Johnson is the victim and slave of all; and, unhappily for himself and unfortunately for the country, there is no ground for hope that he will ever free himself from their malign influence.

It is a common report, and a common report founded upon the statements of those best acquainted with the President, that he lives in continual fear of personal harm, and that he anticipates hostile congressional action in an attempt to impeach him and deprive him of his office. He best of all men knows whether he is justly liable to impeachment; and he ought to know that Congress cannot proceed to impeach him, unless the offences or misdemeanors charged and proved are of such gravity as to justify the proceeding in the eyes of the country and the world.

There is nothing vindictive or harsh in the American character. The forbearance of the American people is a subject of wonder, if it is not a theme for encomium. They have assented to the pardon of many of the most prominent rebels; they have seen the authors of the war restored to citizenship, to the possession of their property, and even to the enjoyment of patronage and power in the government; and, finally, they have been compelled, through the policy of the President, to submit to the dictation, and in some sense to the control, of the men whom they so recently met and vanquished upon the field of battle. The testimony of Alexander H. Stephens everywhere suggests, and in many particulars exactly expresses, the policy of the President.

Mr. Stephens asserts that the States recently in rebellion were always entitled to representation in the Congress of the United States; and Mr. Johnson must accept the same position; for, if the right were once lost, it is impossible to suggest how or when it was regained. It is also known, that, while the Johnston-Sherman negotiations were pending, Mr. Davis received written opinions from two or more persons who were then with him, and acting as members of his Cabinet, upon the very question in dispute between Congress and Mr. Johnson, — the rights of the then rebellious States in the government of the United States. These opinions set up and maintained the doctrine that the rebel States would be at once entitled to representation in the government of the country, upon the ratification or adoption of the pending negotiations. It may not be just to say that the President borrowed his policy from Richmond; but it is both just and true to say that the leaders of the rebellion have been incapable of suggesting a public policy more advantageous to themselves than that which he has adopted. The President knows that the people have been quiet and impartial observers of these proceedings; that the House of Representatives has never in public session, nor in any of its caucuses or committees, considered or proposed any measure looking to his impeachment.

The grounds of his fear are known only to himself; but its existence exerts a controlling influence over his private and public conduct.

Associated with this fear, and probably springing from it, is an intense hatred of nearly all the recognized leaders of the party by which he was nominated and elected to office. Evidence upon this point is not needed. He has exhibited it in a manner and to a degree more uncomfortable to his friends than to his enemies, in nearly every speech that he has made, commencing with that delivered on the 22d of February last.

Superadded to these passions, which promise so much of woe to Mr. Johnson and to the country, is an inordinate, unscrupulous, and unreasoning ambition. To one theme the President is always constant; to one idea he is always true,—"He has filled every office, from that of alderman of a village to the Presidency of the United States." He does not forget, nor does he permit the world to forget, this fact. In some form of language, and in nearly every speech, he assures his countrymen that he either is, or ought to be, satisfied with this measure of success. But have not his own reflections, or some over-kind friend, suggested that he has never been elected President of the United States? and that there yet remains the attainment of this one object of ambition?

Inauguration day, 1865, will be regarded as one

of the saddest days in American annals. We pass over its incidents; but it was fraught with an evil suggestion to our enemies, and it must have been followed by a firm conviction in the mind of Mr. Johnson that he could not thereafter enjoy the confidence of the mass of the Republican party of the country. He foresaw that they would abandon him, and he therefore made hot haste to abandon them. And, indeed, it must be confessed that there was scarcely more inconsistency in that course on his part, than there would have been in continuing his connection with the men who had elected him. His nomination for the Vice-Presidency was an enthusiastic tribute to his Union sentiments; beyond a knowledge of these, the Convention neither had nor desired to have any information. Mr. Johnson was and is a Union man; but he was not an anti-slavery man upon principle. He was a Southern State-Rights man. He looked upon the national government as a necessity, and the exercise of any powers on its part as a danger. His political training was peculiar. He had carried on a long war with slaveholders, but he had never made war upon slavery. He belonged to the poor white class. In his own language, he was a plebeian. The slaveholders were the patricians. He desired that all the white men of the South, and of Tennessee especially, should be of one class, — all slaveholders, all patricians, if that were possible; and he himself, for a time, became one. Failing in this, he was satisfied when all became non-slaveholders, and the patrician class ceased to exist. Hence, as far as Mr. Johnson's opinions and purposes are concerned, the war has accomplished every thing for which it was undertaken. The Union has been preserved, and the patrician class has been broken down.

Naturally, Mr. Johnson is satisfied. On the one hand, he has no sympathy with the opinion that the negro is a man, and ought to be a citizen; and, on the other hand, he shares not in the desire of the North to limit the representation of the South so that there shall be equality among the white men of the country. He is anxious rather to increase the political strength of the South. He fears the growing power of the North. The same apprehension which drove Calhoun into nullification, and Davis, Stephens, and others into rebellion and civil war, now impels Mr. Johnson to urge the country to adopt his policy, which secures to the old slaveholding States an eighth of the political power of the nation, to which they have no just title whatever. To the North this is a more flagrant political injustice than was even the institution of slavery. He once expressed equal hostility towards Massachusetts and South Carolina, and desired that they should be cut off from the main land, and lashed together in the wide ocean. The President appears to be reconciled to South Carolina; but, if the hostility he once entertained to the two States had been laid upon Massachusetts alone, he ought to have felt his vengeance satisfied when her representatives entered the Philadelphia Convention arm in arm with the representatives of South Carolina, assuming only, what is not true, that the sentiment of Massachusetts was represented in that Convention. As a perfect illustration of the President's policy, two men from Massachusetts should have been assigned to each member from South Carolina, as foreshowing the future relative power of the white men of the two States in the government of the country. The States of the North and West will receive South Carolina and the other rebel States as equals in political power and rights, whenever those States are controlled by loyal men; but they are enemies to justice, to equality, and to the peace of the country, who demand the recognition of the rebel States upon the unequal basis of the the existing Constitution.

Of these enemies to justice, equality, and the peace of the country, the President is the leader and the chief; and, as such leader and chief, he is no longer entitled to support, confidence, or even personal respect. He has seized upon all the immense patronage of this government, and avowed his purpose to use it for the restoration of the rebel States to authority, regardless of the rights of the people of the loyal States. He has thus become the ally of the rebels, and the open enemy of the loyal white men of the country. The President, and those associated with him in this unholy project, cannot but know that the recognition of the ten disloyal States renders futile every attempt to equalize representation in Congress. The assent of three-fourths of the States is necessary to the ratification of an amendment to the Constitution. The fifteen old slave States are largely interested in the present system, and they will not consent voluntarily to a change. The question between the

President and Congress is, then, this: Shall the ten States be at once recognized, — thus securing to the old slave States thirty Representatives and thirty electoral votes to which they have no title; or shall they be required to accept, as a condition precedent, an amendment to the Constitution which provides an equal system of representation for the whole country? It is not enough, in the estimation of the President, that the loyal people should receive these enemies of the Union and murderers of their sons and brothers as equals; but he demands a recognition of their superiority and permanent rule in the government by a voluntary tender of an eighth of the entire representative force of the republic. When before were such terms ever exacted of the conqueror in behalf of the conquered? If the victorious North had demanded of the vanquished South a surrender of part of its representative power in the government, as a penalty for its treason, that demand would have been sustained upon the principles of justice, although the proceeding would have been unwise as a measure of public policy. As it is, the victorious North only demands equality for itself, while it offers equality to the vanquished South. Was there ever a policy more just, wise, reasonable, and magnanimous?

Yet the President rejects this policy, deserts the loyal men of the North by whom he was elected, conspires with the traitors in the loyal States and the rebels of the disloyal States for the humiliation, the degradation, the political enslavement, of the loyal people of the country. And this is the second great conspiracy against liberty, against equality, against the peace of the country, against the permanence of the American Union; and of this conspiracy the President is the leader and the chief. Nor can he defend himself by saying that he desires to preserve the Constitution as it was, for he himself has been instrumental in securing an important alteration. "The Constitution as it was" has passed away, and by the aid of Mr. Johnson.

Nor can he say that he is opposed to exacting conditions precedent; for he made the ratification of the anti-slavery amendment a condition precedent to his own recognition of their existence as States clothed with authority. Thus is he wholly without proper excuse for his conduct. Nor can he assert that the rebel States are, and ever have been, States of the Union, and always and ever entitled to representation and without conditions; for then is he guilty of impeachable offences in demanding of them the ratification of the constitutional amendment, in dictating a policy to the Southern States, in organizing provisional governments, in inaugurating constitutional conventions, in depriving officers elected or appointed by authority of those States of their offices, and, in fine, in assuming to himself supreme authority over that whole region of country for a long period of time. Thus his only defence of his present policy contains an admission that he has usurped power, that he has violated the Constitution, that he is guilty of offences for which he ought to be impeached. Thus do the suggestions which the President tenders as his defence furnish conclusive evidence that his conduct is wholly indefensible.

While, then, the President cannot defend his conduct, it is possible for others to explain it.

Its explanation may be found in some one or in several of the following propositions: —

1. That the rebel leaders have acquired a control over the President, through the power of some circumstance not known to the public, which enables them to dictate a policy to him.

2. That he fears impeachment, and consequently directs all his efforts to secure more than a third of the Senate, so as to render a conviction impossible.

3. That he seeks a re-election, and purposes to make the South a unit in his favor, as the nucleus around which the Democratic party of the North must gather in 1868.

4. That he desires to re-instate the South as the controlling force in the government of the country.

In reference to the first proposition, we are restricted to the single remark, that it is not easy to imagine the rebels capable of making any demand upon the Executive which, in his present state of mind, he would not be prepared to grant. He has pardoned many of the leaders and principal men of the rebellion, and some of them he has appointed to office. He has resisted every attempt on the part of Congress to furnish protection to the loyal men of the South, and he has witnessed and discussed the bloody horrors of Memphis and New Orleans with cold-blooded indifference. Early in his term of office, he offered an immense reward for the person of Jefferson Davis; and now that the accused has been in the official custody of the President, as the head of the army, for more than fifteen months, he has neither proclaimed his innocence and set him at liberty, nor subjected him to trial according to the laws of the land. Davis is guilty of the crime of treason. Of this there can be no doubt. He is indicted in one judicial district. The President holds the prisoner by military authority; and the accused cannot be arraigned before the civil tribunals. Davis was charged by the President with complicity in the assassination of Mr. Lincoln. There is much evidence tending to sustain the charge; but the accused is neither subjected to trial by a military commission, nor turned over to the civil tribunals of the country. These acts are offences against justice; they are offences against the natural and legal rights of the accused, however guilty he may be; they are offences against the honor of the American people; they are acts in violation of the Constitution. If the elections of 1866 are favorable to the President, they will be followed by the release of Davis, and the country will see the end of this part of the plot.

Upon any view of the President's case, it is evident that he has thrown himself into the arms of the South, and that his personal and political fortunes are identified with Southern success in the coming contest. He claims to stand upon the Baltimore platform of 1864, and to follow in the footsteps of President Lincoln. The enemies of President Lincoln are reconciled to this assumption, by the knowledge that Mr. Johnson's counsellors are the Seymours, Vallandigham, Voorhees, and the Woods. Mr. Johnson, under these evil influences of opinion and counsel, has succeeded in producing a division of parties in this country corresponding substantially to the division which Demosthenes says existed in Greece when Philip was engaged in his machinations for the overthrow of the liberties of that country. "All Greece is now divided into two parties, — the one composed of those who desire neither to exercise nor to be subject to arbitrary power, but to enjoy the benefits of liberty, laws, and independence; the other, of those who, while they aim at an absolute command of their fellow-citizens, are themselves the vassals of another person, by whose means they hope to obtain their purposes."

The Republican party desires liberty, independence, and equal laws for all people: the presidential party seeks to oppress the negro race, to degrade the white race of the North by depriving every man of his due share in the government of the country, and, finally, to subject all the interests of the republic to the caprice, policy, and passions of its enemies.

The presidential party is composed of traitors in the South who had the courage to fight, of traitors in the North who had not the courage or opportunity to assail their government, of a small number of persons who would follow the fortunes of any army if they could be permitted to glean the offal of the camp, and a yet smaller number who are led to believe that any system of adjustment is better than a continuance of the contest.

The presidential party controls the patronage of the government; and it will be used without stint in aid of the scheme to which the President is devoted.

It only remains to be seen whether the courage, capacity, and virtue of the people are adequate to the task of overthrowing and crushing the conspiracy in its new form and under the guidance of its new allies. The Republican party carries on the contest against heavy odds, and with the fortunes of the country staked upon the result.

One hundred and ninety-one men have been recognized as members of the present House of Representatives. There are fifty vacancies from the ten unrecognized States; consequently a full House contains two hundred and forty-one members. One hundred and twenty-one are a majority, — a quorum for business, if every State were represented. Of the present House, it is estimated that forty-six members are supporters of the President's policy. If to these we add the fifty members from the ten States, the presidential party would number ninety-six, or twenty-five only less than a majority of a full House, No view can be taken of the present House of Representatives more favorable to the Republican party, — possibly the President's force should be increased to forty-eight men. It is worthy of observation, that neither the Philadelphia Convention nor the President has breathed the hope that the Republicans can be deprived of a majority of the members from the loyal States. The scheme is to elect seventy-one or more men from the loyal States, and then resort to revolutionary proceedings for the consummation of the plot. The practical question — the question on which the fortunes of the country depend—is, Will the people aid in the execution of the plot contrived for their own ruin? Upon the face of things, we should say that it is highly improbable that the new party can make any important gains; indeed, it seems most improbable that the President can survive the effect of his own speeches. But we must remember that he is supported by the whole Democratic party, and that that party cast a large vote in 1864, and that in 1862 the Republican majority in the House was reduced to about twenty.

In the Thirty-eighth Congress the Democratic party had ten or fifteen more votes than are now needed to secure the success of the present plot. To be sure, the elections of 1862 occurred at the darkest period of the war. The young men of the Republican party were in the army, and but a small number of them had an opportunity to vote. There was still hope that a peace could be made through the agency of the Democratic party. These circumstances were all unfavorable to the cause of the patriots.

The Democratic party is now weaker than ever before. Its identity with the rebellion is better understood. The young men of the country, in the proportion of three to one, unite themselves with the Republican party. As an organization, considered by itself, the Democratic party is utterly powerless and hopeless.

The defection of Mr. Johnson, however, inspires the leaders with fresh courage. It is possible for them to enjoy the patronage of the government for two years at least, and it is barely possible for them to secure the recognition of the ten rebel States, or, in equivalent words, the ten Democratic States, to the Union.

This combination is formidable; but its dangerous nature is due to the facts that Mr. Seward's name and means of influence are still powerful in the State of New York, and that he has joined himself to the new party and become an instrument in the hands of designing men for the organization of another rebellion. Outside of New York, Mr. Johnson's gains in the elections will be so small that the Union majority will remain substantially as in the present Congress; nor can we conceive that the gains in that State will be adequate to the necessities of the conspirators. It is probable that the undertaking will prove a failure: but it should never be forgotten that the country is in peril; that it is in peril in consequence of the uncertain political character of the State of New York; and that that uncertain character is justly attributable to the conduct of Mr. Seward. If, then, Mr. Johnson succeed in the attempt to change the character of this government by setting aside the Congress of the loyal States, Mr. Seward will be responsible, equally with Mr. Johnson, for the crime.

Reverting to the statement already made, that neither Mr. Johnson nor any of his supporters can even hope to secure a majority of the members elected from the States represented in the present Congress, it only remains for us to consider more specifically the scheme of revolution and usurpation in which these desperate men are engaged. The necessary preliminary condition is the election of seventy-one members of Congress from the twenty-six States. To these will be added fifty persons from the ten unrepresented States, making one hundred and twenty-one, or a majority of Congress if all the States were represented. This accomplished, the way onward is comparatively easy.

When the Thirty-ninth Congress re-assembles in December next, Mr. Johnson and his Cabinet may refuse to recognize its existence, or, recognizing it as a matter of form, deny its legitimate authority.

He would summon the members of the Fortieth Congress to assemble in extra session immediately after the 4th of March. Fifty persons would appear claiming seats as representatives from the ten States. The Republicans would deny their right to seats, — the supporters of the President would maintain it. The supporters of the President, aided directly or indirectly by the army and police, would take possession of the hall, remove the Clerk, and organize the assembly by force.

Whether this could be done without bloodshed in Washington and elsewhere in the North remains to be seen; but as far as relates to the organization of the House, there can be no doubt of the success of the undertaking. We should then see a united South with the President at the head, and a divided North; the army, the navy, the treasury, in the hands of the rebels. This course is the necessity of Mr. Johnson's opinions and position. It is the natural result of the logic of the rebels of the South and of the Democratic party of the North. Mr.

Johnson believes that the present Congress intends to impeach him and remove him from office. Admit that this fear is groundless, yet, if he entertains it, he will act as he would act if such were the purpose of the two Houses. Hence he must destroy the authority of Congress. Hence he arraigns its members as traitors. Hence he made the significant, revolutionary, and startling remark, in his reply to Reverdy Johnson as the organ of the Philadelphia Convention, "*We have seen hanging upon the verge of the government, as it were, a body called, or which assumed to be, the Congress of the United States, but in fact a Congress of only a part of the States.*" This is a distinct, specific denial of the right of Congress to exist, to act, to legislate for the country. It is an impeachment of all our public doings since the opening of the war, of all our legislation since the departure of Davis and his associates from Washington. It is an admission of the doctrine of secession; for, if the departure of Davis and his associates rendered null and void the authority of Congress, then the government, and of course the Union, ceased to exist. The constitutional amendment abolishing slavery is void; the loan acts and the tax acts are without authority; every fine collected of an offender was robbery; and every penalty inflicted upon a criminal was itself a crime. The President may console himself with the reflection that upon these points he is fully supported by Alexander H. Stephens, late Vice-President of the so-called Confederacy.

We quote from the report of his examination before the Committee on Reconstruction.

"*Question.* Do you mean to be understood, in your last answer, that there is no constitutional power in the government, as at present organized, to exact conditions precedent to the restoration to political power of the eleven States that have been in rebellion?

"*Answer.* That is my opinion.

"*Question.* Assume that Congress shall, at this session, in the absence of Senators and Representatives from the eleven States, pass an act levying taxes upon all the people of the United States, including the eleven, is it your opinion that such an act would be constitutional?

"*Answer.* I should doubt if it would be. It would certainly, in my opinion, be manifestly unjust, and against all ideas of American representative government."

Thus it is seen that these two authorities concur in opinion; although it must be confessed that the late Vice-President of the so-called Confederate States in urbanity of manner and in the art of diplomacy far surpasses the late Vice-President (as Mr. Johnson, if his logic does not fail him, must soon say) of the so-called United States.

Having thus impeached the existing Congress and denied its authority, the way is clear for the organization of a Congress into which members from the ten States now excluded shall be admitted.

Representatives who do not concur in these proceedings will have only the alternative of taking seats among the usurpers, and thus recognizing their authority, or of absenting themselves and appealing to the people. The latter course would be war, — civil war, with all the powers of the government, for the time being, in the hands of the usurpers. The absenting members would be treated as rebels, and any hostile organization would be regarded as treasonable. Thus would the rebels be installed in power, and engaged in conducting a war against the people of the North and West.

If, on the other hand, the representatives from the West and North should deem it wiser to accept the condition, and await an opportunity to appeal to the country, how degrading and humiliating their condition! They might for a time endure it; but finally the people of the North would rise in their might, and renew the war with spirit and power, and prosecute it until the entire rebel element of the country should be exterminated. The success of Mr. Johnson in the elections is to be followed, then, by usurpation and civil war. It means this, or it means nothing. The incidents of the usurpation would be, first, that the old slave States would secure thirty Representatives in Congress and thirty electoral votes, or an eighth of the government, to which they have no title whatever unless the negroes should be enfranchised, of which there would be then no probability; and, secondly, that two white men in the South would possess the political power of three white men in the North. The results of the usurpation would be strife and civil war in the North, and, finally, the overthrow of the usurpers by force, to be followed, possibly, by an exterminating war against the rebel population of the South.

Already has one of Mr. Johnson's agents announced the usurpation in substance, and tendered to the country a defence in advance of the commission of the crime. The defence is simple and logical. Congress refuses to receive the members from ten States. Those States have the same immediate right of representation as the other States. Congress is, therefore, a revolutionary body. Any proceeding which secures the right of all the States to be represented immediately is a constitutional proceeding. This is intelligible. Alexander H. Stephens is the author of this cardinal doctrine of the presidential party. On the other hand, Congress maintains that enemies vanquished in war, though formerly citizens and equals, cannot dictate the terms of adjustment; nor even enjoy the privileges of a Constitution which they have violated and sought to destroy, without a compliance with those terms which the loyal people may deem essential to the public safety.

The issue is well defined. Shall the Union be restored by usurpation, with its attendant polittical inequality and personal injustice to loyal people, and consequent civil war, or by first securing essential guaranties for the future peace of the country, and then accepting the States recently in rebellion as equals, and the people of those States as friends and citizens with us of a common country?

The question is not whether the Union shall be restored: the Republican party contemplates and seeks this result. But the question is, Shall the Union be restored by usurpation, — by a policy dictated by the rebels, and fraught with all the evils of civil war? The seizure of the government in the manner contemplated by Johnson and his associates destroys at once the public credit, renders the public securities worthless for the time, overthrows the banking system, bankrupts the trading class, prostrates the laborers, and ends, finally, in general financial, industrial, and social disorder.

POLICY AND JUSTICE IN PUBLIC AFFAIRS.

AN ADDRESS DELIVERED BEFORE THE MERCANTILE LIBRARY ASSOCIATION, BOSTON, WEDNESDAY EVENING, NOV. 7, 1866.

WHEN I accepted the invitation of your committee, it was implied, if not expressed, that I should discuss passing political topics; and you will naturally expect me, in the beginning, to declare with emphasis the satisfaction we all feel that certain grave questions concerning the fortunes of the country have been settled by the judgment of the people, at the October and November elections. But I think I ought not to omit to express the obligations which are due from us to two persons, whose names have not, as far as I know, been often, or perhaps ever, associated together, to whom we are largely indebted for these successes. I refer to Mr. Seward, the Secretary of State, and to "Nasby," of the "Toledo Blade," both of whom, with undiscriminating zeal, have supported the policy of the President, — although some persons suspect that they are both satirists. Those gentlemen, in the profusion of their arguments in behalf of the executive policy, have convinced nearly every person who has listened to the one, or read the productions of the other, of the unsoundness of that policy which they have undertaken to maintain.

In connection with the recent elections and their results, there are two facts which ought not to pass without observation. One is, that by very meagre majorities we have carried the great States of Pennsylvania and New York. In the latter State, in a vote probably not much less than three-fourths of a million, we have maintained the ascendency of the Republican party, and secured the election of a Union man for Governor, by a majority not exceeding twelve or fifteen thousand voters,—not more than two per cent of the entire voting force of that State. This fact shows conclusively that the contest is not yet over, that the battle is to be fought on other fields and with other issues. The second great fact is, that the State of Maryland, one of the border States,—a State in which more has been done than in any other of the border States, except, possibly, Missouri,—has surrendered, under the influence of the President and Governor Swann, to rebel associations and to rebel control. While this result, as far as Maryland is concerned, was not unexpected, I regard it as the omen of a happy future, in the conclusion I reach that the people of this country cannot long be blind to the great truth, that there is no security for republican principles or for the prevalence of Union sentiments in any State which during this century has been cursed by the institution of slavery, except in rallying the entire force of that State to the support of the Union and of free government.

The subject on which I speak to-night, is not novel, and my plan of discourse is simple. I shall discuss the topic announced,—"Policy and Justice in Public Affairs." By "policy," I mean that course of conduct which proceeds from the opinions of men, with reference to what it may seem to them wise to do under a given condition of things, without regard to the justice of their proceedings. Said Mr. Burke, a long time ago, "Justice is the great standing policy of civil society; and any eminent departure from it under any circumstances lies under the suspicion of being no policy at all." One of the most eminent men of antiquity declares that "it is not possible to found a lasting government upon injustice, perjury, and treachery. These may succeed for once, and borrow for a while from hope a gay and flourishing appearance; but time soon reveals their weakness, and they fall into ruin of themselves. As in every structure the lowest parts should be the firmest, so the grounds and principles of all our actions should be just and true." We shall learn, if we have not been taught the lesson sufficiently already, that it is not possible in government to discard justice, and rely upon mere human policy.

There are in governments, and in the affairs of government, three forms which injustice may take. First, it may be recognized in the Constitution of the government itself; secondly, in the policy of the government with reference to domestic affairs; and, lastly, in the policy of the government in its foreign relations. I propose, in the first place, to call your attention to a few signal instances of the effects of injustice in the conduct of nations, chiefly in their domestic affairs, with the design of gathering therefrom, if possible, some force of argument by which I may dissuade you from the purpose, if purpose you have, of re-establishing this government upon the principles of manifest injustice.

Some of us have not forgotten the story of the partition of Poland; and we know very well, that, from the time of its partition, the Poles, exiles from their native land, have been the enemies, in every capital in Europe, of the governments that participated in or sanctioned that injustice. They have been the promoters of revolution, and the disturbers of the public peace everywhere. We remember, also, the injustice of Austria in respect to Hungary; and it does not require any stretch of the imagination to accept the inference, that, in the recent conflict between Austria and Prussia, the power of Austria to resist the demands and the material forces of Prussia was very much diminished by the circumstance that she did not enlist heartily the support of the Hungarian portion of her empire. We know very well, too, the injustice of England towards Ireland. For many centuries, England has been unjust in every particular to the Irish people; and now we see, that not only are there disorder and violence in Ireland, but that the disaffection extends to this country, and disturbs the British possessions on the American continent. It is also true that, at a more recent period, England, desiring to see us prostrated under the power of the rebellion, lent herself to the support of the rebels, and contributed, indirectly, to the destruction of our commerce upon the ocean. Through the policy of Great Britain, piratical corsairs were put afloat, sailing under the flag of the Confederate States, with no port into which they could enter, no prize court anywhere which could adjudge whether the prizes taken by those corsairs were legal prizes or not; establishing, as a matter of fact, a new principle of maritime law, — that the man who walks the quarter-deck may decide whether the prize he takes is lawfully captured or not; and Great Britain to-day is powerless relatively, because she consented to and permitted that unjust policy in maritime affairs. She is not able to make war upon any nation that has a single port. Nay, more than that: if there be a nation on the face of the globe that has not a port, and that nation should engage in a contest with Great Britain, she may employ the maritime capacity of the United States, or of any other commercial power, and drive British commerce from the ocean. Great Britain has not the capacity to maintain her population from her own soil, and hence she is dependent, for her supply of bread, upon her commercial resources. When Prussia and Austria combined for the purpose of wresting Schleswig and Holstein from Denmark, England was disposed to resist the wrong. She was finally compelled, however, to withdraw from the contest; for she saw that Prussia and Austria, acting upon her own rules of maritime law, could, either directly or indirectly, put afloat privateers or quasi ships of war, that would drive her commerce from the seas. Great Britain cannot regain her position as a maritime nation until she recedes from her doctrine in regard to the "Alabama" and the "Shenandoah," compensates this country for the losses we have sustained, and incorporates into the maritime law of the world a provision which shall at once discard and denounce the policy on which she acted during the rebellion.

In another instance, a longer time ago, England suffered by a similar unjust policy. Our ancestors, prior to the Revolution, contended, as they had a right to contend under the principles of the feudal law, that they were a self-governing people, independent of Parliament, having here their properly and legally constituted representative assemblies, with the king at the head of the colonial governments, as he was at the head of the government at home. The Parliament of Great Britain undertook to assert a different principle, and to maintain that the colonies here were subject to the people and Parliament of Great Britain, contrary to the charters, and contrary to the principles of the feudal system. This injustice led to the Revolution, and to the separation of the American colonies from the British government.

We, in our own experience, have had a signal illustration of the impolicy of injustice in the government. In the years 1787, 1788, and 1789, when our ancestors were framing the Constitution of the United States, the pretension was set up by two of the States particularly, — South Carolina and Georgia, — that slavery should be recognized by the Constitution; that twenty years should be allowed for the importation of such persons as any State chose to import; and, by the general consent of the country, three-fifths of the people who were held as slaves in the slave States were counted as of the basis of representation. The result of that arrangement was, as we very well know, that for forty years at least, from 1820 to 1860, there was no union between the States of the North and of the South. The tendency of the government was to disunion, to separation, to division, and war. Finally, the result came which was inevitable from the first, — division, war, conflict, and the sacrifices through which the people have passed.

If we can gather any instruction from this experience of our own, or from the experience of other countries, we ought to accept the lesson which is taught, and resolve, now and for ever, that this government shall not be reconstructed except upon the principles of justice. It is with that end in view that I speak to-night. Justice in the constitution of a government tends to justice and unity in its administration. Injustice in government tends constantly to division of opinion, diversity of ideas, conflict of policies, and finally to war. Reconstruction of the government implies that in some way or other it has been broken; it implies separation; it implies division; it implies that there are parts of the nation that are not in their ordinary and accustomed relations to the whole; and it implies the right, on the part of those sections that are performing their ordinary functions, to judge of the time when, and the circumstances under which, the other parts are to be restored to their former relations. I have, in times past, discussed the legal condition of the revolted and rebel States to the government of the country. For one, I discuss that question no longer. I am disposed to accept the existing facts, without a particular inquiry as to the legal relations which these ten States sustain to the government. There are certain things which we know perfectly well. We know that in 1861 the Senators and Representatives from these States went out of the Congress of the United States; that they organized another government; that they confederated themselves, contrary to the Constitution of the United States; that for four years and more they carried on a war, by sea and by land, against this government; and that during all that period of time, and until now, they have not been represented in the Government of the United States. I accept the facts, and thereupon I maintain that they are not to be represented until the people, and the representatives of the people, who are loyal to this government, consent that they shall be represented.

In the work of reconstruction, there are four classes of people who are specially to be considered. They are, first, the loyal people of the North. The constitutional amendments which have been proposed by Congress, and which have been sanctioned by the people in these elections, furnish protection, as far as constitutional provisions can furnish protection, to the represented States. I may make a remark here which I think not out of place. The constitutional amendments may now be considered as the settled policy of the country. The men who have voted to sustain Congress in this contest have unquestionably declared that nothing less than the adoption of the constitutional amendments shall be accepted as a condition precedent to the restoration of those States to the Union. Of that there can be no doubt. But it is worthy of observation, that, on the day when Tennessee was admitted into the Union, by the vote of the House of Representatives a proposition to declare, that, whenever either of the other ten States ratified these constitutional amendments, such State should be admitted, was laid on the table by a decisive majority. This action indicated very distinctly, that, while the members of Congress were agreed that nothing less than the ratification of the constitutional amendments should be accepted, they were not prepared to say that nothing more should be demanded. In 1861 Congress passed a resolution, declaring that the war was prosecuted for the sole purpose of restoring the Union; and now, since the fall of Richmond, since the surrender of Lee, since the overthrow of the Confederacy, and the prostration of the rebel power at every point, men appear, and say, "In 1861 you said that you were prosecuting the war for the sole purpose of restoring the Union; and now that you have an opportunity to restore the Union, and these States are all ready to return, you refuse to receive them." And they talk about "betrayal of confidence" and "breach of trust"! It is a case very much like this. I have a controversy with my neighbor as to the title to a piece of land, and he offers me a thousand dollars for my claim, whatever it may be. I refuse to accept it; a suit is instituted and prosecuted, as far as the law will allow it to be prosecuted; the verdict of the jury and the judgment of the court are against me; and then I turn around and say, "I have concluded to receive the thousand dollars you offered me at the beginning of the controversy, and give you a title to the land." My antagonist will say very properly, "You are too late. I made the offer originally for the purpose of avoiding further controversy. You refused my terms. You are vanquished, and I shall now assert my rights." We made the proposition to the South in the hope that it would be accepted. But there can be no pretence for asking us now, after prosecuting the war at such expense, to accept a reconstruction of the Union on the basis of the proposals of 1861. So, during the war, Mr. Lincoln, in September, 1862, issued his monitory proclamation to the South, that if, in one hundred days, the people did not lay down their arms and return to the Union, he would proclaim the emancipation of all the slaves. They treated the proposition with scorn; and on the 1st of January, 1863, the proclamation was issued. Legally, all the slaves were then emancipated; and when the rebel armies, in April and May, 1865, surrendered, emancipation became an accomplished fact. And yet, in Virginia, they are taking a census of the slaves, as they were held in 1863, and estimating their value; intending, whenever they have an opportunity, with the help of their Northern allies, to put their hands into the public treasury and compensate themselves for that loss, as they call it. Again, Congress makes a proposition, or makes a declaration (suppose it were a proposition, which it is not), that these States may be received into the Union whenever they ratify the pending amendment. Several of them have already declined it. They have not been encouraged to ratify this amendment by the President. Congress will assemble in December next; and, this amendment not then having been ratified, the whole matter will be open for consideration. It will be for the representatives of the loyal people of the country to determine what further, under the circumstances, ought to be done.

But the rights of the loyal people of the North are in a good degree protected, with reference to the equality of representation, by the constitutional amendment. We have obtained security by the constitutional amendment, as far as security can be obtained, for the payment of the public debt, and for the exclusion of the rebel debt.

Another class that ought to be protected, and whose rights ought to be secured upon the restoration of the Union, are the men who have been engaged in the rebellion. I have a word to say in their behalf; for while I am disposed to exact of them, and of the States to which they belong, every condition necessary for the public security, I am willing that, as individuals, they should be relieved from all unnecessary punishment or penalties. But it is one of their misfortunes, that the man at the head of the government ostensibly in their interest has betrayed the loyal people of the North; and by that betrayal he has rendered himself incapable of doing any thing in behalf of the rebels of the South. If to-night you were to hear that Mr. Johnson was closeted with Stephens, or with Wade Hampton, or with General Johnston, you, and the whole country, would be alarmed. You would fear that some combination or conspiracy was to be made or entered into, prejudicial to your rights. But if the lamented Lincoln were at the head of the government, and you were to hear that he had gone to Fortress Munroe, to visit Jefferson Davis, in his ample quarters there, now including Carroll Hall, or that any number of the men engaged in the rebellion were at Washington in consultation with the President, you would feel no anxiety. You would know that Mr. Lincoln, whatever might be his desire to relieve the difficulties in the way of these men, however he might be disposed to benefit them, to aid them, would still be true to the country. The country having that confidence in him, he could do almost any thing that he thought necessary for the welfare of the rebels. But it is the misfortune of the Southern people, that this man, who has betrayed the loyal sentiment of the country, by that betrayal has rendered himself incapable of doing any thing in their behalf. Before the next two years have passed away, the rebels will more completely despise and contemn the Executive than does any man in the North to-day. He has not only betrayed the loyal people of the North, but he has betrayed even the rebels of the South; so that there will be no man, two years hence, who can say, "President Johnson has been my true friend."

Next, it is not in his power to do any thing for the loyal white people of the South, or for the loyal black people of the South. Whenever this government is reconstructed, it should be upon a basis which will secure the rights of those two large classes of people. The pivot on which all our policy must turn hereafter is the right of the negro to vote. Whether it be agreeable to us or not, we shall finally reach the conclusion that there can be no safe policy for us except in securing to the negro the right of suffrage. In this city, yesterday, you elected a colored man as representative, and in the neighboring city of Charlestown, another colored man, as I understand, has been elected to the same office. I know nothing of the men. It may be that they are not, personally, as well qualified as some others; but I accept their election as an indication of the purpose of this people, at least, to make no distinction on account of race or color. I accept the election as an indication also that the people of this city, and of this State, are prepared to accept the services of the colored people of the South, in any and every capacity for which they are fitted. We have had one hundred and eighty-six thousand of them in the armies of the Republic; they are four million strong; several hundred thousand of them are able-bodied male citizens. If you deny them the elective franchise, then one of two things hereafter is to happen, — either that you discard entirely their services in the field, or else that you accept their services, or compel them to do service, while you deny them all power in the government of the country. Nothing can be more unjust than the latter course. If there be reasons why women and children should not enjoy the elective franchise, one of those reasons is, that, in the very nature of the case, they cannot be called upon to defend with their persons and their lives the government which is set up; and therefore, if they were allowed to vote, a government might be established by their suffrages which would not command the support, and would not receive the sanction, of the men who are to peril their lives in its defence. The first essential condition of a government which exists by force (and no government can exist upon any other foundation) is, that those who are to jeopard their lives in its defence shall have a voice in saying what that government is to be. For the future, then, you have either to reject the military services of the men of this mighty race, four million strong, numbering as many people as the great State of New York, or else you will compel them to serve the country, to defend institutions and support a government in whose organization and administration they have no part. We hear a great deal of equality before the law; and I observe by the papers to-day, that Governor Throckmorton, of Texas, has asked the Legislature of that State to pass laws for the protection of the colored people. The great fact is, that nobody is protected, as a general thing, under any government, if you consider the people in races or classes, except those who participate in the government. The people of England who are protected, whose rights are secure, and who are respected by the government, are the men who possess the elective franchise; those who do not possess this right are to a great extent neglected. The fault of John Bright, in his contest for the extension of suffrage, is, that he does not put it upon a sufficiently broad basis. In England, the necessity of the country is, that every man, as a man, shall vote; such is the necessity of every country. Do you suppose it would have been possible, from 1861 to 1865, to have obtained the services of two million six hundred thousand men, by voluntary contributions, in any country not free? If there had been no slavery in the South, if the four million of colored people had been free, and in the enjoyment of all their political rights, and if their sympathies had been with the men engaged in the rebellion, our final success would have been improbable in the highest degree.

The strength of a country is in the universal right of the people to take part in its government, — a right which belongs to man as man, and not to any of his incidents, whether of education or property. Whenever a man enjoys the elective franchise, an inducement is held out to him to educate himself so as to be worthy of the privileges which it confers, and capable of discharging the duties which it imposes. The whole community is interested, also, in providing that each man, who by his vote may affect the fortunes of every other man, is educated so as to discharge that high duty in the wisest possible way. Universal suffrage is security for every thing desirable of a social, political, or public character. The people of England, when they obtain the right to vote, — as soon they will, and the more speedily if we do justice to the negro population of this country, — will accomplish much in behalf of liberty there, here, and everywhere. The aristocratic party will be prostrated under the power of the masses. The throne may last: that is comparatively immaterial with reference to the liberties and fortunes of the people; but the necessity of the English nation is, first universal suffrage, then the exercise of that power so as to abolish the laws of entail and primogeniture, and to overthrow the aristocracy of Great Britain as a privileged class. We have an interest in all this. The people of England, and the throne of England, to some extent, as far as we know, sympathized with us in our great struggle: the hostility under which we suffered from first to last, and the policy which thwarted us everywhere, on land and sea, originated with the aristocracy of Great Britain.

The extension of suffrage to the negroes of the South brings with it all the blessings of good government. It brings security to the South. I recollect, that, in one of the two conversations I have had with Mr. Johnson, he said, "If you extend suffrage to the negroes, there will at once be quarrels between the whites and blacks, and bloodshed." This result is likely to happen, but the apprehension of it is not a sufficient reason for inaugurating a system of manifest and permanent injustice. It is hardly possible, in the nature of things, that so great a revolution should be effected in the South as the extension of suffrage to several hundred thousand colored people, without resistance on the part of the whites. But that resistance will be temporary, it will be local. After the first year, or first two years, it will be unknown. On the other hand, if you refuse to extend the right of suffrage to the negroes of the South, do you expect peace? Consider. One hundred and eighty-six thousand of these men have been in the military service of the country. General Saxton, in his testimony before the Committee on Reconstruction, said that it was within his knowledge that the negroes of the South were organized and armed. Within the last six weeks, I have received letters from officers of the army in Alabama, saying that they had been approached by leading negroes who suggested the necessity, on their part, of removing certain offensive whites who had oppressed them. Do you expect that without suffrage there is to be peace? Such an expectation is vain. On the other hand, the whites of the South are organized. General Thomas, in his testimony before the Reconstruction Committee, said he had evidence from every one of the eleven States that there were secret hostile organizations among the whites. Here, then, you have two armies in the South, ready to be let loose upon each other. How is the danger to be avoided? By extending suffrage to the negroes. Do this, and at once you enlist in their behalf a certain number of white men. There are loyal whites in the South, who will sympathize and co-operate with the blacks. You at once divide the public sentiment of the South, you divide the governing powers of the South, and you render it certain that neither party will undertake to subjugate the other by force of arms, especially if at Washington there shall be a man in the executive chair who will be as swift to suppress insurrection whenever instituted in behalf of slavery and the interests of slaveholders, as to suppress insurrection in behalf of liberty and the rights of man.

Further, if we extend the right of suffrage to the negroes of the South, we have everywhere a public sentiment in the South more or less strong in favor of this government. I have said that the constitutional amendments which have been presented to the country, and which now have been ratified by the people, are right as far as they go; but they do not by any means go far enough to save the country in the exigency in which we find ourselves. The amendment reduces the representation of the old slave States about eighteen from their present number, and about thirty from the number to which those States will be entitled if the policy of the President shall be carried out. The States are still left in the control of rebels. They will send thirty Senators to the Senate, and about eighty members to the House of Representatives, all of whom will be pledged, under all circumstances, to resist the policy of this government, if it be upon the loyal side. Do you expect Representatives in Congress to differ materially from the constituency at home? Perhaps no more specious argument has been suggested than that we should accept loyal men from these States whenever such present themselves. That is to say, for the practical purposes of government, accept any and every man whose disloyalty cannot be proved; for that is the question to be submitted to the House and Senate upon the application of a person from either of those States for a seat in either branch. Do you suppose that in South Carolina, where the right to vote is limited to white people, anybody in the interest of the government is, during this generation, to be elected to Congress? Certainly not. Under the influence of the power you may exercise in the Senate and House, they may elect men whose disloyalty cannot be proved; but they will be sure to elect men who are disloyal in fact, and for all the purposes that the South has in view. It is necessary to inject into the South a loyal political force. This can be done by using the negro population, composed as it is of persons who have been loyal to the government under all circumstances. The result would be, that in each of those States we should have a large minority on the side of the government; and in Mississippi, Louisiana, and South Carolina, a majority of the people are colored persons. The result of extending the elective franchise to these persons would be, that either loyal white men or loyal black men would be sent to Congress, and either would be preferable to disloyal white men. Is it wise or reasonable to suppose that there is to be, speedily, any change of Southern public sentiment? The doctrine of secession, the doctrine that a State has the right to secede from this Union, is now an ancient doctrine. It was taught by Mr. Calhoun as early as 1820. Two generations of young men have grown up under its influence. The testimony of Mr. Stephens before the committee was, that there had been no change of public sentiment in the Southern country, as far as he knew, in reference to the doctrine of secession. It is true, also, that many men in the South who profess to be Union men are Union men only to this extent: that in 1861 they thought it unwise to make war or to secede at that time; but they yet believe in the theory that a State has the right to secede from the Union whenever it pleases. To-day the press of the South is in favor of secession; all the schools of the South are in the interest of secession; the college and the church are all on the side of secession; the women of the South teach their children to hate the Union. Do you expect that out of the white population of the South, for the next two or three generations at least, there will be a class of men true to this government? If you have that expectation, most certainly you and your posterity will be disappointed. There is no way, then, in which we can secure a loyal majority or a loyal political force in any of the rebel States, except to invite and to accept the services of the loyal black man.

We must still further accept, as a great truth with reference to the reconstruction of the government, that the disloyal white people are to vote also. In Arkansas, in 1864, a law was passed, under a provision of its Constitution, disfranchising the disloyal men. A decision of the Supreme Court of Arkansas has restored them to their political rights. The contest which has been going on in Maryland for the last few weeks, and which finally culminated yesterday in the triumph of the secessionists over the loyal people of that State, has rendered it certain, that, in the near future, all the disloyal people of Maryland are to exercise the elective franchise. In Kentucky and Delaware, they are not disfranchised at all. In Missouri and West Virginia, the contest goes on, but the result is certain. The loyal people in those States, upon the issue of excluding the disloyal people, are to be defeated. Therefore you must accept, as the first fact in the work of reconstruction, that the disloyal people are to exercise political power. How is that power to be met, or resisted, or controlled in any degree? Only in one way, — by extending the elective franchise to the loyal colored people of the South.

Next, make these men citizens, and they become producers and consumers on a much larger scale than they will be if they are kept as a vassal race. All the interests of business, in New York, Boston, Cincinnati, Chicago, are concerned in the freedom and elevation of this great class of American citizens. Therefore it happens that the material and political interests of the country now combine and concur in the policy of conferring upon these men all their just rights.

The Thirty-ninth Congress assembles in December next; and the Fortieth Congress is already elected, with a House in which two-thirds, at least, will be opposed to the Executive policy. The Senate, by a larger majority than heretofore, will also be opposed to that policy. What I desire to consider is, How shall the power which has thus been newly conferred upon the representatives of the people be exercised? I think that it may be exercised with reference to two great matters of permanent, public interest. One I have already considered, — the extension of the elective franchise to the colored people; and I pause a moment to suggest to you that there are two ways in which this result can be accomplished. One is, by holding these ten States just as they are, subject to the control of Congress, representing the people of this country, until those States, of their own motion, shall do justice to the colored people. We have governed this country for the last four years without their aid; and, if it be necessary to govern it four or ten years more without their aid, it can be done, with entire safety to all. Yet it is, without doubt, conformable to the theory of our institutions, that every portion of the people of the country should be represented. It is a necessity of our condition, that they should be represented only by loyal men; and you can secure loyal men only by securing a loyal constituency. The governments existing at the present time in those so-called States are governments instituted by or through the agency of the President and the military authorities of the country. Not more than one or two of the Constitutions under which those several States are acting has ever been submitted to the people. Those governments are, in the eye of the Constitution and the Government of the United States, without any valid authority whatever. Congress may, whenever it sees fit, abolish them, institute territorial governments, and in those territorial governments declare who shall vote and who shall not vote. Congress may institute negro suffrage, if it pleases, and build up States from the beginning, where there shall be equality of rights and loyalty to the Government of the United States. Most likely the result to which all the public policy of the country now tends is the destruction of these false governments that have been set up, and the establishment of constitutional governments in their stead. I take it that the people of the country are not influenced by the suggestion of the President, that, when power is in his hands, there is no danger of centralization; but when Congress undertakes to exercise authority, although the members of the lower house are every two years amenable to the people, there is great danger of centralization of power!

The other matter which will require the attention of Congress is this: whether a person holding the office of President of the United States, if he be guilty of high crimes and misdemeanors, is liable to be impeached and tried, and deprived of his office, or not. When the election was pending, if I supposed that any political advantage was to be gained by a suggestion of this sort, I certainly would scorn myself if I were to make it merely for the purpose of securing a party triumph or party advantage. Now that the election is over, no reason whatever remains for arraigning the President, unless it be a reason connected with the safety and the welfare of the country.

What are the facts? The President of the United States cannot be arraigned because he is disagreeable to us; he cannot be arraigned because he has betrayed a party; he cannot be arraigned because he has deserted principles to which we supposed he was committed; he cannot, perhaps, be arraigned because he has disgraced and humiliated us in the presence of the world. If he is to be arraigned at all, it must be for some substantial, well-grounded cause; some offence that he has committed under the Constitution, which shall be so proved that no man can doubt as to whether he committed it or not, and which is so heinous in its character as to leave no room even for his friends and supporters in this country, much less for the world and for posterity, to decide that he was illegally and unjustly condemned. I allude now to this feature in our prospective policy for this purpose, and for this alone. I observe, from conversation and from the newspapers, that there are those who are opposed to the policy of the President, who yet contend that he ought not to be arraigned, though he be guilty even of the gravest offences. They assert that even then it would be bad policy. I am here to-night to do something, if I may, to induce the country to abandon mere policy, and to be governed in all its public action by the principles of justice.

While the President is not to be arraigned because he is disagreeable, or because he has been false to former professions, yet, if he has been guilty of any substantial and wilful violation of the Constitution or of the laws of the land, then in the name of justice, and without regard to short-sighted policy, he should be arraigned and tried. There are certain things we know. We know that he appointed men to office, in those eleven States, who neither did take nor could have taken the oath of office imposed by the law of the land, passed July 2, 1862. In that act it was declared that no man should hold any office, military, naval, or civil, unless he had first taken an oath that he had never given support, countenance, or encouragement to the enemies of the country, in armed hostility thereto. We know that the President again and again appointed men to office, in violation of that law. That law also said that no man should receive either compensation or salary for the performance of any official duty until he had first taken the oath prescribed. These men were appointed in the Treasury Department; the Congress of the United States had made an appropriation for the payment of all officers in that department; yet these men, so appointed to office, and so entering upon the performance of the duties of their respective offices, without first taking the oath prescribed by the law of the land, were not paid. The President is appointing men to office who were at the last session of Congress rejected by the Senate for the very same offices in which again they have been placed. The Constitution of the United States says that these offices shall be filled by the President, "by and with the advice and consent of the Senate." The Senate refused its consent, and yet these men in various cases have been appointed to the offices, for which they had been nominated previously and rejected.

I refer to these matters, not for the purpose of asking here whether they constitute such offences under the laws and Constitution as would justify the arraignment of the President, but for the purpose of showing that the suggestion that an inquiry should be made into his official conduct is not without some grave foundation in the facts that are before the country. And, my friends, if, in the office of President, we find a man who is guilty of offences rendering him liable to impeachment under the Constitution, it would be no misfortune to the country, if he should be arraigned, condemned, deprived of his office, and declared incapable, for ever after, of holding office; but it would be a misfortune of the gravest character, if a President, so guilty, should escape. Will you arraign the judge of a small tribunal, who passes judgment upon the rights of men to the amount of a hundred dollars, if he appears drunk in his seat, or if he accepts a bribe of a sixpence from a suitor, and allow the President of the United States, the chief magistrate of the land, the highest officer, we may say, judged by his power, upon the face of the earth, to escape, when guilty, merely because some people think it bad policy to disturb the public peace by questions of such a nature? The administration of justice is never a public misfortune; in the case I am considering, it will be a warning to all men who shall hereafter aspire to the Presidency, and all who shall occupy the place, that there are certain things that cannot be done with impunity. There is nothing that so injures and debauches the public mind as unbridled ambition for the great office. There is no evil connected with our public affairs which is fraught with greater danger to the country than the evil of presidential aspirations. Every Executive, or nearly every Executive, has used his power with reference to a re-election. Mr. Lincoln, as far as I know, was the exception. The most that ever he said, in reference to his re-election, was this: "I have never desired to hold this place for four years more; but I have desired to receive the approval of the people for what I have done." With this exception, every Executive in modern times has sought to secure his own re-election. If, under the guidance of the Constitution and in conformity to the strictest principles of justice, the President shall be arraigned and condemned, it will be a warning to every man who may hold the seat he now occupies, or who may aspire to it. Each successor will understand that he cannot with safety disgrace and humiliate the country in its own presence, and in the presence of the representatives of foreign nations; that he cannot with impunity announce that a Congress which has had the power to guide and control the nation during a contest unparalleled in our history, and unexampled in the history of any other country, is a body "called, or which assumed to be, the Congress of the United States, but in fact a Congress of only a part of the States, hanging upon the verge of the government:" nor can he proclaim with impunity, after such a proceeding, that he could have made himself dictator; nor speak of the officers of the government, who are the servants of the people, to do their will, and not mere Executive minions, as satraps and dependants; nor tolerate a Secretary of State who puts the question to the people whether they will have the man who is in office for President, or for king. It should be understood by all the people of the country, that the office of President is too great and too sacred to be trifled with, that it is an office created by the people for their benefit, that he who sits in the chief seat of power in this country is but their first servant, and that they will never consent that the question shall be suggested whether such a person is to be dictator or king.

Then the two great questions for the consideration of the country during the coming two years are, first, whether the President is liable, justly, under the Constitution, to be removed from his office; and, if so liable, there then can be no question about proceeding constitutionally, firmly, faithfully, to the end: and, secondly, whether the people of this country, without reference to race or color, are to be regarded as men in the reconstruction of the government. The Republican party will live or die, it will swim or sink, upon this issue. In 1868, however men may seek to avoid the issue, it will be simply this, — whether the people of the ten States, without regard to color, shall be endowed with the elective franchise; and if, before 1868, these ten States are restored to political power in the government of this country, and the rights of the colored people disregarded, then this party, which rose in 1856 as the party against the extension of slavery, which in 1860 and 1861 accepted the challenge to battle, which in 1863, through its chosen leader, proclaimed emancipation, will have ceased to exist; for there will be nothing in the future to command the services or enlist the efforts of its best men. If in 1868 the question is already settled against the negro, the enthusiastic and determined men of the Republican party will have no longer an interest in fighting its battles; the fifteen thousand majority of the State of New York will disappear; New York, Pennsylvania, and other States will enroll themselves with the ten triumphant States of the South; and the North will see itself again reduced to an abject and servile condition in the government of the country. But if we, as a people, accept fearlessly and in faith the issue before us, which is the issue of the equality of all men under the laws, and reconstruct the government as a government of the people, by the people, and for the people, then a triumphant and glorious future awaits us. We have two years in which to make up this issue. I think I see very clearly that it will be made up on our side in behalf of liberty, equality, freedom, and justice for all men; that we shall hold high the banner above the smoke and dust and turmoil of mere party strife, so that it may be seen not only by the people of this country, but by the people of the whole world. Thus we shall give to the masses of England, who are now struggling to emancipate themselves, an additional reason for effort and an additional motive for success. Finally, this government is not only to be re-established upon the principles of equality; but, through sympathy and the force of our views and the public sentiment which will be here created, England herself is to be redeemed from the aristocratic element by which she is controlled; and, in that country and in this, the day will appear speedily when the masses shall rule, in faith, in justice, and in power.

RECONSTRUCTION, AND ITS RELATIONS TO THE BUSINESS OF THE COUNTRY.

AN ADDRESS BEFORE THE OLD BAY STATE ASSOCIATION, BOSTON, DEC. 27, 1866.

I TRUST no one will suppose that my subject implies any want of confidence in the patriotism of the business men of Boston, of our State, or of the country. I chose to speak upon the topic which has been announced, because I had observed occasionally in the public journals the suggestion that the business men of the country were largely interested in the immediate restoration of the Union, without much regard to the manner of doing the work. For myself, I have never accepted the suggestion, certainly not since the manifestations of patriotism during the war on the part of the business men of our State and of the country, that they would, as a body, be disposed to second any movement for the restoration of the Union not based upon sound principles of public policy. The restoration of the Union means the introduction again, into the government of the country, of that considerable body of people, and that vast extent of territory, engaged in and covered by the rebellion. It implies a renewal of the exercise of power in this government by those men who for thirty years plotted for its overthrow, and for nearly five years carried on a persistent and formidable, and at times apparently successful, rebellion for its destruction. It is therefore no slight matter, that these people at any time, or to any extent, until their spirit and purposes are changed, are to be received into the government of the country. We accept, as far as the persons who have been concerned in the rebellion are to be considered, a body of men who are hostile to this government, who seek its destruction, and who will avail themselves of any opportunity that may present itself in the changing condition of public affairs to accomplish that for which they have fought. Therefore there should be on the part of all, accompanied by a desire for the restoration of the Union, attention to those safeguards and securities which, under the circumstances, it is possible for us either to erect or to take.

Again, consider that the restoration of the Union implies the renewal of power on the part of nearly four million people who, for the present moment, are excluded from all participation in the government of the country. It implies, also, the exercise of power on the part of their posterity and successors through many generations; and if we accept them as they are, with supreme power in their respective localities and States vested in the hands of rebels, with all the institutions which control and mould public sentiment subject to their will, we cannot expect that, in five or ten or twenty or fifty years even, the spirit of rebellion will be extinguished in that section of country. In the ten States that are not represented in the Congress of the United States, there were, in 1860, 4,620,000 white people; there were, at that time, 125,000 free colored persons; there were, also, 3,265,000 slaves,—making an aggregate of colored persons of 3,390,000, and of 4,620,000 white persons. These ten States have an area of 635,454 square miles,—about one-fifth of the entire surface of the Union, including all the territories that are but partially settled this side of the Rocky Mountains, and the vast mountain region between the Mississippi River and the Pacific Ocean. These ten States have a population at present of rather more than eight million; they have an area of 635,000 square miles; they have, for the most part, a fertile soil; they are blessed with a salubrious and agreeable climate; they possess all the natural advantages which insure in the future a vast population. It is therefore a matter of the highest magnitude to so arrange the details of reconstruction, and to proceed upon such principles, as shall secure to the country a loyal public sentiment in all that region. If we leave to these four million rebels local power, undiminished sway in one-fifth of the territory of the Union; if we confide to them and to their care the institutions of government, of education, of religion, of social life; if we assign to them the undisputed control of the press,—what have we to expect in the future except generation after generation influenced by the same principles, and animated by the same purposes, that have controlled the inhabitants of that region for the last thirty-five years? These facts and views give us some idea of the magnitude of the subject with which we are to deal.

For the purpose of showing how the business interests of this country are concerned in the work of restoration, I desire to recall your attention to certain well-known facts, developed by the census of 1860, but indicated quite distinctly in all the censuses that have been taken from 1790 until 1860, showing how the system of slavery has tended to prevent the increase of the population of this vast and inviting region of country, and how also it has contributed to depress labor, to degrade the laborer, and consequently to render that section incapable of producing wealth, as compared with the free States of the country. These facts are well known; but, in the relation in which I speak to-night, I think it not unwise to recall your attention to them. The area of New England, New York, Ohio, Pennsylvania, New Jersey, Maryland, and Delaware — an extensive region of country — is but 213,786 square miles, — just about one-third the area of country covered by the ten unrepresented States. But these twelve States, with an area of but 213,000 square miles, against 635,000 square miles in the ten rebellious States, have a population of 13,682,000 against 8,010,000 in those ten States, nearly half of whom are colored people, showing how much more rapidly population has increased in the free States than in the slave States. In these twelve free States, the population averages sixty-three persons to the square mile, while in the ten rebellious and unrepresented States, the population is but twelve and six-tenths persons to the square mile; that is, the average population in the twelve free States is about five times as large as in the ten unrepresented States. If these ten rebel States, in proportion to their area, had an equal population with the twelve free States, they would number forty million people. That they have not the population is undoubtedly due, in a large degree (not entirely), to the institution of slavery.

Next, it may be well to consider how it is, that slavery has prevented the increase of population in this inviting region of country. First, unquestionably, slavery, as a system of oppression, prevents the increase of population; it deters those seeking a home from migrating into a region of country that is controlled by the institution. In the second place, wherever slavery exists, there must prevail, among the people generally, a system of ignorance from which they cannot escape. It is undoubtedly true, that the people may be in some degree ignorant even where they are free, because it is only by a certain amount of education, acquaintance with the world, experience, knowledge of history, that a man comes to realize the importance of education as a means of prosperity. But wherever the institution of slavery exists, wherever the mass of the people are denied their natural rights, there, of course, the laboring population are in a state of ignorance, because the controlling interests of society are opposed to every system of education. In Great Britain, for example, the interest in education is limited to those classes that are to participate in the government. I have often said, that even in our own State of Massachusetts, where public instruction has existed for about two hundred years, and where there is a strong public sentiment in favor of its continuance, if we were to introduce a system by which the laboring people should be deprived of their natural rights, and especially if they were debarred the exercise of the elective franchise, our system of education would not last thirty years. It is because the mass of the people feel that a system of public instruction is the chief means by which they and theirs are to be elevated from a condition of poverty to affluence, from ignorance to cultivation and refinement, that always and everywhere they support schools and institutions of learning. Therefore, wherever slavery exists, there must be ignorance, and so, wherever slavery exists, there must be a great degree of insecurity, not simply to the slaves themselves, but to every race and every condition of society. The system of slavery being in itself a despotism, and the system of African slavery in this country having proved the truth that every slaveholder was a petty tyrant, life, liberty, and property have always been insecure wherever the system has existed among us.

We have destroyed slavery as a chattel system in the Southern States, although to the dishonor of the government it must be confessed that in several of those States efforts are making to reestablish something like the institution of slavery. What we need now is an Executive who shall use the national authority for the protection of the colored and white loyal people in the States recently in rebellion. We have destroyed the system of slavery in these fifteen States; but we have not destroyed the spirit of slavery: and if, by any plan of restoration, you put local power into the hands of the slaveholding classes; if you give to them the control of those States; if you give to them the exclusive right to be represented in the Congress of the United States, — in some form and in some way, they will devise means for the continued oppression of the class recently in servitude. Therefore it is the duty of the government and of the people, in considering the subject of restoration, not to allow the mind to be diverted at all from the necessity of our condition, which is to so reconstruct this government that oppression shall cease, that ignorance shall be removed, and that there shall be security for life, liberty, and property in all that region of country.

There have been suggested, during the last two years, four different ways of restoring the Union. I call them ways: some of them are poor ways. The first is the President's way, which, upon the views I have been presenting, is really no way at all for the people of this country. It is a way which opens to the South, to the rebel States, and to the rebel leaders, a renewal of power in the government, and consigns all this vast territory and these eight million people to their undisputed control. I trust that the loyal citizens of the country with great unanimity are opposed to this way; and they should be opposed to it as well for its origin as for its results. It is a simple way. The President wishes to invite these ten States back into the Union; to give them, for the present, the representative power which they had under the old Constitution, — representation based upon three-fifths of the slaves, and, after the census of 1870, representation to be based upon the entire negro population of the South, while the negroes are to be excluded from all participation in the government of the country. But the President's way is equally objectionable on account of its origin. You remember very well the proclamation concerning North Carolina, issued in May or June, 1865. It was the beginning of a system of usurpation, which to-day, in its results, is the chief obstacle to the speedy and safe restoration of the government. He assumed, in that proclamation, power which neither he nor any President since the organization of the government had a right to exercise under the Constitution. His premise for the proclamation was the fourth section of the fourth article of the Constitution, which declares that the United States shall guaranty to every State in this Union a republican form of government. After various other non-essential statements, he deduces his conclusions, and proclaims a government in North Carolina, assuming that he was, as the United States, carrying out this provision of the Constitution.

There were two difficulties in the way of his theory. First, he was not the United States; and secondly, the Supreme Court had declared that it was Congress, and Congress only, which could decide whether the government of a State was republican or not. In the case of Luther *vs.* Borden, the Supreme Court held that it was for Congress to decide whether the Constitution of a State was republican, and that every department of the Government of the United States was bound thereby. But the President assumed to be the United States, to erect a government in North Carolina, and to take upon himself authority to decide a question which could be decided only by Congress. This was the beginning of our difficulties with reference to reconstruction. Then the President departed still further. If I am not in error, Mr. Lincoln, during his administration, was very careful, in the provisional governments which he established or authorized, to act exclusively in his capacity as commander-in-chief of the army, and not at all as President clothed with civil authority. And, further, he either appointed an officer of the army to be the provisional or military Governor of a State, or, if civilians were appointed, they received commissions in the military service. But Mr. Johnson acted differently, and not only did not proceed in the reconstruction of the government as commander-in-chief of the army, but he exercised authority merely in his civil capacity. He not only did not go to the army of the United States; he not only did not go exclusively among the loyal people of the country; but he pardoned rebels, exercising therein a high function which he could exercise only as President of the United States; restoring to their civil rights men who had participated in the rebellion, and then appointing them Governors of these various States or districts of country. I think the nation has already reached the conclusion, that, whether we look to the grounds on which these governments are established, or to the results that are likely to flow from them, they are to be regarded as unconstitutional and invalid organizations.

Another plan of restoring the Union is to admit these ten States respectively whenever they shall ratify severally the pending amendment to the Constitution of the United States. The character of this amendment I need not detail to you. The very day that the House of Representatives voted to admit Tennessee to her place as a State in the Union, a bill was laid on the table, which declared, that, whenever any one of the States recently in rebellion should ratify the constitutional amendment, it should be admitted to representation in the government of the country. The constitutional amendment, as far as understood by the radical men in the Congress of the United States, meant this, and nothing more: that it was a condition precedent to the recognition of the right of those States to be represented, — a condition which we would not dispense with, but a condition which we were not bound to regard as the sole condition. It was so treated at the time, by many members of the House of Representatives. Finally, I am bound to declare that it would be in the highest degree unwise and unsafe for the people of the country to accept these States, when the constitutional amendment shall be ratified by the country, or by them respectively; and the reasons are apparent. Like the President's policy, the amendment turns over the ten States to the control of rebels. The amendment itself only by indirection obtains security for the recognition of the rights of the negroes. It will be practicable for the white people of the ten States to exclude the negroes from all voice in the government of them. The old slave States will lose eighteen of their present Representatives; but still I have no doubt, that, on the whole, the mass of the rebel leaders in the South will prefer the loss, rather than the extension of the right of suffrage to negroes. They will still have their two Senators from each State, and an aggregate of about seventy members in the House of Representatives; they will still be a compact and powerful organization, for the purposes of thwarting and overthrowing the government.

As a matter of policy, setting aside the question of right, it will be unfortunate for the people of the country to admit any system of restoration which allows the ten States to continue a unit in opinion with reference to the question of the existence of the government. As a matter of policy, we must divide the public sentiment of these States; divide their local governments, placing some of them on the side of the Union; securing representation by loyal men, even though those loyal representatives be black men. It is the most dangerous of all propositions that the old slave States should hereafter be represented in the government of this country as a unit upon the question which is vital to us, — whether the government shall exist; therefore, for one, I look for such a policy in the work of restoration as will secure to the government of the United States a loyal support. If we cannot have the united force of the fifteen former slave States, let us at least take a portion. If South Carolina has a majority of black people, I prefer that she should have loyal black rather than disloyal white representatives. And therefore I say, secondly, that the constitutional amendment, right in itself and necessary as a condition precedent to the restoration of the Union, is wholly insufficient as a final and complete measure of pacification; and it is better for the country to reject it altogether, and fight out the battle upon the plain issue of human rights, equal and exact justice to all men, than to accept this as a complete and final measure of restoration.

There is a third proposition, that the Union shall be restored, the constitutional amendment being adopted, whenever these States shall inaugurate a system of impartial, restricted suffrage, whenever they shall be ready to declare that any man who can read the Constitution of the United States, or write his own name, or who owns property of the value of two hundred dollars, is entitled to the right of franchise; the law to apply to the black man and the white man alike. I regard this plan of restoration as delusive and dangerous in the highest degree. In Massachusetts, where there is a system of public instruction, where there are public schools that furnish as good an education as was afforded by Harvard College eighty years ago, we may with some degree of propriety say that no man shall be entitled to vote unless he can read and write; for we place before him the means of knowledge. But are you to say this to the three million people who are in those ten States, and who have been denied every opportunity and every means of acquiring education; men, women, and children who are ignorant because it has been, and is to-day, as far as the public sentiment is expressed, a crime to teach them? When you erect schools by charity, the enemies of freedom give them to the flames, and the Southern horizon is lighted up by the fires of the burning houses that the North has erected for the education of the negroes. When you have said that no person can vote in the ten States except on these conditions, you have offered an additional inducement to the rebels to prevent the education of the freedmen. If you consent to the reconstruction of this government upon the basis that those only shall vote in the ten States who can read and write, you have excluded the whole negro population of the South from the ballot-box, and you have placed, perhaps for a century, power in the hands of the rebel slaveholding classes of that region of the country. I think this one objection alone is sufficient to condemn the proposition for impartial, restricted suffrage.

I come, then, to what I believe offers the only safe way out of our present difficulties. The constitutional amendment recognizes all persons born in this country as citizens of the country; but, after all, it is insufficient and untrustworthy, unless you add thereto universal suffrage in the ten States. I do not mean to say that I suppose that the extension of the elective franchise to the negro population of the South will at once remove all our difficulties. I do not expect that there will be then everywhere peace. I suppose there will be resistance on the part of the whites, and very likely there will be blood shed in some places, and lives may be lost; but after a little excitement and some resistance, after a few struggles, the people of the South will come to the conclusion that they had better submit. Out of the four million white people of the South, we may expect that a million will ally themselves with the government. They will be willing to unite with the negro population for the restoration of the State governments upon a loyal basis. When we have secured this, we may then consider that other question, which some persons desire to have considered before all other things in the matter of restoration, — the question of amnesty to the rebels, either partial or universal. I agree that not much time can pass after the restoration of the rebel States to the Union before the men who have participated in the rebellion will be restored to their political rights. I expect this result, and, upon the whole, I desire it; but what I seek most to guard against is the restoration, upon dangerous conditions, of the States that have been disloyal to the Union. What is the aspect of public affairs in the South to-day? What are we to expect, if the government shall be restored upon an unjust basis? It is humiliating to admit, but it is nevertheless true, that the South, as a whole, is in a more unpromising condition to-day than it was a year and a half since. It is not too much to say, that throughout these ten States, from Virginia to Texas, there is one grand carnival of all the spirits of disquiet, disorder, and bloodshed; and I cannot refrain from the remark that this condition of things is due, in a large measure, to the course which Mr. Johnson has chosen to pursue. If he had refrained from issuing a proclamation of peace; if he had been disposed to wield the great powers of the government in the interests of loyalty and of the Union, it would have been in his hand to have maintained order and peace throughout that whole region of country. But what is its condition to-day? The Civil Rights Bill, passed by Congress by a constitutional majority notwithstanding the opposition of the President, is a dead letter. The Freedmen's Bureau Bill is disregarded. I have received letters from officers of the army, stationed throughout the South with small squads of men, in which they declare that they are powerless to serve the country, and protect the loyal blacks or whites in that region. They are insulted by the rebels. The army of the republic, through its officers or their representatives, is constantly insulted, its power disregarded, and the authority of the government everywhere contemned. We know, too, for the testimony is conclusive, that colored men, freemen, are murdered frequently; not a single case, here and there, but by tens and hundreds; and from Texas it is reported that even more than a thousand have been thus sacrificed. Throughout the whole South the black people are insecure in their lives, in their persons, and in their rights, and nowhere in that vast region of country is there power to protect them. I know not, in the history of nations, a more melancholy example than that which this government exhibits to-day in the condition of the Southern country. I say further, after most careful reflection, that I see no possible way out of these difficulties while the present chief magistrate is at the head of the government. Congress is strong; it has received the support of the people; it has now a two-thirds majority in each House, to be increased in the Fortieth Congress; and it can pass whatever measures it prefers, notwithstanding the President's veto. But, after all, it is helpless to execute; it has no hand by which it can wield or control the powers of the government. Therefore I say, that, during the two years following the 4th of next March, if Mr. Johnson continues to be President of the United States, no efficient steps can be taken for the restoration of the government. Disorder will still be the rule in the South. To-day we know very well that citizens of the North who went South during the last twelve or eighteen months to develop the resources and apply their skill and industry to that country, are preparing to abandon it and to come away. There is little probability that the next year will yield an amount of cotton equal to the product of the year 1866.

I make no prediction as to what the future has in store for us with reference to the President; but I only say, that, if he continues in office during the two years to come, I know not of any means by which human life can be protected, by which human rights shall be regarded as sacred, or by which any efficient means can be taken for the restoration of the ten States to their ancient place in the government of the country. We have, then, before us, for these two years for the South, ignorance, poverty, and misrule.

Further, the transfer of the government of that region of country to the rebels, to the slaveholders, means repudiation of all the public debts which those ten States owe. Virginia is indebted $43,000,000, exclusive of what she incurred on account of the rebellion. Returning to the census of 1860, we find that the average annual product in the free States was $131 for each person. In the slave States, the annual product was $70 for each person; giving an excess in favor of the free States of $61. If you compare Massachusetts, a good representative of the free States, with Maryland, the most prosperous of the old slave States, you will find, that, exclusive of her returns for commerce in 1860, the annual product in Massachusetts was $235 for each person, and in Maryland only $96, an excess, however, of nearly fifty per cent over the average of the South, but still giving a balance of $139 in favor of Massachusetts. And this balance, this excess, is due, not to any superior physical capacity on the part of the people of the North, not due to any superior intellectual or natural ability, but due simply to the fact that our people are educated, and to the consequent fact that here labor is honored by all classes of people. In the South, the laboring population is ignorant, labor is considered dishonorable, and, as a natural consequence, the laboring classes produce very little. The political economical problem to be worked out by the people of this country is to re-establish government in the South; to restore those States to the Union upon such a basis that the laboring people shall be educated, and labor consequently made honorable. You will see the productive power of the people of the South thereby increased fifty to one hundred per cent. Therefore it is of importance to business men, not so much with reference to this year or the next two years, — for I suppose business men will consider this matter in a broad view, and for a long period of time, for a period of ten, twenty, or fifty years, — that the government be reconstructed upon the right basis.

Let us consider another fact. In those ten States there were, in the year 1860, eight million people. If you can so educate those eight million people as that their abilities shall be applied to the work of production as efficiently as the people of the North apply their abilities, and the average should go up from $70 for each person to $131, the average of the North, you will thereby add in a single year to the production of the South the sum of $487,946,000. A fifth of the entire public debt of the United States would be added to the resources of the country in a single year, if you could give to the people of the South the productive power which is exhibited and enjoyed by the people of the North.

The continuance of the existing state of things at the South, or the restoration of the Union according to the President's way, or upon the mere ratification of the amendments to the Constitution, or upon the system of impartial but restricted suffrage, means, then, repudiation of the State debts. Does anybody suppose Virginia can pay a debt of $43,000,000 unless she is regenerated, unless her people are able so to improve their powers of production as to augment the resources of that region far beyond its previous development? New England must be carried to Virginia and North Carolina, Ohio must be carried to Georgia and Alabama, New York must be carried to South Carolina, before the natural advantages of that country will be so developed as to enable the people to pay the debts they owe. And, again, the restoration of this government, with the South a unit against the Union, means repudiation of the debt of the United States. I do not stop to dwell upon that.

It is also to be observed, that, unless the South can be restored upon a basis such as I have indicated, there can be no resumption of specie payments for a long period of time. One difficulty in reference to the resumption of specie payments is this: that three, four, or five hundred million of our public securities are owned abroad. Whenever there is a panic on the other side of the Atlantic, as there was upon the opening of the late Continental war, and there is a demand for gold, these securities will be worth more in our markets than they are in foreign markets, and they will be sent here in quantities of twenty-five, fifty, or a hundred million dollars, according to the necessities or the fears of the people on the other side; the proceeds drawn from our banks, if they should be paying specie; and the banks consequently will be compelled to suspend. Therefore one of the difficulties which we have to encounter, and which we must look in the face while we have so large a public debt, a portion of which is owned abroad, is, that, whenever there is a panic in Europe, there will be a demand upon the banks and upon the people of this country for specie. One of the benefits to be derived from the restoration of order in the South is, that you apply the labor of that section of country to the production of those articles which are a substitute for specie. We produce grain in the West in vast quantities; but the condition of transportation between the West and the Atlantic coast is such that we cannot expect to export quantities of grain sufficient to meet an exigency such as I have indicated. But, if we can apply the labor of the South in the most productive way, we can augment the quantity of cotton produced from two to four, six, eight, or even to ten million bales, and supply Europe, supply, indeed, the whole world, with the kind of cotton which this country produces. Cotton is perhaps the nearest to specie of any product of the soil. When the Southern country is cut up into small holdings, when the negro population shall be stimulated to produce cotton by the incentive which stimulates us all, personal pecuniary advantages, the South will produce many million bales of cotton annually in excess of any previous production. Cotton will be a substitute for specie; and, in the nature of the case, it is the chief means upon which we can rely to meet the balances abroad. Until the South is regenerated, until the labor of that section of country is wisely and profitably applied to the production of cotton, it is a very grave question, whether, in view of the large amount of our public debt owned abroad, the banks of this country can resume and maintain specie payments.

In the next place, until there is a restoration of

the Union upon sound principles, there must be a degree of weakness in the government, which cannot by any means be overcome. If we have ten, twelve, or fourteen States known to be hostile to the government, what is our condition for protecting our rights? I am not alarmed in regard to any attempt on the part of other governments to interfere with the United States; but it is a humiliation to every American citizen, that the country is in such a condition that we cannot assert our rights under any circumstances and against all odds. Mr. Johnson, as you have seen, has just sent two ambassadors to Mexico. Laboring under the delusion that he has restored this government to peace, order, and quiet, he thinks the time has come when he can interfere in Mexico, and undertake to manage Maximilian, Juarez, and all the rest who are contending for supremacy in that distracted country. As far as Mr. Johnson is concerned, I think he had better not interfere in the affairs of other governments until he has clearer evidence of his success in managing the affairs of his own country.

I may be justified in an observation rather aside from my theme. The people of this country will not hesitate to declare their rights in reference to the claims upon England for depredations by the "Alabama" and other piratical corsairs upon our commerce; they will not hesitate to maintain the ancient traditional doctrine of this country, that it is an offense for any foreign nation to attempt by force or by external pressure to establish a monarchy upon this continent; they will not hesitate to declare their opinions upon every question concerning the rights of the people: but I take it for granted that neither the Congress of the United States nor the people will intrust Mr. Johnson or Mr. Seward with any power whatever to interfere in the affairs of Mexico, to press our claims for compensation on Great Britain, or to offer any offense to the Emperor of the French. They know perfectly well that we can delay all these questions until after the 4th of March, 1869; and then, if we choose to interfere in the affairs of Mexico, we may do it with the certainty that we shall have the power to execute what we undertake; if we choose to demand compensation from Great Britain, we can do it with every reason to believe that she will concede what we shall consider right and just. They also know that the French emperor will withdraw his troops from Mexico long before the 4th of March, 1869; that it is not for us now to assert offensively any right we may have, however just it may be; that in our strength we can afford to rest, confident that the time is not far distant when there will be an executive department of the government representing the judgment and opinion and purpose of the people of this country, and an executive department disposed to execute this purpose under the Constitution, and according to the laws of the land. The South itself will come soon to the opinion that those who demand universal suffrage and the restoration of the government upon sound principles are, after all, its best friends. The South will discover soon, that Mr. Johnson himself, whether intentionally or not, is in reality its worst enemy. No man has done more to injure the cause of the South than he.

Of all things, the necessity of the Southern people, when the rebellion was overthrown, was this: that the man in the presidential chair should enjoy the confidence of the loyal citizens of the country. Enjoying their confidence, he could have done those things in behalf of the South which were necessary for its prosperity and security; but such is the popular impression now in regard to Mr. Johnson throughout the whole North, that he is utterly incapable of taking any step for the support of the just rights of the people of that section. Mr. Lincoln's death was as great a calamity to the South as to the North. By his death they were deprived of the benign influence of his administration, and the conduct of his successor led them to expect a restoration of the ancient order of things, when they controlled the policy of the United States. in that expectation they are to be disappointed; but it has had an evil effect. They have undertaken to assume authority and to exercise power in their respective localities as though the ancient order of things had been restored already, and now the work of restoration upon sound principles is made more and more difficult. But, from what I know of the purpose and opinion of Congress, I do not hesitate to say that the great majority of the loyal members of the two houses are in favor of declaring, by solemn resolution or public act, that the governments set up in these ten States are illegal and invalid. It is their purpose also, by legislative authority, to establish governments in those districts, — call them territorial governments, or what you will; and, in the act establishing those governments, to decide that all loyal male citizens shall be entitled to the right of suffrage.

I believe the time has come when we ought to cut clear of all theories and of all speculations concerning the rights of the people of that section of the country, growing out of their ancient relations to the Government of the United States. It is our duty to establish institutions upon the fundamental principles of natural justice, beginning at the foundation, recognizing the rights of men because they are men, and building up governments republican in form; and, whether the time necessary for the consummation of this plan be one year, or five years, or ten years, we shall appeal to the people to maintain that policy unto the end.

TEST-OATH FOR ATTORNEYS IN THE COURTS OF THE UNITED STATES.

REMARKS IN THE HOUSE OF REPRESENTATIVES, JAN. 22, 1867.*

MR. BOUTWELL, from the Committee on the Judiciary, reported House Bill No. 239, to prescribe an oath for public officers and members of the bar, and for other purposes, with an amendment in the nature of a substitute therefor, by striking out all after the enacting clause, and inserting the following: —

"That no person shall be permitted to act as an attorney or counsellor in any court of the United States who has been guilty of treason, bribery, murder, or other felony, or who has been engaged in any rebellion against the Government of the United States, or who has given aid, comfort, or encouragement to the enemies of the United States in armed hostility thereto.

SEC. 2. *And be it further enacted,* That the first section of this act is hereby declared to be a rule of every court of the United States.

SEC. 3. *And be it further enacted,* That it shall be the duty of the judge or judges of any such court, when the suggestion is made in open court that any person acting as an attorney or counsellor of said court, or offering or proposing to so act, is barred by the provisions of this act,

* On the twenty-third day of January, the bill passed by a vote of one hundred and eight yeas to forty-two nays.

or whenever said judge or judges shall believe that such person is so barred, to inquire and ascertain whether such person had been guilty of treason, bribery, murder, or other felony, or whether he has been engaged in any rebellion against the Government of the United States, or whether he has given aid, comfort, or encouragement to the enemies of the United States in armed hostility thereto; and if the court shall be of opinion that such person has been guilty of treason, bribery, murder, or other felony, or that he has been engaged in any rebellion against the Government of the United States, or that he has given aid, comfort, or encouragement to the enemies of the United States in armed hostility thereto, to exclude and debar such person from the office of attorney or counsellor of said court: and any person who shall testify falsely in any examination made by any court as aforesaid shall be guilty of perjury, and liable to the pains and penalties of perjury."

Mr. Boutwell. — Mr. Speaker, the amended bill having been read by the clerk, I shall be saved the necessity of a minute explanation. It is very well known that the majority of the Supreme Court has declared the test-oath unconstitutional, as far as by act of Congress the attempt was made to apply it to counsellors and attorneys in the courts of the United States. The purpose of this bill is to provide by a rule, which, under the Constitution and by the decisions of the courts of the United States, it is entirely competent for the legislative department of the government to make and prescribe, that certain persons shall not hold the office of attorney or counsellor in any national court. It provides that persons who are guilty of certain offences shall be debarred from that office in all of the courts of the United States.

We believe, as a committee, that it is entirely competent for Congress to declare, not only what the rules of the Supreme Court shall be in reference to this particular class of cases, but in reference to every case which can possibly arise in the judicial administration of the law. Congress, by the Constitution, has power to enact all laws necessary and proper for the administration of the executive and judicial departments of the government; and nothing can be more eminently proper than that persons who have been guilty, as is in this bill set forth, of treason, bribery, murder, or other felony, or who have participated in any rebellion against the Government of the United States, or have given aid, comfort, counsel, or encouragement to the enemies of the United States in armed hostility thereto, should be deprived of the privilege of appearing as officers of the government in any court of the United States.

It is not a punishment. The opinion of the court that persons are guilty of any of the offences enumerated in this bill is not evidence elsewhere by which those persons are to be deprived of any right whatever. It does not even deprive them of the power of practising in the vocation of attorneys or counsellors, but merely says that persons who are of such character and such known repute, based upon the actual facts of their lives, are unworthy to appear in the judicial tribunals of the country, to come in contact with the officers of the law, to exercise over the chief judicial magistrates of the land an influence deleterious to the public morals. If there be five judges upon the bench of the highest tribunal who will not enact rules and enforce proper regulations by which they may protect themselves from the foul contamination of conspirators and traitors against the constitution of the country, then the time has already arrived when the legislative department of the government should exercise its power and declare who shall be officers of the government in the administration of the law in the courts of the Union; and this bill is for that purpose. I am directed by the Committee on the Judiciary to report the bill.

[After debate by several members, Mr. Boutwell proceeded.]

If the House will pardon me, I think that by the record I can demonstrate concisely that Congress is justified in this proceeding. The gentleman from New Jersey [Mr. Rogers] was pleased to say that this bill contemplates a new mode of trial. No one better knows than the gentleman from New Jersey that the provisions of this bill with reference to an examination into the character of a counsellor are in exact accordance with the practice in every court in this country, and in Great Britain. If it be suggested in open court, that a man has been guilty in any time past of an act which unfits him, either according to law or in the judgment of the court, to pursue his profession and hold office as a practitioner, the court proceeds to inquire whether the suggestions are true, not as a criminal is charged upon the criminal side of a court, but merely for the purpose of reaching an opinion which has only this effect, that it determines the future standing of the party in court, but does not anywhere else affect him in his rights.

Mr. ROGERS. — I desire to ask the gentleman what is the best proof that a man is guilty of the offences referred to in this bill, treason, murder, &c.? Can you prove it in any way except by the production of a record of his conviction?

Mr. BOUTWELL. — Undoubtedly the production of the record of conviction is the best evidence of the guilt of the party; but that is not the only evidence that a court may take. It may go into an examination of charges which have never been brought before a criminal tribunal; and, if the court is convinced that the party is guilty, it has a right to deprive him of the privilege of practising in the court.

Mr. MAYNARD. — I would ask the gentleman from Massachusetts whether this bill amounts to any thing more than a statute declaratory of what the law now is? Every court has a right to inquire into the character of its officers; this House might inquire into the conduct of any one of its members, or of its Clerk or Sergeant-at-arms or Doorkeeper, and, being satisfied of his guilt of the charges brought against him, might set him aside. I would ask if this is any thing more than the embodying in a statute of what the common law of the courts now is.

Mr. BOUTWELL. — There can be no doubt upon that point. And I say, with reference to the recent decision of the Supreme Court, that it is an offence to the dignity and the respectability of the nation, that that tribunal, under the general authority vested in it by the Constitution and the laws, does not protect itself from the contamination of rebels and traitors, until the rebellion itself shall be suppressed, and those men shall be restored by the political department of the government to their former rights as citizens of the country. The Supreme Court failing in the performance of this high and self-protecting duty, the time has arrived when the Congress of the United States, by whose breath alone the Supreme Court enacts rules of any sort or admits any man to the office of counsellor or attorney at its bar, should assume exact and specific authority to declare by solemn law that men who have been guilty of murder or treason or bribery, or who have raised their arms to strike down the government of their country, shall not participate in the administration of the laws of the land until they are absolved from their crimes.

It is not enough that the Supreme Court of the country instructs us that the pardon of the President absolves these men from their iniquities. Sir, that is not enough; the pardon of the President may open the doors of jails and penitentiaries; it may release criminals who are guilty of murder or other felony; but, while I occupy a place upon this floor, never with my consent shall the pardon of the President be a certificate on which a felon may enter into the sacred tribunals of the land, and assist in the administration of justice.

SAME SUBJECT, JAN. 23, 1867.

I WISH, in closing the debate, to state more distinctly than I have stated heretofore, the constitutional and logical argument by which this bill is supported. Among the enumerated powers of Congress is this: —

"To make all laws which shall be necessary and proper for carrying into execution the foregoing powers, and all other powers vested by this Constitution in the Government of the United States, or in any department or officer thereof."

Following the enumeration of judicial powers, the Constitution declares: —

"In all the other cases before mentioned, the Supreme Court shall have appellate jurisdiction, both as to law and fact, with such exceptions and under such regulations as the Congress shall make."

Further authority is given by the Constitution to Congress in these words: —

"But the Congress may by law vest the appointment of such inferior officers as they may deem proper in the President alone, in the courts of law, or in the heads of Departments."

These provisions of the Constitution sustain Congress in the exercise of two kinds of power: First, in the enactment of all laws which Congress deems necessary and proper to carry into effect any of the powers vested in any department of the government; and, secondly, the authority is given to Congress to confer on the courts of law, as well as on the departments of the government, power to appoint such inferior officers as may by Congress be authorized.

We maintain this bill by maintaining the doctrine that an attorney in a court is an officer of the government. We maintain the doctrine by the ancient theory and rule, as old as the British law, of the official character of a counsellor or attorney. From the very first he has been regarded as an officer of the court. The Supreme Court, in giving the decision which has been considered, admit that an attorney is an officer of the court, although they deny that he is an officer of the government. The admission, which can be easily comprehended by any man, overturns the singular theory of the court. The Supreme Court itself is a department of the government. Every court inferior to the Supreme Court is a branch or judicial agency of the government; and therefore when you have demonstrated or admitted, as the Supreme Court in this decision has admitted, that an attorney is an officer of the court, it follows as a necessary consequence, from which there can be no logical, legal, or constitutional escape, that the attorney is an officer of the government, because the court itself is either a department or a branch or agency of the government.

Under section thirty-five of the Judiciary Act of 1789, provision is made by law for the appointment of these officers by the court; and, as I said yesterday, the court derives its power to appoint attorneys from that act. But for that act they would be driven back upon the ancient common-law doctrine, under which the party himself was required to appear in court and defend his cause. The thirty-fifth section is as follows: —

> "*And be it further enacted,* That in all courts of the United States the parties may plead and manage their own causes personally, or by the assistance of such counsel or attorneys-at-law as by the rules of the said courts, respectively, shall be permitted to manage and conduct causes therein."

Therefore the authority of the court to appoint an attorney is derived from the Judiciary Act of 1789, framed by the fathers of the Constitution; and, without the authority of that act, the court would not to-day possess constitutional or legal power to admit a single attorney to the performance of his ordinary functions in any court of the United States. They are entirely devoid of power to enact rules for their own government, except through the act of March 2, 1793, which provides, —

> "That it shall be lawful for the several courts of the United States from time to time, as occasion may require, to make rules and orders for their respective courts, directing the returning of writs and processes, the filing of declarations and other pleadings, the taking of rules, the entering and making up judgments by default, and other matters, in the vacation and otherwise, in a manner not repugnant to the laws of the United States, &c."

They have power by the authority of law to make their rules, and that is the only power they have on the subject. The law limits this power by declaring that they shall not make any rules except such as are in conformity to the laws of the United

States. The Supreme Court of the United States, many years ago, through the decision of Justice Story, recognized the authority of the Congress of the United States in this matter. He says: —

> "So far as the acts of Congress have adopted the forms of process and modes of proceeding and pleadings in the State courts, or have authorized the courts thereof to adopt them, and they have been actually adopted, they are obligatory, but no further. But no court of the United States is authorized to adopt by rule any provisions of State laws which are repugnant to or incompatible with the positive enactments of Congress upon the subject of the jurisdiction or practice or proceedings in such court." — *Reary et al.* vs. *The Farmers' and Merchants' Bank of Memphis*, 16 Peters, p. 94.

It is from the Constitution and laws, and decisions of the courts, then, that we derive the authority to pass any rule which we think necessary and proper for the performance of the duties devolved upon the courts of the country. If we have authority to give the courts power to make their own rules, we have authority to prescribe exactly and definitely the rules by which the courts shall be governed; and, upon this statement of the matter, I submit the bill to the House.

GOVERNMENT OF THE INSURRECTIONARY STATES.*

REMARKS UPON THE BILL TO PROVIDE FOR THE MORE EFFICIENT GOVERNMENT OF THE INSURRECTIONARY STATES, FEB. 9, 1867.

[Mr. Raymond, of New York, having the floor, suggested that the Bill should be recommitted to the Committee on Reconstruction.]

ONLY a few days since, a bill of a different sort from that now pending was before this House; and a majority of the House — I believe the gentleman from New York [Mr. Raymond] was of that majority — desired to refer the whole subject to the Committee on Reconstruction. The various propositions were so referred. They have been considered by that committee; and I believe I am guilty of no breach of confidence when I say that never has any report been made which was so unanimously supported by its different members as the one now under consideration; nor has any bill submitted by that committee ever been so carefully considered as this.

We have now spent two days and more in the discussion of the present measure. We have but eight or ten days in which, as a legislative body, we can act. I hold that it would be the greatest of public calamities, if this Congress should adjourn without an expression, both on the part of the

* See Appendix II.

House and of the Senate, of the opinions entertained by the representatives of the country in reference to this measure. It is now to be seen plainly, that, if the bill be recommitted, there can be no proper reconsideration of the subject by a new committee, no conclusion reached, no report made, much less any action had, even by this branch of the government, within the period to which we are limited by the Constitution of the country for the consideration of this measure, and the passage of a law over the President's objections.

To-day there are eight million and more of people, occupying six hundred and thirty thousand square miles of the territory of this country, who are writhing under cruelties nameless in their character, — injustice such as has not been permitted to exist in any other country in modern times; and all this because in this capitol there sits enthroned a man who, as far as the executive department is concerned, guides the destinies of the republic in the interest of rebels; and because, also, in those ten former States, rebellion itself, inspired by the executive department, wields all authority, and is the embodiment of law and power everywhere. Until in the South this obstacle to reconstruction is removed, there can be no effectual step taken toward the re-organization of the government; and, argue as gentlemen may, no way can be devised for the removal of this obstacle in the South, except to confide the work to Grant and Sherman and Sheridan, — the men who overthrew the rebellion when it was flagrant in the field, but not, as now, organized in the government. They will crush out the despotisms which have been set over the people, and prepare a way for the inauguration of civil authority. You might as well expect to build a fire in the depths of the ocean as expect to reconstruct loyal civil governments in the South until you have broken down the rebel despotism which everywhere holds sway in that vast region of country.

Therefore, sir, after all this debate, considering the magnitude of the question, the peril in which the country is involved, I, for my part, feel it to be my duty to insist that we shall hold this business in our hands as the representatives of the people, and take the judgment of the House upon the question whether all power shall be surrendered to the rebels of the South, or whether we shall exert the constitutional authority we possess over the army (which is our servant to-day, and will be our servant in the interest of loyalty through all this contest), and thus break down the governments which have been illegally set up, lay a basis on which we may be able to build civil institutions, and, as soon as we have the opportunity, prepare a way for their establishment. But it is the vainest of delusions, the most dangerous of aspirations, to contemplate, or even to hope for, the reconstruction of civil government, until the rebel despotisms in those ten States shall be broken up.

GOVERNMENT OF THE REBEL STATES.*

REMARKS UPON THE BILL TO PROVIDE FOR THE MORE EFFECTUAL GOVERNMENT OF THE INSURRECTIONARY STATES, FEB. 13, 1867.

I AM aware that no measure can be more unpalatable to the American people than one which provides for a military government; and there is no position in which I can myself be placed, in the performance of a public duty, more disagreeable than that of an advocate of military rule. I shall, however, make no apology for proceeding to the discussion of the measure before the House by the aid of commonplace and inartificial processes of examination and reasoning. It is my purpose, first to examine this bill in connection with the amendments that are now pending, moved by the chairman of the committee on the part of the House, with the design of relieving, if possibly I may, the force of some objections which have been made to its passage. I shall then consider the amendments proposed by the gentleman from Ohio [Mr. Bingham] and the gentleman from Maine [Mr. Blaine], for the purpose of showing that those amendments are inconsistent with the vote of the House taken yesterday in reference to a bill for the reconstruction of Louisiana, and that they are also vitally and dangerously inconsistent with any measure for the perma-

* See Appendix II. and III.

nent restoration of the rebel States to their position and influence as members of the government. Then, in conclusion, I design to present certain general views bearing upon the question of military authority in the ten rebellious States; showing, that, in a large degree, the present condition of things has arisen from the policy of the President, — a policy for which we are in no proper sense responsible, but which, in its effects, compels us, as the representatives of the people and as the law-making power in the government, bound to protect all who are within the jurisdiction of the Union in their rights of person, property, and liberty, to resort to measures which otherwise we could neither approve nor contemplate.

It has been objected, that the committee did not propose, in connection with this bill, any measure or measures for the restoration of civil authority in the ten States recently in rebellion. The objection is well founded, and the omission may have been a mistake on the part of the committee. If so, it is due in some degree, as far as I am concerned, to an error of opinion as to what the House was prepared to do. I refer now to the vote upon the passage of the bill for the re-organization of Louisiana.

It will be very well remembered, that, on former occasions during the existence of this Congress, any proposition contemplating universal manhood suffrage was not only unanimously opposed on the other side of the House, but it failed to receive the united or even the general support of members upon this side of the House. It therefore naturally came to be believed in the committee, that if we should report a measure which provided for universal manhood suffrage, either in one of these States or in the ten States, we should fail to combine in its favor the entire support even of the loyal party. I have now to say that it is one of the most noteworthy facts in the history of this great contest, that the bill providing for civil government in Louisiana, which passed the House yesterday, was discussed to some extent on this side, and for two consecutive hours without interruption on the other side, and was not, I believe, opposed by any gentleman upon the ground that it provided for universal manhood suffrage in the State of Louisiana. Only one gentleman on the other side adverted incidentally, as far as I heard, to the fact that there was such a provision in the bill.

Mr. FINCK. — Will the gentleman yield?

Mr. BOUTWELL. — Yes, sir.

Mr. FINCK. — One of my objections to the bill was, that it proposed to disfranchise the white people of Louisiana, and confer suffrage on the colored people. I made that point distinctly.

Mr. BOUTWELL. — I referred to the gentleman [Mr. Finck], and I believe I did not misinterpret the force of his observations. It was a passing, incidental objection, instead of being in the forefront of the reasons why the bill for the reconstruction of Louisiana should not be adopted by the House. I have therefore to say for myself, that I was in error as to what this House, representing the country, was prepared to do; and, without submitting to the interruption which is indicated by the gentleman from Kentucky [Mr. Hise], I congratulate the House and the country, and give notice to that gentleman and to all those of the border States who sympathize with him in opinion, that the time manifestly has passed when there can be a struggle or a question whether the colored people of the South are to participate, as other men participate, in the government of the country.

Speaking generally of the bill under consideration, it has two advantages which I think of primary, nay, I may say of vital, importance to the future welfare of the republic. One is that it contains a distinct declaration for all political purposes, that the governments which have been set up in the ten States recently in rebellion are mere pretexts, pretended governments, having no vital or binding force upon the people of the respective States, and being in no sense entitled to the recognition of the country.

The declaration is of importance to the future of the country, considered with reference to its effect upon those governments; but it is of more importance considered with reference to the possible action of the Supreme Court of the United States. If it be true, as has been asserted by the gentleman from Ohio [Mr. Bingham], that on former occasions, and especially upon the re-enactment of the Freedmen's Bureau Bill, Congress did virtually admit that those ten States were States in the Union, then the reasons for the passage of this bill are vastly increased. If Congress being the political department of the government, entitled under the Constitution to decide what form of government in any State is the legal government, has heretofore used language which can be so interpreted properly as to support these pretended State governments at the South, then it is of vital necessity that that policy should be reversed, and another declaration made. If it happen, as possibly it may, that the Supreme Court of the United States shall declare that those ten States are States in the Union, entitled to all the rights and privileges of States, and shall base that declaration upon any act of Congress, then those States are restored, as far as the judiciary can restore them, and nothing remains for Congress, and for the people, but to accept that conclusion, or else to enter into an undesirable and dangerous controversy with the chief judicial tribunal of the land.

In the preamble of this bill, these words are found: "Whereas the pretended State governments of the late so-called Confederate States," &c.; thus declaring that these governments are merely pretended State governments. While the preamble will not in itself, as matter of law, bind the legal tribunals of the country, the text of the bill is connected with the proposition in the preamble by the use of such language as that there can be no mistake as to the true import of the whole considered as a measure of legislation. In the third section, we have said, —

> "And all legislative or judicial proceedings or processes to prevent or control the proceedings of said military tribunals, and all interference by said pretended State governments with the exercise of military authority under this act, shall be void and of no effect."

We have declared, then, in the preamble and in the text of the bill, that these are pretended, not real State governments. How will that declaration made by Congress affect the action of the Supreme Court? As is very well known, in the case of Luther *vs.* Borden, the Supreme Court held that Congress is the department of the government that is to decide, in case of two governments set up in a State, which of the two is republican in form. They also decided another point which has not yet attracted the attention of the country. It was held in general terms, that it is in the power of Congress to inspect the Constitution of a State where there is but one form of government, and to decide whether that particular Constitution is republican or not. The court illustrated the proposition by saying, that, if a State should establish a military government, it would be in the power of Congress to set it aside, and to institute proceedings for the organization of a government republican in form.

The Supreme Court, looking at these ten States, before they can discern judicially the existence of States must find State governments; and, if this bill be passed, they will fail entirely to find any State government whatever. They must also further find that the State government existing in any State has been recognized by the Congress of the United States, and therefore judicially the Supreme Court will have no capacity to see in either of these ten States any existing government; and therefore for judicial purposes there is no State. It follows, then, that with the object which we have in view, which is to keep in our own hands, as the political department of the government, the re-organization of these ten States, this bill, in its present form, is of vital importance to the future welfare of the country. It retains in the hands of Congress and of the people the control of a most important question; none other than this: whether these ten States shall be admitted into the Union under the lead and management of disloyal men, or whether they shall be admitted under the lead, and by the direction and influence, of loyal men. This is the question before the country.

The remark has been made, that the committee did not contemplate any thing but a military governnment for these States. This statement is negatived by the concluding clause of the preamble, which is in these words: —

> "And whereas it is necessary that peace and good order should be enforced in said so-called States until loyal and republican State governments can be legally established," &c.

I may remark here that the gentleman from New York [Mr. Raymond] admitted that life, liberty, and property were not protected in these ten States; and it follows, as a matter of course, that somebody, for the time being, is bound to furnish that protection. What I ask the House to accept is the fact that there is no other practicable way of furnishing protection to life, liberty, and property in these ten States, except through the instrumentality of a bill conferring great powers upon the military department of the government, but powers not to be exercised without authority of law, powers not to be exercised independently of Congress, but to be exercised precisely as the police of a city exercise the powers confided to them. They derive their authority from the law, and they exercise the powers intrusted to them in obedience to principles of law. They are always responsible to the people as the source of law. The military department in its operations in these ten States, whether considered with reference to the people of the whole country or considered with reference to the powers that they exercise, will be but as the police of a city acting under authority of law and in consonance with the principles of law, possessing vast power, exercising great authority, but always in subjection to law. The moment the military authorities depart from the principles of law, the moment they attempt to assume or assert any authority not confided to them, they become utterly powerless in the presence of the majesty of the people, who will revoke the delegated authority with the same judgment and the same certainty with which they conferred it. It follows, therefore, that fifty or sixty thousand men of the army who may be intrusted with power in those States will be, with reference to the people of those States and of the country, but as the police of a city.

I pass over the second section of this bill. I believe, that, as reported by the committee, it is constitutional, and I believe also that the amendments suggested by the gentleman from Pennsylvania would be constitutional. But the main feature of this section, whether accepted as reported by the committee or amended as suggested by the chairman, is that which gives to the general of the army, subject, of course, to the authority vested by the Constitution in the President as commander-in-chief of the army, authority to designate five officers of the rank of major-general or brigadier-general, and appoint them severally to the command of the five districts created and established by this bill.

In passing, I venture to make a single observation for the purpose of relieving gentlemen upon the point suggested by my friend from Ohio [Mr. Schenck], that it was not competent for Congress to detail officers of the army by rank. I do not at all concur in that idea, if by "detailing" is meant designating certain officers by name or by rank, and assigning them to the performance of specified services. The President is undoubtedly commander-in-chief of the army and navy; but, by a provision of the Constitution, Congress has power to make rules for the regulation and government of the army and navy. The President is required to command the army in subordination to the rules and regulations which Congress may prescribe. There would be no doubt of the authority of Congress to send a fleet to the Indian Ocean for the protection of American commerce, and to detail Admiral Farragut by name, and assign to him a certain number of vessels belonging to the navy, and direct him to proceed to the Indian Ocean for the purpose of protecting the commerce of the United States. The authority of the President over the navy is precisely the same as is his authority over the army.

Objection is made to another provision of this

bill, found in the third section, which authorizes the military officers to allow local civil tribunals to take jurisdiction of and to try offenders. It has been suggested, that this provision is equivalent to a recognition of the State governments which have been set up in those States, and that, in some way or to some degree, it conflicts with the provisions contained in the preamble, and in the text of the last paragraph of the third section of the bill. I think that this provision is not subject justly to any such interpretation. We establish military authority in that vast district of country. We give to our military officers supreme, but not necessarily exclusive, jurisdiction over all local affairs; and by this provision we put it in the power of the military officers to use the existing legal tribunals. The officer does not use a local tribunal because it was instituted by the State, and derives its powers from the State; but he uses it, if he uses it at all, because he finds it there, because he finds the people acquainted with its administration, and because he can make it useful in protecting the property, the liberty, and the lives of the persons within his jurisdiction. But no authority, no valid argument, can be deduced from this provision, in favor of the pretended State governments which have been set up. Our action in this case will be analogous with the conduct of President Lincoln when my friend and colleague [Mr. Banks] was in command in Louisiana. I remember that at that time a proclamation was issued by the President, declaring the Constitution of Louisiana, except those parts of it which related to slavery, the law of Louisiana for the time being.

I was myself slightly disturbed by the fear that the President thereby recognized the old Constitution as binding upon the people because it had been the Constitution of the State: but, with his usual clearness, the President made the distinction, and said, that finding the Constitution there, and finding the people familiar with it, he recognized and enforced it; but not because it had any vital power or legal existence arising out of the fact that it had been previously the Constitution of the State.

Mr. BANKS.—Will my colleague allow me to say, the Constitution of Louisiana was recognized, as he has suggested, only for the purpose of the election, or with a view to the establishment, of a government immediately by the people, and not as a semi-frame of government? It was recognized for a special purpose.

Mr. BOUTWELL.—Undoubtedly it was for a special purpose. I did not introduce the subject for the purpose of saying that it was otherwise, but only to show that it was competent for the authorities of the United States to use the institutions and framework of government found in the rebellious States and thus to accomplish what is desired, whether it be the protection of life, liberty, and property, or whether it be the reconstruction of the government itself. They are used, not because they have been established in those States at some previous time, but because they are convenient instruments for doing what we desire to have done. They derive their power, not from the fact that they have been established as institutions of the State at some previous time, but from the fact that we endow them with life for certain purposes, whether those purposes be temporary or permanent. In this case, as in the case of Louisiana, we propose to use the existing institutions and tribunals for certain purposes, for a limited period of time, and only until another system can be introduced.

Mr. BANKS. — I desire to say a word further.

Mr. ELDRIDGE. — Will the gentleman allow me to ask him a question?

Mr. BOUTWELL. — I will first yield to my colleague.

Mr. BANKS. — There is one other distinction to which the attention of my colleague ought to be called. That distinction is, that the Constitution of Louisiana which was recognized was in the hands of loyal men. But the civil governments indirectly recognized in this bill are in the hands of the enemies of this country.

Mr. BOUTWELL. — Very well; that for our purpose is a distinction of no consequence whatever, for the reason that the military officers having control over these tribunals will deprive them of power from time to time, and to such extent as may be necessary for the security of life and liberty and property. If the tribunals referred to fail to such a degree, and for such periods of time as to render it probable that they cannot be used as instruments of good government, then they will be thrust aside altogether. And so it would have been with the Constitution of Louisiana, if, in the experiment which was tried, it had failed to accomplish that which the President desired; to wit, to aid in the restoration of civil government in that State. Had it failed to do that, the President would not have hesitated to put the hand of military power upon that Constitution at once.

Mr. Eldridge. — If the gentleman from Massachusetts will now allow me a moment, I will say that I understand the gentleman to admit that the whole government of these people will be under the control of the military officer who may be in command of the district or department, subject alone to his supreme will, unless he shall concede, if he shall see fit, a certain amount of jurisdiction to the civil officers. Now, I would inquire of the gentleman, in the first place, what laws these military officers are to administer, — whether they are to be the laws of their own will, which they are to administer upon their own impulse and discretion, or whether the laws and Constitution of the United States, and the laws and Constitution of the State of Louisiana. Are these the laws that they are to administer, or are they to administer martial law alone?

Mr. Boutwell. — I think I understand what the gentleman desires to express. I may say, in one word, that the supreme power undoubtedly will be for a time in the military officers. But that power is limited by this bill in various ways, and by the Constitution of the United States, as I will undertake to point out.

But, before entering upon that branch of the subject, I desire to refer to what has been said in reference to the suspension, by this bill, of the writ of *habeas corpus*.

Mr. Banks. — Let me say just one more word right here.

Mr. Boutwell. — Very well.

Mr. Banks. — I wish to say one word in confirmation of what my colleague has said, — that it was the distinct understanding of the military authorities and those they represented in the experiment in Louisiana, that, if it had resulted in placing disloyal men in office, the whole affair would have been immediately suppressed.

Mr. Boutwell. — I have no doubt of it. As I was about to say, there is not in the terms in this bill any suspension of the writ of *habeas corpus*. If it be true, as is asserted in the preamble of the bill, that these are pretended State governments, and not real State governments, then they have no power whatever over the privilege of the writ of *habeas corpus*.

The privilege of the writ is a privilege which can be enjoyed only under those governments which are legitimate and recognized. Therefore, when we declare that the governments in these ten States are pretended governments and not real governments, then, as far as those governments are concerned, they neither have nor can have any power over the writ of *habeas corpus* in any form. Hence it follows that this bill is broader in its provisions than the mere suspension of the writ of *habeas corpus*, as far as the tribunals of the so-called States are concerned. The bill not only suspends their functions in that particular, but it suspends by its power all their functions. So far as the courts of the United States are concerned, there is no suspension of the writ of *habeas corpus*, but only a regulation of the mode in which the privilege of the writ shall be enjoyed by the people. With reference to this point, the amendment introduced by the gentleman from Ohio [Mr. Bingham] seems to me very proper; and I trust that it may be adopted.

I come now to certain provisions of the bill, which limit the authority of the military officers. It is declared, first, —

> "That it shall be the duty of each officer assigned as aforesaid to protect all persons in their rights of person and property, to suppress insurrection, disorder, and violence, and to punish, or cause to be punished, all disturbers of the public peace and criminals."

Then it is declared in the fourth section, that —

> "All persons put under military arrest by virtue of this act shall be tried without unnecessary delay, and no cruel or unusual punishment shall be inflicted;"

using in this respect the language of the Constitution.

The fifth section provides, —

> "That no sentence of any military commission or tribunal hereby authorized, affecting the life or liberty of any person, shall be executed until it is approved by the officer in command of the district."

Under the general principles of law and practice, no capital punishment can be inflicted until the sentence shall have been approved first by the military commander of the district, and then referred to the President of the United States, and approved also by him. Thus we impose upon the officers those obligations which are imposed upon other departments of the government by the Constitution of the United States. We place, then, always in the presence of these officers, the political power of the government to arrest their proceedings at any time, if they are harsh, unjust, unwise, or oppressive in any degree.

Mr. ELDRIDGE. — I desire to ask the gentleman whether he considers that this bill secures to a person accused of a capital offence the right of trial by a jury of his peers?

Mr. BOUTWELL. — It does not.

Mr. ELDRIDGE. — Is it not, then, in direct conflict with that provision of the Constitution which declares that a party charged with crime shall be entitled to a trial by jury, to be confronted with the witnesses against him, &c.?

Mr. BOUTWELL. — Mr. Speaker, the Constitution provides that "the privilege of the writ of *habeas corpus* shall not be suspended, unless when, in cases of rebellion or invasion, the public safety may require it." Now, sir, there is a distinction which can properly be made, but which, as far as I have observed, has not been indicated upon this floor. It is this: that the power of Congress to suspend the writ of *habeas corpus* is not confined to periods of rebellion or invasion; but it arises when there is a case of rebellion or invasion, and it ceases to exist only when, in the judgment of the law-making power, the occasion has passed. Therefore the people of these ten States are to-day, not only without civil governments, — that has been declared by the executive department, and it is also affirmed in this bill, — but they are also in that condition, even if the existing governments are valid, when it is in the power of Congress to suspend the writ of *habeas corpus* for the reason that a case of rebellion exists. Although war is no longer flagrant in that part of the country, it still is true, as is confessed by gentlemen on all sides, that, as an effect and consequence and incident of the rebellion, there is no real protection to life, person, or property. There was a case of rebellion, and the consequences remain.

Therefore the case of rebellion having arisen, the consequences, incidents, and facts of that case yet continuing, the power of the government over the people of these vast regions of country, aside from the rights of conquest, is as supreme and exclusive as it was over the sections of country subjugated by the arms of the republic, during the time while the rebellion was flagrant in other quarters.

Mr. Raymond. — If it does not interrupt the gentleman from Massachusetts, — and I understand it does not, — I desire to ask him a question on one point which seems to me a point of distinction in that matter. The gentleman maintains, inasmuch as the invasion, the rebellion, the endangerment of the public safety continued, therefore the suspension of the writ of *habeas corpus* continued.

Mr. Boutwell. — The power to suspend the privilege of the writ continues.

Mr. Raymond. — But as I understand it, by proclamation duly authorized by law, that state of rebellion has been legally ended, and therefore this is a new exercise of power. It is not the continuance of a previous exercise of power; but a new state of things having arisen, the war having been ended, and proclaimed ended, in accordance with law, this is a new exercise of that power.

Mr. BOUTWELL. — The proclamation of the President had no other effect, as I understand, than to declare that flagrant war was at an end; but no proclamation of the President, whatever may be the terms in which it is couched, can ever deprive the legislative department of its constitutional authority to decide for itself, in the case of rebellion, that the privileges of the rebels shall be suspended. The President cannot deprive the legislative department of the government of the power of deciding for itself when the case of rebellion exists, and when the effects and consequences of that rebellion terminate. The power is here, and no paper proclamation of the President can ever divest us of it.

Mr. ELDRIDGE rose.

Mr. BOUTWELL. — I fear all my time will be consumed with these interruptions. I will yield to the gentleman from Wisconsin, and then decline to yield to all others.

Mr. ELDRIDGE. — I understand the gentleman to claim the suspension of the writ of *habeas corpus* itself justifies the holding of the person charged with crime, and the depriving him of an immediate trial. I do not understand that the suspension of the writ of *habeas corpus* has any such effect; but, on the contrary, I hold the provisions of the Constitution still apply, that he is entitled to be tried speedily by an impartial jury, and be confronted with the witnesses against him, and to have the assistance of counsel for his defence.

Mr. BOUTWELL. — I have only to say that in my

view, so far as these ten States are concerned, when the exigency exists, it is competent for Congress to declare that they shall be governed by martial law; to declare that pretended State governments have no power to grant writs of *habeas corpus*, or do any other act of government, except as they derive it from military authority. The military government for the time being will be supreme, but not necessarily exclusive, because these military officers may, as provided in this bill, grant to the local tribunals an opportunity to dispose of questions as they may arise among the people.

Mr. Speaker, passing from the provisions of the bill, I wish to call the attention of the House to the amendment offered by the gentleman from Ohio [Mr. Bingham] and the amendment offered by the gentleman from Maine [Mr. Blaine], which are similar in character. I observe that these amendments are supported by a number of gentlemen on this side of the House. Without examining into the details of the amendments, I do not hesitate to say, that any general proposition for the restoration of these States to the Union upon any basis set forth in general terms in an act of Congress is fraught with the greatest danger to the future peace and prosperity of the republic.

The reason is apparent: yesterday we passed a bill providing for the admission of Louisiana to the Union. I will refer now to the provisions of that bill for the purpose of deducing therefrom an argument against the amendments proposed by the gentleman from Maine and the gentleman from Ohio.

In that bill we have taken the greatest care to

secure a loyal governor for Louisiana while the process of reconstruction is going on. We have taken the utmost security that the legislative council shall be composed of loyal men, that no person shall be elected a delegate to the constitutional convention or to the legislature who has had any thing whatever to do with the rebellion.

And for what purpose have we taken all these securities? For this purpose alone, as I apprehend, that we may present loyal men as the principal figures in the reconstruction of Louisiana. We clothe loyal persons with authority, so that the people of Louisiana, loyal and rebel, may see that all power in the new State, under the policy of Congress, is given to loyal men, and also that disloyal men are carefully excluded. I need not dwell upon the well-known and potent fact, that, when you create a State, when you give power to a governor, when you appoint a legislative council, when you select judges, it is of the first importance that they be loyal men, if you desire to construct a loyal State.

How will it be under the amendment proposed by the gentleman from Ohio? He lays down a general rule under which each of these nine States is permitted to reconstruct itself, and obtain admission into the Union. What is to be the effect of this measure? The legislative departments of those nine States are all now in the hands of disloyal men. Every governor, every judge, is a disloyal man. The majority in each of the legislative assemblies is composed of disloyal men. When it is ascertained, as it will be ascertained if the amendment of the gentleman from Ohio prevail, that certain things are to be done in order to secure admission into Congress, what happens? The disloyal authorities proceed at once to do that which the gentleman from Ohio says they must do before they are admitted into Congress. Disloyal men in these States become the central figures in the government. They become the source of power.

The effect of this will be that these nine States will appear here with their constitutions framed as you demand, the constitutional amendment adopted, and negro suffrage provided for, but every officer elected or appointed will be a disloyal man. Am I told that the pending amendment to the Constitution excludes certain persons? To be sure it does; but the number excluded is very small in proportion to the whole number of disloyal people in those States. Nothing remains except for the disloyal to select those who are also disloyal, but who will not come under the ban of the constitutional amendment. The consequence is, that the timid, whether black or white, who adhere to authority, who naturally place confidence in those who possess power, will be the sport of disloyal men. Thus you permit disloyal men to set up and control the governments which are to be formed in these ten States. Therefore I protest with all the power I can command against any general proposition for the admission of the States into the Union; and, in that protest, I do not mean to be understood as entertaining the opinion that these States ought not to be restored as speedily as possible. But I assert and maintain that either the bill which passed yesterday should be passed for these several States as they may appear qualified to take their places in the Union, or one somewhat like that proposed by my colleague [Mr. Banks]. Consider the States separately, and provide that the men who are intrusted with the organization shall be loyal men; secure a loyal government, loyal judges, loyal legislatures, a loyal convention for framing the State constitutions, and thereby you secure loyalty among the people of each of the new States. If you allow power to pass into the hands of the disloyal people of the South, they will without doubt reconstruct governments as you demand. They possess all the means of information; they command in a large degree the intellect of the South; they control the institutions of learning; the clergy is in their interest. Having already the chief means of influence and power, if in addition we allow them the offices in the incipient States, they will rally to their support enough of the people to control the States for a long period of time. Therefore I am of the opinion that, if we were to pass bills to-morrow for the reconstruction of every one of these States, the bills should be separate; they should be framed like the bill passed yesterday in relation to Louisiana, that thereby we may have the influence of the military officers in support of the new State governments we desire to establish.

I hold further that we are driven to this extreme measure, because the policy of the President has failed, for some reason or other, to secure to the people of the South protection of life, liberty, or property. I have in my desk a statement in detail, which I suppose, and have reason to believe, is very imperfect, but which contains the names of forty persons murdered in Arkansas within a comparatively brief period of time. Although many of the murderers are known, not one of them has been brought to justice, or even arraigned before any tribunal.

There are now, as far as I understand, but four methods which can be resorted to for reconstructing the governments of the rebel States. The first mode is to admit all the Southern States upon the plan suggested by the gentleman from Ohio [Mr. Bingham]. I have already indicated, as clearly as I am able, the objections to that plan. I consider it nothing more and nothing less than a proposition to put all those State governments into the hands of the rebels. Therefore I am opposed, as strenuously as I can be opposed to any thing, to the passage of that measure.

The second plan is to leave the rebel States as they now are. Are gentlemen prepared to do that? Are they prepared to continue this grand carnival of disquiet, disorder, bloodshed, and murder throughout the South? We shall be false to our duty, if we permit the existing condition of things to continue one day beyond the time when we can relieve ourselves from the circumstances in which we are placed.

The third plan is to follow the example set in the case of Louisiana by the bill which we passed yesterday. We may follow that example as speedily as possible, even though we pass the bill now before the House. The bill for a military government over the rebel States does not interfere at all with the reconstruction of North Carolina or Arkansas, or any other State, should Congress deem either in a fit condition to be received into the Union of States.

But in the mean time, as I believe, it is necessary to establish some sort of government which shall protect the people in their rights; and I know of no means whatever, except to employ the military forces for that purpose. I do not participate at all in the apprehension that the military will in any degree deviate from the strict line of their duty. I do not apprehend that they will oppress any man, or that they will do any thing from malice, or for any unjust purpose. I believe that temporarily they will be safe depositaries of the public power, and that we can at least do that which thus far the government has failed to do since the suppression of the rebellion, protect our friends against the injustice and wrongs under which they have suffered for now more than two years, and under which they are writhing in the very agony of death.

REMARKS UPON THE AMENDMENTS OF THE SENATE TO THE BILL TO PROVIDE FOR THE MORE EFFICIENT GOVERNMENT OF THE INSURRECTIONARY STATES, FEB. 18, 1867.*

I AM aware that the provisions of this bill have already been discussed very thoroughly by the House, and I have had my full share of the opportunity for discussion. If I did not believe that the bill, in the form in which it now comes to us from the Senate, was fraught with great and permanent danger to the country, I would not attempt to resist further its passage.

* See Appendix IV.

I ask the House to consider the position in which we are placed at the present time. In proceeding, I make a remark which seems to be necessary, but I do not make it for any party purpose; yet I cannot reach the object I have in view without stating a fact of a party nature. That fact is, that the majority here, representing the majority of the loyal people of the country, has the control of the government for a period of two years or more. We have every reason to believe that the government will be continued in the hands of loyal men.

In any event, in these two years we ought to be able, and I am sure we shall be able, to reconstruct the government upon a loyal basis. But, in any event, nothing worse can happen to us, and nothing worse can happen to the country, than the reconstruction of the government on a disloyal basis. If it is to be reconstructed upon a disloyal basis, there are two things which I seek: first, that we who believe ourselves to be loyal to the government and to the country shall not in any degree be responsible for the reconstruction of the rebel States in the hands of disloyal men; and, secondly, that, if it is to be the fortune of the country that it shall be reconstructed upon a disloyal basis and by the agency and under the control of disloyal men, then I desire to postpone that calamity to the latest day possible.

There can be no doubt, however, that during this session, or during the existence of the Fortieth Congress, if the majority acts according to its means and its opportunities, it cannot fail to secure the reconstruction of these ten States, and their restoration to the Union, through the agency of loyal men and by loyal means.

My objection to the proposed substitute of the Senate is fundamental; it is conclusive. That substitute provides, if not in terms, at least in fact, by the measures which it proposes, for the reconstruction of the State governments at once, through the agency of disloyal men. That great fact, which, if this substitute shall be concurred in, will be near to us, ought to restrain us from any action in favor of this measure, though we be compelled to separate, on the 4th of March next, without having done any thing whatever for the restoration of the rebel States.

I do not believe that the people of this country are prepared to accept a measure of restoration which looks to the re-introduction of disloyal men, first, into the governments of the ten States, and then into the government of the country. If that be their feeling, it is our duty to resist the reconstruction of these ten States through any such agency, or with any such certain result near at hand.

I pass over the provisions in the second section of the substitute, by which all power is put into the hands of the President of the United States, with the remark that the House bill gave authority to the general of the army, of which by the amendment he is deprived. The Civil-Rights Act, if it be enforced by the President according to its terms and its intention, he being the commander-in-chief of the army, is sufficient for the protection of liberty, of persons, of rights, and of life throughout these ten States. And, if that be so, the necessity for the passage of a military bill, with power in the hands of the general of the army, for the government of the Southern States, arises from the fact that the President thus far has failed to exercise the power conferred on him by the Civil-Rights Act. By this remark, I do not say whether he is guilty or not of any neglect of duty. But he has not used the power which the laws of the country have placed in his hands for the protection of the loyal people of the ten States recently in rebellion. Until you have some assurance that the vast powers which he already possesses are to be exercised in behalf of loyalty and justice and life, will you clothe him anew, will you give him additional power, will you concede to him entire and unrestricted control of the army, when he now has means to do that which we desire to have done, if he did not for some purpose, or under some influence, neglect to exercise the authority which he already possesses?

I come now to that provision of the proposed substitute which is even of graver import: I refer to the provision found in the fourth section, wherein we give up to the present leaders of the South the business of re-organizing the State governments. Under the substitute, no one man, from Jefferson Davis, if he be released from Fortress Monroe, down to the humblest soldier that trained in the armies of the rebellion, or practised the nefarious business of a guerilla, is deprived of the right of suffrage.

The fifth section of this bill proposes, in effect,

if not in terms, universal amnesty and the restoration to political power, as far as the franchise is concerned, of every man in the ten States. The pending constitutional amendment deprives certain persons of the right to hold office; but the power of this government and the power of the States is not in the right of individuals to hold office, but it is in the immensely superior power of the people to elect to office, and in the assurance that those elected to office will represent the men by whom they are elected. By the bill as now amended, you transfer the re-organization of these ten States to the rebels; you give to rebels the chief places in the work of reconstruction, possessing, as they do for the time being, the means of influence, of trust, of power; and, submitting all authority to them, you expect them to reconstruct loyal State governments.

Now is the time when we ought to cherish and nourish the loyal sentiment of the people. We ought to take security that the men under whose guidance these States are to be reconstructed shall be loyal men. We ought to exclude from the business of reconstructing South Carolina, for example, the Orrs, the Pickens, the Magraths, and all those who participated in the rebellion. We ought to seek out the loyal men, and confide to them the great work. Let them be the standard-bearers of the republic; let them rally the loyal people, black and white, to the support of the Union. On the other hand, this bill leaves the whole matter of reconstruction open to anybody and everybody in the Southern country who may choose to engage in the business. The result will be, that, in these several States, the ancient rebel party will resist reconstruction for a time; but, when in a particular State they see that it is inevitable, they will take the business into their own hands, and reconstruct governments according to their own ideas, with their representative men in places of power and trust. They will then come here with every condition precedent fully satisfied. Every black man will be secured in the right to vote. The controlling rebel party will organize the States, soon or late, in their own interest. They will organize the militia; they will control the polls; they will manage the elections; and do you expect that the negroes, unaccustomed to political struggles, timid, careworn, broken down in spirit to some degree by the institution of slavery, can in five or even ten years overthrow the rebels, and deprive them of power, although the negroes and the loyal whites should be a majority in those States?

Hence, by this bill in its present form, we exchange power to reconstruct these governments in the interest of loyalty, and accept in its place mere declarations upon paper; we exchange authority for promises; we neglect to do our own duty in the work of reconstruction, in the vain hope that men who have been rebels will do, in the interest of loyalty and the government, that which we ourselves, intrusted with vast powers for the public good, are either afraid to do or are incapable of doing.

These, in brief, are my objections to the passage of the substitute. So great, so enormous, do the objections appear, that by no process of reasoning can I overcome them. I see the three million newly emancipated slaves of the South surrendered over again to the control of their former masters, when we have the power, by following in some form of language the bill which we passed here with reference to Louisiana, to reconstruct these States through the agency of loyal men, in the interest of loyalty, and thus make this government compact and firm as one great republican State with many members, in which everywhere loyalty shall be in the ascendant, and treason shall be odious.

APPENDIX.

I.

Joint Resolution proposing an Amendment to the Constitution of the United States.

Be it resolved by the Senate and House of Representatives of the United States of America in Congress assembled (two-thirds of both houses concurring), That the following article be proposed to the legislatures of the several States as an amendment to the Constitution of the United States, which, when ratified by three-fourths of said legislatures, shall be valid as part of the Constitution; namely: —

ARTICLE XIV.

SECTION 1. All persons born or naturalized in the United States, and subject to the jurisdiction thereof, are citizens of the United States and of the State wherein they reside. No State shall make or enforce any law which shall abridge the privileges or immunities of citizens of the United States; nor shall any State deprive any person of life, liberty, or property, without due process of law, nor deny to any person within its jurisdiction the equal protection of the laws.

SEC. 2. Representatives shall be apportioned among the several States according to their respective numbers, counting the whole number of persons in each State, excluding Indians not taxed. But when the right to vote at any election for the choice of electors for President and Vice-President of the United States, representatives in Congress, the executive and judicial officers of a State, or the members of the legislature thereof, is denied to any of the male inhabitants of such State, being twenty-one years of age, and citizens of the United States, or in any way abridged, except for participation in rebellion or other crime, the basis of representation therein shall be reduced in the proportion which the number of such male citizens shall bear to the whole number of male citizens twenty-one years of age in such State.

Sec. 3. No person shall be a senator or representative in Congress, or elector of President and Vice-President, or hold any office, civil or military, under the United States, or under any State, who having previously taken an oath as a member of Congress, or as an officer of the United States, or as a member of any State legislature, or as an executive or judicial officer of any State, to support the Constitution of the United States, shall have engaged in insurrection or rebellion against the same, or given aid or comfort to the enemies thereof. But Congress may, by a vote of two-thirds of each house, remove such disability.

Sec. 4. The validity of the public debt of the United States, authorized by law, including debts incurred for payment of pensions and bounties for services in suppressing insurrection or rebellion, shall not be questioned. But neither the United States nor any State shall assume or pay any debt or obligation incurred in aid of insurrection or rebellion against the United States, or any claim for the loss or emancipation of any slave; but all such debts, obligations, and claims shall be held illegal and void.

SEC. 5. That Congress shall have power to enforce, by appropriate legislation, the provisions of this article.

SCHUYLER COLFAX,
Speaker of the House of Representatives.

LAFAYETTE S. FOSTER,
President of the Senate pro tempore.

Attest:

EDWARD MCPHERSON,
Clerk of the House of Representatives.

J. W FORNEY,
Secretary of the Senate.

Received at Department of State, June 16, 1866.

II.

A Bill to provide for the more Efficient Government of the Insurrectionary States.

Whereas the pretended State governments of the late so-called Confederate States of Virginia, North Carolina, South Carolina, Georgia, Mississipppi, Alabama, Louisiana, Florida, Texas, and Arkansas were set up without the authority of Congress and without the sanction of the people; and whereas said pretended governments afford no adequate protection for life or property, but countenance and encourage lawlessness and crime; and whereas it is necessary that peace and good order should be enforced in said so-called States until loyal and republican State governments can be legally established: therefore —

Be it enacted by the Senate and House of Representatives of the United States of America in Congress assembled, That said so-called States shall be divided into military districts and made subject to the military authority of the United States as hereinafter prescribed: and for that purpose Virginia shall constitute the first district; North Carolina and South Carolina the second district; Georgia, Alabama, and Florida the third district; Mississippi and Arkansas the fourth district; and Louisiana and Texas the fifth district.

SEC. 2. *And be it further enacted*, That it shall be the duty of the general of the army to assign to the command of each of said districts an officer of the regular army, not below the rank of brigadier-general, and to detail a sufficient military force to enable such officer to perform his duties and enforce his authority within the district to which he is assigned.

SEC. 3. *And be it further enacted*, That it shall be the duty of each officer assigned as aforesaid to protect all persons in their rights of person and property, to suppress insurrection, disorder, and violence, and to punish, or cause to be punished, all disturbers of the public peace and criminals, and to this end he may allow civil tribunals to take jurisdiction of and to try offenders, or, when in his judgment it may be necessary for the trial of offenders, he shall have power to organize military commissions or tribunals for that purpose, any thing in the Constitution and laws of the so-called States to the contrary notwithstanding; and all legislative or judicial proceedings, or processes to prevent or control the proceedings of said military tribunals, and all interference by said pretended State governments with the exercise of military authority under this act, shall be void and of no effect.

SEC. 4. *And be it further enacted*, That courts and judicial officers of the United States shall not issue writs of habeas corpus in behalf of persons in military custody, unless some commissioned officer on duty in the district wherein the person is detained shall indorse upon said petition a statement certifying, upon honor, that he has knowledge, or information, as to the cause and circumstances of the alleged detention, and that he believes the same to be wrongful; and further, that he believes that the indorsed petition is preferred in good faith, and in furtherance of justice, and not to hinder or delay the punishment of crime. All persons put under military arrest by virtue of this act shall be tried without unnecessary delay, and no cruel or unusual punishment shall be inflicted.

SEC. 5. *And be it further enacted,* That no sentence of any military commission or tribunal hereby authorized, affecting the life or liberty of any person, shall be executed until it is approved by the officer in command of the district, and the laws and regulations for the government of the army shall not be affected by this act, except in so far as they conflict with its provisions.

III.

An Act to provide for the more Efficient Government of the Insurrectionary States.

Whereas the pretended State governments of the late so-called Confederate States of Virginia, North Carolina, South Carolina, Georgia, Mississippi, Alabama, Louisiana, Florida, Texas, and Arkansas, were set up without the authority of Congress, and without the sanction of the people; and whereas said pretended governments afford no adequate protection for life or property, but countenance and encourage lawlessness and crime; and whereas it is necessary that peace and good order should be enforced in said so-called States, until loyal and republican State governments can be legally established: therefore —

Be it enacted by the Senate and House of Representatives of the United States of America in Congress assembled,

That said late so-called Confederate States shall be divided into military districts and made subject to the military authority of the United States, as hereinafter prescribed, and for that purpose Virginia shall constitute the first district; North Carolina and South Carolina the second district; Georgia, Alabama, and Florida the third district; Mississippi and Arkansas the fourth district; and Louisiana and Texas the fifth district.

SEC. 2. *And be it further enacted*, That it shall be the duty of the general of the army to assign to the command of each of said districts an officer of the army, not below the rank of brigadier-general, and to detail a sufficient military force to enable such officer to perform his duties and enforce his authority within the district to which he is assigned.

SEC. 3. *And be it further enacted*, That it shall be the duty of each officer assigned as aforesaid to protect all persons in their rights of person and property, to suppress insurrection, disorder, and violence, and to punish, or cause to be punished, all disturbers of the public peace and criminals, and to this end he may allow local civil tribunals to take jurisdiction of and to try offenders, or, when in his judgment it may be necessary for the trial of offenders, he shall have power to organize military commissions or tribunals for that purpose, any thing in the Constitution and laws of any of the so-called Confederate States to the contrary notwithstanding; and all legislative or judicial proceedings or processes to prevent or control the proceedings of said military tribunals, and all interference by said pretended State governments with the exercise of military authority under this act, shall be void and of no effect.

SEC. 4. *And be it further enacted*, That courts and judicial officers of the United States shall not issue writs of habeas corpus in behalf of persons in military custody, except in cases in which the person is held to answer only for a crime or crimes exclusively within the jurisdiction of the courts of the United States within said military districts, and indictable therein, or unless some commissioned officer on duty in the district wherein the person is detained shall indorse upon said petition a statement certifying, upon honor, that he has knowledge or information as to the cause and circumstances of the alleged detention, and that he believes the same to be wrongful; and, further, that he believes that the indorsed petition is preferred in good faith and in furtherance of justice, and not to hinder or delay the punishment of crime. All persons put under military arrest by virtue of this act shall be tried without unnecessary delay, and no cruel or unusual punishment shall be inflicted.

SEC. 5. *And be it further enacted*, That no sentence of any military commission or tribunal hereby authorized, affecting the life or liberty of any person, shall be executed until it is approved by the officer in command of the district, and the laws and regulations for the government of the army shall not be affected by this act, except in so far as they conflict with its provisions.

Passed the House of Representatives, February 13, 1867.

Attest: EDWARD McPHERSON, *Clerk*.

IV.

An Act to provide for the more Efficient Government of the Rebel States.

Whereas no legal State governments, or adequate protection for life or property, now exist in the rebel States of Virginia, North Carolina, South Carolina, Georgia,

Mississippi, Alabama, Louisiana, Florida, Texas and Arkansas; and

Whereas it is necessary that peace and good order should be enforced in said States until loyal and republican State Governments can be legally established: therefore —

Be it enacted by the Senate and House of Representatives of the United States of America in Congress assembled, That said rebel States shall be divided into military districts, and made subject to the military authority of the United States, as hereinafter prescribed, and for that purpose Virginia shall constitute the first district; North Carolina and South Carolina the second district; Georgia, Alabama, and Florida the third district; Mississippi and Arkansas the fourth district; and Louisiana and Texas the fifth district.

SEC. 2. *And be it further enacted,* That it shall be the duty of the President to assign to the command of each of said districts an officer of the army not below the rank of brigadier-general, and to detail a sufficient military force to enable such officer to perform his duties and enforce his authority within the district to which he is assigned.

SEC. 3. *And be it further enacted,* That it shall be the duty of each officer assigned as aforesaid to protect all persons in their rights of person and property, to suppress insurrection, disorder, and violence, and to punish, or cause to be punished, all disturbers of the public peace and criminals, and to this end he may allow local civil tribunals to take jurisdiction of and try offenders, or, when in his judgment it may be necessary for the trial of offenders, he shall have power to organize military commissions or tribunals for that purpose, and all interference under color of State authority, with the exercise of military authority, under this act, shall be null and void.

SEC. 4. *And be it further enacted,* That all persons put

under military arrest by virtue of this act shall be tried without unnecessary delay, and no cruel or unusual punishment shall be inflicted, and no sentence of any military commission or tribunal hereby authorized, affecting the life or liberty of any person, shall be executed until it is approved by the officer in command of the district, and the laws and regulations for the government of the army shall not be affected by this act, except in so far as they may conflict with its provisions; *Provided*, That no sentence of death under this act shall be carried into effect without the approval of the President.

SEC. 5. *And be it further enacted*, That when the people of any one of said rebel States shall have formed a Constitution of government in conformity with the Constitution of the United States in all respects, framed by a convention of delegates elected by the male citizens of said State, twenty-one years old and upward, of whatever race, color, or previous condition, who have been resident in said State for one year previous to the day of such election, except such as may be disfranchised for participation in the rebellion, or for felony at common law, and when such Constitution shall provide that the elective franchise shall be enjoyed by all such persons as have the qualifications herein stated for electors of delegates, and when such Constitution shall be ratified by a majority of the persons voting on the question of ratification who are qualified as electors for delegates, and when such Constitution shall have been submitted to Congress for examination and approval, and Congress shall have approved the same, and when said State, by a vote of its Legislature, elected under said Constitution, shall have adopted the amendment to the Constitution of the United States, proposed by the Thirty-ninth Congress, and known as "Article XIV.," and when said Article shall have became a part of the Constitution of the United States, said State shall be declared entitled to representation in Congress, and senators and representatives shall be admitted therefrom on their taking the oath prescribed by law, and then and thereafter the preceding sections of this act shall be inoperative in said State;

Provided, That no person excluded from the privilege of holding office by said proposed amendment to the Constitution of the United States, shall be eligible to election as a member of a Convention to frame a Constitution for any of said rebel States, nor shall any such person vote for members of such Convention.

SEC. 6. *And be it further enacted, That, until the people of said rebel States shall by law be admitted to representation in the Congress of the United States, any civil governments which may exist therein shall be deemed provisional only, and in all respects subject to the paramount authority of the United States, at any time to abolish, modify, control, or supersede the same. And in all elections for officers of such provisional governments, all persons shall be entitled to vote, and none others, who are entitled to vote under the provisions of the fifth section of this act; and no person shall be eligible to any office under such provisional governments who would be disqualified from holding office under the provisions of the third section of said Constitutional Amendment.*

NOTE.—Appendix II. is the bill reported by the Committee on Reconstruction. Appendix III. is the bill as it passed the House of Representatives. Appendix IV. is the bill which became a law on the 2d of March, 1867, over the veto of the President.

The House bill was amended by the Senate, and, on the 16th of February, the Senate returned the amended bill to the House.

The part which precedes the proviso to the fifth section is the Senate bill. On the 19th of February, the House, by a vote of 98 to 73, non-concurred with the Senate. On the same day, the Senate voted to insist upon its amendments. On the 20th of February, the House receded, and concurred, with two amendments, which are printed in Italics. The Senate then concurred in these amendments. The proviso to the fifth section was proposed by Hon. James F. Wilson, of Iowa. The sixth section was proposed by Hon. Samuel Shellabarger, of Ohio.

INDEX.

INDEX.

THE END.

Cambridge: Stereotyped and Printed by John Wilson and Son.

www.ingramcontent.com/pod-product-compliance
Lightning Source LLC
LaVergne TN
LVHW021059110826
845150LV00001B/114

9781425566173